SCHAUM'S OUTLINE OF

THEORY AND PROBLEMS

of

INTERMEDIATE ACCOUNTING I

•

by

JAMES A. CASHIN

Professor of Accounting
Hofstra University

SAUL FELDMAN

Associate Professor of Accounting
Hofstra University

and

JOEL J. LERNER

Chairman, Faculty of Business
Sullivan County Community College

SCHAUM'S OUTLINE SERIES

McGRAW-HILL BOOK COMPANY

New York   St. Louis   San Francisco   Auckland   Düsseldorf   Johannesburg
Kuala Lumpur   London   Mexico   Montreal   New Delhi   Panama
Paris   São Paulo   Singapore   Sydney   Tokyo   Toronto

0-07-010202-3

2 3 4 5 6 7 8 9 10 11 12 13 14 15 16 17 18 19 20   SH SH   7 9 8 7

Library of Congress Cataloging in Publication Data

Cashin, James A

    Schaum's outline of theory and problems of inter-
mediate accounting.

    (Schaum's outline series)

    Continues the work by J. A. Cashin and J. J.
Lerner published in 1973-1974 under title: Schaum's
outline of theory and problems of accounting I-II.

    Includes index.

    1. Accounting.   2. Accounting—Problems, exer-
cises, etc.   I. Feldman, Saul, 1916- joint
author.   II. Lerner, Joel J., joint author.   III. Title.   IV. Title: Outline of theory and problems of
intermediate accounting.

HF5625.C36   657'.076   75-29495
ISBN 0-07-010202-3

Preface

This volume, the third in the Schaum's Outline Series in Accounting, covers the first part of the Intermediate Accounting course. As in the preceding volumes, the *solved problems* approach is used, with emphasis on the *practical application* of basic accounting concepts. The student is provided with:

1. concise definitions and explanations, in easily understood terms

2. examples which illustrate the concepts and principles developed in each chapter

3. chapter review questions with answers

4. fully worked-out solutions to a large range of representative problems (against which students can check their own solutions)

5. sample comprehensive examinations with answers and solutions typical of those used by two-year and four-year colleges

Intermediate Accounting I and its sequel, *Intermediate Accounting II,* parallel the full-year intermediate course offered in most schools. The subject matter has been carefully coordinated with leading textbooks, so that any topic can easily be found from the Table of Contents or the Index.

Intermediate Accounting I is the most significant course in the college accounting program, as it covers in great depth the principles and procedures introduced in the introductory course. Thus, earlier learning is greatly reinforced. It is especially important that the student throughly understand the complex concepts covered in Intermediate I as most other accounting courses cover more specialized areas.

The first four chapters of this volume summarize introductory course material, and will be especially helpful to those whose introductory courses emphasized managerial concepts, information systems, computer methods and other concepts, rather than accounting principles and procedures.

The new requirements relating to present value concepts are presented in both text and problems concerned with imputed interest, receivable and payable amounts, plant property amounts, amortization of discount and premium, and similar transactions. An Appendix showing present value tables for compound interest and ordinary annuity is also included.

Significant advances have been made in accounting theory and practice in recent years and the many recent pronouncements of the American Institute of Certified Public Accountants, the Financial Accounting Standards Board, the Securities and Exchange Commission and others are included and explained throughout the volume. *Intermediate Accounting I* will provide excellent preparation and review for the theory and practice sections of the Uniform CPA Examination and for advanced accounting courses.

Intermediate Accounting I will also serve the needs of those who must understand the basic financial statements and be able to interpret significant relationships and trends, such as majors in management, finance, general business, economics and business education. It will also be helpful to bankers, financial analysts, managers and others who may need to make use of methods of computing financial ratios and other financial measurements and statistics.

Among the many individuals the authors have to thank for contributions to this volume, they would like to make special mention of the assistance they received from Philip Malafsky, Joan Mastca, and the following members of a student panel: Charles Banker, Shelby Goldgrab, Elaine Miliano, Vincent Newman and Gary Reynolds.

JAMES A. CASHIN
SAUL FELDMAN
JOEL J. LERNER

CONTENTS

CONTENTS

CONTENTS

CONTENTS

CONTENTS

Chapter 1

Accounting Principles

1.1 INTRODUCTION

Our rapidly changing economic environment has made the role of the accountant an increasingly important one. Statements of financial position are at the core of our society's operation and are subject to close scrutiny by a variety of interested parties — business executives, union leaders, investors, creditors, and government agencies, to name just a few. As a result, the onus is on the accountant to present the financial picture of the on-going business organization—be it profit or nonprofit—so that it is fair, complete and open to analysis.

1.2 FINANCIAL REPORTING

The theoretical foundation developed over the years by such organizations as the AICPA and the AAA includes fundamental underlying assumptions which allow for certain basic premises as well as the Generally Accepted Accounting Principles (GAAP) which provide a framework for professional judgment.

EXAMPLE 1.

The theoretical structure of financial reporting is depicted graphically in Fig. 1-1.

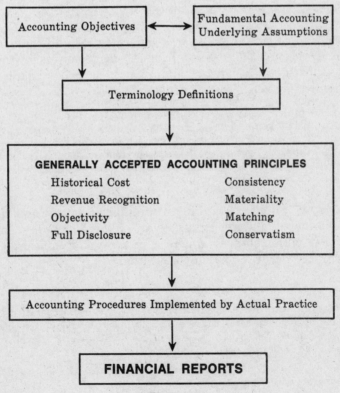

Fig. 1-1

The process of *recording, classifying* and *summarizing* the day-to-day activities of the business firm requires considerable judgment on the accountant's part. Since so much reliance is placed on financial reports, it is imperative that the accounting system be designed to generate information that will meet the needs of users, both internal (the board of directors, corporation officers, employee groups) and external (investors and creditors).

1.3 GENERALLY ACCEPTED ACCOUNTING PRINCIPLES

The eight Generally Accepted Accounting Principles are described below. While some of the more important ones include a brief illustration, applications of all principles can be found throughout the book.

(1) **Historical Cost.** The properties and assets acquired by an enterprise, as well as the expenses incurred by it, are generally recorded *at cost* (the cash or equivalent exchanged). When noncash assets (such as stocks, bonds or machinery trade-ins) are used, cost is defined as the cash value of the acquired asset. Costs are spread over the accounting periods which benefit from the expenditures.

(2) **Revenue Recognition.** Revenues are realized when *the market value of output can be determined and supported* and *the transaction is essentially complete.*

EXAMPLE 2.

The timing of revenue recognition varies according to the type of transaction. In the case of *merchandise* sales, revenues are realized at the *point of sales*, when goods are delivered and title has passed. *Fees income* represents *fully rendered services.* For *long-term projects* such as construction, revenue can be recognized as a *percentage of the contract price based on the relationship between actual cost to date and total estimated costs to completion.*

(3) **Objectivity.** The financial statements generated by a business entity's books *must be supported by evidence.* When business documents showing the details of a completed transaction do not or cannot exist, estimates based on informed judgments which can be verified are included.

EXAMPLE 3.

Company B purchased an electric typewriter for $400. Based upon their experience with similar machines and the experience of the typewriter vendor, it was decided to use eight years as the *estimated life* in the depreciation calculation. The depreciation expense would therefore amount to $50 each year.

(4) **Full Disclosure.** For accurate interpretation, it is required that accounting reports include financial statements and *accompanying notes* which call attention to events and circumstances which may have a significant effect on potential future earnings and/or a company's position.

EXAMPLE 4.

With an eye toward eventual merger, the Photo Mart Corporation entered into negotiations with one of its suppliers, Frames, Ltd., to acquire 45% of that company's outstanding stock. Close to an agreement at the end of its fiscal year, Photo Mart issued its financial statement with the following note:

At June 30, negotiations were virtually complete for the acquisition of 45% of all outstanding stock of Frames, Ltd. for $2,350,000.

(5) **Consistency.** Any change in accounting procedures usually has some effect on current or past income. Since it is important that income data be interpreted

and compared over time, the consistency principle requires that any deviation in procedures *from those of the preceding year* be clearly defined as a footnote to the financial statements or possible retroactive restatement.

EXAMPLE 5.

Suppose that at the beginning of its new fiscal year, a firm changes its inventory procedure from FIFO to LIFO in an effort to reduce its amount of taxable income. At the year end, the accountant prepares the financial statements and includes a note reading:

> In our opinion the aforementioned financial statements present fairly the financial position of ABC Company at December 31, 19—, and the results of its operations and the changes in its financial position for the year ended, in conformity with Generally Accepted Accounting Principles *applied on a basis consistent with that of the preceding year.*

(6) *Materiality.* Under this principle, the relative importance of data is considered. The decision as to what is material and what is unimportant requires judgment rather than inflexible rules.

EXAMPLE 6.

Blue Company has reported net income in excess of $200,000 for many years. It has established a rule that all shop supplies and small tools purchased, which cost under $100, shall be treated as an *expense* regardless of when used. This is acceptable accounting under the principle of *materiality.*

(7) *Matching.* In determining net income, it is necessary to match related costs and expenses to revenues for the reporting period. The cost of the product sold and all expenses incurred in generating the sale should be matched against the respective revenues. (See Chapter 4 for illustrations of this principle.)

(8) *Conservatism.* Current theory advocates that in situations where data are unclear or conflicting, the accountant's judgment should be in the direction of understatement rather than overstatement. It is important to note that the seven principles previously discussed take precedence over conservatism.

1.4 FUNDAMENTAL UNDERLYING ASSUMPTIONS

Some of the broad theoretical concepts on which the GAAP are based include:

(1) *Separate-entity.* Revenues, costs and expenses apply to the *business entity* rather than its owners. The accounting system is concerned primarily with three types of entities: the proprietorship, the partnership and the corporation. A business entity may take other forms for reporting purposes; among these might be a group of corporations operating under common control, a corporate division which operates autonomously, a specific nonprofit organization or a government unit.

(2) *Going-concern.* The accountant assumes, in preparing the records or financial statements of any business, that the firm will continue in existence for the foreseeable future. This is to be contrasted with a liquidation viewpoint.

(3) *Money measuring unit.* It is assumed that the dollar is the best measuring unit of business transactions. Thus, only those transactions which can be quantified in terms of money are measured and recorded.

(4) *Time period.* So that accounting data can serve the decision-making process, it is necessary that it be provided on a systematic basis of time intervals. Comparison of reported results from one period to the next is useful in determining performance patterns.

Summary

(1) Accounting, as a field of thought, contains certain basic premises. These are called the Fundamental Underlying _____ .

(2) The preparation of financial statements and their analysis rely heavily on _____ _____ .

(3) The primary external users of financial statements are _____ and _____ _____ .

(4) The _____ principle holds that historic *cost* is the appropriate basis for initial accounting recognition.

(5) The methods of performing work are known as _____ .

(6) In order to provide a foundation for new or revised opinions on accounting problems, the American Institute of Certified Public Accountants and, more recently, the Financial Accounting Standards Board issue _____ as a basis for comment and review before opinions are formulated.

(7) A company adopting the LIFO inventory method in its first year of operation would have to continue to use this method (or disclose its justifiable reasons for a change) in accordance with the _____ Principle.

(8) Treating the purchase of an "asset" of less than $50 as an expense item (on condition that this will not materially distort the net income) is allowed under the Principle of _____ .

Answers: (1) Assumptions; (2) Generally Accepted Accounting Principles; (3) investors, creditors; (4) historical cost; (5) accounting procedures; (6) Accounting Research Bulletins; (7) Consistency; (8) Materiality.

Solved Problems

1.1. On January 2, 19X1 Baker Company paid $6,000 for a three-year Fire and Casualty Insurance Policy. At December 31, 19X2, a question arose regarding the amount of Insurance Expense to be properly shown on Baker's income statement for the current year and the amount of the asset Prepaid Insurance for the balance sheet. Explain which of the following possibilities is best.

   (a) Use the redemption value of $1,400.

   (b) Use $2,000, which is one third of the original cost.

   (c) Use $2,300, which is the current cost of a one-year policy.

SOLUTION

The historical cost principle states that cost is the appropriate basis for initial accounting recognition and subsequent allocations; therefore, the current year's expense should be (b), or $2,000. The redemption table value (a) is inappropriate since it does not apply to an on-going business. Possibility (c) is also inappropriate since it is not a one-year policy.

1.2. Doe Company issued 15,000 shares of common stock (par value $1), whose market value is $2.50 each, in exchange for 10 acres of industrial land. The land was assessed for tax purposes at $22,000 and was recently appraised by competent appraisers for $37,750. What is the proper value for land on the balance sheet at the year end?

SOLUTION

Land should be reported on the end-of-year balance sheet as $37,500 (15,000 × $2.50), since measurement of an asset acquired in a noncash transaction is the fair market value of the asset *or* the cash equivalent of the stock issued.

Assessed values are rarely equivalent to fair market values. Since the fair market value of land is so close to the value established for the stock offered in exchange, that amount should be used on the balance sheet.

1.3. Felson Company owns several rental properties. The rent collected during 19X2 was $40,000 and included advance payments by several tenants. The following account balances are shown in its general ledger at two successive balance sheet dates. In accordance with generally accepted accounting principles, determine Rent Income for the 19X2 income statement.

	Dec. 31, 19X1	Dec. 31, 19X2
Rent Receivable	$ 6,500	$ 5,800
Unearned Rent Income	10,000	12,000

SOLUTION

Actual Cash Received in 19X2	$40,000
Add: 19X2 Accrued Receivable	5,800
	$45,800
Less: 19X1 Accrued Receivable	(6,500)
Total	$39,300
Add: Deferred from 19X1	10,000
Less: Unearned in 19X2 and Deferred to 19X3	(12,000)
Rent Income	$37,300

Revenue should be recognized in accordance with the *realization concept*. This results in adding certain revenue (e.g. accrued receivables) to the current period's reportable income. Conversely, rent received from tenants in advance for services to be performed is entered in an unearned rent income account until the service is rendered.

1.4. For the return of ten of its product box tops plus 50¢ in mailing costs, the Fox Cereal Company offers a silver table setting as a premium. The company's accountant, in establishing the liability for the premiums to be redeemed, estimates that on the basis of past records and industry data, 60% of the tops from cereal boxes sold will never be redeemed. Discuss the degree of objectivity involved in this estimate.

SOLUTION

It is known that all coupons (box tops) will not be redeemed. It is proper accounting to match the premium expense with the revenue produced. In order to do this, the purchase of the premium —table settings—would be debited to an asset account such as "Premiums—Silverware"; and credited to Accounts Payable or Cash. Then the adjustment for the expense could be entered upon the 40% return. Assuming data from past records supports this 40%, it is appropriate and within the realm of objectivity to use this data.

1.5. For each of the following statements, identify the Generally Accepted Accounting Principle(s) to which it refers and indicate whether the interpretation is accurate.

(*a*) Anticipate no profits and recognize all possible losses.

(*b*) Lower of cost or market should be used in valuing all investments of a temporary nature.

(*c*) Reported net income is affected more by judgment than by fact.

(*d*) The cost principle primarily affects only the income statement.

(*e*) When in doubt, be conservative.

(*f*) The only way to have an informed financial statement reader is to report every fact and bit of information, regardless of how minor or insignificant.

(*g*) Consistency means that one can never change to another method of valuing inventory.

SOLUTION

(*a*) This relates to the principle of *conservatism*. It stresses caution against the overstatement of earnings through two approaches. First, all costs, expenses and potential losses that are related to the period should be included in the period's statements. This is done even if it is necessary to make an estimate of these costs or losses based upon an informed judgment. Secondly, as far as recognition of gains or profits is concerned, this principle holds that where several alternates for an accounting determination exists, each having reasonable support, the one with the *least favorable immediate influence* on the proprietor's equity should be selected.

(*b*) This also relates to the principle of *conservatism* as well as the principle of *full disclosure*. Assuming a material decline in the market value of bonds or equity securities carried as investment assets, the loss should be disclosed on the current income statement in accordance with relevant APB opinions. In addition, the *lower net realizable value* should be disclosed on the balance sheet. This conservative point of view would not wait for the *loss* to be fixed by a sale.

(*c*) This statement relates to the principle of *objectivity*. Many elements entering into the calculation of net income require estimates based upon informed judgments. Examples are the depreciation of plant assets, write-off of intangible assets, estimated costs for warranty work on products sold, etc. Occasionally, one must decide during which period to report income based on an informed judgment.

(*d*) This statement relates to the *cost* principle. Defining the initial amount of accounting recognition of an asset affects the amount of depreciation shown on the income statement. The treatment required for subsequent major, extraordinary repair, overhaul of equipment and additions to assets also affects the amount of depreciation expense as well as repair expense shown. Applying the principle to a noncash acquisition of raw materials aids in establishing the cost to be used for materials.

(*e*) This rule is debated within professional accounting circles. The degree of *conservatism* to be applied is based on professional opinion which may differ among accountants.

(f) This statement relates to the principle of *full disclosure*. Including all explanatory data should not be carried to an extreme. The judgment of the auditor must be used in meeting the obligations of the audit but not confusing the reader with unnecessary information. Only items which are *material* should be included.

(g) This statement relates to the principle of *consistency*. It is basically incorrect. When good accounting reasons exist for a change, the change should be made. However, the effect, such as the amount, of the change must be reported, consistent with the *full disclosure* principle. An example is the change from the FIFO to the LIFO method of inventory.

1.6. The NoDoze Company has the following receivables at the end of Year 19X1.

Accounts Receivable—Trade	$185,000
Notes Receivable—Trade	60,000
Notes Receivable—Officers	30,000
Accrued Interest Receivable	2,000

NoDoze secured a $100,000 loan in July, for which it assigned $125,000 of Accounts Receivable. Notes Receivable—Trade with a face value of $40,000 have been discounted and are not yet due. The Notes Receivable—Officers have been on the books for many years; several are from officers no longer with the company. What is the required information for the annual statements in accordance with the principle of *full disclosure*?

SOLUTION

The Assignment of a large part of Accounts Receivable—Trade must be disclosed. The statement that $125,000 was the basis for collateral and reference to the current liability, Loans Payable, is preferably made as a footnote or parenthetically among the current assets.

Since part ($40,000) of the face value of Notes Receivable represents unmatured notes which are still payable to the discounting party, a *contingent liability* exists. The preferred treatment is to disclose such a liability in a footnote to the financial statements; however, it may be included parenthetically in current assets or among current liabilities. The Notes Receivable—Officers is more involved, since a question has been raised as to their collectibility. If it is determined that these notes cannot be collected, they should be written off as *bad debts*. It is probable that most of the $30,000 due from officers will have to be classified as noncurrent with full disclosure in a footnote.

It is interesting to note that a *Summary of Significant Accounting Policies* has been prescribed by APB Opinion No. 22, "Disclosure of Accounting Policies." In addition to the above, policies to be described in this manner are changes in accounting policy and the justification thereof, depreciation methods, inventory pricing methods, accounting for research and development costs, and translation of foreign currencies. Should any accounting principle used in audited financial statements differ from an official position as set forth by the APB or the Financial Accounting Standards Board, these departures must be fully disclosed in either notes attached to the statements or in the reports of the independent auditors.

1.7. Consider the situation below and state your opinion on the proposed action in light of the principle of conservatism.

> After occupying an old building on leased property for 17 years of a 20-year lease, the tenant company constructed a new frame building on the premises. This was done because the old building was unsatisfactory and the owner refused to make repairs. All improvements on the land revert to the owner at the end of the lease. Renewal of the lease is possible, but no assurance exists. Should the cost of the new frame building be written off in one year or recovered over some longer period?

SOLUTION

The company in question is the tenant. The potential use of the new building just constructed is three years, unless the lease is renewed. The company knew that ownership would pass to the landlord at the end of the lease, without a sale of any kind. Therefore, the company must have felt a compelling business need to construct this new building. This is a situation where a determination must be made among several alternatives, each of which can be said to have reasonable support. One could argue that there exists a clear indication by the tenant company that it expects to renew the lease. This would result in a recovery by depreciation expense over the next 23 years (three years remaining plus twenty years of the new lease). At the same time, one could argue that there is no evidence to indicate a contractual agreement for a new lease and that, therefore, the principle of conservatism must be employed. This would require the recovery of the cost of the building over the next three years. In any case, the cost of the new building should *not* be charged entirely to the current year. (See Problem 1.6 for additional comment on this principle.)

1.8. The Output Corporation had adopted the FIFO inventory method using a periodic inventory. When its accountant realized that, because of rapidly rising costs during the current year, gross margin and net income would be distorted, he wished to change to a weighted average procedure for the year-end Cost of Goods Manufacturing and Ending Inventory but did not believe he could do so because of *consistency*. Was he correct?

SOLUTION

No. While comparability of annual financial statements is essential if favorable and unfavorable trends in the business are to be identified, a material economic event such as this would justify a change in accounting policy. As long as full disclosure is made in a footnote to the financial statements, there is no reason that this company cannot change its inventory costing procedure.

1.9. Industrial Builders, Incorporated operates with long-term construction contracts often extending over two or more years, and uses the *completed-contract* method of recognizing income. All costs, including heat, insurance, etc., are accumulated in a separate Construction-in-Process account and identified by job number. Interim billings by the company are debited to Accounts Receivable and credited to a balance sheet account, Revenue Billed on Construction Contracts. No income is recognized prior to completion of the contract and collection of all or a major portion of the funds. Does this procedure violate the GAAP?

SOLUTION

No. Accounting statements are designed to focus on usefulness, feasibility and appropriateness. Certain industries which have unique timing for the receipt of income or the basis of income accrual warrant an exception. It is permissible to allow for special treatment of specific items where there is a clear precedent in the industry based on a real need or rationale. In this situation, it is appropriate to defer income and all related costs and expenses until the construction contract is completed. This procedure matches costs and expenses with related income.

Chapter 2

Accounting Procedures

Accounting has been defined by the AICPA Committee on Terminology as "the act of recording, classifying and summarizing in a significant manner and in terms of money, transactions and events which are, in part at least, of a financial character, and interpreting the results thereof." This chapter presents relationships between the various records used by the accountant in the preparation of financial reports.

2.1 THE JOURNAL

A *transaction* can be defined as *any event which results in a change in asset, liability or capital accounts*. The various transactions of a business are supported by sales invoices, cash register tapes, purchase invoices, check stubs, etc.

The *journal* is the record of original entry for accounting data. Transactions are recorded in chronological order; each entry includes (1) the date, (2) the accounts to be debited and credited, (3) the debit and credit amounts, and (4) an explanation of the transaction.

The general journal is usually supplemented by a system of special journals which group repetitive transactions by type. Typically included in such a system are the purchases journal, sales journal, cash receipts journal and cash disbursements journal. Non-repetitive entries, such as corrections and adjustments, are made in the general journal.

EXAMPLE 1.

BOOKS OF ORIGINAL ENTRY POSTED AS OF DECEMBER 31, 19X1

PURCHASES JOURNAL

Date	Account Cr.	P.R.	Acct. Pay. Cr.	Pur. Dr.	Store Supp. Dr.	Office Supp. Dr.	Sundry		
							Acct. Dr.	P.R.	Amt.
Mar. 16	Schop Corp.	√	500		500				
	Total		46,725	23,150	11,675				11,900
			(211)	(511)	(114)				(√)

SALES JOURNAL

Date	Account Debited	P.R.	Accounts Receivable Dr. Sales Cr.
Mar. 28	Sapre Company	√	950
	Total		32,305
			(112/411)

CASH RECEIPTS JOURNAL

Date	Account Credited	P. R.	Cash Dr.	Sales Disc. Dr.	Acct. Rec. Cr.	Sales Cr.	Sundry Acc. Cr.
Mar. 30	Borak Company	√	2,254	46	2,300		
	Total		36,402	143	21,286	7,510	7,749
			(111)	(412)	(112)	(411)	(√)

CASH DISBURSEMENTS JOURNAL

Date	Check No.	Account Debited	P. R.	Cash Cr.	Pur. Disc. Cr.	Acct. Pay. Dr.	Sundry Acc. Dr.
Mar. 31	47	Salaries Expense	551	2,810			2,810
		Total		15,120	370	11,700	3,790
				(111)	(513)	(211)	(√)

GENERAL JOURNAL

Date	Description	P. R.	Debit	Credit
Mar. 19	Accounts Payable, Bronner Co.	211	200	
	Purchases Returns & Allowances	532		200
	Defective goods received.			

2.2 THE LEDGER

On a monthly basis, journal totals are transferred or *posted* to the ledger accounts. *The ledger contains the accounts for the business entity.* It is used to classify and summarize transactions as well as to prepare financial statements. It is also a valuable source of information for management purposes, providing, for example, the total sales and net income for the period, or the cash balance at the end of the period.

Accounts may be termed *real* (permanent) or *nominal* (temporary). Real accounts are the asset, liability and capital accounts which appear in the balance sheet and are not closed out at the end of the accounting period. The closing balances for one period become the opening balances for the next. Nominal accounts, on the other hand, are those revenue and expense accounts which are closed out to income. The net balance of these accounts (the excess of revenue over expense or vice-versa) is then transferred to the balance sheet capital account (see Example 7).

It is customary to establish subsidiary ledgers to provide detailed information in support of certain accounts and amplification of general ledger balances. For example, Accounts Receivable in the general ledger summarizes the total accounts due, while its corresponding subsidiary ledger shows transactions by customer. Such a system not only simplifies billing, but also reduces the degree of detail required in the general ledger.

Where subsidiary ledgers are used, transactions are posted to the subsidiary ledger accounts at the time journal entries are recorded. The total of these journals is posted to the control account at the end of the month.

EXAMPLE 2.

The Mastcar Corporation's sales journal and corresponding subsidiary ledgers for the month of January are shown on page 11.

SALES JOURNAL   S-1

Date	Account Debited	P. R.	Accounts Receivable Dr. Sales Cr.
Jan. 1	J. Smith		500
7	R. Roberts		350
9	M. Carey		605
25	J. Smith		300
			1,755

ACCOUNTS RECEIVABLE SUBSIDIARY LEDGER

J. Smith

Jan. 1 S-1 500	
25 S-1 300	

R. Roberts

Jan. 7 S-1 350	

M. Carey

Jan. 9 S-1 605	

EXAMPLE 3.

At the end of the month, Mastcar's sales journal total is posted to the accounts receivable control account. A trial balance of the subsidiary ledger should agree with the control account balance.

Control Account
General Ledger

Accounts Receivable

Jan. 31 S-1 1,755	

Subsidiary Ledger
Trial Balance

J. Smith	800
R. Roberts	350
M. Carey	605
	1,755

2.3 THE WORKSHEET

To bring the ledger accounts up to date, the accountant prepares an informal record called *the worksheet* in which he makes the adjusting and closing entries and prepares the financial statement data.   The steps in completing the worksheet are:

(1) Enter the trial balance figures from the ledger.

(2) Make the adjusting entries.

(3) Compute adjusted trial balances and extend figures to the cost of goods manufactured, income statement and balance sheet columns.

(4) Total the cost of goods manufactured columns* and transfer the balance to the debit column of the income statement.

(5) Total the income statement and balance sheet columns and enter the net income or loss.

EXAMPLE 4.

Given the Mastcar Corporation trial balance and year-end adjustments on page 13, its worksheet would appear as shown in Fig. 2-1.

---

* Normally included for a manufacturing company.

MASTCAR CORPORATION   Worksheet   Year Ending December 31, 19X1

	ACCOUNTS	TRIAL BALANCE Debit	TRIAL BALANCE Credit	ADJUSTMENTS Debit	ADJUSTMENTS Credit	COST OF GOODS MANUFACTURED Debit	COST OF GOODS MANUFACTURED Credit	INCOME STATEMENT Debit	INCOME STATEMENT Credit	BALANCE SHEET Debit	BALANCE SHEET Credit
1	Cash	44750								44750	
2	Accounts Receivable	35300								35300	
3	Allowance for Doubtful Accounts		1250		(2) 750						2000
4	Finished Goods	60300		(5) 43100	(6) 60300					43100	
5	Work in Process	25600		(5) 31500	(6) 25600					31500	
6	Direct Materials	22100		(5) 27600	(6) 22100					27600	
7	Prepaid Expenses (control)	7500			(1) 4000					3500	
8	Plant Assets (control)	545450								545450	
9	Accumulated Depr. Plant Assets		138400		(4) 20000						158400
10	Accounts Payable		32500								32500
11	Income Tax Payable				(7) 3000						3000
12	Accrued Liabilities				(3) 2500						2500
13	Common Stock $5 par		450000								450000
14	Retained Earnings		50500								50500
15	Income Summary			(6) 60300	(5) 43100			60300	43100		
16	Manufacturing Summary			(6) 25600	(5) 31500	25600	31500				
17	" "			(6) 22100	(5) 27600	22100	27600				
18	Sales		510000						510000		
19	Direct Materials Purchases	160800				160800					
20	Direct Labor	145000				147200					
21	Factory Overhead (control)	46750		(3) 2200		68250					
22	" "			(1) 3300							
23	" "			(3) 300							
24	Selling Expenses (control)	41000		(4) 18000				41000			
25	General Expenses (control)	35600		(1) 800				39150			
26				(2) 750							
				(4) 2000							
27	Interest Expense	500						500			
28	Income Tax	72000		(7) 3000				75000			
		1182650	1182650	240950	240950	423950					
30	Cost of Goods Manufactured						364850	364850			
						423950	423950	520800	553100	731200	698900
33	Net Income							32300			32300
								553100	553100	731200	731200

Fig. 2-1

Mastcar Corporation
Trial Balance
December 31, 19X1

Cash	$ 44,750	
Accounts Receivable	35,300	
Allowance for Doubtful Accounts		$ 1,250
Finished Goods	60,300	
Work in Process	25,600	
Direct Materials	22,100	
Prepaid Expenses (control)	7,500	
Plant Assets (control)	545,450	
Accumulated Depreciation, Plant Assets		138,400
Accounts Payable		32,500
Common Stock, $15 par		450,000
Retained Earnings		50,500
Sales		510,000
Direct Materials Purchases	160,800	
Direct Labor	145,000	
Factory Overhead (control)	46,750	
Selling Expenses (control)	41,000	
General Expenses (control)	35,600	
Interest Expense	500	
Income Taxes	12,000	
	$1,182,650	$1,182,650

Adjustments for the current year are as follows:

(1) Prepaid insurance of $4,000 has expired during the year, 80% being applicable to Factory Overhead and 20% to General Expenses.

(2) An analysis of accounts receivable shows that the Allowance for Doubtful Accounts should be $2,000.

(3) Unpaid payroll amounts at the end of the year are: direct labor, $2,200; factory supervision, $300.

(4) Depreciation for the year was $20,000, chargeable 90% to Factory Overhead and 10% to General Expenses.

(5) Inventories at December 31, 19X1 are: Finished Goods, $43,100; Work in Process, $31,500; Direct Materials, $27,600.

(6) The opening inventories are to be closed out to the appropriate summaries.

(7) The estimated federal income tax for the year is $15,000.

2.4   FINANCIAL STATEMENTS

Financial statements are prepared using the worksheet as the prime source of data. The *Statement of Cost of Goods Manufactured,* the *Income Statement,* and the *Balance Sheet* are typical formal reports.   (See Chapters 3 and 4 for detailed discussions.)

EXAMPLE 5.

The financial statements of the Mastcar Corporation appear below.

Mastcar Corporation
Statement of Cost of Goods Manufactured
year ended December 31, 19X1

Work in Process Inventory, January 1		$ 25,600
Direct Materials:		
Inventory, January 1	$ 22,100	
Purchases	160,800	
Available for Use	$182,900	
Less: Inventory, December 31	27,600	
Cost Put in Production	$155,300	
Direct Labor	147,200	
Factory Overhead	68,250	
Total Manufacturing Costs		370,750
Total Work in Process During Period		$396,350
Less: Work in Process Inventory, December 31		31,500
Cost of Goods Manufactured		$364,850

Mastcar Corporation
Income Statement
year ended December 31, 19X1

Sales		$510,000
Cost of Goods Sold:		
Finished Goods Inventory, January 1	$ 60,300	
Cost of Goods Manufactured	364,850	
Goods Available for Sale	$425,150	
Less: Finished Goods Inventory, December 31	43,100	
Cost of Goods Sold		382,050
Gross Profit on Sales		$127,950
Operating Expenses:		
Selling Expenses	$ 41,000	
General Expenses	39,150	
Total Operating Expenses		80,150
Net Operating Income		$ 47,800
Other Expense:		
Interest Expense		500
Income Before Income Taxes		$ 47,300
Income Taxes		15,000
Net Income		$ 32,300

Mastcar Corporation
Balance Sheet
December 31, 19X1

ASSETS

Current Assets			
Cash		$ 44,750	
Accounts Receivable	$ 35,300		
Less: Allowance for Doubtful Accounts	2,000	33,300	
Inventories:			
Finished Goods		43,100	
Work in Process		31,500	
Direct Materials		27,600	
Prepaid Expenses		3,500	
Total Current Assets			$183,750

Plant Assets			
Plant Assets (Control)		$545,450	
Less: Accumulated Depreciation, Plant Assets		158,400	
Total Plant Assets			$387,050
Total Assets			$570,800

LIABILITIES

Current Liabilities			
Accounts Payable		$32,500	
Income Tax Payable		3,000	
Accrued Liabilities		2,500	
Total Liabilities			$ 38,000

STOCKHOLDERS' EQUITY

Common Stock, $15 par		$450,000	
Retained Earnings		82,800*	
Total Stockholders' Equity			532,800
Total Liabilities & Stockholders' Equity			$570,800

* Balance, January 1	$50,500
Net income, Year 19X1	32,300
Balance, December 31	$82,800

2.5 ADJUSTING AND CLOSING ENTRIES

After the completion of the worksheet and financial statements, entries must be made in the journal in order to bring the ledger accounts up to their current balances as reflected on the financial statements. This procedure is part of the *accrual basis* of accounting, which requires that a given period's expenses be matched against its revenues.

Adjusting entries are entered in the general journal and posted to the ledger after the financial statements have been formalized.

EXAMPLE 6.

The adjustment entries posted in columns 3 and 4 of Fig. 2-1 are recorded below.

Entry 1	Factory Overhead (control)	3,200	
	General Expense (control)	800	
	Prepaid Expenses (control)		4,000
Entry 2	General Expense (control)	750	
	Allowance for Doubtful Accounts		750
Entry 3	Direct Labor	2,200	
	Factory Overhead (control)	300	
	Accrued Liabilities		2,500
Entry 4	Factory Overhead (control)	18,000	
	General Expense (control)	2,000	
	Accumulated Depreciation, Plant Assets		20,000

Entry 5	Finished Goods	43,100	
	Work in Process	31,500	
	Direct Materials	27,600	
	Income Summary		43,100
	Manufacturing Summary		31,500
	Manufacturing Summary		27,600
Entry 6	Income Summary	60,300	
	Manufacturing Summary	25,600	
	Manufacturing Summary	22,100	
	Finished Goods		60,300
	Work in Process		25,600
	Direct Materials		22,100
Entry 7	Income Taxes	3,000	
	Income Taxes Payable		3,000

Closing entries are also made at this time. A summary account—variously called the Expense and Income Summary, Profit and Loss Summary, etc.—is set up; each expense account is credited so as to produce a zero balance, and the total amount for the closed-out accounts is debited to the Expense and Income Summary. Similarly, the individual revenue accounts are closed out by debiting, and the total is credited to the summary account. The result is zero balances in all nominal accounts for the new fiscal year, while the Expense and Income Summary shows the net income or loss for the year just ended.

EXAMPLE 7.

We again refer to the accounts of the Mastcar Corporation to illustrate closing entries (see columns 5, 6, 7 and 8 of Fig. 2-1 for worksheet presentation).

Entry 1	Manufacturing Summary	59,100	
	Cost of Goods Manufactured	364,850	
	Manufacturing Summary		47,700
	Direct Materials Purchased		160,800
	Direct Labor		147,200
	Factory Overhead (control)		68,250
Entry 2	Sales	510,000	
	Income Summary		510,000
Entry 3	Income Summary	477,700	
	Finished Goods, December 31	43,100	
	Selling Expense (control)		41,000
	General Expense (control)		39,150
	Interest Expense		500
	Income Taxes		15,000
	Cost of Goods Manufactured		364,850
	Finished Goods, January 1		60,300
Entry 4	Income Summary	32,300	
	Retained Earnings		32,300

2.6 REVERSING ENTRIES

Since adjusting entries set up temporary accrued balances, reversing entries (the exact opposite of adjustments) are made to correct the balances for the new accounting period.

EXAMPLE 8.

From the Mastcar Corporation's accounts, the following reversing entries have been made.

Entry 1	*Accrued Liabilities*	2,500	
	Direct Labor		2,200
	Factory Overhead (control)		300
Entry 2	*Income Taxes Payable*	3,000	
	Income Taxes		3,000

Summary

(1) The accounting process is composed of three major elements: _____
_____ .

(2) Books of original entry are called _____ . The complete set of accounts appears in the _____ .

(3) Assets, liabilities and capital accounts are known as _____ accounts while income and expense accounts are referred to as _____ accounts.

(4) In order to facilitate adjusting entries, the accountant uses an informal record called the _____ .

(5) The worksheet is retained by the _____ and (is/is not) presented with the formal statements.

(6) A heading for two columns that may appear in a manufacturing worksheet that would not appear in a mercantile worksheet is _____ .

Answers: (1) recording, classifying and summarizing; (2) journals, ledger; (3) real, nominal; (4) worksheet;
(5) accountant, is not; (6) Cost of Goods Manufactured.

Solved Problems

2.1. State whether each of the following transactions should be recorded in the cash receipts journal, cash disbursements journal, sales journal, purchases journal or general journal.

(*a*) Purchase of merchandise on account.

(*b*) Purchase of merchandise for cash.

(c) Receipt of cash from a customer in settlement of an account.

(d) Cash sales for the month

(e) Payment of salaries.

(f) Sales of merchandise for cash.

(g) Sales of merchandise on account.

(h) Cash refund to customer.

(i) Sale of a fixed asset for cash.

(j) Notes payable sent to creditor in settlement of an account.

SOLUTION

(a) Purchases   (f) Cash receipts

(b) Cash disbursements   (g) Sales

(c) Cash receipts   (h) Cash disbursements

(d) Cash receipts   (i) Cash receipts

(e) Cash disbursements   (j) General journal

2.2.   William Drew began business on March 1. The transactions completed by the Drew
Company for the month of March are listed below. Establish the necessary journals
and record the transactions.

March 1:   Deposited $14,000 in bank account for the operation of Drew Company

March 2:   Paid rent for the month, $600, Check #1

March 4:   Purchased equipment on account from Andon Equipment, $10,000

March 7:   Purchased merchandise on account from Baily Company, $1,200

March 7:   Cash sales for the week, $1,650

March 10:   Issued Check #2 for $150, for store supplies

March 11:   Sold merchandise on account to Manny Company, $600

March 12:   Sold merchandise on account to Nant Company, $350

March 14:   Paid biweekly salaries of $740, Check #3

March 14:   Cash sales for the week, $1,800

March 16:   Purchased merchandise on account from Cotin Company, $1,100

March 17:   Issued Check #4 to Baily Company for March 7 purchase, less 2%

March 18:   Bought $250 worth of store supplies from Salio Supply House on account

March 19:   Returned defective merchandise of $200 to Cotin Company and received
            credit

March 19:   Sold merchandise on account to Olin Company, $645

March 21:   Issued Check #5 to Andon Equipment for $500, in part payment of equip-
            ment purchase

March 22: Received check from Nant Company in settlement of their March 12 purchase, less 2% discount

March 22: Purchased merchandise from Canny Corporation for cash, $750, Check #6

March 23: Cash sales for the week, $1,845

March 24: Purchased merchandise on account from Baily Corporation, $850

March 25: Sold merchandise on account to Pallit Corporation, $740

March 26: Purchased additional supplies, $325, from Salio Supply House

March 27: Received check from Manny Company in settlement of their March 11 purchase

March 30: Cash sales for the week, $1,920

March 30: Received $300 on account from Olin Company

March 31: Paid biweekly salaries, $810. Check #7

SOLUTION

GENERAL JOURNAL   J-1

Date	Description	P. R.	Debit	Credit
Mar. 19	Accounts Payable, Cotin Co.	21 / √	200	
	Purchase Returns and Allowances	52		200
	Defective goods.			

CASH RECEIPTS JOURNAL   CR-1

Date	Account Credited	P. R.	Cash Dr.	Sales Disc. Dr.	Acct. Rec. Cr.	Sales Cr.	Sundry Acct. Cr.
Mar. 1	Drew Company, Capital	31	14,000				14,000
7	Sales	√	1,650			1,650	
14	Sales	√	1,800			1,800	
22	Nant Company	√	343	7	350		
23	Sales	√	1,845			1,845	
27	Manny Company	√	600		600		
30	Sales	√	1,920			1,920	
30	Olin Company	√	300		300		
			22,458	7	1,250	7,215	14,000
			(11)	(42)	(12)	(41)	(√)

CASH DISBURSEMENTS JOURNAL   CD-1

Date	Check No.	Account Debited	P. R.	Cash Cr.	Pur. Disc. Cr.	Acct. Pay. Dr.	Sundry Acct. Dr.
Mar. 2	1	Rent Expense	54	600			600
10	2	Store Supplies	14	150			150
14	3	Salaries Expense	55	740			740
17	4	Baily Company	√	1,176	24	1,200	
21	5	Andon Equipment	√	500		500	
22	6	Purchases	51	750			750
31	7	Salaries Expense	55	810			810
				4,726	24	1,700	3,050
				(11)	(51)	(21)	(√)

PURCHASES JOURNAL

P-1

Date	Account Cr.	P. R.	Acct. Pay. Cr.	Pur. Dr.	Store Supp. Dr.	Office Supp. Dr.	Sundry Acct. Dr.		
							Acct.	P. R.	Amount
Mar. 4	Andon Equipment	√	10,000				Equip.	19	10,000
7	Baily Company	√	1,200	1,200					
16	Cotin Company	√	1,100	1,100					
18	Salio Supply House	√	250		250				
24	Baily Corporation	√	850	850					
26	Salio Supply House	√	325		325				
			13,725	3,150	575				10,000
			(21)	(51)	(14)				(√)

SALES JOURNAL

Date	Account Debited	P. R.	Accounts Receivable Dr. Sales Cr.
Mar. 11	Manny Company	√	600
12	Nant Company	√	350
19	Olin Company	√	645
25	Pallit Corporation	√	740
			2,335
			(12)(41)

2.3.   A review of the Bronner Corporation's books, which have not yet been closed, provides the following closing information as of December 31, 197–.   Prepare (a) year-end adjustments and (b) required reversing entries.

(1)   The building occupied by the corporation cost $220,000.   The estimated useful life is 50 years with no expected scrap value.   Straight-line depreciation is used.

(2)   An aging of the accounts receivable at December 31 indicates $4,200 to be a reasonable estimate of uncollectible accounts.   The allowance for doubtful accounts shows a credit balance of $600.

(3)   Bonds of $100,000, bearing 6% interest and held for investment, pay interest semiannually on April 1 and October 1.

(4)   Accrued wages as of December 31 amounted to $10,654.

(5)   The prepaid insurance account at the end of the year shows a balance of $16,000. The unexpired portions of the policies as of December 31 are $9,400.

(6)   Mortgage Notes Payable of $140,000 are outstanding at December 31.   Interest at the rate of 6% is payable semiannually on March 31 and September 30.   No entry has been made for the accrued interest since the last semiannual payment.

SOLUTION

(a)   **ADJUSTING ENTRIES**

(1)   Depreciation Expense—Building   4,400
              Accumulated Depreciation—Building   4,400
                  ($220,000 × 1/50)

(2)   Uncollectible Accounts Expense   3,600
              Allowance for Uncollectible Accounts   3,600
                  ($4,200 − $600)

(3)	Accrued Interest Receivable	1,500	
	Interest Income		1,500
	($100,000 × 6% × 1/4)		
(4)	Wages Expense	10,654	
	Accrued Wages Payable		10,654
(5)	Insurance Expense	6,600	
	Prepaid Insurance		6,600
	($16,000 − $9,400)		
(6)	Interest Expense	2,100	
	Accrued Interest Payable		2,100
	($140,000 × 6% × 1/4)		

(b) **REVERSING ENTRIES**

(1)	None required		
(2)	None required		
(3)	Interest Income	1,500	
	Accrued Interest Receivable		1,500
(4)	Accrued Wages Payable	10,654	
	Wage Expense		10,654
(5)	None required		
(6)	Accrued Interest Payable	2,100	
	Interest Expense		2,100

2.4. Below are the balance sheet account balances for Stevemarc Corporation as of December 31, 19X1. Prepare a classified balance sheet.

Accounts Receivable	$ 128,400
Accounts Payable	102,000
Accumulated Depreciation, Building	120,000
Accumulated Depreciation, Equipment	26,000
Allowance for Doubtful Accounts	4,600
Appropriation for Plant Expansion	68,000
Appropriation for Treasury Stock	42,000
Bonds (6%, 10-year debentures)	1,000,000
Building	696,700
Cash	1,655,000
Common Stock, $25 par (40,000 shares authorized, 30,000 shares issued)	750,000
Common Stock Subscribed	100,000
Common Stock Subscriptions Receivable	60,000
Discount on Preferred Stock	60,000

Equipment	$216,000
Goodwill	125,000
Land	30,000
Merchandise Inventory	442,500
Notes Receivable	75,000
Notes Payable	38,000
Organization Costs	15,000
Paid-in Capital from Sale of Treasury Stock	22,000
Premium on Bonds Payable	36,000
Premium on Common Stock	15,000
Preferred Stock, 6%, $100 par (20,000 shares authorized, 10,000 shares issued)	1,000,000
Prepaid Expenses	32,000
Taxes Payable	24,000
Treasury Stock (at cost)	42,000
Unappropriated Retained Earnings	230,000

SOLUTION

Stevemarc Corporation
Balance Sheet
December 31, 19X1

ASSETS

Current Assets			
Cash		$1,655,000	
Accounts Receivable	$ 128,400		
Less: Allowance for Doubtful Accounts	4,600	123,800	
Notes Receivable		75,000	
Merchandise Inventory		442,500	
Common Stock Subscriptions Receivable		60,000	
Prepaid Expenses		32,000	
Total Current Assets			$2,388,300
Fixed Assets			
Building	$ 696,700		
Less: Accumulated Depreciation Building	120,000	$ 576,700	
Equipment	$ 216,000		
Less: Accumulated Depreciation Equipment	26,000	190,000	
Land		30,000	
Total Fixed Assets			796,700
Intangible Assets			
Goodwill	$ 125,000		
Organization Costs		15,000	
Total Intangible Assets			140,000
Total Assets			$3,325,000

LIABILITIES AND STOCKHOLDERS' EQUITY

Current Liabilities

Accounts Payable	$ 102,000	
Notes Payable	38,000	
Taxes Payable	24,000	
Total Current Liabilities		$ 164,000

Long-term Liabilities

Bonds (6%, 10-year debentures)	$1,000,000	
Add: Premium on Bonds Payable	36,000	
Total Long-term Liabilities		1,036,000
Total Liabilities		$1,200,000

Paid-in Capital

Preferred Stock, 6%, $100 par (20,000 shares authorized, 10,000 shares issued)	$1,000,000		
Less: Discount on Preferred Stock	60,000	$ 940,000	
Common Stock, $25 (40,000 shares authorized, 30,000 shares issued)	$ 750,000		
Add: Premium on Common Stock	15,000	765,000	
Common Stock Subscribed		100,000	
From Sales of Treasury Stock		22,000	
Total Paid-in Capital			$1,827,000

Retained Earnings

Appropriated Retained Earnings:			
For Plant Expansion	$ 68,000		
For Treasury Stock	42,000		
Total Appropriated Retained Earnings		$ 110,000	
Unappropriatd Retained Earnings		230,000	
Total Retained Earnings			340,000
Total			$2,167,000
Less: Treasury Stock (at cost)			42,000
Total Stockholders' Equity			$2,125,000
Total Liabilities and Stockholders' Equity			$3,325,000

2.5. The Richard Janowitz Manufacturing Company has the following accounts in its pre-closing trial balance at December 31, 19X1

Direct Materials Purchases	$ 75,700	Finishing Goods Inventory	$ 85,000
Direct Materials Inventory	29,500	Sales	360,000
Direct Labor	113,500	Selling Expense	18,000
Factory Overhead	76,000	General Expense	12,000
Work in Process Inventory	35,000		

Inventories at December 31 were:

Direct Materials	$31,400
Work in Process	28,200
Finished Goods	80,000

Prepare a statement of Cost of Goods Manufactured.

SOLUTION

Richard Janowitz Manufacturing Company
Cost of Goods Manufactured
December 31, 19X1

Work in Process Inventory, January 1, 19X1		$ 35,000
Direct Materials		
Inventory, January 1, 19X1	$ 29,500	
Purchases	75,700	
Available for Use	$105,200	
Less: Inventory, December 31, 19X1	31,400	
Put in Production	$ 73,800	
Direct Labor	113,500	
Factory Overhead	76,000	
Total Manufacturing Costs		263,300
Total Work in Process During Period		$298,300
Less: Work in Process Inventory, December 31, 19X1		28,200
Cost of Goods Manufactured		$270,100

2.6. Based on the data in Problem 2.5, show the necessary journal entries for December 31 to (a) adjust the inventory accounts, (b) close the accounts to the manufacturing summary, (c) close the manufacturing summary.

SOLUTION

(a)	Manufacturing Summary	64,500	
	Work in Process Inventory		35,000
	Direct Materials Inventory		29,500
	Work in Process Inventory	28,200	
	Direct Materials Inventory	31,400	
	Manufacturing Summary		59,600
	Expense and Income Summary	85,000	
	Finished Goods Inventory		85,000
	Finished Goods Inventory	80,000	
	Expense and Income Summary		80,000
(b)	Manufacturing Summary	265,200	
	Direct Materials Purchases		75,700
	Direct Labor		113,500
	Factory Overhead		76,000
(c)	Expense and Income Summary	270,100	
	Manufacturing Summary		270,100

2.7.　At the end of January, 19X1 the S. Lashinsky Company has the following trial balance:

Cash	$ 34,750	
Marketable Securities	15,000	
Accounts Receivable	41,300	
Allowance for Doubtful Accounts		$ 2,200
Finished Goods, Product A	32,400	
Finished Goods, Product B	56,200	
Work in Process, Department 1	22,900	
Work in Process, Department 2	22,600	
Materials	25,400	
Prepaid Expenses	5,800	
Machinery and Equipment	115,700	
Accumulated Depreciation, Machinery and Equipment		35,000
Buildings	257,000	
Accumulated Depreciation, Buildings		55,000
Land	50,000	
Accounts Payable		48,600
Wages Payable		6,500
Income Taxes Payable		4,200
Mortgage Note Payable (due 1990)		75,000
Common Stock, $25 par		350,000
Retained Earnings		85,400
Sales		175,800
Cost of Goods Sold	115,600	
Factory Overhead, Department 1	300	
Factory Overhead, Department 2	50	
Factory Overhead, Department 3		100
Selling Expenses	24,600	
General Expenses	13,500	
Interest Expense	650	
Interest Income		150
Income Taxes	4,200	
	$837,950	$837,950

Prepare the company's (a) income statement and (b) classified balance sheet.

SOLUTION

S. Lashinsky Company
Income Statement
month of January, 19X1

Sales		$175,800
Less: Cost of Goods Sold		115,600
Gross Profit on Sales		$ 60,200
Operating Expenses		
Selling Expenses	$24,600	
General Expenses	13,500	38,100
Net Income from Operations		$ 22,100
Other Expenses (net):		
Interest Expense	$ 650	
Less: Interest Income	150	500
Income Before Income Taxes		$ 21,600
Income Taxes		4,200
Net Income		$ 17,400

S. Lashinsky Company
Balance Sheet
January 31, 19X1
ASSETS

Current Assets			
Cash		$ 34,750	
Marketable Securities		15,000	
Accounts Receivable	$41,300		
Less: Allowance for Doubtful Accounts	2,200	39,100	
Inventories			
Finished Goods	$88,600		
Work in Process	45,500		
Materials	25,400	159,500	
Prepaid Expenses		5,800	
Total Current Assets			$254,150

Plant Assets	Cost	Accumulated Depreciation	Book Value	
Mach. & Equipment	$115,700	$35,000	$ 80,700	
Buildings	257,000	55,000	202,000	
Land	50,000		50,000	
Total Plant Assets	$422,700	$90,000		332,700
Deferred Charge				
Factory Overhead Underapplied				250
Total Assets				$587,100

LIABILITIES AND STOCKHOLDERS' EQUITY

Current Liabilities			
Accounts Payable		$ 48,600	
Wages Payable		6,500	
Income Taxes Payable		4,200	
Total Current Liabilities			$ 59,300
Long-term Liabilities			
Mortgage Note Payable (due 1990)			75,000
Total Liabilities			$134,300
Stockholders' Equity			
Common Stock, $25 par		$350,000	
Retained Earnings	$85,400		
Add: Net Income	17,400	102,800	
Total Stockholders' Equity			452,800
Total Liabilities and Stockholders' Equity			$587,100

2.8. Based upon the income statement below, prepare the necessary entries to close the accounts.

J. Epstein Company
Income Statement
year ended December 31, 197—

Sales Revenue			
Gross Sales			$700,000
Less: Sales Returns and Allowances		$ 15,300	
Cash Discounts on Sales		12,400	27,700
Net Sales			$672,300
Cost of Goods Sold			
Beginning Inventory		$ 58,700	
Purchases	$400,000		
Less: Purchase Returns and Allowances	12,100		
Net Purchases	$387,900		
Transportation-in	43,200	431,100	
Goods Available for Sale		$489,800	
Less: Ending Inventory		45,600	
Cost of Goods Sold			444,200
Gross Profit on Sales			$228,100
Operating Expenses			
Selling Expenses			
Sales Salaries and Commissions	$ 30,000		
Sales Travel	15,000		
Advertising and Promotion	28,000		
Delivery Expense	7,000		
Other Selling Expenses	5,000	$ 85,000	
General and Administrative Expenses			
Administrative Salaries	$ 32,000		
Insurance	8,000		
Depreciation of Office Equipment	3,000		
Other Administrative Expenses	12,000	55,000	
Total Operating Expenses			140,000
Net Operating Income			$ 88,100
Other Revenues			
Interest	$ 7,000		
Dividends	3,000	$ 10,000	
Other Expenses			
Interest Expense		2,100	7,900
Income Before Taxes			$ 96,000
Federal and State Income Taxes			50,000
Net Income			$ 46,000

SOLUTION

CLOSING ENTRIES

Entry 1	Inventory	45,600	
	Sales Income	700,000	
	Purchase Returns and Allowances	12,100	
	Interest Income	7,000	
	Dividend Income	3,000	
	Income Summary		767,700

Entry 2	*Income Summary*	721,700	
	Inventory		58,700
	Sales Returns and Allowances		15,300
	Cash Discounts on Sales		12,400
	Purchases		400,000
	Transportation-in		43,200
	Sales Salaries and Commissions		30,000
	Sales Travel		15,000
	Advertising and Promotion		28,000
	Delivery Expense		7,000
	Other Selling Expense		5,000
	Administrative Salaries		32,000
	Insurance		8,000
	Depreciation of Office Equipment		3,000
	Other Administrative Expenses		12,000
	Interest Expense		2,100
	Federal and State Income Taxes		50,000
Entry 3	*Income Summary*	46,000	
	Retained Earnings		46,000

Chapter 3

The Balance Sheet

3.1 CLASSIFICATION OF THE BALANCE SHEET

The *Balance Sheet,* also known as the Statement of Financial Position, presents the assets, liabilities and capital of a business entity at a specific date. Since the balance sheet is an expansion of the basic accounting equation, accounts are generally classified under the three basic headings:

1. *Assets*: Resources the business owns
2. *Liabilities*: Claims against those resources
3. *Capital or Stockholders' Equity*: The difference between assets and liabilities

In preparing a balance sheet, the general practice is to arrange the assets in the order of liquidity and the liabilities in order of expected payment. By placing the items in a current to long-term sequence, the emphasis is on current solvency. While a variety of captions exist, those listed below are generally accepted.

ASSETS

(1) **Current Assets.** Current assets are those which are reasonably expected to be converted into cash or used during the normal operating cycle of the business, or within one year, whichever is longer. They would include cash in banks and on hand, marketable securities used in current operations of the company and accounts receivable, inventory and short-term prepayments.

NOTE: Negative accounts, known as *contra assets,* under the current asset classification might include Allowance for Doubtful Accounts and Notes Receivable Discounted.

(2) **Investments.** Long-term investments are usually held for ownership control, appreciation or regular income and include investments in stocks and bonds, advances to subsidiaries and affiliates, and land or other long-lived assets held for investment rather than for current use of the business. Although long-term investments are usually carried at cost, it is advisable to show parenthetically the current market quotations or other estimates of current value.

(3) **Property, Plant and Equipment.** Investments in long-lived physical properties to be used in the production of goods and services are included in this category. This classification discussed in Chapters 10 and 11 may be broken down into three groups:

(*a*) *Assets subject to depreciation.* Buildings, equipment and machinery, furniture, etc.

(*b*) *Assets subject to depletion.* Mineral deposits, oil, timber and those assets which are extracted and used up physically.

(c) *Land.* Land used for business purposes is considered to have a perpetually useful life and is carried at cost with no depreciation or depletion charges.

(4) **Intangible Assets.** These are long-term assets that have no physical existence but are rights having value. Although most balance sheets list intangible assets in one total, a detailed balance sheet would generally separate them into two categories:

(a) Limited legal and useful life—Patents, copyrights

(b) No definite life—Trademarks, goodwill

Intangible assets are recorded at cost. According to APB Opinion No. 17, all intangibles must be amortized; systematic charges should be made to periods benefited and the period of amortization should not exceed 40 years (see Chapter 12).

LIABILITIES AND STOCKHOLDERS' EQUITY

(5) **Current Liabilities.** Current liabilities are obligations whose liquidation is expected to require the use of existing current assets or the creation of other current liabilities. This classification includes accounts and notes payable, income taxes payable, cash dividends payable, etc.

(6) **Deferred Credits.** These credits represent income received but not yet earned and are included in the total of liabilities because they involve a commitment to provide goods and services in the future. Their balances are properly carried forward until the company meets its responsibilities through performance or delivery of goods.

(7) **Long-term Liabilities.** These are obligations with a maturity longer than one year which are not to be liquidated from current assets. Included in this classification are bonds payable, long-term notes payable, mortgage payable, long-term service contracts, etc. Installments due and advances earned in the current period should be shown under current liabilities while the balances are carried as long-term liabilities.

NOTE: A negative liability account (*contra liability*) such as *discount on bonds payable* can be handled in one of two ways: (i) as a separate valuation account or (ii) as a parenthetical notation reflecting the amount deducted to arrive at the net amount shown in the balance sheet.

(8) **Owners' Equity.** The sole proprietorship is represented by a single capital account and is the cumulative result of the owner's investments and withdrawals as well as profits and losses. In the partnership, a capital account is established for each partner; it summarizes his investments, withdrawals and shares of profits and losses, measuring his individual equity in the business.

However, in the corporation's equity account, a distinction is made between capital originating from the stockholder's investment (paid-in capital) and capital originating from income (retained earnings).

Paid-in Capital. For accounting purposes, paid-in capital consists of two components:

1. *Capital stock.* That portion of the stockholder's investment carried at par value or, in the case of a no-par issue, at the total purchase price or some value set by law. Ledger capital stock accounts should show class, par value, shares authorized, issued and outstanding.

2. *Additional paid-in capital.* This includes both positive and negative elements. Additional paid-in capital from shares issued and sold at a price above par or stated value is credited to a separate account with a title descriptive of capital source (i.e. Premium on Common Stock). When stock is sold at less than par, a discount is reported and an account such as Discount on Capital Stock is debited.

Capital arising from transactions other than the sale of stock, such as donations of property or sale of treasury stock at amounts greater than cost, is also considered additional paid-in capital.

EXAMPLE 1.

Typical ledger accounts for stock issues show

Preferred 5% stock, $100 par (1,000 shares authorized and issued)	$100,000
Common stock, $25 par (40,000 shares authorized, 20,000 issued)	500,000

EXAMPLE 2.

The balance sheet paid-in capital section is presented as follows:

Paid-in Capital

Preferred 5% Stock, $100 par (1,000 shares authorized and issued)	$100,000	
Discount on Preferred Stock	5,000	$ 95,000
Common Stock, $25 par (40,000 shares authorized, 20,000 issued)	$500,000	
Premium on Common Stock	20,000	520,000
Gain on Sale of Treasury Stock		10,000
Donated Capital		8,000
Total Paid-in Capital		$633,000

Retained Earnings. Net income increases retained earnings, while dividends decrease it. If there is an excess of dividends and losses over profits, this will result in negative earnings, or a *deficit*. A balance in retained earnings is added to paid-in capital while a deficit is subtracted. Retained earnings may be *appropriated* and unavailable for dividends (i.e. for the purpose of plant expansion, contingencies or sinking funds). Those earnings that are free for dividends with no restrictions are called *unappropriated retained earnings*.

EXAMPLE 3.

Retained earnings may be presented on the balance sheet as shown below.

Retained Earnings		
Appropriated:		
For Plant Expansion	$40,000	
For Contingencies	10,000	$ 50,000
Unappropriated		125,000
Total Retained Earnings		$175,000

3.2 FORMS OF THE BALANCE SHEET

Account Form. This form presents the assets by sections on the left side and the liabilities and equity balanced against it on the right side. Depending on the type of reader, an appropriate degree of condensation will be applied. While management demands detailed and complete information, usually supplied by supplementary schedules, stockholders are more interested in condensed financial statements. Therefore, related items are frequently combined (e.g. finished goods, work in process and raw materials may be combined and listed as inventory).

EXAMPLE 4.

A model balance sheet in account form is shown in Fig. 3-1.

Report Form. In order to avoid the use of facing pages, an alternative arrangement is to list the liability and equity sections directly below the assets on the same page.

Statement of Financial Position. Some companies prefer to emphasize their current financial position and to report working capital. This vertical presentation may be summarized as:

Current Assets − Current Liabilities = Working Capital

All Other Assets − All Other Liabilities = Stockholders' Equity

EXAMPLE 5.

In the illustration below, the Statement of Financial Position uses the figures of the model balance sheet for the Mastcar Corporation (see Example 4).

Mastcar Corporation
Statement of Financial Position
December 31. 197—

Current Assets		$166,000
Less: Current Liabilities		62,000
Working Capital		$104,000
Add:		
Investments		31,000
Fixed Assets		141,000
Intangible Assets		15,000
Deferred Charges		25,000
Total Assets less Current Liabilities		$316,000
Deduct:		
Long-term Liabilities	$80,000	
Deferred Credits	4,000	84,000
Net Assets		$232,000
Stockholders' Equity		
Paid-in Capital		$185,000
Retained Earnings		47,000
Stockholders' Equity		$232,000

3.3 STATEMENT ANALYSIS

It should be clear from the foregoing discussion that the balance sheet provides a basis for analyzing and interpreting the business entity's operations—for a given period and over time. A primary area of concern to financial statement users is a firm's *solvency* (its ability to meet its financial obligations when due). This is measured by (1) *working capital*—the excess of current assets over current liabilities, and (2) *the current ratio*—the relationship between current assets and current liabilities which, to be acceptable, should be at least 2 to 1.

Mastcar Corporation
Balance Sheet
December 31, 197–

ASSETS

Current Assets			
Cash			$ 62,000
Accounts Receivable	$ 24,000		
Less: Allowance for Doubtful Accounts	2,000	22,000	
Notes Receivable		16,000	
Inventories (FIFO)		58,000	
Prepaid Insurance		8,000	
Total Current Assets			$166,000
Investments			
Common Stock of Claire Co. (cost)	$ 21,000		
Bonds of Sapre Corporation (cost)	10,000		
Total Investments			31,000
Fixed Assets			
Land	$ 45,000		
Buildings	$86,000		
Less: Accumulated Depreciation, Buildings	26,000	60,000	
Equipment	$52,000		
Less: Accumulated Depreciation, Equipment	16,000	36,000	
Total Fixed Assets			141,000
Intangible Assets			
Goodwill	$10,000		
Patents	5,000		
Total Intangible Assets			15,000
Deferred Charges			
Organization Costs			25,000
Total Assets			$378,000

LIABILITIES

Current Liabilities			
Accounts Payable	$ 36,000		
Notes Payable	10,000		
Dividends Payable	16,000		
Total Current Liabilities			$ 62,000
Contingent Liabilities			
Notes Receivable Discounted (A. Miles, Due February 15, $1,800)			
Long-term Liabilities			
Bonds Payable	$ 50,000		
Less: Discount on Bonds Payable	5,000	$ 45,000	
Mortgage Payable (6%, Due 1990)		35,000	
Total Long-term Liabilities			80,000
Deferred Credits			
Rent Collected in Advance			4,000
Total Liabilities			$146,000

STOCKHOLDERS' EQUITY

Paid-in Capital			
Preferred 6% Stock, $100 Par (1,000 shares authorized & issued)	$100,000		
Less: Discount on Preferred Stock	5,000	$ 95,000	
Common Stock, $25 par (5,000 shares authorized; 3,000 shares issued)	$ 75,000		
Add: Premium on Common Stock	15,000	90,000	
Total Paid-in Capital		$185,000	
Retained Earnings		47,000	
Total Stockholders' Equity			232,000
Total Liabilities and Stockholders' Equity			$378,000

Fig. 3-1

EXAMPLE 6.

With reference to the Mastcar Corporation's statement of financial position (Example 5), working capital is shown as $104,000 ($166,000 in current assets less $62,000 in current liabilities). The current ratio (current assets divided by current liabilities) is 2.677:1 or $2.68 in current assets available to cover every $1 of current liabilities.

The advantage of using the current ratio is that it shows *how many times* current liabilities can be covered, and thus is a better measure of short-run solvency than a simple dollar value of working capital.

Analysis of solvency indicators for successive periods is also useful in determining performance trends.

EXAMPLE 7.

Mastcar Corporation
Current Ratio
19X2, 19X1 and 19X0

	19X2	19X1	19X0
Current Assets	$166,000	$155,000	$150,000
Less: Current Liabilities	62,000	73,000	75,000
Working Capital	$104,000	$ 82,000	$ 75,000
Current Ratio	2.68	2.12	2.0

Steady improvement in the current ratio over three years' operations indicates increasing stability which might be looked on favorably by grantors of short-term loans.

Summary

(1) An alternative name for the balance sheet is the statement of _____.

(2) The general practice in preparing a balance sheet is to arrange the assets in the order of their _____ and liabilities according to their expected _____.

(3) Negative assets are sometimes called _____.

(4) Current assets are expected to be realized in one operating cycle or in a period_____ _____ year, whichever is longer, while fixed assets are expected to have useful lives extending into _____ periods.

(5) Long-term investments are carried at____but it is advisable to show their_____ value.

(6) Deferred credits represent revenue _____ but not yet _____.

(7) Possible future claims against the business are known as _____ and are usually shown as _____ to the financial statements.

(8) Capital originating from stockholders' investments is known as_____ while capital originating from earnings is known as _____.

(9) Restrictions on retained earnings are termed _____ and are segregated because they are unavailable for _____.

(10) A ratio to measure a firm's solvency is the_____ratio while the _____ _____ is used to evaluate a company's ability to meet currently maturing obligations.

Answers: (1) financial position; (2) liquidity, payment dates; (3) contra assets; (4) within one, subsequent; (5) cost, current; (6) received, earned; (7) contingent liabilities, footnotes; (8) paid-in capital, retained earnings; (9) appropriated earnings, dividends; (10) current, working capital amount.

Solved Problems

3.1. On December 31, the balance sheet of the I. Sochet Corporation includes the following classifications:

ASSETS	LIABILITIES AND STOCKHOLDERS' EQUITY
Current Assets	Current Liabilities
Long-term Investments	Contingent Liabilities
Fixed Assets	Long-term Liabilities
Intangible Assets	Deferred Credits
Deferred Charges	Capital Stock
	Paid-in Capital
	Retained Earnings

Indicate the proper balance sheet classification for each of the following items:

(a) Equipment purchased at cost of $125,000.

(b) Bonds payable (20 years), $60,000.

(c) Unamortized discount on bonds payable, $6,000.

(d) A petty cash fund, $250.

(e) Common stock, $50 par, 5,000 shares authorized and $250,000 issued.

(f) Premium on common stock, $12,000.

(g) Cash in the First Union Bank, $26,500.

(h) Inventory of work in process, $22,400.

(i) 20% ownership of the common stock of Carlind Corporation, $82,000.

(j) Net income, $85,200.

(k) Income taxes payable on earnings, $42,000.

(l) Appropriation for plant expansion, $15,000.

(m) Unearned revenue that will be earned in the next three years, $62,500.

(n) Ownership of patents at cost, $12,000.

(o) Possible law suit arising from negligence, $50,000.

(p) Three notes receivable discounted at the bank, totaling $8,600.

SOLUTION

(a) Fixed Assets

(b) Long-term Liabilities

(c) Long-term Liabilities (deduction)

(d) Current Assets

(e) Capital Stock

(f) Paid-in Capital

(g) Current Assets

(h) Current Assets

(i) Long-term Investments

(j) Retained Earnings

(k) Current Liabilities

(l) Retained Earnings

(m) Deferred Credits

(n) Intangible Assets

(o) Contingent Liabilities

(p) Contingent Liabilities

3.2. The balance sheet of the Sullivan Company, which has been prepared by the bookkeeper, is shown below. List your criticisms of this financial statement.

Sullivan Company
Balance Sheet
for the year ended December 31, 197–

ASSETS

Current Assets	
Cash in Banks	$20,000
Accounts Receivable from Various Sources	
(net of reserves for bad debts)	12,000
Inventories	8,000
Total Current Assets	$40,000
Other Assets	
Treasury Stock	15,000
Fixed Assets (net)	20,000
Total Assets	$75,000

LIABILITIES AND STOCKHOLDERS' EQUITY

Current Liabilities		
Accounts Payable		$10,000
Accrued Salaries Payable		1,000
Total Current Liabilities		$11,000
Long-term Liabilities		
Mortgage Note Payable		12,000
Stockholders' Equity		
Capital Stock	$42,000	
Surplus	10,000	
Total Stockholders' Equity		52,000
Total Liabilities and Stockholders' Equity		$75,000

SOLUTION

The following criticisms may be made:

(1) The heading covers a period of time and not a specific date.

(2) Accounts Receivable should be listed at its gross figure, not *net*.

(3) Allowance for Doubtful Accounts should be substituted for the caption, Reserve for Bad Debts.

(4) The above account should be listed separately.

(5) Treasury Stock is not an asset but should be subtracted from Stockholders' Equity with the number of shares listed.

(6) Fixed assets should not be shown as net. The major categories should be listed.

(7) Accumulated Depreciation should be shown separately as a deduction from Fixed Assets, preferably by major categories.

(8) The mortgage does not show any details (i.e. rate of interest, maturity date).

(9) The capital stock account does not list necessary details: par value, number of shares authorized, issued and outstanding.

(10) Surplus is an incorrect term. It should be Retained Earnings.

3.3. From the list of accounts below, compute working capital.

Accumulation Depreciation, Equipment	$18,500
Accounts Payable	18,400
Accounts Receivable	14,500
Allowance for Doubtful Accounts	2,500
Cash	28,000
Dividends Payable	6,000
Equipment	154,000
Inventory	40,000
Long-term Advances	12,400
Notes Payable (Long-term)	42,000
Notes Payable (Short-term)	20,000
Treasury Stock	8,000

SOLUTION

Current Assets			
Cash		$28,000	
Accounts Receivable	$14,500		
Less: Allowance for Doubtful Accounts	2,500	12,000	
Inventory		40,000	
Total Current Assets			$80,000
Current Liabilities			
Accounts Payable		$18,400	
Notes Payable (Short-term)		20,000	
Dividends Payable		6,000	
Total Current Liabilities			44,400
Working Capital			$35,600

3.4. Based upon the following accounts, prepare (a) the retained earnings section of the balance sheet and (b) a retained earnings statement.

Appropriation for Contingencies

Dec. 31 Transfer to Retained Earnings 10,000		Jan. 1 Balance 40,000	

Appropriation for Plant Expansion

	Jan. 1 Balance 70,000
	Dec. 31 Transfer from Retained Earnings 15,000

Retained Earnings

Mar. 25	Dividend	6,000	Jan. 1	Balance	120,000
June 24	Dividend	6,000	Dec. 31	Net Income	108,000
Sept. 23	Dividend	6,000	Dec. 31	Appr. for	
Dec. 20	Dividend	6,000		Contingencies	10,000
Dec. 31	Appr. for Plant Exp.	15,000			

SOLUTION

(a)
Retained Earnings			
Appropriated			
For Contingencies		$ 30,000	
For Plant Expansion		85,000	$115,000
Unappropriated			199,000
Total Retained Earnings			$314,000

(b)

Statement of Retained Earnings
December 31, 19X1

Appropriated Retained Earnings			
Appropriated for Contingencies, Jan. 1 Balance	$ 40,000		
Less: Transfer, Dec. 31	10,000	$ 30,000	
Appropriated for Plant Expansion, Jan. 1 Balance	$ 70,000		
Add: Appropriation, Dec. 31	15,000	85,000	
Total Appropriated Retained Earnings			$115,000
Unappropriated Retained Earnings			
Balance, Jan. 1		$120,000	
Add: Net Income	$108,000		
Transfer from Approp. for Contingencies	10,000	118,000	
		$238,000	
Less: Dividends Declared	$ 24,000		
Transfer to Approp. for Plant Expansion	15,000	39,000	
Total Unappropriated Retained Earnings			199,000
Total Retained Earnings			$314,000

3.5. The working capital of the Rickosi Corporation was $82,000 before the following transactions occurred:

(1) Issued a 5-year, 6% note for $40,000.

(2) Bought 30% of Ajax Company for investment purposes, $65,000.

(3) Fully depreciated machinery was sold for $1,800.

(4) Treasury stock was purchased for $10,000.

(5) Sold an additional 6,000 shares of common stock, par $50, for $32,000.

(6) A 60-day, 6%, $5,000 bank note was paid in full, $5,050.

(7) Purchased raw materials on account for $21,000.

(8) Office equipment costing $8,000 was purchased, $2,000 was paid in cash and the balance by a 3-year, 6% note.

    (9) Sold the rights to a patent for $6,000.

    (10) Received 1,000 shares of common stock, par $50, as a donation.

(a) Determine whether each transaction increases, decreases or has no effect on working capital.

(b) Compute the new working capital amount.

SOLUTION

(a) Increases: 1, 3, 5, 9.   Total: $79,800.
     Decreases: 2, 4, 8.   Total: $77,000.
     No change: 6, 7, 10.

(b)

Working Capital Balance		*$82,000*
Increases in Working Capital	*$79,800*	
Less: Decreases	*77,000*	
Increase in Working Capital (Net)		*2,800*
Working Capital (New)		*$84,800*

3.6.   From the information below, prepare the stockholders' equity section of the balance sheet.

Preferred 6% Stock, $100 par (5,000 shares authorized and issued)	$500,000
Discount on Preferred Stock	20,000
Common Stock, $50 par (20,000 shares authorized, 15,000 shares issued)	750,000
Premium on Common Stock	35,000
Donated Capital	6,000
Appropriated Retained Earnings	41,000
Unappropriated Retained Earnings	74,000
Treasury Stock (1,000 shares at cost)	40,000

SOLUTION

STOCKHOLDERS' EQUITY

Paid-in Capital		
Preferred 6% Stock, $100 par (5,000 shares authorized and issued)	$500,000	
Less: Discount on Preferred Stock	20,000	$ 480,000
Common Stock, $50 par (20,000 shares authorized, 15,000 issued)	$750,000	
Add: Premium on Common Stock	35,000	785,000
Donated Capital		6,000
Total Paid-in Capital		$1,271,000
Retained Earnings		
Appropriated	$ 41,000	
Unappropriated	74,000	
Total Retained Earnings		115,000
Total		$1,386,000
Less: Treasury Stock (1,000 shares at cost)		40,000
Total Stockholders' Equity		$1,346,000

3.7. Presented below are balance sheet accounts and balances for the Lovelace Corporation as of December 31, 19X1. Prepare a classified balance sheet, incorporating retained earnings details.

Accounts Receivable	$ 65,800
Accounts Payable	112,000
Accumulated Depreciation, Buildings	120,000
Accumulated Depreciation, Equipment	25,000
Allowance for Doubtful Accounts	4,600
Appropriation for Plant Expansion	68,000
Appropriation for Treasury Stock	42,000
Bonds (6%, 10-year debentures)	1,000,000
Buildings	696,700
Cash	1,655,000
Common Stock, $25 par (40,000 shares authorized, 30,000 shares issued)	750,000
Common Stock Subscribed	100,000
Common Stock Subscriptions Receivable	60,000
Discount on Preferred Stock	60,000
Equipment	216,000
Goodwill	125,000
Land	30,000
Merchandise Inventory	442,500
Notes Receivable	75,000
Notes Payable	38,000
Organization Costs	95,000
Paid-in Capital from Sale of Treasury Stock	22,000
Premium on Bonds Payable	44,400
Premium on Common Stock	15,000
Preferred Stock, 6%, $100 par (20,000 shares authorized, 10,000 shares issued)	1,000,000
Prepaid Expenses	32,000
Taxes Payable	24,000
Treasury Stock (at cost)	42,000
Unappropriated Retained Earnings	230,000

SOLUTION

Lovelace Corporation
Balance Sheet
December 31, 19X1

ASSETS

Current Assets

Cash		$1,655,000	
Accounts Receivable	$ 65,800		
Less: Allowance for Doubtful Accounts	4,600	61,200	
Notes Receivable		75,000	
Merchandise Inventory		442,500	
Common Stock Subscriptions Receivable		60,000	
Prepaid Expenses		32,000	
Total Current Assets			$2,325,700

Fixed Assets

Buildings	$ 696,700		
Less: Accumulated Depreciation, Buildings	120,000	$ 576,700	
Equipment	$ 216,000		
Less: Accumulated Depreciation, Equipment	25,000	191,000	
Land		30,000	
Total Fixed Assets			797,700

Intangible Assets

Goodwill		$ 125,000	
Organization Costs		95,000	
Total Intangible Assets			220,000
Total Assets			$3,343,400

LIABILITIES

Current Liabilities

Accounts Payable		$ 112,000	
Notes Payable		38,000	
Taxes Payable		24,000	
Total Current Liabilities			$ 174,000

Long-term Liabilities

Bonds (6%, 10-year debentures)		$1,000,000	
Add: Premium on Bonds Payable		44,400	
Total Long-term Liabilities			1,044,400
Total Liabilities			$1,218,400

STOCKHOLDERS' EQUITY

Paid-in Capital

Preferred Stock, 6%, $100 par (20,000 shares authorized, 10,000 shares issued)	$1,000,000		
Less: Discount on Preferred Stock	60,000	$ 940,000	
Common Stock, $25 (40,000 shares authorized, 30,000 shares issued)	$ 750,000		
Add: Premium on Common Stock	15,000	765,000	
Common Stock Subscribed		100,000	
Sale of Treasury Stock		22,000	
Total Paid-in Capital			$1,827,000

Retained Earnings
   Appropriated

For Plant Expansion	$ 68,000			
For Treasury Stock	42,000			
Total Appropriated Retained Earnings		$ 110,000		
Unappropriated Retained Earnings		230,000		
Total Retained Earnings			340,000	
Total			$2,167,000	
Less: Treasury Stock (at cost)			42,000	
Total Stockholders' Equity				$2,125,000
Total Liabilities and Stockholders' Equity				$3,343,400

3.8. Present a revised balance sheet of the following data in proper form, changing titles of accounts where needed.

ASSETS

Current Assets		
Cash in Bank		$125,000
Investments in Affiliated Companies		30,000
Accounts Receivable	$ 12,500	
Less: Accounts Payable	10,000	2,500
Notes Receivable	$ 14,000	
Less: Notes Payable	6,000	8,000
Treasury Stock (at cost)		9,900
Merchandise Inventory		36,000
Discount on Common Stock		6,000
Total Current Assets		$217,400
Fixed Assets		
Buildings	$ 85,000	
Less: Reserve for Building Expansion	19,000	$ 66,000
Equipment		50,000
Patents (10 years)		6,000
Goodwill		12,000
Prepaid Expenses		4,000
Total Fixed Assets		138,000
Total Assets		$355,400

LIABILITIES

Income Tax Payable	$ 2,900
Premium on Preferred Stock	5,000
Bonds Payable (20 years)	50,000
Total Liabilities	$ 57,900

STOCKHOLDERS' EQUITY

Paid-in Capital			
Prefered Stock	$100,000		
Common Stock	140,000		
Total Paid-in Capital		$240,000	
Retained Earnings		20,000	
Reserves			
For Doubtful Accounts	$ 2,500		
For Buildings	25,000		
For Equipment	10,000		
Total Reserves		37,500	
Total Stockholders' Equity			297,500
Total Liabilities and Stockholders' Equity			$355,400

SOLUTION

ASSETS

Current Assets			
Cash in Bank		$125,000	
Accounts Receivable	$ 12,500		
Less: Allowance for Doubtful Accounts	2,500	10,000	
Notes Receivable		14,000	
Merchandise Inventory		36,000	
Prepaid Expenses		4,000	
Total Current Assets			$189,000
Investments			
In Affiliated Companies			30,000
Fixed Assets			
Buildings	$ 85,000		
Less: Accumulated Depreciation, Buildings	25,000	$ 60,000	
Equipment	$ 50,000		
Less: Accumulated Depreciation, Equipment	10,000	40,000	
Total Fixed Assets			100,000
Intangible Assets			
Patents		$ 6,000	
Goodwill		12,000	
Total Intangible Assets			18,000
Total Assets			$337,000

LIABILITIES

Current Liabilities			
Accounts Payable		$ 10,000	
Income Tax Payable		2,900	
Notes Payable		6,000	
Total Current Liabilities			$ 18,900
Long-term Liabilities			
Bonds Payable (Due 199–)			50,000
Total Liabilities			$ 68,900

STOCKHOLDER'S EQUITY

Paid-in Capital			
Preferred Stock	$100,000		
Add: Premium on Preferred Stock	5,000	$105,000	
Common Stock	$140,000		
Less: Discount on Common Stock	6,000	134,000	
Total Paid-in Capital		$239,000	
Retained Earnings			
Appropriation for Building Expansion	$ 19,000		
Unappropriated	20,000	39,000	
Total		$278,000	
Less: Treasury Stock (at cost)		9,900	
Total Stockholders' Equity			268,100
Total Liabilities and Stockholders' Equity			$337,000

3.9. Prepare a classified balance sheet for the Robert Green Company from the following account balances as of December 31, 197–.

Accounts Payable	$ 16,400	Goodwill	$16,000
Accounts Receivable	24,500	Income Taxes Payable	9,000
Accrued Salaries Payable	4,000	Inventory	46,000
Accumulated Depreciation, Buildings	5,000	Investment in Bonds of Bradley Corporation	25,000
Accumulated Depreciation, Equipment	2,000	Investment in Common Stocks of Phillips Company	10,000
Allowance for Doubtful Accounts	1,500	Land	30,000
Appropriation for Contingencies	10,500	Mortgage Payable	25,000
		Notes Payable	12,000
Bonds Payable	40,000	Notes Receivable	36,000
Buildings	45,000	Paid-in Capital from Sale of Treasury Stock	12,000
Cash in Bank	18,000		
Cash on Hand	2,500	Patents	12,000
Common Stock, $50 par (200 shares authorized & issued)	100,000	Premium on Bonds Payable	4,000
		Premium on Common Stock	8,000
Dividends Payable	6,600	Prepaid Insurance	8,000
Equipment	19,000	Retained Earnings	36,000

SOLUTION

Robert Green Company
Balance Sheet
December 31, 197—

ASSETS

Current Assets		
Cash on Hand and in Bank		$20,500
Accounts Receivable	$24,500	
Less: Allowance for Doubtful Accounts	1,500	23,000
Notes Receivable		36,000
Inventory		46,000
Prepaid Insurance		8,000
Total Current Assets		$133,500
Fixed Assets		
Building	$45,000	
Less: Accumulated Depreciation, Buildings	5,000	$40,000
Equipment	$19,000	
Less: Accumulated Depreciation, Equipment	2,000	17,000
Land		30,000
Total Fixed Assets		87,000
Investments		
Investment in Bonds of Bradley Corporation		$25,000
Investment in Common Stock of Phillips Company		10,000
Total Investments		35,000
Intangible Assets		
Goodwill		$16,000
Patents		12,000
Total Intangible Assets		28,000
Total Assets		$283,500

LIABILITIES

Current Liabilities		
Accounts Payable		$ 16,400
Notes Payable		12,000
Accrued Salaries Payable		4,000
Dividends Payable		6,600
Income Taxes Payable		9,000
Total Current Liabilities		$ 48,000
Long-term Liabilities		
Bonds Payable	$ 40,000	
Add: Premium on Bonds Payable	4,000	$ 44,000
Mortgage Payable		25,000
Total Long-term Liabilities		69,000
Total Liabilities		$117,000

STOCKHOLDERS' EQUITY

Paid-in Capital		
Common Stock, $50 par (2,000 shares authorized & issued)	$100,000	
Add: Premium on Common Stock	8,000	$108,000
Sale of Treasury Stock		12,000
Total Paid-in Capital		$120,000

Retained Earnings
Appropriation for Contingencies	$ 10,500	
Unappropriated	36,000	
Total Retained Earnings		$ 46,500
Total Stockholders' Equity		$166,500
Total Liabilities and Stockholders' Equity		$283,500

3.10. From the solutions in Problems 3.8 and 3.9, compute (*a*) the current ratio and (*b*) working capital.

SOLUTION

(*a*) For Problem 3.8:

$$\frac{\text{Current Assets}}{\text{Current Liabilities}} = \frac{189,000}{18,900} = 10:1$$

The firm has the ability to meet its current obligations by having $10 of current assets for every $1 of current liability.

For Problem 3.9:

$$\frac{\text{Current Assets}}{\text{Current Liabilities}} = \frac{133,500}{48,000} = 2.78:1$$

(*b*) For Problem 3.8:

Current Assets	$189,000
Current Liabilities	− 18,900
Working Capital	$170,100

For Problem 3.9:

Current Assets	$133,500
Current Liabilities	− 48,000
Working Capital	$ 85,500

3.11. From the selected accounts of the Harper Corporation below, (*a*) compute the amount of working capital and (*b*) determine the book value per share of stock.

Bonds Payable	$ 40,000
Premium on Bonds Payable	4,000
Interest Receivable	10,000
Accounts Receivable	80,000
Accounts Payable	15,000
Cash Surrender Value of Life Ins. Policies	18,500
Unappropriated Retained Earnings	50,000
Appropriation for Contingencies	40,000
Appropriation for Plant Expansion	20,000
Additional Paid-in Capital	10,000
Patents	24,000
Leasehold Improvements	16,200
Common Stock, $100 par	500,000
Accumulated Depreciation	4,800
Other Current Assets	130,000
Other Current Liabilities	100,000

SOLUTION

(a)

Current Assets:		
Accounts Receivable	$ 80,000	
Interest Receivable	10,000	
Other Current Assets	130,000	$220,000
Current Liabilities:		
Accounts Payable	$ 15,000	
Other Current Liabilities	100,000	115,000
Working Capital		$105,000

(b)

STOCKHOLDERS' EQUITY

Paid-in Capital		
Common Stock, $100 par	$500,000	
Additional Paid-in Capital	10,000	
Total Paid-in Capital		$510,000
Retained Earnings		
Appropriation for Contingencies	$40,000	
Appropriation for Plant Expansion	20,000	
Total Appropriated Retained Earnings	$ 60,000	
Unappropriated Retained Earnings	50,000	
Total Retained Earnings		110,000
Stockholders' Equity		$620,000

Book Value Computation

$620,000 ÷ 5,000 shares (from $500,000 ÷ $100 par) = $124 per share

3.12. The balance sheet of the Clarisa Corporation at December 31, 197– appears below.

Clarisa Corporation
Balance Sheet
December 31, 197–

ASSETS

Current Assets		
Cash	$ 4,600	
Accounts Receivable	6,900	
Merchandise Inventory	33,400	
Supplies	250	
Prepaid Rent	1,800	$46,950
Fixed Assets		
Equipment	16,000	
Less: Accumulated Depreciation	2,500	13,500
Total Assets		$60,450

LIABILITIES AND STOCKHOLDERS' EQUITY

Current Liabilities		
Accounts Payable	$ 9,200	
Salaries Payable	1,250	
Total Liabilities		$10,450
Stockholders' Equity		50,000
Total Liabilities and Stockholders' Equity		$60,450

Further examination of the corporation's records uncovered the following questionable practices.

(1) Goods shipped to customers in December at a sales price of $2,500 were not billed until January.

(2) Cash included a check of $400 that was marked and returned as "insufficient funds." No payment is expected.

(3) Local taxes of $1,600 were accrued as of December 31. The money had been deposited in a special account to pay the tax debt but neither the accrued tax nor the cash has been reported on the balance sheet.

(4) Clarisa Corporation had been organized in January of the current year by exchanging 450 shares of $100 par common stock for the net assets of the original business.

Prepare a corrected balance sheet as of December 31, 197–.

SOLUTION

Clarisa Corporation
Balance Sheet
December 31, 197—

ASSETS

Current Assets		
Cash	$ 4,200	
Cash Fund for Taxes	1,600	
Accounts Receivable	9,400	
Merchandise Inventory	33,400	
Supplies	250	
Prepaid Rent	1,800	$50,650
Fixed Assets		
Equipment	$16,000	
Less: Accumulated Depreciation	2,500	13,500
Total Assets		$64,150*

LIABILITIES AND STOCKHOLDERS' EQUITY

Current Liabilities		
Accrued Taxes	$ 1,600	
Accounts Payable	9,200	
Salaries Payable	1,250	
Total Liabilities		$12,050
Stockholders' Equity		
Capital Stock	$45,000	
Retained Earnings	7,100**	52,100
Total Liabilities and Stockholders' Equity		$64,150

* Increase in Total Assets: $3,700 ($64,150 − 60,450) or
($1,600 cash fund + $2,500 receivables − $400 cash)

** Computation of Net Income

Stockholders' Equity as reported (before correction)		$50,000
Less: Stockholders' Equity from original incorporation		45,000
Net Income		$ 5,000
Adjustment: Understatement of sales	$2,500	
Loss from insufficient fund check	400	2,100
Adjusted Net Income		$ 7,100

3.13. A condensed balance sheet of the MSC Corporation is shown below. Assume that (1) the book value of plant and equipment, stated in terms of equivalent current dollars, increased by 10%, (2) the equivalent of $50,000 in current dollars has been invested in inventories and (3) realized retained earnings stated in current dollars were computed to be $40,000. Prepare a revised balance sheet in terms of current dollars.

MSC Corporation
Balance Sheet
December 31, 197–

ASSETS

Cash	$ 42,000
Accounts Receivable	28,000
Merchandise Inventory	36,000
Plant and Equipment (net)	84,000
Total Assets	$190,000

LIABILITIES AND STOCKHOLDERS' EQUITY

Current Liabilities	$ 30,000
Long-term Liabilities	15,000
Capital Stock	100,000
Retained Earnings	45,000
Total Liabilities and Stockholders' Equity	$190,000

SOLUTION

In presenting a balance sheet of this nature, it is often helpful to prepare a comparative report showing both mixed dollar and current dollar amounts.

MSC Corporation
Balance Sheet: Mixed and Current Dollars
December 31, 197—

	Mixed Dollars	Current Dollars
ASSETS		
Current Assets		
Cash	$ 42,000	$ 42,000
Accounts Receivable	28,000	28,000
Merchandise Inventory	36,000	50,000
Total Current Assets	$106,000	$120,000
Add: Plant and Equipment (net)	84,000	92,400
Total Assets	$190,000	$212,400
LIABILITIES AND STOCKHOLDERS' EQUITY		
Current Liabilities	$ 30,000	$ 30,000
Long-term Liabilities	15,000	15,000
Total Liabilities	$ 45,000	$ 45,000
Stockholders' Equity		
Capital Stock	100,000	100,000
Retained Earnings	45,000	40,000
Unrealized General Price-level Gain		27,400
Total Liabilities and Stockholders' Equity	$190,000	$212,400

Chapter 4

The Income Statement

4.1 INTRODUCTION

The business entity's *Income Statement*, like the Balance Sheet and Statement of Changes in Financial Position, is an end result of the accounting procedures described in Chapter 2. It may be defined as *a summary of the revenues, expenses and net income of a business entity for a specific period of time,* and is sometimes called the Earnings Statement, Operating Statement or Statement of Profit and Loss.

4.2 ACCOUNTING PRINCIPLES AND POLICIES

In preparing a firm's financial statements, the accountant must consider the *accounting policies* established by its management. Such policies can significantly affect the amount of net income, and must be disclosed, according to APB Opinion No. 22, as an integral part of all *audited* financial reports. Policies of special interest to the analyst, such as inventory, depreciation, pensions and other specified matters, fall into this category, as do unusual applications of GAAP, industry peculiarities which conflict with GAAP and those which differ from existing acceptable alternatives. Another requirement, established by APB Opinion No. 15, is that the published income statement must disclose net earnings or loss per share.

4.3 FORMAT OF THE INCOME STATEMENT

The income statement may be presented in a multiple-step or single-step format. Unlike the balance sheet, which is a position statement at a fixed point in time, the income statement reports activities *over a period of time*. That is, it summarizes net income for the current fiscal period.

MULTIPLE-STEP STATEMENT

The multiple-step income statement presents figures significant in the determination of net income. Its various classifications define the on-going operations of the business entity, providing a perspective as to its flow of revenues and expenses. The usual multiple-step classifications are:

(1) *Revenue from Sales.* In this section, usually called Gross Sales, revenue (income) earned from normal operations is summarized. It is offset by the contra income accounts, Sales Returns and Allowances and Sales Discounts.

(2) *Cost of Goods Sold.* This section includes the cost of goods applicable to the revenue obtained for the period. Its presentation is slightly different for a mercantile than a manufacturing company since the former does not have inventories of raw materials, goods in process, direct labor or manufacturing overhead. It has only furnished goods, called *merchandise inventory*.

EXAMPLE 1.

The cost of goods sold section of a mercantile company's income statement is shown below.

Beginning Inventory			$ 10,000
Add: Merchandise Purchases		$160,000	
Less: Purchase Returns and Allowances	$10,000		
Purchase Discounts	4,000	14,000	
Net Purchases			146,000
Add: Transportation-in			9,000
Merchandise Available for Sale			$165,000
Less: Ending Inventory			15,000
Cost of Goods Sold			$150,000

In the case of a manufacturing company, the *cost of goods manufactured* classification is similar to the mercantile *merchandise purchases* section. However, a separate summary, called the Statement of Cost of Goods Manufactured or Manufacturing Schedule, is generally prepared, citing costs of raw materials, direct labor, manufacturing overhead and work in process.

EXAMPLE 2.

A statement of Cost of Goods Manufactured is typically presented as follows.

Bondai Corporation
Statement of Cost of Goods Manufactured
for year ended June 30, 19X5

Raw Materials				
Inventory, July 1, 19X4			$ 10,000	
Purchases		$100,000		
Less: Purchase Returns and Allowances	$10,000			
Purchase Discounts	4,000	14,000	86,000	
Transportation-in			9,000	
Material Available			$105,000	
Less: Inventory, June 30, 19X5			12,000	
Cost of Material Consumed				$ 93,000
Direct Labor				52,000
Manufacturing Overhead				
Indirect Labor			$ 14,000	
Payroll Taxes			4,000	
Repairs, Insurance, Heat and Miscellaneous			22,000	
Depreciation of Factory Equipment			10,000	50,000
				$195,000
Work in Process, June 30, 19X5		$ 44,000		
Less: Work in Process, July 1, 19X4		14,000		
Net Change in Inventory				(30,000)
Cost of Goods Manufactured				$165,000

An alternate treatment of cost of goods manufactured is given in Problem 4.10.

Once the manufacturing schedule is completed, its bottom line (cost of goods manufactured) is incorporated in the cost of goods sold section of the income statement (see Example 3).

(3) **Gross Profit on Sales.** This figure is the difference between net sales and cost of goods sold. It is frequently divided by net sales to determine the average percentage of margin for the fiscal period. The same ratio is developed for cost of goods sold and it can easily be seen that they are complementary.

EXAMPLE 3.   (details condensed)

Bondai Corporation
Partial Income Statement
for the year ended June 30, 19X5

Gross Sales		$300,000	105%
Less: Sales Returns, Allowances & Discounts		15,000	
Net Sales		$285,000	100%
Cost of Goods Sold			
Add: Beginning Inventory, Finished Goods	$ 20,000		
Cost of Goods Manufactured (per schedule)	165,000		
Goods Available for Sale	$185,000		
Less: Ending Inventory, Finished Goods	35,000		
Cost of Goods Sold		150,000	52.6%
Gross Profit on Sales		$135,000	47.4%

(4) **Operating Expenses.** These are often classified according to the major *functions* of the business (i.e. selling, general and administrative). Terminology may differ as appropriate; however, taxes on income, extraordinary items and prior period adjustments must be segregated at the bottom of the statement.

Selling expenses typically include sales salaries, commissions, related payroll costs, advertising, store display costs, store supplies used, etc.

General and administrative expenses include officer and office salaries and related payroll taxes, telephone and communication costs, heat, light and power costs, postage and office supplies, legal and accounting costs, etc.

(5) **Other Income and Expense** includes all other miscellaneous recurring items. Other income includes interest, dividends, rents and royalties; other expense includes interest and miscellaneous expenses.

(6) **Income Taxes.** Total income taxes due is presented as a single figure on the income statement and is applied against the subtotal, *Net Income before Income Taxes*. Income from normal operations is often supplemented by a gain or loss from extraordinary items. The amount directly applicable to income from normal operations is taxed at normal rates. Extraordinary items are often taxed at *lower* capital gains rates. The applicable tax for each extraordinary item should be deducted and the net amount shown on the income statement.

NOTE: Property, payroll and excise taxes are properly allocated to the various business functions as normal operating expenses.

(7) **Net Income.** The excess of revenues over expenses. In the multiple-step format, separate captions are generally shown for *Income before Taxes*, *Income before Extraordinary Items* and *Net Income*.

(8) **Extraordinary Items.** Those events and transactions which are *material* in amount and which are *significantly different* from the regular activities of the business (APB Opinion No. 9). Extraordinary or nonrecurring earnings, when included in the income statement, are shown below (separately from) regular earnings.

EXAMPLE 4.

The all-inclusive concept incorporates extraordinary items into the income statement (see Section 4.4).

Bondai Corporation
Partial Income Statement
for year ending June 30, 19X5

Income Before Extraordinary Items	*$25,000*
Extraordinary Gain:	
Sale of Timberland, $31,000,	
Net of Applicable Taxes, $15,000 (Note C)	*16,000*
	$41,000
Extraordinary Loss:	
Fully Deductible Fire Loss, $40,000, Net of	
Applicable Taxes, $19,000 (Note C)	*21,000*
Net Income	*$20,000*

SINGLE-STEP STATEMENT

A simple, condensed statement devoid of all classification except the general groupings: (1) *revenues,* and (2) *cost* and *expenses* has been developed for stockholders' reports and other special uses. Section labeling is at a minimum. The single-step format does not recognize intermediate stages such as gross profit from operations or income before extraordinary items. All income, including rents, interest, dividends, etc., is included in the first section. All costs and expenses are shown in the next, including Federal and state taxes on income. This form tends to be compact and relatively uncluttered at the sacrifice of information. Generally the costs and expenses are classified on the object basis rather than the functional basis.

When the *object basis* is used, the *nature* of each cost and expense rather than whether it serves manufacturing, selling, general and administrative, or some other function is the controlling factor. Examples of this classification are such broad captions as materials, supplies and services purchased, salaries and wages, and depreciation. The *functional basis*, on the other hand, expands the income statement so that it includes major classifications such as cost of goods sold, sales revenues and operating expenses as major headings, with applicable subfunctions in each category.

It should be noted that the required separation of ordinary and extraordinary items resulting from application of APB Opinion No. 9 also applies to the condensed *single-step* form. The treatment of extraordinary items is discussed in Section 4.4.

EXAMPLE 5.

The figures cited for extraordinary gains and losses in the income statement below are consistent with those given in Example 4, but are classified on the *functional basis.*

Bondai Corporation
Single-Step Income Statement
for year ended June 30, 19X5

Revenues		
Sales, less Returns, Allowances and Discounts		$285,000
Other Income; Dividends, Interest and Rent		5,000
Total Revenues		$290,000
Cost and Expenses		
Cost of Goods Sold (Note 1)	$150,000	
Selling Expenses	40,000	
General and Administrative Expenses	50,000	
Other Expenses	12,000	
Income and Property Taxes	13,000	
Total Costs and Expenses		265,000
Income before Extraordinary Items		$ 25,000
Extraordinary Gain (net of applicable tax, $15,000)		16,000
Extraordinary Loss (net of applicable tax, $19,000)		(21,000)
Net Income		$ 20,000
Per Share of Common Stock (Note 2):		
Income before Extraordinary Items	$2.50	
Extraordinary Items, Net of Income Taxes	(.50)	
Net Income	$2.00	

NOTE 1. Includes Cost of Goods Manufactured of $165,000 less a $15,000 increase in the Inventory of Finished Goods.

NOTE 2. Earnings per share based upon average shares of 10,000.

4.4   INCOME STATEMENT CONCEPTS

Extraordinary Items

There have existed over the years differences with respect to the income statement regarding the proper presentation of extraordinary items as well as adjustments and corrections from prior periods. Two procedures are now considered acceptable alternative treatments:

(1) **Current Operating Performance Concept.**   Extraordinary items are omitted from the income statement and are closed directly to the statement of retained earnings.

(2) **All-inclusive Concept.**   Extraordinary items are shown separately on the income statement after Net Income from Regular Operations but before Net Income. This procedure is required by the SEC and recommended by the AICPA in Opinions Nos. 9 and 30 (see Example 4).

Other Material Gains and Losses

APB Opinions Nos. 9 and 30 not only defined clearly what could be considered extraordinary items but also clarified treatment of material gains and losses not of an extraordinary nature. Items such as write-downs and write-offs of inventories and receivables (which do not fulfill the dual criteria of being both infrequent in occurrence and unusual in nature) fall into this latter category and are relegated to operating expense sections or to a separate section called *Other Income and Expense,* both of which appear before the income before extraordinary items figure.

Prior Period Adjustments

APB Opinion No. 9 also includes a provision for *prior period adjustments,* defined as those rare, material, nonrecurring adjustments which (*a*) are directly related to the business operations of particular prior periods, (*b*) are not attributable to business events subsequent to the date of financial statements for the prior period, (*c*) are determined by persons other than internal management and (*d*) were not determinable during the prior period under consideration. Items which meet all four requirements are not included in the calculation of net income but are reported instead (net of tax) in the statement of retained earnings. Settlement of income tax claims or litigation are examples of prior period adjustments.

EXAMPLE 6.

In 19X5 the Bondai Corporation learned that it would receive a rebate of $15,000 on taxes paid for the fiscal year ended June 30, 19X1. The financial statement below for 19X5 reflects this prior period adjustment (assume all other figures).

Retained Earnings, July 1, 19X4	*$175,000*
Corrections in Retained Earnings Applicable to Prior Periods—Tax Rebate	*15,000*
Corrected Retained Earnings Balance, July 1, 19X4	*$190,000*
Add: Net Income per Income Statement	*20,000*
Retained Earnings, June 30, 19X5	*$210,000*

Prior period items *not* in fulfillment of the four characteristics established by APB Opinion No. 9 should be treated as current period income or expense within the body of the income statement, with an appropriate footnote or parenthetical explanation.

EXAMPLE 7.

Changes in estimates from prior periods are no longer considered prior period adjustments. An increase in estimated bad debt losses would therefore be added to the allowance account and charged as a current period expense.

Accounting Errors

APB Opinion No. 20 states that errors made during previous periods and discovered subsequently should be reported as prior period adjustments. Examples are arithmetic mistakes, oversights, the use of inappropriate estimates, etc. These adjustments follow the same guidelines previously discussed, and for the most part, are reported in the appropriate section of the income statement.

4.5 COMBINED INCOME AND RETAINED EARNINGS STATEMENT

Some companies combine these two statements in an effort to present a complete picture of both the elements of net income and the changes in retained earnings. All that is required is to continue beyond net income (or net loss) by adding the beginning balance of retained earnings and deducting dividends declared and any other charges against retained earnings.

Summary

(1) In the process of measuring periodic net income, the accountant must make use of _____ which, in turn, is based upon the Generally Accepted Accounting Principles.

(2) The requirement that audited statements carry a statement of significant accounting policies was set down in APB Opinion No.____.

(3) The income statement may be presented in either the _____ or the _____ format.

(4) A manufacturing schedule is made up of the cost of material consumed, _____ _____, the various manufacturing overhead components and the beginning and ending _____ inventories.

(5) The gross profit ratio is found by _____.

(6) When costs and expenses are grouped on the functional basis, some typical functions are _____ and _____.

(7) A major revision in the presentation of extraordinary gains and losses was required by APB Opinion No.____.

(8) Adjustments which are rare, material, nonrecurring, and arise from prior period economic events are called_____.

(9) A simplified form of the income statement, which avoids detailed classifications of revenues and expenses, is called the _____.

(10) Setting out the effect of an extraordinary capital gain, net of any applicable capital gains tax or ordinary tax, is required by APB Opinion Nos. 9 and 30 and is referred to as the _____ procedure.

Answers: (1) judgment; (2) 22; (3) multiple-step, single-step; (4) direct labor, work in process; (5) dividing gross profit by net sales; (6) cost of goods sold, selling, and general and administrative; (7) 9; (8) prior period adjustments; (9) single-step form; (10) net-of-tax.

Solved Problems

4.1. Assuming that a manufacturing corporation uses the multiple-step income statement and a supporting manufacturing schedule, indicate in what sections and on which form each of the following accounts would appear.

MANUFACTURING SCHEDULE	INCOME STATEMENT
M-1 Raw Material Consumed	I-1 Revenue
M-2 Direct Labor	I-2 Cost of Goods Sold
M-3 Manufacturing Overhead	I-3 Gross Profit on Sales
M-4 Work-in-Process Inventory	I-4 Operating Expenses
	I-5 Other Financial Income and Expenses
	I-6 Extraordinary Items

(1) Purchase of raw materials

(2) Transportation-in, raw materials

(3) Inventories: Raw materials, end of year

(4) Work in process, end of year

(5) Finished goods, beginning of year

(6) Finished goods, end of year

(7) Sales returns and allowances

(8) Purchases returns and allowances

(9) Wages of production personnel

(10) Wages of office personnel

(11) Wages of store personnel

(12) Executive wages

(13) Commissions to salesmen

(14) Factory rent

(15) Indirect labor

(16) Insurance on factory buildings and equipment

(17) Insurance on storage warehouse for raw materials

(18) Taxes on factory property

(19) Sales income

(20) Advertising costs

(21) Depreciation of office equipment

(22) Bond interest expense

(23) Rental and dividend income

(24) Uninsured fire loss

(25) Provision for Federal and state income taxes

SOLUTION

(1) M-1	(6) I-2	(11) I-4	(16) M-3	(21) I-4
(2) M-1	(7) I-1	(12) I-4	(17) M-3	(22) I-4
(3) M-1	(8) M-1	(13) I-4	(18) M-3	(23) I-5
(4) M-4	(9) M-2	(14) M-3	(19) I-1	(24) I-6
(5) I-2	(10) I-4	(15) M-3	(20) I-4	(25) between I-5 and I-6

4.2. State how you would report each of the following items on a corporation's income statement and related schedules in conformity with the various pronouncements of the AICPA:

(a) A material loss resulting from spring floods which ruined merchandise with a value in excess of insurance coverage.

(b) A loss arising from the sale of securities held as a long-term investment (not considered material).

(c) Amortization of the balance in the patent account.

(d) Settlement of a ten-year-old claim for income tax refund in the corporation's favor (material).

(e) Collection of accounts receivable previously written off.

(f) Settlement of a material liability claim brought against the company several years ago.

(g) Revision of a depreciation rate established five years ago and apparently in error.

(h) A large charge caused by the writing off of obsolete inventory.

SOLUTION

(a) Extraordinary loss.

(b) Under Financial Income and Expenses, classified such as Loss on Securities.

(c) General and Administrative Expenses.

(d) Prior period adjustment.

(e) Credited to Allowance to Bad Debts; no effect upon income.

(f) Prior period adjustment.

(g) Any change in depreciation is spread over the remaining life of the asset.

(h) Operating Expenses.

4.3. From the following income data extracted from the records of Leech Company, Inc. for the current year, prepare a multiple-step income statement following the recommendations of APB Opinion No. 9.

Merchandise inventory, beginning of year	$ 48,920
Merchandise inventory, end of year	38,990
Purchase returns and allowances	8,050
Sales	947,320
Excise taxes on sales (debit balance)	16,430
Depreciation on buildings and equipment (70% selling; 30% administrative)	46,800
Dividends declared	20,000
Royalty revenues	24,650
Rental revenues	15,770
Interest on notes payable	9,840
Transportation-in, merchandise	43,960
Purchases, merchandise	387,440
Property taxes (70% selling; 30% administrative)	34,300
Selling expenses:	
Salaries and wages	102,560
Purchased services	27,870
Materials and supplies	13,460

Administrative expenses:

Salaries and wages	$141,390
Purchased services	44,220
Materials and supplies	10,620
Provision for Federal income taxes	49,500
Flood loss (Tax, $65,000)	130,000

SOLUTION

Leech Company, Inc.
Income Statement
for year ended December 31, 19X5

Revenues			
Gross Sales		$947,320	
Less: Excise Tax on Sales		16,430	
Net Sales			$ 930,890
Cost of Goods Sold			
Purchases		$387,440	
Less: Purchase Returns and Allowances		8,050	
		$379,390	
Add: Transportation-in		43,960	
Delivered Cost of Purchases		$423,350	
Merchandise Inventory, Beginning January 1	$48,920		
Merchandise Inventory, Ending December 31	38,990		
Add: Net Change in Inventory		9,930	
Cost of Goods Sold			433,280
Gross Profit from Operations			$ 497,610
Operating Expenses			
Selling Expenses			
Salaries and Wages	$102,560		
Services	27,870		
Materials and Supplies	13,460		
Depreciation (70%)	32,760		
Property Taxes (70%)	24,010		
Total Selling Expenses		$200,660	
General and Administrative Expenses			
Salaries	$141,390		
Services	44,220		
Materials and Supplies	10,620		
Depreciation (30%)	14,040		
Property Taxes (30%)	10,290		
Total General and Administrative Expenses		220,560	
Total Operating Expenses			421,220
Operating Income			$ 76,390
Other Income and Expenses			
Royalties Earned	$ 24,650		
Rentals Earned	15,770	$ 40,420	
Less: Interest on Notes Payable		9,840	30,580
Net Income Before Income Taxes			$ 106,970
Provision for Federal Income Tax			(49,500)
Income Before Extraordinary Items			$ 57,470
Extraordinary Items			
Flood Loss ($130,000 less tax, $65,000)			65,000
Net Loss (to Retained Earnings)			$(7,530)

4.4   Using the *net-of-tax* method recommended in APB Opinions Nos. 9 and 20 and a tax
rate of 40%, prepare revised year-end statements for the Dolsey Corporation from
the pretax data given below.

Income before extraordinary items	$ 40,000
Extraordinary items:	
Loss on sale of timberland	(10,000)
Net income	$ 30,000
Retained earnings	
Beginning balance	$ 85,000
Less: Damages paid on prior period lawsuit	15,000
As restated	$ 70,000
Add net income, 19X1	30,000
	$100,000
Less: Dividends paid during 19X1	20,000
Ending Balance	$ 80,000

SOLUTION

Dolsey Corporation
Partial Income Statement
for year ended December 31, 19X1

Income Before Taxes and Extraordinary Items		$40,000
Less: Applicable Income Taxes		16,000
Income Before Extraordinary Items		$24,000
Extraordinary Items:		
Loss on Sale of Land	$10,000	
Less: Applicable Income Taxes	4,000	6,000
Net Income		$18,000

Dolsey Corporation
Statement of Retained Earnings
December 31, 19X1

Beginning Balance (previously reported)		$85,000
Deduct: Prior Period Adjustment	$15,000	
Less: Applicable Income Taxes	6,000	9,000
As Restated		$76,000
Add: Net Income for 19X1		18,000
		$94,000
Less: Dividends paid during 19X1		20,000
Retained Earnings (ending balance)		$74,000

4.5. During an audit of the Bolshop Theatre Corporation's books, it was discovered that
through inadvertent omission no depreciation had been taken for the past two years
on machinery having an original cost of $12,000, no salvage value and a ten-year life.
The machine was being depreciated on a straight-line basis.

Using the principles in various APB Opinions, for the current year, (a) state
the accounting change involved, (b) give the entry to record the accounting change,
showing computations, (c) give the depreciation entry and (d) briefly explain how
these entries would appear on the corporation's statements.

SOLUTION

(a) The accounting change required is a *correction of an error*.

(b) Debit: *Depreciation Correction of Prior Years (Prior Period Adjustment)*   *2,400*

Credit: *Accumulated Depreciation ($12,000 × 2/10 = $2,400)*   *2,400*

(c)   *Depreciation Expense, Machinery*   *1,200*

Accumulated Depreciation   *1,200*

To record the annual depreciation on machinery at 10% (1/10).

(d) The depreciation correction of $2,400 would be reported on the statement of retained earnings as a prior period adjustment (assuming that it is material). The depreciation expense of $1,200 would be reported on the income statement as a normal expense and the total accumulated depreciation would be a contra asset item on the balance sheet.

4.6. In accordance with APB Opinion No. 15, show the reporting of earnings per share in the income statement of Sensitivity, Incorporated from the data below. Assume that there were 50,000 shares of common stock outstanding during the entire year, including no preferred or dilutive shares.

Sales		$330,000
Cost and Expenses		210,000
		$120,000
Income Taxes		20,000
Income before Extraordinary Items		$100,000
Extraordinary Items		
Gain on Sale of Fixed Assets	$20,000	
Less: Applicable Income Taxes	5,000	15,000
		$115,000
Loss on Sale of Investments	$ 5,000	
Less: Applicable Income Taxes	1,000	4,000
Net Income		$111,000

SOLUTION

APB Opinion No. 15 requires that earnings per share be shown in a manner consistent with income statement presentation. In this case, therefore, earnings per share amounts should be shown for income before extraordinary items, extraordinary items and net income, as follows:

Income before Extraordinary Items	*$2.00*
Extraordinary Items	*.22*
Net Income (per share)*	*$2.22*

* $100,000 divided by 50,000 shares = $2.00

$ 11,000 Gain (net of taxes and loss) divided by 50,000 shares = $ .22.

4.7. After closing entries were posted on December 31, 19X5, selected accounts of **Happy Electronics, Incorporated** showed the total debits and credits given below. (a) Prepare a statement of cost of goods manufactured for the year and (b) derive the cost of goods sold.

	DEBITS	CREDITS
Materials Inventory	$ 46,512	$ 21,902
Work in Process Inventory	32,852	17,656
Materials Purchased	216,604	216,604
Purchase Discounts on Materials	2,500	2,500
Transportation-in	4,910	4,910
Direct Labor	248,616	248,616
Manufacturing Overhead	342,412	342,412
Finished Goods Inventory	18,766	8,656
Selling Expenses	126,200	126,200
Administrative Expenses	114,200	114,200
Sales Revenue	652,100	652,100
Expense and Income Summary	924,318	924,318

SOLUTION

Happy Electronics, Incorporated
Cost of Goods Manufactured
for year ended December 31, 19X5

(a)

Materials		
Inventory 1/1/X5		*$ 21,902*
Purchases	*$216,604*	
Less: Purchase Discounts	*2,500*	*214,104*
Transportation-in		*4,910*
Materials Available		*$240,916*
Less: Inventory 12/31/X5		*24,610*
Cost of Materials Used		*$216,306*
Direct Labor		*248,616*
Manufacturing Overhead		*342,412*
Total Manufacturing Costs		*$807,334*
Work in Process, 12/31/X4	*$ 17,656*	
Work in Process, 12/31/X5	*15,196*	
Net Change		*2,460*
Cost of Goods Manufactured		*$809,794*

(b)

Deduct: Increase in Finished Goods Inventory		
December 31, 19X5	*$ 10,110*	
December 31, 19X4	*8,656*	*1,454*
Cost of Goods Sold		*$808,340*

4.8. From the information in Problem 4.7, prepare the cost of goods sold section for Happy Electronics' income statement.

SOLUTION

Cost of Goods Sold	
Beginning Inventory, Finished Goods	*$ 8,656*
Cost of Goods Manufactured (per manufacturing schedule)	*809,794*
Goods Available for Sale	*$818,450*
Less: Ending Inventory, Finished Goods	*10,110*
Cost of Goods Sold	*$808,340*

4.9.	From the income statement below, using the all-inclusive concept, prepare (*a*) a revised income statement and (*b*) a statement of retained earnings. Assume that the balance in the retained earnings account at the beginning of the year was $105,000.

T. Randolf Corporation
Income Statement
year ended December 31, 19X4

Net Sales		$360,000
Gain on Sale of Treasury Stock		16,000
		$376,000
Less: Cost of Goods Sold	$170,000	
Operating Expenses	75,000	
Loss on Disposal of Equipment	13,000	
Reserve for Contingencies	20,000	
Dividends on Common Stock	15,000	
Provision for Income Taxes	50,000	343,000
Net Income for the Year		$ 33,000

SOLUTION

(*a*)
T. Randolf Corporation
Income Statement
year ended December 31, 19X4

Sales	$360,000
Cost of Goods Sold	170,000
Gross Profit on Sales	$190,000
Operating Expenses	75,000
Income from Operations	$115,000
Extraordinary Item	
Loss on Disposal of Equipment	13,000
	$102,000
Provision for Income Taxes	50,000
Net Income	$ 52,000

(*b*)
T. Randolf Corporation
Statement of Unappropriated Retained Earnings
December 31, 19X4

Balance, January 1, 19X4		$105,000
Net Income		52,000
Total		$157,000
Dividends Declared on Common Stock	$15,000	
Appropriation to Reserve for Contingencies	20,000	35,000
Balance, December 31, 19X4		$122,000

4.10.	The following balances appear on the books of the Ross Manufacturing Company on December 31. All adjustments except for final inventories and Federal income taxes (48%) have been made. The company had 5,000 shares of common stock outstanding as of December 31, 197–.

Sales	$300,000	Sales salaries	$25,000
Materials purchased	50,000	Advertising	18,000
		Office salaries	9,000
Inventories, January 1:			
Raw materials	20,000	Rent of office	2,000
Work in process	16,000	Depreciation,	
Finished goods	15,000	office equipment	1,200
Direct labor	30,000	Depreciation,	
Indirect labor	12,000	store equipment	1,000
Superintendence	9,000	Depreciation,	
Light, heat and power	15,000	plant equipment	3,000
Machinery repairs	2,000	Sales returns and allowances	3,000
Sundry factory expense	6,000	Miscellaneous general expense	2,600

The final inventories were: raw materials, $16,000; work in process, $18,000; and finished goods, $14,000. Prepare (a) a manufacturing statement and (b) a multiple-step income statement showing (c) earnings per share.

SOLUTION

(a)

Ross Manufacturing Company
Statement of Cost of Goods Manufactured
year ended December 31, 197—

Material Costs		
Inventory, January 1		$ 20,000
Purchases		50,000
		$ 70,000
Less: Inventory, December 31		16,000
Cost of Materials Consumed		$ 54,000
Direct Labor		30,000
Manufacturing Expenses		
Indirect Labor	$12,000	
Superintendence	9,000	
Light, Heat and Power	15,000	
Machinery Repairs	2,000	
Sundry Factory Expense	6,000	
Depreciation, Plant Equipment	3,000	47,000
		$131,000
Work in Process		
Inventory, December 31	$18,000	
Inventory, January 1	16,000	2,000
Cost of Goods Manufactured		$129,000

(b)

Ross Manufacturing Company
Income Statement
year ended December 31, 197—

Revenues		
Gross Sales	$300,000	
Less: Sales Returns and Allowances	3,000	
Net Sales		$297,000

Cost of Goods Sold		
Finished Goods Inventory, January 1	$ 15,000	
Cost of Goods Manufactured	129,000	
	$144,000	
Less: Finished Goods Inventory, December 31	14,000	$130,000
Gross Profit on Sales		$167,000
Operating Expenses		
Selling Expenses		
Advertising	$18,000	
Depreciation of Store Equipment	1,000	
Sales Salaries	25,000	$ 44,000
General Expenses		
Depreciation of Office Equipment	$ 1,200	
Office Salaries	9,000	
Office Rent	2,000	
Miscellaneous General Expense	2,600	14,800	58,800
Net Income before Federal Income Taxes		$108,200
Less: Federal Income Taxes		51,936
Net Income		$ 56,264

(c)	Earnings per Share (5,000 shares)	$ 11.25

4.11. Selected accounts in the ledger of AJL Corporation after year-end adjusting entries at December 31, 197– were as follows:

Building rental expense	$ 10,800
Depreciation, office equipment	800
Dividends paid ($2.00 per share)	20,000
Franchise amortization	750
Gain on sale of securities	9,000
Insurance expense	640
Inventory, January 1	10,000
Office and administrative salaries	21,000
Payroll taxes	2,000
Repairs and maintenance	760
Purchases	305,000
Sales	452,600
Sales returns and allowances	2,000
Sales salaries and commissions	45,000
Supplies used	700
Taxes and licenses	2,600
Uncollectible accounts expense	600

The gain on sale of securities is taxable at the capital gains rate of 30%. The company is subject to income tax rates of 22% on the first $25,000 of net income before taxes and 48% on all above that amount. The ending inventory is valued at $9,200. (a) Prepare an income statement for 197– in the single-step form and in accordance with the recommendations of the Accounting Principles Board. (b) Determine the net income per share before extraordinary items, its effect and the net result.

SOLUTION

AJL Corporation
Income Statement
year ended December 31, 197—

Net Sales		$450,600
Costs and Expenses		
Cost of Goods Sold	$305,800	
Building Rental Expense	10,800	
Depreciation, Office Equipment	800	
Franchise Amortization	750	
Insurance Expense	640	
Office and Administrative Salaries	21,000	
Payroll Taxes	2,000	
Repairs and Maintenance	760	
Sales Salaries and Commissions	45,000	
Supplies Used	700	
Taxes and Licenses	2,600	
Uncollectible Account Expense	600	
Income Taxes	21,892*	
Total Expenses		413,342
Net Income before Extraordinary Items		$ 37,258
Extraordinary Items		
Gain on Sale of Securities	$ 9,000	
Less: Applicable Income Tax Deduction	2,700	6,300
Net Income		$ 43,558
Net Income per Share before Extraordinary Items		$ 3.73+
Extraordinary Items Effect per Share		.63+
Net Income per Share		$ 4.36+

* $450,600 − (305,800 + 85,650) = $59,150 times tax rate

Examination I

Chapters 1-4

Part I. *Circle T for true, F for false.*

1. T F Generally accepted accounting principles apply only to CPA reports.

2. T F The revenue principle refers to the goods and services a business transfers to its customers.

3. T F The cost principle means that a business should buy at the lowest cost.

4. T F Accounting has been defined authoritatively as the act of recording, summarizing and interpreting financial transactions.

5. T F The books of original entry are the first books that were put into use by the business.

6. T F The worksheet is an informal record that aids in determining the necessary adjusting and closing entries at the end of the period.

7. T F An alternative title for an income statement is statement of *financial position*.

8. T F Current assets are expected to be realized in one year or in the normal operating cycle, whichever is longer.

9. T F When expenses are classified on a *functional* basis, some typical examples are materials and supplies, and wages and salaries.

10. T F The multiple-step income statement form shows intermediate stages in arriving at profit and loss.

11. T F Interperiod tax allocation means that income taxes are allocated between years.

Part II. *Circle the letter identifying the best answer.*

1. The organization that has been most active in developing generally accepted accounting principles is:

    a. The American Accounting Association

    b. The Internal Revenue Service

    c. The American Institute of Certified Public Accountants

2. The matching principle refers to:

    a. comparing the current operations with that of the preceding year

    b. relating revenue to cost incurred to produce that revenue

    c. matching all accounting forms

    d. comparing ending inventory with beginning inventory

3. Adjusting entries are necessary to:
    a. correct and update accounts at the end of the period
    b. balance the books for the year
    c. record the sales for the year
    d. close out expenses for the year

4. Accrued expenses:
    a. decrease assets
    b. decrease liabilities
    c. increase liabilities
    d. increase controlling accounts

5. Working capital represents:
    a. capital invested in the business
    b. current assets divided by current liabilities
    c. earnings retained in the business
    d. current assets less current liabilities

6. Deferred credits represent revenue:
    a. received but not yet earned
    b. earned but not yet received
    c. credited by a supplier
    d. credited to accounts receivable

7. The operating cycle refers to the time period:
    a. for manufacturing the product
    b. changes in the business cycle
    c. circulation of liabilities and capital in the business
    d. expenditure of cash for inventories, converting them to receivables, then back to cash

8. Extraordinary losses and gains are:
    a. seldom encountered in business
    b. disclosed separately from operating income or loss
    c. prior period adjustments
    d. not material in amount

9. An example of a "prior period adjustment" is a:
    a. bad debt loss from a sale two years ago
    b. loss on obsolete inventory
    c. settlement of a lawsuit or income tax case which arose in a prior period
    d. correction made in a prior period

10. The "current operating performance concept" requires that:

    a. all income be included for the period

    b. all expenses be recorded

    c. only usual and recurring items be included in the income statement

    d. unusual and nonrecurring items be included in income

Part III. *Complete the following statements.*

1. The principle of _____ requires disclosure of all matters of relative importance.

2. The complete sequence of procedures which is repeated each period in accounting is called the _____.

3. The accounting record which aids in classifying transactions is called the _____.

4. The books of original entry are called _____.

5. Expenses which grow with time but are not recorded until payment, or when the accounting period ends before payment, are termed _____.

6. The five types of accounts are_____.

7. The net assets of a corporation are represented by _____ _____ and as a group are termed_____.

8. In most balance sheets in this country assets are arranged in order of_____ and liabilities in order of_____.

9. "Prior period adjustments" must be _____in amount; excluded from current income and included in_____.

10. The form of income statement which shows all ordinary income at the top of the statement and all ordinary expenses below is called the_____form.

Part IV. *Solve the following problems.*

1. The financial information for the Sage Corporation is as follows for the year 19X1.

Current assets	$250,000
Total assets	500,000
Current liabilities	100,000
Total liabilities	150,000
Average receivables	50,000
Average inventory	120,000
Sales, all on account	600,000
Gross profit percentage of sales	30%
Net income percentage of sales	10%

Compute the following for the year:

- (*a*) Working capital
- (*b*) Current ratio
- (*c*) Accounts receivable turnover
- (*d*) Day's sales in receivables
- (*e*) Inventory turnover
- (*f*) Cost of goods sold
- (*g*) Net income
- (*h*) Net income as a percentage of stockholders' equity

2. The records of the Matthews Company show the following changes in account balances for 19X6:

	Changes during 19X6	
	Dr.	Cr.
Current assets	$ 95,000	
Plant and equipment	210,000	
Accumulated depreciation		$ 40,000
Current liabilities		20,000
Capital stock, $10 par		100,000
Discount on capital stock	5,000	
Retained earnings		150,000
	$310,000	$310,000

In addition, cash dividends of $30,000 were declared and paid during the year. Equipment which cost $20,000 was sold at the book value of $5,000. There were 10,000 shares of capital stock issued during the year.

Prepare a Statement of Changes in Financial Position for the year.

Answers to Examination I

Part I

1. F,   2. T,   3. F,   4. T,   5. F,   6. T,   7. F,   8. T,   9. F,   10. T,   11. F

Part II

1. c,   2. b,   3. a,   4. c,   5. d,   6. a,   7. d,   8. b,   9. c,   10. d

Part III

1. materiality;   2. accounting cycle;   3. ledger;   4. journals;   5. accrued expenses;   6. assets, liabilities, owners' equity, income, and expense;   7. capital stock, paid-in capital and retained earnings; stockholders' equity;   8. liquidity, payment;   9. material, retained earnings;   10. single-step

Part IV

1. (a) Working capital: $150,000 ($250,000 − $100,000)

   (b) Current ratio: 2.5 to 1 ($250,000 ÷ $100,000)

   (c) Accounts receivable turnover: 12 times ($600,000 ÷ $50,000)

   (d) Day's sales in accounts receivable: 30 days (365 ÷ 12)

   (e) Inventory turnover: 3.5 times ($600,000 × 70% ÷ $120,000)

   (f) Cost of goods sold: $420,000 ($600,000 × 70%)

   (g) Net income amount: $60,000 ($600,000 × 10%)

   (h) Net income as a percentage of stockholders' equity: 17.1%
        [$60,000 ÷ $350,000 ($500,000 − $150,000)]

2.

Matthews Company
Statement of Changes in Financial Position
year ended December 31, 19X6

Source of Working Capital

Operations During the Year		
Net Income (1)		*$180,000*
Add: Depreciation (2)		*55,000*
Working Capital from Operations		*$235,000*
Sale of Equipment	*$ 5,000*	
Sale of Capital Stock (3)	*95,000*	*100,000*
Total Sources of Working Capital		*$335,000*

Uses of Working Capital

Purchase of Equipment (4)	*$230,000*	
Declaration of Cash Dividends	*30,000*	
Total Uses of Working Capital		*260,000*
Increase in Working Capital (5)		*$ 75,000*

Computations:

(1) Increase of $150,000 + dividends declared $30,000 = $180,000 net income

(2) Increase of $40,000 + acc. dep. on retirement $15,000 ($20,000 − book value $5,000)
     = $55,000 depreciation expense

(3) Increase of $100,000 − discount of $5,000 = $95,000 net on sale of stock

(4) Increase of $210,000 + equipment retired $20,000 = $230,000 purchases of plant and equipment

(5) Increase in current assets $95,000 − increase in current liabilities $20,000
     = $75,000 increase in working capital

Chapter 5

Cash and Temporary Investments

5.1 THE NATURE OF CASH

Cash is that current asset which is available for payment of current liabilities and the regular operating expenses of the business. It includes deposits with banks as well as petty cash funds, currency and coins, personal checks, bank drafts, money orders and cashiers' checks. The term excludes such items as postage on hand, IOU's, postdated checks, sinking funds in the hands of a bond trustee, etc.

5.2 CASH BUDGETS

A *cash budget* is a statement of estimated cash receipts, disbursements and balances for a given time period. This time period is determined by operating patterns and industrial peculiarities. Cash budgets may be (1) long-term policy budgets covering several years or (2) short-term operating budgets covering a year or less. The basic distinction between the two lies in the fact that the short-term budget is used in planning for borrowings or the investment of temporary idle funds whereas the long-term forecast can be used in planning for capital expenditures, dividend policy, etc.

5.3 FORECASTING CASH RECEIPTS, DISBURSEMENTS AND BALANCES

The main source of cash for any business is the revenue from the sale of its goods and/or services. There are also some miscellaneous cash sources, such as interest, dividends, commissions, etc. When forecasting cash receipts, it must be remembered that a lag between sales and cash collection usually results from conducting business on credit. Collection patterns based on past experience therefore provide the basis for approximating the flow of cash into the enterprise.

EXAMPLE 1.

The Costello Recreation Company has found that payments are made on its trade receivables according to the following pattern: 75% in the first month after sale, of which 25% occur in the ten days after bills are issued; 23% in the next month; 2% allowance for uncollectibles. Its billings amounted to $93,280 in December and $89,000 in November. January cash receipts from receivables are forecasted as follows:

Estimated Receivables from December, 19X1 (0.75 × $93,280)	$69,960
Estimated Receivables from November, 19X1 (0.23 × $89,000)	20,470
Total Receivable Collection, January, 19X2	$90,430

The sales pattern is also useful in forecasting cash disbursements. Expenditures for raw materials, supplies, salaries and wages, etc. are largely controlled by expected sales. At the same time, payments for other items may follow a consistent pattern each month and not be dependent on sales volume (e.g. salaries for key management personnel, rental payments, etc.). Still other expenditures may depend on a combination of contractual arrangements and sales volume.

Generally, cash forecasts are prepared on a monthly basis for several months at a time. The projected balance is compared to the amount established as necessary to finance regular operations; this sometimes appears within the budget as the *cash balance desired*. When the relationship between projected receipts and disbursements results in the availability of a significant amount of excess (free) cash, such funds are usually invested. Conversely, if a cash deficiency exists, plans will be made to obtain the necessary funds from either existing excess cash or short-term loans (see Problem 5.10).

EXAMPLE 2.

The Costello Recreation Company's cash budget for January is shown below.

Costello Recreation Company
Cash Budget
January 197—

Cash on Hand, January 1, 197–		$ 42,500
Estimated Receipts		
Cash Sales	$75,230	
Trade Receivables	90,430	
Miscellaneous	18,500	184,160
Total Cash Available		$226,660
Estimated Disbursements		
Merchandise	$93,850	
Supplies	33,250	
Salaries and Wages	19,500	
Payroll Witholdings	5,650	
Equipment	20,400	
Bank Loan	10,000	
Miscellaneous	12,600	195,250
Estimated Cash Balance, January 31, 197–		$ 31,410
Cash Balance Desired		25,000
Free Cash		$ 6,410

5.4 INVESTMENT OF IDLE CASH

Idle cash is defined as those funds which will not be needed in the immediate future for the daily operations of the business. Such funds are invested in marketable securities (generally short-term notes or bonds) to generate additional income. Marketable securities are those which have relatively stable prices and are salable on a day-to-day basis.

5.5 TRANSACTIONS INVOLVING MARKETABLE SECURITIES

Marketable securities are recorded at cost upon acquisition. Cost includes the actual purchase price plus brokers' fees, transfer taxes and any other costs incidental to acquisition.

EXAMPLE 3.

On January 2, Ace Electronics, Incorporated purchased $100,000 ($100 par value) of a new bond issue at par. These were 6% bonds with interest payable on June 30 and December 31. The cash outlay is

Cash outlay: Bonds	$100,000
Brokerage fees	75
Total cash outlay	$100,075

The journal entry required to record the transaction is

Marketable Securities (A. T. & T. Bonds)	100,075	
Cash		100,075

EXAMPLE 4.

On March 1, Ace Electronics sells the bonds at the market price of 101 plus accrued interest for the period January 2 to March 1. The cash received on the sale is

Market price of bonds sold ($101 × 1,000)	$101,000
Accrued interest for two months	1,000
Total value of bonds sold	$102,000
Less: Brokerage, etc.	75
Net cash received	$101,925

The journal entry to record the sale is

Cash	101,925	
Marketable Securities		100,075
Interest Income		1,000
Gain on Sale of Securities		850

To record the sale of A. T. & T. bonds at 101.

5.6 MARKETABLE SECURITIES AND FINANCIAL STATEMENTS

By definition, marketable securities represent highly liquid assets. As such, their financial statement presentation is of special interest to creditors and other analysts concerned with a firm's debt-paying ability. In the current asset section of the balance sheet, these temporary investments may be listed in one of two ways:

(1) At cost, with a parenthetical notation showing current market value, or

(2) At lower-of-cost-or-market, which requires the establishment of a separate valuation account for reduction of the asset. This method is not allowed for income tax purposes. The position of the American Institute of Certified Public Accountants, with respect to marketable securities, is that

> . . . where market value is less than cost by a substantial amount and it is evident that the decline in market value is not due to a mere temporary condition, the amount to be included as a current asset should not exceed the market value. . . . It is important that the amounts at which current assets are stated be supplemented by information which reveals for temporary investments, their market value at the balance-sheet date. . . . (Accounting Research and Terminology Bulletins, Final Edition)

EXAMPLE 5.

Ace Electronics' fiscal year ends on April 30, 19X2. Suppose that instead of selling the A. T. & T. bonds (Example 4), these securities were held and were selling on the open market at $99\frac{1}{2}$ on April 30. The investment, with a market valuation of $99,500, represents a loss on paper of $575 from the original recorded cost. The year-end balance sheet would reflect the current status of these bonds as follows:

Investment in A. T. & T., 6% Bonds (Market Value, $99,500)   *$100,075*

5.7   PETTY CASH

Imprest cash is the term used for a petty cash fund of fixed amount from which the firm makes payments for small bills that are most conveniently paid in cash. The size of the fund should be sufficient to meet the normal needs of the business for two to three weeks. As disbursements are made, vouchers are prepared and placed in the fund. Thus, at any one time, the total of these vouchers plus the remaining cash should equal the total size of the original fund. The fund is restored periodically to its original amount by a company check drawn to Petty Cash.

EXAMPLE 6.

On February 1, Ace Electronics establishes a petty cash fund in the amount of $500 for the purpose of paying small freight bills. On February 23, the receiving clerk requests reimbursement for freight bills paid in the amount of $469.32. The journal entries for the establishment of the fund and for the reimbursement of the fund are

February 1, 19X2	*Petty Cash Fund*	*500*	
	Cash		*500*

To record the establishment of a petty cash fund for the payment of freight bills.

February 23, 19X2	*Incoming Freight and Cartage*	*469.32*	
	Cash		*469.32*

To record the freight paid from the petty cash fund and to reimburse the fund for the total amount expended.

5.8   RECONCILIATION OF BANK BALANCES

The cash balance on a company's books seldom agrees with the balance on its monthly bank statement. Differences between these two amounts result from one or more of the following:

(1)   Cash received at the end of the month which is not deposited in the bank until the following month (deposit in transit)

(2)   Checks issued by the company which have not cleared the bank (outstanding checks)

(3)   Bank charges for services rendered during the past month

(4)   Notes receivable collected by the bank

(5)   Recording and handling errors made by either the bank or the company

The process of reconciling these two amounts requires a review of all cash transactions for the period on the company's books *and* on the bank statement. Many differences involve time lags which are self-correcting over time. However, errors on the company's books must be corrected, and the bank must be advised if there are errors in its records. This is the essence of the reconciliation.

EXAMPLE 7.

The Reinhardt Restaurant ledger account for cash in bank shows a debit balance of $8,848.63 on June 30. The bank statement at that date shows $11,345.20. The restaurant had receipts for June 30 of $1,520.60 The restaurant was open until late in the evening and the receipts for June 30 were deposited July 1. Bank service charges shown on the bank statement were $12.81. The bank statement also disclosed a credit of $3,030.00 representing the proceeds of a note receivable of $3,000.00 and interest of $30.00.

Comparing the returned checks with the cash disbursements book showed that the following checks had not yet cleared the bank: #107, $185.27; #108, $267.51; and #109, $687.20. The review of checks also showed that check #97 in the amount of $83.21 for raw materials was erroneously entered in the cash disbursements book as $38.21. A check of $35.00 from James Smith, a customer, was returned marked NSF (not sufficient funds) and charged to the account. Included among the checks was one for $60.00, issued by the Reinhardt Brewery, which was erroneously charged to the Reinhardt Restaurant account by the bank.

The bank balance is reconciled to the book balance as follows:

The Reinhardt Restaurant
Bank Reconciliation
June 30, 197—

Balance per bank statement			$11,345.20
Add: Deposit in transit			1,520.60
			$12,865.80
Deduct: Outstanding checks			
	#107	$185.27	
	#108	267.51	
	#109	687.20	1,139.98
			$11,725.82
Add:	Bank error, Reinhardt Brewery check	$ 60.00	
	Recording error, check #97	45.00	
	NSF check, James Smith	35.00	
	Bank service charges	12.81	152.81
			$11,878.63
Deduct: Proceeds of note (interest, $30.00)			$ 3,030.00
Balance per books			$ 8,848.63

5.9 FORMS OF BANK RECONCILIATION

There are two principal forms for reconciling bank accounts: (1) reconciling the bank balance to the book balance, and (2) reconciling both bank and book balances to corrected balances. The first form, that used in the preceding reconciliation, is similar to the form generally used in reconciling other accounts. It simply shows the items which account for the difference between the bank balance and the book balance.

The second form has two sections, one pertaining to the bank data, the other to company data. If the bank makes an error such as charging the account for a check drawn by another company, it is not necessary for the company to make an entry on its books. The bank will ordinarily make the correction of its balance promptly after the company has notified the bank. Many accountants prefer this form because all reconciling items which require entries on the books are shown together in the company section, which facilitates recording.

EXAMPLE 8.

The following example uses the form in which both bank and book balances are brought to corrected balances.

The Reinhardt Restaurant
Bank Reconciliation
June 30, 197—

BANK SECTION

Balance per bank statement			*$11,345.20*
Add:	*Deposit in transit*	*$1,520.60*	
	Bank error, Reinhardt Brewery check	*60.00*	*$ 1,580.60*
			$12,925.80
Deduct: Outstanding checks			
	#107	*$185.27*	
	#108	*267.51*	
	#109	*687.20*	*$ 1,139.98*
Correct cash balance			*$11,785.82*

COMPANY SECTION

Balance per ledger			*$ 8,848.63*
Add:	*Proceeds of note collected*		
	by bank (interest $30.00)		*3,030.00*
			$11,878.63
Deduct: Recording error, check #97		*$45.00*	
	NSF check from James Smith	*35.00*	
	Bank service charges	*12.81*	*92.81*
Correct cash balance			*$11,785.82*

The adjusting journal entry would be

Cash	*2,937.19*	
Raw Materials	*45.00*	
Accounts Receivable, J. Smith	*35.00*	
Miscellaneous Expense, Bank Charge	*12.81*	
Notes Receivable		*3,000.00*
Interest Income		*30.00*

The net cash debit of $2,937.19 is the difference between $8,848.63, the book balance before adjustment, and $11,785.82, the correct cash balance.

5.10 RECONCILIATION OF CASH RECEIPTS AND DISBURSEMENTS

Another reconciliation device, often called the *proof of cash* or *four column form,* provides a more complete record than the usual reconciliation. Here the bank and book beginning and ending balances for the period are reconciled on the same forms with the reconciliation for bank and book *total* receipts and disbursements. This form is especially helpful in auditing cash receipts and cash disbursements.

Generally, the figures from the previous month's reconciliation are inserted in the first column, then the cash receipts for the month are reconciled, then the cash disbursements are checked out. The reconciliation for the end of the current month appears in the final column.

EXAMPLE 9.

A reconciliation of cash receipts, disbursements and balances (proof of cash) for the Reinhardt Restaurant (Example 7) is illustrated and discussed below. The necessary additional information was obtained from the bank statement and from the company cash books.

The Reinhardt Restaurant
Reconciliation of Cash Receipts, Disbursements, and Balances
(Proof of Cash)
June 30, 197—

Description		Balance, May 31	Receipts	Disbursements	Balance, June 30
Balances per bank statement	(1)	$13,150.75	$18,603.10	$20,408.65	$11,345.20
Deposits in transit					
May 31	(3)	675.20	(675.20)		
June 30	(4)		1,520.60		1,520.60
Outstanding checks					
May 31	(6)	(1,275.18)		(1,275.18)	
June 30	(7)			1,139.98	(1,139.98)
Bank service charge	(8)			(12.81)	12.81
NSF check	(9)			(35.00)	35.00
Recording error	(10)			(45.00)	45.00
Bank error	(11)			(60.00)	60.00
Proceeds of note collected	(5)		(3,030.00)		(3,030.00)
Balance per books	(2)	$12,550.77	$16,418.50	$20,120.64	$8,848.63

In preparing the proof of cash, each adjustment must be carefully considered since two columns are affected. Basically, it is a process of adding or subtracting from the bank totals to arrive at the book figures for the current month, as follows (description column numbers are keyed to explanations):

(1) The bank statement figures for the *opening balance* (reconciliation balance from May statement), *total receipts* (found by adding all deposits for month when total figure is not provided in statement), *total disbursement*s made by bank [opening balance ($13,150.75) plus total receipts ($18,603.10) less *closing balance* ($11,345.20) equals total disbursements ($20,408.65)], and *closing balance* are entered in appropriate columns of the form.

(2) Book figures for opening cash balance (obtained from May reconciliation), total receipts, total disbursements and closing balance for current month are entered.

Reconciling the receipts column:

(3) The deposit in transit for May ($675.20) is deducted from June bank deposits since it was recorded in the books in May.

(4) The June 30 deposit in transit ($1,520.60), not recorded by the bank in June, is added to both receipts and balance columns since it was recorded in the books in June.

(5) The proceeds of the note ($3,030) included in the bank statement balance must be deducted from both receipts and the June 30 balance since it was not entered in the books.

Reconciling the disbursements column:

(6) The outstanding checks for May ($1,275.18) are deducted from the opening balance and disbursements columns since they were recorded in the books in May.

(7) The outstanding checks for June ($1,139.98) are added to the bank disbursement total since they are properly June charges. This amount is deducted from the June total to reflect the reduction in available cash.

(8) Since the June bank charge of $12.81 was not recorded in the company's books, it is deducted from total disbursements and added to the closing bank balance.

(9) The NSF check ($35) charged to Reinhardt by the bank is deducted from disbursements and added to the June 30 balance since it does not represent a payment.

(10) The recording error ($45) and bank error ($60) are also deducted from disbursements and
& (11) added to the June 30 balance since the book balance does not reflect these payments.

Once the proof of cash is completed, necessary adjusting entries are made in the journals; these were illustrated in Example 8.

Summary

(1) Cash budgets may be _____ or _____ .

(2) An _____ of a fixed amount is used to make small cash payments.

(3) The two forms of bank reconciliation are where_____
_____ and _____ .

(4) The form which reconciles cash receipts and cash disbursements as well as the beginning and ending balances is called the_____ .

(5) The two principal differences between the bank balance and the cash book balance are _____ and _____ .

(6) The forecast of cash transactions is called a_____ .

(7) The most important factor in cash budgeting is the _____ .

(8) Cash not needed in the immediate future in a business is called_____ .

(9) Securities which have relatively stable prices and are usually held for short periods are called_____ .

(10) The cost of marketable securities includes the purchase price,_____
and _____ .

Answers: (1) long-term, short-term; (2) imprest cash fund; (3) the bank balance is reconciled to the book balance, both balances are reconciled to a corrected balance; (4) proof of cash or four-column form; (5) deposits in transit, outstanding checks; (6) cash budget; (7) forecast of revenue; (8) idle cash; (9) marketable securities; (10) brokerage fees, transfer taxes.

Solved Problems

5.1. From the data given below, (*a*) compute the adjusted balance of the cash account on the company's books, (*b*) compute the book cash balance before adjustment and (*c*) show the entries required to bring the company's books up to date.

Balance per bank statement	$18,240
Receipts recorded on the books but not yet deposited in bank	1,147
Note collected by bank but not recorded by the company	3,030
Bank service charges not recorded on the company's books	15
Outstanding checks	6,125

SOLUTION

(*a*)

Balance per bank	$18,240
Add: Deposit in transit	1,147
	$19,387
Less: Outstanding checks	6,125
Adjusted balance per books	$13,262

(*b*)

Less: Note collected by bank	3,030
	$10,232
Add: Bank service charge not recorded	15
Unadjusted balance per books	$10,247

(*c*) The journal entry to correct the books of account is calculated as follows:

Cash collected by bank for note not recorded	$ 3,030
Less: Bank service charge not recorded by company	15
Net increase in cash	$ 3,015

Thus,

Cash in Bank	3,015	
Bank Charges	15	
Notes Receivable		3,000
Interest Income		30

5.2. The bank reconciliation shown below was prepared for the U.S. Medallion Company, Incorporated at November 30, 197–.

Balance per bank		$32,974
Add: Deposit in transit	$1,240	
Check incorrectly charged by bank	75	
Bank service charges	5	
Customer's check returned by bank marked "insufficient funds"	150	1,470
		$34,444
Less: Error in recording check in payment of invoice	$ 27	
Proceeds of bank loan not recorded	2,500	
Outstanding checks	1,860	4,387
		$30,057

(*a*) Reconstruct the above bank reconciliation to show the adjusted balance per books and (*b*) prepare the journal entry to adjust the ledger account balance.

SOLUTION

(a) Since in this case both the bank balance and the unadjusted balance per books are known, the solution can be approached from either end. The key is to identify those items which affect the balance per books to arrive at the adjusted balance.

Unadjusted balance per books		$30,057
Add: Proceeds of bank loan not recorded	$2,500	
Error in recording check in payment of invoice	27	2,527
		$32,584
Less: Customer's check returned	$ 150	
Bank service charges	5	155
Adjusted balance per books		$32,429
Add: Outstanding checks		1,860
		$34,289
Less: Check incorrectly charged by bank	$ 75	
Deposit in transit	1,240	1,315
Balance per bank		$32,974

(b) The journal entry to adjust the cash balance is

Cash in Bank	2,372	
Accounts Receivable (bad check)	150	
Bank Charges	5	
Notes Payable, Bank		2,500
Accounts Payable		27

See Section 5.9.

5.3. Compute the net cash flow from operations based on the following data for the fiscal year just ended.

	197–	
	Dec. 31	Jan. 1
Net profit for the year ended (accrual basis)	$50,000	
Accounts receivable	40,400	$30,400
Inventories	60,000	55,000
Miscellaneous prepayments	3,200	4,000
Accrued liabilities	1,600	3,600
Accounts payable	30,000	48,000
Accumulated depreciation (no retirements during year)	34,000	28,000

SOLUTION

Net Income		$50,000
Add: Decrease in Miscellaneous Short-term Prepayments	$ 800	
Depreciation Expense (Increase in Accumulated Depreciation)	6,000	6,800
		$56,800
Less: Increase in Accounts Receivable	$10,000	
Increase in Inventories	5,000	
Decrease in Accrued Liabilities	2,000	
Decrease in Accounts Payable	18,000	35,000
Increase in Cash During the Year		$21,800

5.4. The management of Merox, Incorporated is faced with the problem of estimating the cash to be collected from customers during the month of September and the amount of funds it will need to pay for merchandise purchases during that month. The following information is available:

	Balances August 31	Estimated for September
Accounts receivable:		
July sales (10% of total)	$ 20,000	
August sales (50% of total)	140,000	
Accounts payable (1% discount available)	50,000	
Sales:		
Cash		$ 40,000
Credit		280,000
Purchases:		
Cash		20,000
On credit (subject to 1% discount)		180,000

Sales on credit are collected as follows: 50% in month of sale, 40% in the month following sale, and 8% in the second month following sale; 2% are generally never collected. 70% of purchases on credit are paid witihin the discount period in the month goods are purchased and the balance is paid within the discount period in the following month.

For the month of September, prepare schedules showing (a) total estimated receipts and (b) total estimated disbursements for merchandise purchases.

SOLUTION

(a)

Collections from Customers	
Cash Sales, September	$ 40,000
Accounts Receivable	
September Sales (50% × $280,000)	140,000
August Sales ($140,000 × 80% or $280,000 × 40%)	112,000
July Sales ($20,000 × 80% or $200,000 × 8%)	16,000
Total Estimated Receipts for September	$308,000

(b)

Disbursements for Merchandise Purchases	
Cash Purchases, September	$ 20,000
Accounts Payable	
September Purchases ($180,000 × 70% × 99%)	124,740
August Purchases ($50,000 × 99%)	49,500
Total Estimated Disbursements, September	$194,240

5.5. Continuing with Problem 5.4, investigation and analysis of Merox, Incorporated's prior operations reveal the following additional information pertinent to the month of September:

(1) Operating expenses consist of variable costs totaling 10% of monthly sales.

(2) Fixed operating overhead is $25,000 per month.

(3) Cash dividends of $20,000 must be paid in accordance with the July resolution of the Board of Directors.

(4) Regular quarterly installment of estimated corporate income tax ($15,000) for the current year is due.

(5) Payments on loans from individuals totaling $11,760 including interest are due.

In the past, the maximum cash balance maintained by the company has been $20,000, which is also its cash balance at September 1. Management now feels that a minimum balance of $40,000 is desirable.

Calculate the amount of money Merox must borrow from the bank in order to maintain this new minimum cash balance

SOLUTION

Cash in bank, September 1		$ 20,000
Estimated Cash Collections from Sales (from Problem 5.4a)		308,000
Total Cash available during September		$328,000
Disbursements		
Merchandise Purchases (from Problem 5.4b)	$194,240	
Operating Expenses		
Variable Costs ($320,000 × 10%)	32,000	
Fixed Operating Costs	25,000	
Dividends	20,000	
Tax Payment on Estimated Corporate Income Tax	15,000	
Loans Payable (including interest)	11,760	
Total Disbursements, September		298,000
Expected Cash Balance, September 30		$ 30,000
Desired Cash Balance		$ 40,000
Anticipated Cash Balance		30,000
Amount to be Borrowed		$ 10,000

5.6. On June 1, the Givens Company adopted an imprest cash fund procedure for the payment of small bills. The operations of the fund for the months of June and July are summarized below.

June 1:   Established the fund by drawing a company check for $2,000, cashing it at bank and delivering the cash to the petty cash cashier.

June 18:   The Vouchers Payable Department received a request from the petty cash fund cashier for the replenishment of the fund. Supporting the request was a summary of disbursements along with appropriate signed petty cash vouchers, as follows:

Factory expenses	$ 293
Special small tools	212
Salesmens' travel expenses	387
Administrative expenses	746
Miscellaneous expenses	225
Total	$1,863

June 19:   A check in the amount of $1,863 to replenish the petty cash fund was delivered to the petty cash fund cashier.

June 30:   In connection with the audit of the company for the fiscal year ended June 30, an independent CPA counted the petty cash fund and found the following:

Cash in the petty cash fund box		$1,156
Employees' checks dated July		125
Expense vouchers properly approved:		
Miscellaneous factory expenses	$ 55	
Salesmens' travel expenses	185	
Office supplies	245	
Postage	100	
Miscellaneous expenses	134	719
Total		$2,000

No attempt was made to replenish the fund at June 30.

July 12:   The employees' checks held in the fund as of June 30 were cashed and the proceeds given to the petty cash fund cashier.

July 26:   The Vouchers Payable Department received a request from the petty cash fund cashier to replenish the fund and a check was drawn that same day. The vouchers accompanying the request are summarized as follows:

Factory supplies	$ 367
Miscellaneous factory overhead	65
Salesmens' travel expenses	250
Postage and office supplies	486
Miscellaneous expense	156
Total	$1,324

Record the above transactions, using a general journal format.   Be sure to make any adjustment that may be required at the end of the company's fiscal year.

SOLUTION

Givens Company
General Journal

June 1	Petty Cash Fund		2,000	
	Cash			2,000
	To record the establishment of a petty cash fund at June 1.			
June 18	Factory Expenses, Miscellaneous		293	
	Factory Expenses, Small Tools		212	
	Selling Expenses, Travel		387	
	Administrative Expenses		746	
	Miscellaneous Expenses		225	
	Vouchers Payable			1,863
	To record vouchers submitted by petty cash fund cashier for the above expenses.			
June 19	Vouchers Payable		1,863	
	Cash			1,863
	To record check drawn to replenish petty cash fund.			

ADJUSTING ENTRIES

June 30	Due from Employees	125	
	Factory Expenses, Miscellaneous	55	
	Salesmens' Travel Expenses	185	
	Postage and Office Supplies	345	
	Miscellaneous Expenses	134	
	Petty Cash Fund		844

To bring the book balance of the petty cash fund to its actual cash balance of $1,156 at June 30 and to record all outlays from the fund to the end of the fiscal year.

REVERSING ENTRIES

July 1	Petty Cash Fund	844	
	Due from Employees		125
	Factory Expenses, Miscellaneous		55
	Salesmens' Travel Expenses		185
	Postage and Office Supplies		345
	Miscellaneous Expenses		134

To reverse adjusting entry at June 30 re: petty cash adjustment for cash actually on hand.

July 12 *No entry required since it appears that the employees' checks were cashed and the cash given directly to the petty cash fund cashier without being deposited into the company's regular bank account. If that had not been done, it would have been necessary to draw a regular company check to reimburse the fund.*

July 26	Factory Expenses, Supplies	367	
	Factory Expenses, Miscellaneous	65	
	Salesmens' Travel Expenses	250	
	Postage and Office Supplies	486	
	Miscellaneous Expenses	156	
	Vouchers Payable		1,324
	Vouchers Payable	1,324	
	Cash in Bank		1,324

Replenishment of petty cash fund with check drawn same day.

5.7. Information pertaining to the Wright Corporation's summary of cash transactions and bank statement for the month of March is presented below.

(1) Outstanding checks as of March 31, including #4328 certified by the bank in the amount of $1,250. $ 8,794.25

(2) Bank service charge for February, not recorded by the company.   10.20

(3) Proceeds of a bank loan for 60 days in the amount of $5,000 with interest at 9% per annum not recorded by bank.   4,925.00

(4) Check #4285 was entered in the cash disbursements books as $952.10. The bank paid the proper amount.   925.10

(5) The bank charged the Wright Corporation for printing a check book and the charge had not been recorded.   8.75

(6) During the month of March, the Wright Corporation deposited a check from one of its customers, the Tully Company, Incorporated. This check was returned by the bank marked NSF. The Wright Corporation has made no entry to record this.   1,075.62

(7) Customer's note, face amount $600, collected by the bank and credited by the bank to the account of the Wright Corporation. The company has made no entry for this item. $ 606.00

(8) Deposit of March 31 credited by the bank on April 1.   5,284.25

(9) Adjusted cash balance as of March 31.   15,148.86

(*a*) Prepare a bank reconciliation as of March 31, reconciling the adjusted cash book balance with the bank statement. What was the unadjusted balance per cash book at March 31? What was the balance per bank statement at March 31?

(*b*) Prepare the journal entry (or entries) at March 31 to bring the unadjusted balance per cash book into agreement with the adjusted balance of $15,148.86.

SOLUTION

(*a*)

The Wright Corporation
Bank Reconciliation
March 31, 197—

Adjusted cash balance at March 31, per books	(9)		$15,148.86
Add: Bank service charges for February	(2)	$ 10.20	
Cost of printing checkbook	(5)	8.75	
NSF check, Tully Corporation	(6)	1,075.62	1,094.57
			$16,243.43
Less: Proceeds of bank loan	(3)	$4,925.00	
Proceeds of customer's note (interest $6)	(7)	606.00	
Check #4285 entered in cash book as $952.10, paid by bank in the correct amount, $925.10	(4)	27.00	5,558.00
Unadjusted balance per cash book, March 31			$10,685.43
Adjusted cash book balance at March 31			$15,148.86
Add: Outstanding checks	(1)	$8,794.25	
Less: certified check #4328		1,250.00	7,544.25
			$22,693.11
Less: Deposit in transit, March 31	(8)		5,284.25
Balance per bank			$17,408.86

NOTE: The individual items comprising the reconciliation are keyed with the facts of the problem.

(*b*) The correcting journal entry is

Cash in Bank	4,463.43	
Accounts Receivable, Tully Corporation	1,075.62	
Bank Service Charges	10.20	
Printing Expense	8.75	
Bank Discount Expense	75.00	
Notes Receivable		600.00
Notes Payable, Bank		5,000.00
Miscellaneous Expenses		27.00
Interest Income		6.00

Unadjusted cash book balance at March 31		$10,685.43
Items increasing cash balance	$5,558.00	
Items decreasing cash balance	1,094.57	4,463.43
Adjusted cash balance at March 31		$15,148.86

5.8. The Azalea Feed Company is a wholesale establishment that operates on a fiscal year ending December 31. In November of 19X1 the company's president asks you, the independent CPA, for assistance in preparing the cash budget for the first few months of 19X2 and provides the following information.

(1) Management feels that the 19X2 sales pattern will parallel the sales pattern for 19X1. Sales in 19X1 were as follows (December, 19X1 sales are based upon orders presently on hand and which will be shipped during that month).

January	$180,000	July	$175,000
February	210,000	August	275,000
March	300,000	September	250,000
April	270,000	October	200,000
May	240,000	November	300,000
June	200,000	December	400,000

Total $3,000,000

(2) At December 31, 19X1, Accounts Receivable will total $190,000; all uncollectible accounts arising from sales prior to November have been written off. The pattern of sales collections is as follows:

During month of sale	60%
In the first month after sale	30%
In the second month after sale	9%
Uncollectible	1%

(3) The purchase price for items sold by the company averages 60% of the selling price. Inventory on hand at December 31, 19X1 is expected to amount to $420,000, of which $15,000 represents obsolete items. This obsolete inventory will be sold during January at 40% of its normal selling price on a C.O.D. basis. The company has found it desirable in the past to maintain a level of inventory at the end of each month equal to the anticipated sales level for the next three months. All purchases made during a particular month are paid for by the tenth of the following month. At December 31, 19X1 accounts payable for purchases are expected to be $185,000.

(4) Fixed operating expenses average $60,000 per month, including depreciation of $10,000. Variable expenses amount to 15% of sales. Payment for these expenses is made as follows:

	During Month Incurred	In Following Month
Fixed expenses	50%	50%
Variable expenses	60%	40%

(5) Additional expenses will involve: annual property taxes of $25,000 which are paid in equal installments on December 31 and March 31, and unusual advertising and promotional costs which will require cash payments of $5,000 in February and $20,000 in March.

(6) Cash dividends of $10,000 will be paid each quarter on the fifteenth day of the third month of the quarter.

(7) Monthly equipment replacements are estimated at $2,500 for 19X2.

(8) The company's income tax liability for 19X1 will amount to $115,000. Payments of $26,250 were made against this liability in 19X1 each quarter. The balance of the tax due for 19X1 will be paid on March 15, 19X2. The company expects that its income tax liability for 19X2 will amount to $110,000. This estimated tax will be paid in four equal installments on April 15, June 15, September 15, and December 15, 19X2.

(9) At December 31, 19X1, the company will be indebted to its bank for a loan in the amount of $140,000. The repayment schedule for this loan requires the company to pay back $10,000 on principal on the last day of each month plus interest at $\frac{3}{4}\%$ on the unpaid balance at the beginning of the month.

(10) The cash balance at December 31, 19X1 is expected to amount to $70,000.

Prepare a cash forecast statement by months for the first three months of 19X2, showing the anticipated cash balance at the end of each month.

SOLUTION

Azalea Feed Company
Cash Flow Forecast
for the three-month period ended March 31, 19X2

RECEIPTS	January	February	March
Cash Balance, Beginning of Month	$ 70,000	$ 46,250	$(6,925)
Collections of Receivables (Schedule B)	255,000	216,000	259,200
Sale of Obsolete Merchandise (See Below)	10,000	—	—
Total Cash Available	$335,000	$ 262,250	$ 252,275
DISBURSEMENTS			
Payment for Merchandise Purchased	$185,000	$ 171,000	$ 144,000
Fixed and Variable Expenses (Schedule E)	90,200	79,700	89,600
Property Taxes			12,500
Advertising and Promotional Costs		5,000	20,000
Dividends			10,000
Equipment Replacement	2,500	2,500	2,500
Balance of 19X1 Income Taxes			10,000
Loan Repayment, Principal	10,000	10,000	10,000
Interest on Loan	1,050	975	900
Total Cash Expenditures	$288,750	$ 269,175	$ 299,500
Anticipated Cash Balance (Deficit) at End of Month	$ 46,250	$(6,925)	$(47,225)

Computation of proceeds on sale of obsolete inventory:

Cost of obsolete inventory, $15,000 = 60% of selling price

Selling price of obsolete inventory = $25,000

$25,000 × 40% = $10,000 (proceeds of sale)

Azalea Feed Company
Subsidiary Schedules to Cash Flow Forecast
for the three-month period ended March 31, 19X2

A. COMPUTATION OF ACCOUNTS RECEIVABLE AT JANUARY 1, 19X2

Month of Sale	Sales	% Remaining	Amount
November, 19X1	$300,000	10%	$ 30,000
December, 19X1	400,000	40%	160,000
Total receivables at January 1, 19X2			$190,000

NOTE: The problem states that bad debt amounts *prior to November 1* have been written off. Therefore, the receivables at January 1, comprising balances from November and December sales, still include the 1% for bad debts.

B. COLLECTIONS OF RECEIVABLES

Month of Sale	Balance January 1, 19X2	Sales	Collections		
			January	February	March
November, 19X1	$ 30,000		$ 27,000	$ —	$ —
December, 19X1	160,000		120,000	36,000	—
January, 19X2		$180,000	108,000	54,000	16,200
February, 19X2		210,000	—	126,000	63,000
March, 19X2		300,000	—	—	180,000
Totals			$255,000	$216,000	$259,200

C. INVENTORY REQUIREMENTS, END OF MONTH

End of Month	Covering Sales for	Anticipated Sales	Cost of Sales at 60%	Total at End of Month
January, 19X2	February, 19X2	$210,000	$126,000	
	March, 19X2	300,000	180,000	
	April, 19X2	270,000	162,000	$468,000
February, 19X2	March, 19X2	300,000	$180,000	
	April, 19X2	270,000	162,000	
	May, 19X2	240,000	144,000	486,000
March, 19X2	April, 19X2	270,000	$162,000	
	May, 19X2	240,000	144,000	
	June, 19X2	200,000	120,000	426,000

D. SCHEDULE OF REQUIRED PURCHASES

	January	February	March
Required inventory level at end of month (see Schedule C)	$468,000	$486,000	$426,000
Cost of goods sold for current month	108,000	126,000	180,000
Cost of goods to be available	$576,000	$612,000	$606,000
Inventory on hand at beginning of month[1]	405,000	468,000	486,000
Anticipated purchases during the month	$171,000	$144,000	$120,000

[1]Total inventory at December 31, 19X1 amounts to $420,000, of which $15,000 represents obsolete merchandise and will be sold as such in January, 19X2.

E. PAYMENT SCHEDULE FOR FIXED AND VARIABLE EXPENSES

Variable Expenses Month	Variable Expenses at 15% of Sales	To Be Paid In		
		January	February	March
December, 19X1	$60,000	$24,000	$ —	$ —
January, 19X2	27,000	16,200	10,800	—
February, 19X2	31,500	—	18,900	12,600
March, 19X2	45,000	—	—	27,000
Total Variable Expenses		$40,200	$29,700	$39,600
Fixed Expenses		50,000	50,000	50,000
Total Fixed and Variable Expenses		$90,200	$79,700	$89,600

5.9.   During the audit of the cash account of the Stroud Company, the independent CPA obtained the information presented below after satisfying himself as to the credibility and validity of the cash books, the bank statement and the returned checks, except as noted.

(1) A summary of the cash books before adjustments for June, 19X5:

Balance, June 1, brought forward	$ 23,000
Receipts	212,715
	$235,715
Disbursements	175,960
Unadjusted balance per books, June 30, 19X5	$ 59,755

(2) A summary of the bank statement for June, 19X5:

Balance per bank, June 1, 19X5	$ 23,800
Deposits	211,500
	$235,300
Disbursements	189,700
Balance per bank statement, June 30, 19X5	$ 45,600

(3) Bank reconciliation as of May 31, 19X5:

Balance per bank statement, May 31, 19X5		$ 23,800
Add: Deposit in transit		2,100
		$ 25,900
Less: Outstanding checks:		
#6221	$300	
#0980	650	
#0981	750	
#0983	800	
#0984	275	
#0986	125	
		2,900
Balance per books, May 31, 19X5		$ 23,000

(4) On June 1, 19X5, the Stroud Company discounted its own 90-day note with the bank. The bookkeeper recorded a cash receipt of $18,000, forgetting that the bank would deduct $315 as interest.

(5) Bank charges for June were $25, plus a $20 service charge for the collection of a foreign draft in May. These charges had not been recorded.

(6) Outstanding checks at June 30, 19X5 totaled $5,600 exclusive of checks #6221 and #0984.

(7) In June the bank returned two NSF checks in the amounts of $500 and $200. The check for $500 was redeposited but the $200 check was still on hand as of June 30. The usual practice of the company bookkeeper is to record dishonored checks as reductions of receipts. When they are redeposited they are recorded as regular cash receipts. If the company cancels its own checks, those are recorded as reductions of cash disbursements.

(8) Check #6221 in the amount of $300, listed in the outstanding checks as of May 31, 19X5, was actually drawn three years ago. Efforts to locate the payee were fruitless and it was agreed that the check should be cancelled.

(9)   All outstanding checks as of May 31, 19X5 were returned with the bank statement for June, 19X5 except for checks #6221 and #984.   An examination of certain checks returned with the bank statement disclosed the following:

Number	Date Drawn	Amount	Explanation
0981	May 28, 19X5	$ 570	Recorded in cash disbursements as $750.
1032	June 12	275	Replacement for check #984 originally returned by the payee because it had been made out to him personally, instead of to the corporation owned by the payee.
—	June 19	900	A counter check drawn by the president of Stroud for travel expenses. The president had forgotten to tell the bookkeeper.
—	June 21	250	During the month the bookkeeper noted that these
	June 22	300	two checks were missing. They had been stolen, presented for payment at the bank and paid, even though they lacked any signature.
1097	July 3	15,000	Originally issued on June 30, 19X5 but postdated for July 3. This check had not been recorded in the June disbursements since it was not supposed to have been deposited until July 3.

(10)   The cash receipts of June 30, 19X5 amounting to $3,700 were mailed to the bank on that day but did not arrive at the bank until July 2.

Prepare a four-column "proof of cash" reconciling cash receipts and disbursements as recorded on the bank statement and the company's books for the month of June, 19X5.   Be sure to arrive at the cash figure that will be shown in the company's financial statements as of June 30, 19X5.

SOLUTION

Stroud Company
Reconciliation of Cash Receipts, Disbursements and Cash Balance
(Proof of Cash)
at June 30, 19X5

	Ref.	Balance May 31	Receipts	Payments	Balance June 30
Balances per bank statement	(2)	$23,800	$211,500	$189,700	$45,600
Deposits in transit: May 31	(3)	2,100	(2,100)		
June 30	(10)		3,700		3,700
Outstanding checks: May 31	(3)	(2,900)		(2,900)	
June 30	(6)			5,600	(5,600)
Bank error	(9)			(550)	550
Dishonored checks returned by bank	(7)		(700)	(700)	
Corrected totals per bank		$23,000	$212,400	$191,150	$44,250
Balances per ledger	(1)	$23,000	$212,715	$175,960	$59,755
Error in recording check #981	(9)			(180)	180
Cancelled check #6221	(8)			(300)	300
Cancelled check #984	(9)			(275)	275
Record counter check of June 19	(9)			900	(900)
Record check #1097	(9)			15,000	(15,000)
To correct entry of June 1, discount on note not entered	(4)		(315)		(315)
Record bank charges	(5)			45	(45)
Corrected totals per books		$23,000	$212,400	$191,150	$44,250

Notes to Solution

(1) The reference column has been inserted here so that the student can follow the solution from the text of the problem.

(2) The last column of the solution shows the adjusted balance per books.

(3) The use of this particular type of reconciliation is recommended especially where the accountant is at all uncertain as to the correctness of the books of account since it enables him to find errors quickly.

5.10. The Matador Corporation wants to expand its level of operations for the coming year. After investigation, management determined that the following would be necessary: (1) additional investment in receivables and inventory and (2) a minimum cash balance of $50,000. The corporation's forecast of operations for the coming year shows the following estimated monthly cash balances (cash deficiencies are shown in brackets):

January	$ 90,000
February	60,000
March	(75,000)
April	(200,000)
May	(125,000)
June	125,000
July	350,000
August	400,000
September	80,000
October	(225,000)
November	(300,000)
December	(60,000)

It has been the practice of management to undertake investments and to make loans on the fifteenth of each month in an amount equal to the projected cash surplus or deficiency for the month. These changes in the investment or loan position are made in multiples of $5,000. Excess cash is invested in short-term government bonds bearing 6% interest. Borrowings are made at the local bank where the interest charge is $8\frac{1}{2}\%$.

(a) Prepare a schedule showing the net interest cost (interest expense less interest income on temporary investments) of short-term borrowing to finance the operations for the coming year. All computations are to be carried to the nearest dollar.

(b) How much long-term or permanent capital needs to be raised if Matador is to avoid short-term borrowing? Which method of financing would you recommend? Why?

SOLUTION

The schedule presented in answer to the problem makes the following assumptions:

(1) Interest earned or interest expense is calculated at the applicable rate for one month from the fifteenth of one month to the fifteenth of the next.

(2) Interest for the month of December is calculated from the fifteenth to the thirty-first.

(3) There was no investment or loan position at the beginning of the year.

(a)

The Matador Corporation
Schedule Showing Net Cost of Short-term Borrowing
Minimum Balance $50,000

Month	Expected Cash Balance at End of Month	Amount in Excess or (Under) Minimum Balance	Investment		Borrowings	
			Amount	Interest Earned (6%)	Amount	Interest Expense (8½%)
January	$ 90,000	$ 40,000	$ 40,000	$ 200	$ —0—	$ —0—
February	60,000	10,000	10,000	50	—0—	—0—
March	(75,000)	(125,000)	—0—	—0—	125,000	885
April	(200,000)	(250,000)	—0—	—0—	250,000	1,771
May	(125,000)	(175,000)	—0—	—0—	175,000	1,240
June	125,000	75,000	75,000	375	—0—	—0—
July	350,000	300,000	300,000	1,500	—0—	—0—
August	400,000	350,000	350,000	1,750	—0—	—0—
September	80,000	30,000	30,000	150	—0—	—0—
October	(225,000)	(275,000)	—0—	—0—	275,000	1,948
November	(300,000)	(350,000)	—0—	—0—	350,000	2,479
December	(60,000)	(110,000)	—0—	—0—	110,000	779
Totals				$4,025		$9,102
Less: Interest earned						4,025
Net cost of short-term borrowing						$5,077

(b) To avoid all short-term borrowing, the company would have to raise $350,000 in permanent capital since this was the largest amount borrowed. This amount could be either in the form of long-term debt or equity capital. Which method to use would depend on a host of complex factors. Among these are the following:

(1) The ability of the company to use financial leverage or "trade on the equity."

(2) The use to which these permanent funds could be put.

(3) The ability of the company to borrow on a short-term basis.

(4) The costs associated with borrowing on a long-term basis or of raising the funds through the sale of equity securities.

There is no question but that the net cost of permanent capital will exceed the net cost of short-term borrowing. If the company raises its needs in the form of long-term capital there will be large sums of money to invest which, according to the facts we know, can only be invested at a 6% return.

Chapter 6

Receivables

6.1 RECEIVABLES DEFINED

The term *accounts receivable* generally denotes all claims involving a future inflow of cash. These receivables result from business transactions involving sales of goods and services, loans and miscellaneous claims. The accounting procedures surrounding the creation of receivables as well as the controls over the credit granting function and the collection process are, therefore, of considerable importance.

6.2 TRADE RECEIVABLES

Trade receivables represent the sale of goods and services in the normal course of business operations and account for the major portion of a firm's revenue-producing activities. The *open account*, or *trade account*, created by a transaction between business concerns is generally *unsecured* (an informal arrangement rather than a legal agreement) and *non-interest-bearing*. This can be contrasted to retail trade receivables, which typically involve the addition of an interest or service charge to revolving charge accounts and installment agreements.

Trade receivables sometimes take the form of commercial credit instruments such as promissory notes or time drafts. Since these are signed agreements, a measure of legal commitment is provided and the holder may borrow against them (see Section 6.7).

6.3 OTHER RECEIVABLES

Revenue is sometimes generated from sources other than trade receivables. Among these are short-term advances to customers or subcontractors, insurance claims, claims for rebates on taxes or other overpayments, sale of plant and equipment and accruals of interest, rent, royalties, etc. Such receivables are properly classified as current assets when collection is expected within one year and as other assets or miscellaneous assets if a longer collection period is anticipated.

6.4 VALUATION OF TRADE RECEIVABLES

Trade receivables are generally recognized at the time goods are sold and title passes, or when the service provided is actually performed. The valuation placed on the receivables depends on *the amount due, the time of collection* and *the probability of collection*.

Determining the amount due. The amount actually paid by the customer often includes a variety of charges and discounts which the seller may impose on the quoted price.

(1) *Trade discounts* represent the difference between the gross or recommended list price and the net price to the buyer before other discounts and charges. The receivable and resulting revenue are both recorded at the *net* price.

EXAMPLE 1.

    The Sincerely Yours Greeting Card Company provides a 35% trade discount on orders having a resale value of up to $500, and a 50% discount on orders of $1,000 or more. The Forget-Me-Not Card Shop ordered $400 worth of merchandise, which was billed at the net price of $260. Cards Unlimited placed an $1,100 order; the net price billed ($550) reflected the higher discount rate.

(2) *Cash discounts* are offered as an incentive for prompt payment. They represent the difference between the *cash price* and the amount realized.

EXAMPLE 2.

    When the Sincerely Yours Greeting Card Company shipped Cards Unlimited's $1,100 order on May 1, its invoice carried the terms 2/10, n/30. Taking advantage of the cash discount, Cards Unlimited remitted $539 ($1,100 − $550 − $11) on May 8. The additional 2% discount represents the saving of an effective interest rate of 36.7% per annum to the buyer.

    The seller may record cash discounts as they are taken or by establishing a system for anticipating them. The latter method more closely records receivables and revenues at their *net realizable amounts*. When cash discounts are anticipated and the customer pays after the discount period, the allowance account is offset by a credit to Sales Discounts Forfeited.

EXAMPLE 3.

    Suppose that Sincerely Yours records cash discounts when they are taken. The accounting entry on May 1 reflects the gross amount (or the amount after trade discount):

May 1	*Accounts Receivable*	*550*	
	Sales		*550*

When Cards Unlimited's payment is received on May 8, the entry is

May 8	*Cash*	*539*	
	Cash Discounts	*11*	
	Accounts Receivable		*550*

If instead, Sincerely Yours followed the practice of anticipating cash discounts, the entries might have been

May 1	*Accounts Receivable*	*550*	
	Sales		*539*
	Allowance for Cash Discounts		*11*
May 8	*Cash*	*539*	
	Allowance for Cash Discounts	*11*	
	Accounts Receivable		*550*

(3) *Credit card fees* enable the seller of retail goods to extend credit to some customers—the credit card holders. Credit card companies generally assume the collection function and charge the seller a fee for this purpose, usually basing it upon a percentage of the sales price. Since the fees are automatic charges, they should be accrued by the seller when the sale is recognized. Sales revenues are recorded at full value while receivables due from the credit card company are recorded at the net amount expected. The difference, representing the fees charged by the credit card company, is recorded as an expense of the period.

(4) *Sales returns and allowances* recognizes the probability that some merchandise will be returned or that an adjustment will be made on the sales price. Since

returns and allowances represent a reduction in receivables and anticipated cash, immaterial amounts should be debited to an expense account when made, with the balance offset against sales revenue in the income statement. Material amounts which can be objectively estimated may be recorded by an adjusting entry at the end of the current period.

EXAMPLE 4.

The Sincerely Yours Greeting Card Company knows that its sales returns average 5% of accounts receivable at the end of any period. At the end of May, the following entry is made to adjust $500,000 in outstanding trade receivables,

Sales Returns and Allowances	25,000	
Allowance for Sales Returns and Allowances		25,000

thus restating its receivables at their net realizable amount.

(5) *Freight allowances* may arise when the customer pays for the transportation of goods even though the seller is obligated to do so. In such cases, both the receivable and the revenue should be valued net of the transportation expense. When goods are sold "f.o.b. shipping point" and the customer is billed for the freight charge, the revenue accounts should reflect only the invoice price of the goods sold. The freight charge in the invoice should be credited to an expense account, such as Transportation-out.

(6) *Sales and excise taxes* itemized separately on invoices should be credited to appropriate liability accounts, such as Sales Taxes Payable. When taxes are included in the selling price of an item, they are in essence costs of production and should be deducted from revenue generated as an expense.

(7) *Container deposits* received from customers create a liability for the seller since it is understood that deposits will be refunded when containers are returned. The container charge should be segregated from the sale amount on the invoice and in the receivables; a separate liability account should be established to avoid overstatement of receivables.

The liability for container refunds is offset by a receivable from the customer for unreturned containers. When containers are not returned, the difference between the amount charged to the customer and the cost of the container to the company is taken as income.

EXAMPLE 5.

The following entries illustrate the container liability account.

(i)   Recording the liability at time of sale:

Accounts Receivable, ABC Manufacturing	300	
Miscellaneous Receivables, Unreturned Containers	5	
Sales Income		300
Liability for Unreturned Containers		5

(ii)   If container is returned:

Liability for Unreturned Containers	5	
Miscellaneous Receivables, Unreturned Containers		5

(iii)   If customer pays for container:

Cash	5	
Miscellaneous Receivables, Unreturned Containers		5
Liability for Unreturned Containers	5	
Container Inventory		3
Income from Sale of Containers		2

Time of collection. It is generally acknowledged that a given amount of money is worth less today than a year from now. Therefore, when it is known that a receivable will not be collected for a long period of time and no interest is being charged, it is customary to assign a *present value* to that account based on an appropriate rate of interest.

EXAMPLE 6.

If a receivable for $3,180 is to be outstanding for an entire year and money is worth 6% per annum, the entry at the time of sale would be

Accounts Receivable	3,180	
Sales		3,000
Interest Income		180

Probability of collection. While the probability of any receivable being ultimately uncollectible is very low, it is a necessary consideration with respect to valuation accuracy. Uncollectibles are estimated to prevent an overstatement of assets and revenues; the estimate serves to reduce gross receivables to an approximation of the net realizable value of short-term funds due from customers.

The valuation account carries a credit balance and is variously titled Allowance for Doubtful Accounts or Allowance for Uncollectible Accounts. On the income statement, the estimated allowance may be shown as a contra asset reducing gross sales, but is more often included as an operating expense or other expense representing a failure of management.

The two principal methods for estimating uncollectibles are an estimate based on a percentage of sales and an estimate based on an analysis of receivables at the end of the accounting period. Uncollectibles may also be recognized on a direct write-off basis. Finally, the possibility does exist that some accounts deemed uncollectible and written off may eventually be collected.

(1) *Estimate based on sales.* When the percentage of sales method is used, the seller examines the relationship between credit sales and uncollectibles in past periods to derive a percentage applicable to credit sales in the current period. This method attempts to match costs and revenues in each period. It assumes a fairly stable relationship between credit sales and uncollectibles and provides a basis for estimation which is in essence an average reflecting past experience. Since this method relies heavily on past experience, it is important to test the adequacy of the established percentage on a periodic basis to allow for any changes in business conditions.

EXAMPLE 7.

The Bishop Company found that uncollectibles in 19X1 and 19X2 averaged 3% of credit sales in each year. Using this percentage to estimate uncollectibles on first quarter 19X3 credit sales of $1,000,000, the journal entry is

Provision for Doubtful Accounts	30,000	
Allowance for Doubtful Accounts		30,000

To record provision for doubtful accounts in the first quarter
based on 3% of $1,000,000 in sales.

(2) *Estimate based on accounts receivable.* This method of estimating uncollectibles depends on an analysis of receivables by age group and probability of collection. It assumes that there is a strong relationship between the age of a receivable and its eventual collection. It has the advantage of identifying specific accounts in need of special attention. The procedure is to prepare an *aged trial balance* at the end of the accounting period, classifying the outstanding amounts

according to whether the account is *not due* or *past due,* based on varying lengths of time.

EXAMPLE 8.

The Franklin Company has asked its accountant to prepare an aged trial balance of accounts receivable as a basis for estimating the amount of its uncollectible accounts. It is presented below.

The Franklin Company
Aged Trial Balance
December 31, 197—

Customer	Amount	Not Yet Due	Past-Due Days					
			Under 30	31–60	61–90	91–120	121–180	Over 180
Brought forward	$601,000	$359,600	$79,700	$58,500	$48,600	$24,800	$ 9,900	$19,900
R. B. Adams	1,600			1,500	100			
J. A. Barton	300		300					
E. M. Bates	400	400						
R. A. Cain	200						100	100
J. D. Englefield	1,500				1,300	200		
Totals	$605,000	$360,000	$80,000	$60,000	$50,000	$25,000	$10,000	$20,000

Once the amount of receivables has been determined for each of the aging categories, experience percentages are applied to arrive at the estimated uncollectible amount. Following is the schedule prepared by the accountant for the Franklin Company.

The Franklin Company
Estimation of Uncollectible Receivables
December 31, 197—

Classification	Balances	Uncollectible %	Estimated Uncollectible Amount
Not yet due	$360,000	2	$ 7,200
Under 30 days past due	80,000	5	4,000
31 to 60 days past due	60,000	10	6,000
61 to 90 days past due	50,000	15	7,500
91 to 120 days past due	25,000	20	5,000
121 to 180 days past due	10,000	45	4,500
Over 180 days past due	20,000	75	15,000
Totals	$605,000		$49,200

The above analysis indicates that approximately $50,000 of accounts receivable may prove to be uncollectible. If the balance in the Allowance for Doubtful Accounts is $20,000, the adjusting entry will be

Provision for Doubtful Accounts	30,000	
Allowance for Doubtful Accounts		30,000

It is important to note that actual write-offs of uncollectibles rarely agree with the balance in the allowance account. If the differences are nominal, it is not necessary to change the balance. Major differences, however, require charges to the current period's Uncollectible Accounts Expense or a similar account before computing extraordinary items. They should not be recorded as extraordinary items or prior period adjustments.

EXAMPLE 9.

With reference to Example 8, suppose that while an allowance account balance of $50,000 was needed, the account showed a balance of $75,000. The adjusting entry to reduce the Allowance for Doubtful Accounts balance is

Allowance for Doubtful Accounts	*25,000*	
Provision for Doubtful Accounts		*25,000*

(3) *Direct write-off method.* Under the direct write-off method, bad debts are recorded only when specific accounts are determined to be definitely uncollectible. Losses are recorded by crediting Accounts Receivable and debiting Bad Debts Expense. Since this method overstates the net realizable value of receivables at the end of the period and does not provide for proper matching of collectibles and associated revenues, it is less desirable for income taxes than the allowance method, although it is an acceptable alternative.

(4) *Collection of receivables previously written off.* When a firm uses the allowance method for estimating uncollectibles, the actual write-off of a receivable is a charge to Allowance for Doubtful Accounts and a credit to Accounts Receivable. If the firm uses the direct charge-off method, the charge is to Bad Debt Expense and a credit to Accounts Receivable. When an account that has been written off is subsequently collected and the firm uses the allowance method, the usual procedure is a reversing entry crediting the recovery to the allowance account and debiting Accounts Receivable. However, if there is a large amount involved and the credit to the allowance account will create an excessive balance, the credit may go instead to a separate account for Bad Debts Recovered. When the direct charge-off method is used, the credit may go either to Bad Debt Expense, if one has been created, or to Bad Debts Recovered.

6.5 INSTALLMENT SALES

The installment contract is a widely used credit instrument which provides for payment over an extended period of time. Selling goods and services on this basis requires special considerations in terms of asset classification and valuation.

Installment receivables are usually carried on the books from 6 to 36 months; however, according to ARB No. 43, they should be classified as current assets when this arrangement represents the normal course of business operations. It is customary to record installment sales at face value less unearned interest and finance charges; interest and finance charges are recognized as revenue only as earned.

6.6 GENERATING CASH FROM ACCOUNTS RECEIVABLE

Accounts receivable may be sold or used as collateral in order to generate immediate cash for the business. These procedures are quite common in some industries while in others they are used to raise funds in times of financial difficulty.

Factoring accounts receivable. When a receivable is sold or *factored*, the risk of credit and all collection efforts are assumed by the buyer, or *factor*. The firm selling the receivables receives its cash immediately, for a fee. Factoring arrangements vary widely, and usually depend on such things as the amount of receivables purchased and the credit standing of the firm's customers. The fees imposed by the factor generally consist of an interest charge on the funds actually borrowed plus a commission of from 1 to 3% of the net amount of receivables purchased.

The factoring of accounts receivable does not raise any particular accounting problems. Cash is debited for receipts from the sale, Accounts Receivable is credited and the factor's commission and interest charges are recorded as expenses. If the factor holds back a percentage of the proceeds as protection against returns and allowances, the seller records that amount as a receivable from the factor.

Assigning receivables. Under this method, the business (*assignor*) pledges the receivables to the lender (*assignee*) as collateral for a loan. The assignor retains all credit risks and generally makes all collections since the customer is rarely notified of the assignment. The assignee generally advances less than 100% of the receivables pledged, which means that the assignor has some equity in the receivables.

For accounting purposes the following procedures should be used:

(1)   Accounts that have been assigned should be transferred to a separate account called Accounts Receivable Assigned.

(2)   Funds received from the assignee should be credited to a Notes Payable, Assignee account.

(3)   Collections on those accounts turned over to the assignee would require a debit to Notes Payable, Assignee and a credit to Accounts Receivable Assigned.

(4)   Charges for interest, commissions, etc. should be handled as period expenses and included in payments to the assignee.

In the balance sheet, the assignor's equity in pledged receivables is indicated by deducting the balance due the assignee from the total receivables assigned.

EXAMPLE 10.

Suppose that the Carstairs Company had accounts receivable of $300,000 plus $40,000 in accounts receivable assigned, of which $25,000 was designated for Notes Payable, Assignee. At the end of the period, its balance sheet would present the following information.

Current Assets		
Accounts Receivable		*$300,000*
Accounts Receivable Assigned	*$40,000*	
Less: Notes Payable to Assignee	*25,000*	
Equity in Assigned Receivables		*15,000*
Total Receivables		*$315,000*

6.7 NOTES RECEIVABLE

For accounting purposes, the term *notes receivable* refers to promissory notes, bills of exchange or trade acceptances. Notes receivable are distinguished by the fact that they are written contractual arrangements for the payment of a specific amount of money, generally plus interest, at a stated time. They are usually *negotiable* or transferable instruments which enable the holder to use them for cash generation in much the same way as is done with accounts receivable.

Valuation of notes receivable. A note is generally recorded at its face value. However, when no interest rate is specified, the face amount of a note is assumed to include some provision for interest. Such non-interest-bearing notes are recorded at face value less an interest charge based on a percentage that is assumed to be reasonable. The Discount on Notes Receivable is taken into income over the life of the note.

EXAMPLE 11.

A one-year note with a face value of $26,500 and no stated interest rate would be recorded as follows, using 6% as a reasonable rate of interest.

Notes Receivable	26,500	
Discount on Notes Receivable		1,500
Sales		25,000
At acquisition.		
Discount on Notes Receivable	125	
Interest Earned		125
Monthly entry to record interest earned.		
Cash	26,500	
Notes Receivable		26,500
At maturity.		

Discounting notes receivable. Notes receivable may be sold or discounted. When a note is *sold* to a bank or finance company *without recourse,* the seller assumes no future liability should the maker of the note default. *Discounting,* on the other hand, is usually done on a recourse basis (i.e. money is borrowed using the note as collateral and the borrower, who endorses the note, becomes contingently liable should the maker default).

The *proceeds* or cash received when a note is discounted may be computed in one of two ways:

(1) The interest or discount charged by the lender is deducted from the *face value* of the note, or

(2) The discount rate may be applied to the *maturity value* of the note.

EXAMPLE 12.

Assume that the non-interest-bearing note for $26,500 (Example 11) is discounted at the local bank the day it is received at a rate of 6%. The amount of cash that the company will receive is computed as follows:

Face amount of note, less interest	$25,000
Interest included therein	1,500
Maturity value	$26,500
Less: Discount at 6%	1,590*
Cash received (proceeds)	$24,910

* The discount is computed on the maturity value of $26,500 while the interest (assumed to be 6%) is computed on the principal of $25,000. The $90 difference between these computed amounts represents an additional finance charge by the bank. Keeping in mind that this note was probably given in exchange for $25,000 worth of sales merchandise, this arrangement can be likened to factoring accounts receivable, where a percentage of the actual value is withheld by the factor as a fee (see Section 6.5). In both cases, the seller receives slightly less than the present cash value of the receivable.

When the note is discounted, the entry to record this would be

Cash	24,910	
Discount on Notes Receivable	1,500	
Financing Expense	90	
Notes Receivable Discounted		26,500

When the note is paid the following entry would be made:

Notes Receivable Discounted	*25,000*	
Notes Receivable		*25,000*

If the note is dishonored at maturity (the maker fails to pay the seller as promised), the entries are

Accounts Receivable	*26,500*	
Cash		*26,500*
Notes Receivable Discounted	*26,500*	
Notes Receivable		*26,500*

Summary

(1)   Receivables from ordinary sales or services are called_____, while receivables from nonrecurring or unusual transactions are called_____.

(2)   The principal methods for estimating the amount of uncollectible accounts are based on_____and_____.

(3)   In the income statement, doubtful accounts expense can be (*a*) a selling expense, (*b*) a general and administrative expense, (*c*) a financial expense, (*d*) a deduction from sales, or (*e*) all of the above.

(4)   In the income statement, a sales discount is considered (*a*) a financial expense or a deduction from sales, (*b*) a general and administrative expense, (*c*) all of the above, or (*d*) none of the above.

(5)   A major adjustment to Allowance for Uncollectible Accounts should be treated, according to the AICPA, as (*a*) a prior period adjustment, (*b*) an extraordinary item, or (*c*) an expense in computing income before extraordinary items.

(6)   The Sherwood Company's schedule of estimated uncollectible accounts shows a balance of $6,500.   If the balance in the allowance account is $9,000, the entry should be (*a*) a debit of $2,500, (*b*) a debit of $1,000, or (*c*) a credit of $2,500.

(7)   Which of the following is *not* a proper deduction in the evaluation of receivables? (*a*) Allowance for Doubtful Accounts, (*b*) Allowance for Sales Discounts, (*c*) Discount Lost, or (*d*) Allowance for Freight Claims.

(8)   If a firm sells its accounts receivables, this is called_____; if it assigns receivables as collateral for a loan, this is called_____.

(9)   Collection of a $50 account previously written off should be credited to_____
_____.

(10)   On the installment basis, a sale is originally recorded (*a*) at face value *plus* unearned interest and finance charges, (*b*) at face value *less* unearned interest and finance charges, (*c*) at face value *plus* interest *minus* finance charges, or (*d*) at face value.

Answers: (1) trade receivables, miscellaneous receivables; (2) a percentage of sales, an analysis of accounts receivable; (3) *e*; (4) *a*; (5) *c*; (6) *a*; (7) *c*; (8) factoring, assignment; (9) Allowance for Uncollectible Accounts; (10) *b*.

Solved Problems

6.1. The Memo Corporation began operations on July 1, and has outstanding receivables of $250,000 at the end of the year. Because of the nature of the enterprise, management wishes to take into account the following in valuing receivables at year end:

Estimated uncollectible accounts	$4,500
Estimated allowances for cooperative advertising	6,000
Estimated cash discounts (sales discounts)	2,200

(a) Prepare a journal entry to recognize the above estimates of management in valuing accounts receivable.

(b) Show the accounts receivable section of the balance sheet at year end.

SOLUTION

(a)
Uncollectible Accounts Expense	4,500	
Cooperative Advertising Expense	6,000	
Sales Discounts	2,200	
Allowance for Uncollectible Accounts		4,500
Allowance for Cooperative Advertising		6,000
Allowance for Sales Discounts		2,200

(b)
Accounts Receivable		$250,000
Less: Allowance for Uncollectible Accounts	$4,500	
Allowance for Cooperative Advertising	6,000	
Allowance for Sales Discounts	2,200	12,700
Accounts Receivable, Net Realizable Value		$237,300

6.2. The Onyx Company acquired a job lot of merchandise at a total cost of $8,000. At list price, the merchandise would bring $15,000. In order to sell the lot as quickly as possible, Onyx sells the entire lot at list less a trade discount of 15% and agrees to allow a cash discount of 1% if the bill is paid within ten days. Normally, Onyx records these sales less the applicable trade discount.

Prepare the necessary journal entries to record (a) the sale and the cost of goods sold, assuming a perpetual inventory system and (b) the collection of the account within the ten-day period.

SOLUTION

(a)
Accounts Receivable	12,750	
Sales		12,750
To record sale of merchandise less the trade discount of 15%.		

Cost of Goods Sold	8,000	
Inventories		8,000
To record the cost of merchandise sold.		

(b)
Cash	12,622.50	
Sales Discounts	127.50	
Accounts Receivable		12,750

6.3. On September 1, the Alwyn Corporation assigned accounts receivables of $75,000 to the Barclay Finance Company and received $67,500 less a 2% financing charge.

Interest is charged at the rate of $1\frac{1}{4}\%$ per month of the unpaid balance. During the month of September, the Alwyn Corporation collected $50,000 on the assigned accounts and remitted that amount to Barclay Finance at the end of the month.

Prepare all necessary journal entries relating to the above transactions for the month of September.

SOLUTION

| September 1 | Assigned Accounts Receivable | 75,000 | |
| | Accounts Receivable | | 75,000 |

NOTE: The purpose of this entry is to segregate the assigned receivables from all others. This may have to be done by agreement with the factor, by state law, or just to indicate on the financial records those accounts which have been assigned.

September 1	Cash	66,150	
	Financing Charges	1,350	
	Notes Payable, Barclay Finance Company		67,500

To record the proceeds of a loan from Barclay Finance and the related finance charge.

| September 30 | Cash | 50,000 | |
| | Accounts Receivable Assigned | | 50,000 |

To record collections on assigned receivables during September.

September 30	Notes Payable, Barclay Finance Company	49,156.25	
	Interest Expense	843.75	
	Cash		50,000

To record the payment of $50,000 to Barclay Finance Company, including interest on $67,500 @ $1\frac{1}{4}\%$ interest.

6.4. On January 1, the beginning balance in Accounts Receivable was $120,000, and the balance in Allowance for Doubtful Accounts was $6,500. At December 31, the balance in Accounts Receivable amounted to $90,000, of which 3% was estimated to be uncollectible. During the year, $7,500 of Accounts Receivable were written off as uncollectible.

(a) Compute the bad debts expense for the year and (b) prepare the necessary journal entry.

SOLUTION

(a) At December 31, the balance in the allowance for bad debts account would be calculated as follows:

Balance at January 1 (credit balance)	$6,500
Charge to allowance during the year as uncollectible	7,500
Balance of account at December 31 (debit balance)	$1,000
Required credit balance at December 31 ($3\% \times \$90,000$)	2,700
Bad debts expense	$3,700

| (b) | Bad Debts Expense | 3,700 | |
| | Allowance for Bad Debts | | 3,700 |

Journal entry required to bring the balance in Allowance for Bad Debts to a credit balance of $2,700 ($3\% \times \$90,000$).

6.5. At June 30, the following balances appeared in the general ledger of the Semloh Corporation:

Accounts receivable (debit balance)	$ 750,000
Allowance for bad debts (debit balance)	6,000
Sales revenue (for the year ended June 30)	1,600,000

For the year ended June 30, prepare the necessary journal entry to recognize bad debts expense under each of the following assumptions:

(a) As a result of aging the receivables, $32,500 of the accounts receivable are considered uncollectible.

(b) The allowance for bad debts is to be increased to a credit balance of $18,500.

(c) The company's usual practice is to recognize 4% of sales as bad debts expense.

SOLUTION

(a)   Bad Debts Expense   38,500
            Allowance for Bad Debts   38,500

        Entry to bring the balance in the allowance for bad debts account to a credit balance of $32,500 to take care of anticipated uncollectible accounts at June 30.

(b)   Bad Debts Expense   24,500
            Allowance for Bad Debts   24,500

        To bring the balance in the allowance for bad debts account to a balance of $18,500.

(c)   Bad Debts Expense   64,000
            Allowance for Bad Debts   64,000

        To increase the allowance for bad debts account by 4% of $1,600,000.

6.6. In examining the accounts receivable balance of the Dendy Corporation at December 31, you discover that included in the total amount of $250,000 are the following items:

Accounts considered uncollectible	$ 1,968
Amounts due from officers of the corporation	17,500
Advances to employees	1,500
Accounts with credit balances resulting from advance payments on contracts	5,000

Prepare a journal entry reclassifying those items which are not trade receivables and writing off any uncollectible accounts.

SOLUTION

There are several points to consider in preparing this entry. In presenting accounts receivable in the balance sheet, (1) items not part of this classification (in this case, amounts due from officers of the corporation and advances to employees) should be shown separately. (2) Uncollectible accounts should be written off as soon as the determination as to their status has been made. (3) Deposits made by customers for goods and services to be delivered *in the future* are not receivables in the technical sense but instead represent, as of the balance sheet date, liabilities for future goods and services to be delivered.

Given the above explanation, the journal entry to accomplish the necessary separation of these items from the main account, Trade Accounts Receivable, is

Due from Officers	17,500	
Due from Employees	1,500	
Allowance for Bad Debts	1,968	
Advance Payments from Customers		5,000
Accounts Receivable		15,968

6.7. From the information presented below, prepare the journal entries necessary to record the transactions of the Hardy Manufacturing Company relating to Notes Receivable:

January 5:   Received a 30-day, 6% note from A. A. Manufacturing Company in the amount of $10,000 in partial payment of its account.

January 15:   Discounted the note from A. A. Manufacturing at the bank. The bank charged 8% interest.

February 4:   The bank notified Hardy Manufacturing that A. A. Manufacturing had dishonored the note and that it was charging Hardy's checking account for the full amount.

SOLUTION

January 5	Notes Receivable	10,000	
	Accounts Receivable, A. A. Manufacturing Company		10,000
	Received a 30-day, 6% note from A. A. Manufacturing in partial payment of its account.		
January 15	Cash	10,005.33	
	Notes Receivable Discounted		10,000.00
	Interest Income		5.33
	To record the proceeds of the note discounted with the bank at a rate of 8%.		

Face amount of note	$10,000.00	
Interest at 6% for 30 days	50.00	
Maturity value	$10,050.00	
Discount on maturity value at 8% for		
20 days ($10,050 × 8% ÷ 18)	44.67	
Cash proceeds	$10,005.33	

February 4	Notes Receivable Discounted	10,000.00	
	Notes Receivable		10,000.00
	Accounts Receivable, A. A. Manufacturing Company	10,050.00	
	Cash in Bank		10,050.00
	To record the notification received from the bank regarding the failure of the A. A. Manufacturing Company to pay the note at maturity.		

6.8. The bookkeeper of the Hillwood Animal Hospital was hired on April 1, 19X1, the beginning of the fiscal year. On March 31, 19X2, before making any adjusting entries, she prepares a trial balance which includes the following items:

Accounts Receivable	$75,000	
Notes Receivable (Trade)	25,000	
Allowance for Uncollectible Accounts	2,400	
Sales		$320,000
Sales Returns and Allowances	1,800	
Cash Discounts on Sales	3,200	

Prepare the appropriate adjusting entry to provide for estimated uncollectibles under each of the following independent assumptions:

(a) Company experience indicates that 75% of all sales are on a credit basis and that on the average 2% of these are uncollectible.

(b) Company policy is to maintain an allowance for uncollectibles equal to 5% of outstanding trade receivables, including notes.

(c) An analysis of the aging of trade receivables indicates that potential uncollectibles on receivables at the end of the year amount to $6,000.

(d) The allowance for uncollectible accounts is increased by 1.5% of gross sales, and an allowance for cash discounts of $450 on outstanding accounts receivable is to be established.

SOLUTION

(a)

| Uncollectible Accounts Expense | 4,800 | |
| Allowance for Uncollectible Accounts | | 4,800 |

To record the current year's provision for uncollectible accounts equal to 2% of the credit sales of $240,000 (75% of $320,000).

Under this method, the allowance for uncollectible accounts is increased each period by the estimated amounts of current revenue that will not be collected, in this case 2% of credit sales. The debit balance in the allowance may be the result of some current year's accounts having been written off.

(b)

| Uncollectible Accounts Expense | 7,400 | |
| Allowance for Uncollectible Accounts | | 7,400 |

To bring the allowance for uncollectible accounts to $5,000 (5% of $100,000), an amount equal to 5% of outstanding trade receivables: $75,000 of open accounts and $25,000 of trade notes.

An amount deemed sufficient to cover estimated uncollectibles on the existing receivables is charged to Uncollectible Accounts Expense each period via a predetermined percentage. This percentage does not allow for differences in the age of receivables at the end of a given period. The credit to the allowance account is for $7,400 in order to offset the debit balance of $2,400 in the account.

(c)

| Uncollectible Accounts Expense | 8,400 | |
| Allowance for Uncollectible Accounts | | 8,400 |

To bring the allowance for uncollectible accounts to $6,000, the estimated amount of uncollectible accounts included in trade receivables at the end of the year.

Under this method the amount charged to Uncollectible Accounts Expense each period is an amount sufficient to bring the balance in the allowance account to an amount deemed sufficient to cover estimated uncollectibles on existing receivables.

(d)

Uncollectible Accounts Expense	4,800	
Cash Discounts on Sales	450	
Allowance for Uncollectible Accounts		4,800
Allowance for Cash Discounts		450

To increase Allowance for Uncollectible Accounts by $4,800 (1.5% of $320,000), and to set up an allowance for cash discounts which customers are expected to take on outstanding accounts receivable.

Under this procedure the amount charged to the expense accounts is an estimate of the amount of current revenue that will not be collected.

6.9. The allowance for uncollectible accounts of the David Charles Sports Supplies Company for the current year is shown below:

Allowance for Uncollectible Accounts

June 30	Write-offs	1,700	April 1	Balance	6,000
Sept. 31	Write-offs	1,100	June 30	Provision	3,600
Dec. 31	Write-offs	2,900	Sept. 31	Provision	2,100
Mar. 31	Write-offs	1,350	Dec. 31	Provision	1,400
			Mar. 31	Provision	1,650

The company sells on a 30-day credit basis and has followed a practice of charging Uncollectible Accounts Expense in an amount equal to 1% of sales. The company's CPA regularly prepares quarterly income statements and makes adjusting entries at the end of each quarter in order to state accurately the quarterly net income figure. At the end of the current fiscal year, the accountant suggests that an aging of accounts receivable be made to test the adequacy of the allowance account. The aging of accounts receivable at March 31, the end of the current fiscal year, showed the following:

Current accounts	$ 81,600
31–60 days	26,450
61–120 days	12,810
121 days–6 months	4,200
Over 6 months old	1,260
Balance in control account, March 31	$126,320

After discussion with the company's sales manager, the CPA estimated that the following percentages represented a reasonable estimate of the uncollectible accounts in each category: current accounts, 3%; 31–60 days, 4%; 61–120 days, 10%; 121 days–6 months, 15%; over 6 months, 40%.

(a) Using the above information, test the adequacy of the balance in the allowance for uncollectible accounts as of March 31.

(b) Assuming that the books have not been closed for the year, prepare any necessary adjusting entries resulting from your analysis.

SOLUTION

(a)

David Charles Sports Supplies Company
Aging Analysis of Accounts Receivable
Current Year

	Balance Due	Estimated Uncollectible, %	Necessary Provision
Current accounts	$ 81,600	3	$2,448
31–60 days old	26,450	4	1,058
61–120 days old	12,810	10	1,281
121–180 days old	4,200	15	630
Over 6 months old	1,260	40	504
	$126,320		$ 5,921

Balance in allowance account:

Balance, April 1	$ 6,000
Provision during the year	8,750
Total credits	$14,750
Write-offs during the year	7,050
Ending balance	$ 7,700
Estimated balance that would be adequate	5,921
Amount by which allowance is overstated	$ 1,779

(b) Journal entry:

Allowance for Uncollectible Accounts	1,779	
Provision for Uncollectible Accounts		1,779

To correct for overstatement in Allowance for Uncollectible Accounts.

6.10. The National Machinery Company is a dealer in heavy construction equipment. Terms of sale are 5/15, n/60. As of January 1, $85,000 of receivables are uncollected, on which $2,500 of cash discounts is still available. During the month of January, the company had sales amounting to $230,000; $2,200 of cash discounts available during the month were not taken. On January 31, total receivables amounted to $105,000, on which discounts were available on $95,000. During the month of February, the company sold equipment for $111,000 and collected $115,000 on receivables. As of February 28, $2,750 of cash discounts were still open on outstanding accounts of $98,500. *All sales are made on open account.*

(a) Prepare journal entries to record the above transactions for the months of January and February, assuming that the company recognizes cash discounts only as taken.

(b) Prepare journal entries to record the above transactions for the months of January and February, under the assumption that the company accounts for all cash discounts that are allowable and for cash discounts not taken.

SOLUTION

(a) Journal entries for cash discounts recognized only when taken:

January 31	Accounts Receivable	230,000	
	Sales		230,000
	To record January sales.		
	Cash	202,950	
	Cash Discounts on Sales (1)	7,050	
	Accounts Receivable (2)		210,000

February 28	Accounts Receivable		111,000	
	Sales			111,000
	To record February sales.			

	Cash		113,500	
	Cash Discounts on Sales	(1)	4,000	
	Accounts Receivable	(2)		117,500

(NOTE TO STUDENT: To follow the solution to this problem it will be necessary to refer to the supporting computations presented below).

Supporting Schedule 1	**January**	**February**
Cash discounts allowable at beginning of month	$ 2,500	$ 4,750*
Cash discounts allowed for month	11,500	5,550
Total discounts available	$14,000	$10,300
Less: Cash discounts open at end of month	$ 4,750	$ 2,750
Cash discounts expired during month	2,200	3,550**
Total	$ 6,950	$ 6,300
Cash discounts taken during the month	$ 7,050	$ 4,000

* 5% of $95,000

** January receivables, discounts still open	$ 95,000
February sales	111,000
Accounts on which discounts were available	$206,000
Less: Accounts on which discounts were taken ($4,000 ÷ 5%)	$ 80,000
Accounts on which discounts are still open ($2,750 ÷ 5%)	55,000
Total	$135,000
Total accounts on which discounts expired	$ 71,000 × 5% = $3,550

Supporting Schedule 2	**January**	**February**
Accounts receivable, beginning of month	$ 85,000	$105,000
Sales during the month	230,000	111,000
Total receivables	$315,000	$216,000
Less: Accounts receivable at end of month	105,000	98,500
Accounts receivable collected during the month	$210,000	$117,500

(b) Journal entries accounting for all cash discounts and those not taken:

January 31	Accounts Receivable	230,000	
	Allowance for Cash Discounts		11,500
	Sales		218,500
	To record January sales, net of 5% discount.		

	Cash	202,950	
	Allowance for Cash Discounts	9,250	
	Accounts Receivable		210,000
	Cash Discounts Not Taken		2,200
	To record January collections on receivables and cash discounts not taken.		

February 28	Accounts Receivable	111,000	
	Allowance for Cash Discounts		5,550
	Sales		105,450
	To record February sales, net of 5% discount.		

Cash   *113,500*

Allowance for Cash Discounts   *7,550*

    Accounts Receivable   *117,500*

    Cash Discounts Not Taken   *3,550*

    *To record cash collections on receivables for February and
cash discounts not taken.*

6.11. In order to obtain a loan secured by receivables, on May 1, 19X1 the Karmell Candy Company assigned accounts totaling $60,000 to a local finance company. The terms of their agreement were that Karmell would receive 85% of the accounts assigned in cash, less a commission charge of 2% of the total. The remaining 15% of the value of the accounts was to be withheld until the finance company had collected the full amount of its loan, at which time any receivables outstanding would revert to the assignor.

On May 31, Karmell received a statement from the finance company indicating that the assignee had collected accounts with a face value of $36,000, and had made an additional charge for interest of 1% of the assigned accounts outstanding as of that date. This charge was to be deducted from the first remittance made by the finance company to Karmell.

On June 30, Karmell received a second statement from the finance company, together with a check for the amount due. The statement indicated that the finance company had collected an additional $16,000 and had made an additional charge for interest of 1% of assigned accounts outstanding as of June 30.

(a) Prepare the journal entries necessary to record the above transactions on the books of the Karmell Candy Company.

(b) Indicate how the above information should be shown on the balance sheet of Karmell at May 31 and June 30.

SOLUTION

(a) Journal entries to record the transactions with the finance company:

   May 1   *Cash*   *49,980*

                Financing Expense   *1,020*

                    Due to Finance Company   *51,000*

                *To record cash received from finance company secured by an
assignment of accounts receivable with a face value of $60,000.
The finance company advanced 85% of these receivables, less
a commission of 2%.*

                Accounts Receivable Assigned   *60,000*

                    Accounts Receivable   *60,000*

                *To segregate the face value of those receivables assigned to
the finance company.*

   May 31   *Due to Finance Company*   *35,760*

                Financing Expense   *240*

                  Accounts Receivable Assigned   *36,000*

                *To record notification from the finance company concerning
the collection of receivables in the face amount of $36,000, less
a 1% interest charge on the balance of receivables still uncol-
lected of $24,000 ($60,000 assigned less $36,000 collected).*

June 30	Cash		680	
	Financing Expense		80	
	Due to Finance Company		15,240	
	Accounts Receivable Assigned			16,000

To record the receipt of $680 from the Finance Company representing the balance due Karmell on the loan agreement as follows:

15% of original amount assigned ($60,000)			$9,000
Open receivables at May 31	$24,000		
Collected in June	16,000		8,000
Due to Karmell at June 30			$1,000
Less: Finance charges, May	$ 240		
Finance charges, June	80		320
Amount Received			$ 680

	Accounts Receivable		8,000	
	Accounts Receivable Assigned			8,000

To return the balance of receivables assigned to the finance company to the regular accounts receivable since the loan to the finance company has been completely paid.

(b) Balance sheet presentation:

(1) *May 31, 19X1* (Preferred solution)

Current Assets		
Accounts Receivable Assigned	$24,000	
Less: Loan Payable to Finance Company	15,240	
Equity in Assigned Receivables		$8,760

As an alternative, Equity in Assigned Receivables may be shown as a total in the balance sheet proper with a footnote containing the detailed information given in the preferred solution.

(2) *June 30, 19X1.* Since there is no longer any liability to the finance company, the balance of the assigned receivables ($8,000) is no longer pledged as collateral. These receivables, therefore, now become a part of the total amount of receivables as of June 30 and should be shown as such. However, since these receivables are now several months old, Karmell should consider the advisability of establishing an allowance for doubtful accounts against them.

6.12. During an audit of the financial records of the Norden Company for 19X1, the following information is extracted:

(1) On December 31, the company sold property which it had held for many years. The land had cost the company $20,300. The sales price was $46,000. The buyer gave Norden a check for $16,000 and a three-year, non-interest-bearing note for $30,000. The profit on the sale of the land, $25,700, was credited to Gain on Sale of Land. From all indications, the fair market value of the note is approximately $24,500.

(2) Until now the company has recognized uncollectible accounts as the specific receivables were deemed to be bad and uncollectible. The auditor has decided that an allowance of $4,750 should be established as of December 31, 19X1.

(3) On June 30, the company received a non-interest-bearing note for $11,000 in payment of a technical fee it had earned. The fee had originally been billed to the client at $10,400. Since the client was short of cash, however, Norden had agreed to accept the note in full settlement. The note had originally been recorded in full with a credit for $11,000 to a fees income account.

(4) A note receivable, face amount $5,000, and on which accrued interest receivable of $150 had been recorded, was discounted at the company's bank at a rate of interest higher than the rate indicated on the note. The proceeds, amounting to $5,099, had been credited to the Notes Receivable and was still outstanding at December 31.

(5) Accrued interest income on bonds of $3,125 as of December 31, 19X1 had not been picked up.

(6) A review of the receivables at December 31 indicates that $2,025 are deemed to be worthless and should be written off.

Prepare any adjusting entries required for the information presented above. Assume that the books have *not* been closed for 19X1.

SOLUTION

Norden Company
General Journal

(1)   Gain on Sale of Land   5,500
       Discount on Notes Receivable   5,500

To defer a portion of the profit on land measured by the difference between the face value of the three-year, non-interest-bearing note in the amount of $30,000 and the fair market value of the note, $24,500. The imputed interest amounts to approximately 7.5% on $24,500, the fair market value of the note at December 31, 19X1.

(2)   Bad Debts Expense   4,750
       Allowance for Bad Debts   4,750

To establish a bad debt allowance account as of December 31, 19X1.

(3)   Fees Income   600
       Interest Earned   300
       Discount on Notes Receivable   300

To recognize interest earned for the period July 1 to December 31, 19X1 and to defer the remainder to 19X2.

(4)   Notes Receivable   5,099
   Interest Income   51
       Accrued Interest Income Receivable   150
       Notes Receivable Discounted   5,000

Correction made for improper recording of note receivable discounted, and to reflect the company's contingent liability for the note to the bank.

(5)   Accrued Interest Income Receivable   3,125
       Interest Income on Bonds   3,125

To record interest earned on bond investments as of December 31, 19X1.

(6)   Bad Debts Expense   2,025
       Accounts Receivable   2,025

To write off worthless accounts at December 31, 19X1.

(NOTE TO STUDENT: According to the problem, the company has been in the habit of writing off accounts directly to expense, as in journal entry above. Presumably, therefore, the allowance established by journal entry (2) is to remain at the amount established.)

Chapter 7

Inventories: General

7.1 NATURE OF INVENTORIES

Inventories represent one of the most important elements of a business. Much of a company's resources is invested in this asset, which is usually its chief source of revenue. In recent years, accountants have given much consideration to the primary inventory problems of (1) determining quantity and (2) determining dollar value, which are discussed here and in the following two chapters.

7.2 CLASSES OF INVENTORIES

In a merchandising business at the retail or wholesale level, inventories consist of goods held for sale in the same form as purchased and are designated *merchandise inventory*. A manufacturing business, in contrast, has several types of inventories: *finished goods, goods in process* and *raw materials*.

Finished Goods. Finished goods are completed products awaiting sale. All costs (i.e. those for raw materials, direct labor and manufacturing overhead) have been incurred. Finished parts of assemblies purchased or produced for use in the completed product, however, are classified as raw materials.

Goods in Process. Goods in process or work in process consists of partly completed goods. Generally, the cost of raw material, direct labor and manufacturing overhead applied to date can be identified and included in the cost of goods in process.

Raw Materials. Raw materials may be obtained directly from natural resources or from production. Thus, they may be produced by the company manufacturing the finished product or purchased as the finished product of another company. Raw materials cost includes the purchase price, freight, receiving, storage and/or other charges necessary to make the finished goods ready for use. *Factory supplies* are auxiliary materials that do not become an integral part of the finished product, such as cleaning supplies, lubricating oils and fuels.

7.3 INVENTORY SYSTEMS

The two principal systems for determining the inventory quantities on hand are *the periodic system* and *the perpetual system*. Both systems may be used simultaneously by companies with different classes of inventory.

The Periodic System. This system requires a physical count of goods on hand at the end of the period. A cost basis (i.e. FIFO, LIFO, etc.) is then applied to derive an inventory value.   This system is widely used because it is simple and requires records and computations primarily only at the end of the period.   It is not as useful as the perpetual system, however, in the planning and control of inventories.

The Perpetual System.   This system calls for a continuous record of receipt and disbursement for every item of inventory.   Physical counts of the quantities on hand are usually made at least once a year and reconciled to the perpetual records.   Most large manufacturing and merchandising companies use the perpetual system to provide continuous control over the quantities and the investment in inventory.   Adequate supplies are assured for production or sale and costly machine shut-downs and customer complaints are minimized.

7.4 INVENTORY COSTING

Inventory cost includes all expenditures relating to inventory acquisition, preparation and readiness for sale.   Any purchase discounts are treated as reductions in the cost of inventory.   Accounting for inventory costs for goods in process and finished goods can be best accomplished by means of a good cost accounting system, a topic which will be treated in depth in later volumes of this series.

In a manufacturing company, the two primary methods for accumulating costs are (1) *by job order* and (2) *by process or operation.*

Job Order Cost System.   This system is generally used by companies which manufacture a number of different products in limited quantities.   The costs for each job are accumulated separately on a *job order cost record* and are included in goods in process until the job is completed.   The completed job and its associated costs are considered finished goods until the job is sold.   Examples of companies using job order cost systems are printing shops and construction companies.

Process Cost System.   This system is used where large amounts of similar units are produced on an assembly-line basis.   The controlling factor is the cost center or department.   Costs of raw material, direct labor and manufacturing overhead are accumulated by cost center rather than by individual job.   The unit cost is obtained by dividing total costs by the quantity produced for the week, month, etc.   Examples of companies using process cost systems are steel mills, paper companies and other large-volume enterprises.

7.5 SPECIAL INVENTORY ITEMS

While most items are included in inventory when received, the technical procedure is to recognize purchases when ownership changes or title passes.   There are cases, however, where the legal rule must be modified because of special circumstances, some of which are described below.

Goods in Transit.   Most goods are shipped *f.o.b. shipping point*, which means that title passes to the buyer when the goods are loaded on the carrier.   When goods are shipped *f.o.b. destination*, title does not pass until the shipment reaches its destination.

Goods on Consignment.   When goods are shipped to dealers on consignment, title does not change until the goods are sold by the *consignee*.   Such goods are reported as inventory of the *consignor* (shipper) until the goods are sold and cash or an account receivable is obtained.   The inventory cost includes all handling and shipping costs incurred in transferring the goods to the consignee.

Segregated Goods. When goods are produced on special order, title may pass at the time goods are segregated. At this point the vendor recognizes a sale and the goods are deducted from inventory. The purchaser records a purchase and an inventory increase when notice of segregation is received from the vendor.

Installment and Conditional Sales. In these cases, even though the buyer receives the merchandise, the seller retains title until the full sales price has been received. Technically, the seller should show goods transferred as inventory with an offset for the equity the buyer has built up through payments. Where the possibility of default is negligible, the seller usually waives his right and permits title to pass. However, there is usually a right to repossession of the product if the contract is not completed.

7.6 COST FLOW METHODS

Since it is likely that during a specified time period a given item may be purchased at a variety of prices, it is necessary to determine which costs relate to units remaining in inventory and which costs relate to units sold. The concept of a *cost flow* refers to the entire flow of costs through the system, from purchase or production of goods to their sale. It does not involve the physical flow of goods. Because the value assigned to inventory has a direct effect on net income for both the current and subsequent accounting period, the objective in selecting a cost flow method is the matching of appropriate costs with revenue.

The main cost flow methods are: *first-in, first-out* (FIFO), *last-in, first-out* (LIFO), *weighted average* and *specific identification*. They all resolve the basic costing problem: What is the combination of costs in the units on hand, and in the units shipped out?

In order to show the effect of the various cost flow methods on inventory, costs of goods sold and net income, the following data will be used in all examples. It will also be assumed that a physical inventory on January 31 shows 600 units on hand; thus, 1,400 units were shipped out during the month.

ACQUISITIONS DURING JANUARY

Date	Type	Units	Unit Cost	Total Amount
Jan. 1	Inventory	300	$10	$ 3,000
Jan. 7	Purchase	800	11	8,800
Jan. 16	Purchase	400	12	4,800
Jan. 30	Purchase	500	13	6,500
	Total Available	2,000		$23,100

Method 1. First-in, First-out (FIFO). Under FIFO, costs are charged off in the order in which they were incurred (i.e. first-price-in, first-price-out). It is further assumed that goods are sold in the same order they were received.

EXAMPLE 1.

Under FIFO, the goods on hand are assumed to be those most recently acquired. The cost assigned to the inventory of 600 units is $7,700, calculated as follows using the periodic inventory system:

INVENTORY: FIRST-IN, FIRST-OUT METHOD (PERIODIC SYSTEM)

Jan. 30	Last Purchase	500 units	$13	$6,500
Jan. 16	Next to Last Purchase	100 units	12	1,200
	Total	600 units		$7,700

EXAMPLE 2.

Keeping in mind that the term first-in, first-out refers to shipments, not *inventory on hand*, the cost of goods sold can be calculated. Since the total goods *available* during January cost $23,100, it follows that the goods shipped cost $15,400 ($23,100 − $7,700), as shown below. The same results will be obtained for FIFO whether the periodic or the perpetual system is used because each withdrawal of units is from the oldest inventory.

COST OF GOODS SOLD:
FIRST-IN, FIRST-OUT METHOD (PERIODIC SYSTEM

Jan. 5	100 issued		$10	$ 1,000
Jan. 10	400 issued { 200		10	4,200
	200		11	
Jan. 18	600 issued		11	6,600
Jan. 28	300 issued		12	3,600
	1,400 issued			$15,400

Most companies use some kind of perpetual inventory record, usually a card form, to know at all times the status of certain critical materials (e.g. raw materials or finished goods items). Generally the form shows columns for goods ordered, received, issued, and balance.

EXAMPLE 3.

A typical perpetual record for one inventory item is shown below.

COMMODITY C: FIFO (PERPETUAL SYSTEM)

Ordered	Date	Received		Issued		Balance	
Memo	Jan. 1	300 @ $10	$ 3,000			300 @ $10	$3,000
	Jan. 5			100 @ $10	$ 1,000	200 @ 10	2,000
	Jan. 7	800 @ 11	8,800			{ 200 @ 10	2,000
						800 @ 11	8,800
	Jan. 10			{ 200 @ 10	2,000		
				200 @ 11	2,200	600 @ 11	6,600
	Jan. 16	400 @ 12	4,800			{ 600 @ 11	6,600
						400 @ 12	4,800
	Jan. 18			600 @ 11	6,600	400 @ 12	4,800
	Jan. 28			300 @ 12	3,600	100 @ 12	1,200
	Jan. 30	500 @ 13	6,500			{ 100 @ 12	1,200
						500 @ 13	6,500
	Total	2,000 units	$23,100	1,400 units	$15,400	600 units	$7,700

Method 2. Last-in, First-out (LIFO). The concept of LIFO is that the latest costs will be matched with sales as they occur. In a period of rising prices, the cost of goods sold will carry the higher costs, the inventory the lower costs under this method.

EXAMPLE 4.

Under LIFO, the inventory at the end of the period is assumed to be goods purchased at the beginning of the period. The inventory to be shown on the balance sheet under LIFO would be $6,300 rather than the $7,700 under FIFO, as calculated below.

INVENTORY: LAST-IN, FIRST-OUT (PERIODIC SYSTEM)

Jan. 1	Beginning inventory	300 units	$10	$3,000
Jan. 7	First purchase	300 units	11	3,300
		600 units		$6,300

EXAMPLE 5.

Since the inventory cost is lower under LIFO, the corresponding cost of goods sold would be *higher*, or $16,800 ($23,100 − $6,300). The details are shown below. Generally, in computing the LIFO amount for cost of goods sold, it is easier to begin with the last purchase and work back until the amount of total shipments is reached. Thus, it would be $500 + 400 + 500 = 1,400$. The second to last purchase was for 800 units, but only 500 units of this receipt were shipped out.

COST OF GOODS SOLD: LAST-IN, FIRST-OUT (PERIODIC SYSTEM)

Jan. 30	Last purchase	500 units	$13	$ 6,500
Jan. 16	Next to last purchase	400 units	12	4,800
Jan. 7	Second to last purchase	500 units	11	5,500
		1,400 units		$16,800

LIFO has several advantages over FIFO in that it (1) permits a more realistic measurement of income by matching current costs with current revenues and (2) produces a smaller tax in a period of rising costs.

EXAMPLE 6.

Since the cost of goods sold under LIFO is $1,400 more than under FIFO ($16,800 − $15,400), the profit for the period would be $1,400 less. At a 50% corporate income tax rate, there would be a saving of about $700 in Federal income taxes. Under both methods, the identical physical items would be on hand and the identical physical items would have been shipped out.

Under the perpetual inventory system, the *cost of units issued* is sometimes summarized at the end of the period rather than having the cost assigned as the goods are issued. When this is done, the cost of goods sold is the same as under the periodic system. However, if costs are applied as each issue is made, the result will be somewhat different.

EXAMPLE 7.

Continuing with our basic data, the cost of goods sold is $16,800 when the cost of units issued is summarized at the end of the period under both perpetual and periodic inventory systems (see Example 5). The procedure for charging costs as goods are issued is shown below. There is a difference of $1,200 if the perpetual system rather than the periodic system is used. The cost of goods sold under the perpetual system is $15,600; under the periodic system, $16,800. Inventory under the perpetual system is $7,500; under the periodic system, $6,300.

COMMODITY C: LIFO (PERPETUAL SYSTEM)

Ordered	Date	Received		Issued		Balance	
Memo	Jan. 1	300 @ $10	$ 3,000			300 @ $10	$3,000
	Jan. 5			100 @ $10	$ 1,000	200 @ 10	2,000
	Jan. 7	800 @ 11	8,800			200 @ 10	2,000
						800 @ 11	8,800
	Jan. 10			400 @ 11	4,400	200 @ 10	2,000
						400 @ 11	4,400
						200 @ 10	2,000
	Jan. 16	400 @ 12	4,800			400 @ 11	4,400
						400 @ 12	4,800
	Jan. 18			400 @ 12	4,800	200 @ 10	2,000
				200 @ 11	2,200	200 @ 11	2,200
	Jan. 28			200 @ 11	2,200		
				100 @ 10	1,000	100 @ 10	1,000
	Jan. 30	500 @ 13	6,500			100 @ 10	1,000
						500 @ 13	6,500
	Total	2,000 units	$23,100	1,400 units	$15,600	600 units	$7,500

Method 3. Weighted Average.　　This method assumes that all units are commingled and no particular batch is held in inventory. An average unit cost (found by dividing total cost of goods available during the period by the total number of these goods) is used for inventory and for cost of goods sold. This is quite different than for FIFO or LIFO unit costs and the results will fall somewhere between those two methods.

EXAMPLE 8.

According to the data, there were 2,000 units available for sale in January at a total cost of $23,100. Therefore, the average unit cost is

$$\$23,100 \div 2,000 = \$11.55$$

Under a periodic system, the inventory cost is

$$600 \text{ units @ } \$11.55 = \$6,930$$

and the cost of goods sold is

$$1,400 \text{ units @ } \$11.55 = \$16,170$$

When the perpetual system is used with the weighted-average method at *date of issue,* it becomes *a moving weighted average method.* A new average cost is computed after each receipt of goods and that cost is applied to subsequent issues until a new receipt of goods is recorded and a new unit cost computed.

EXAMPLE 9.

Recording purchases and issues under the moving weighted average method is illustrated in the form below. Generally, to simplify the computation and costing of issues, many companies round to two decimal places, which results in a very slight discrepancy in the dollar amount.

COMMODITY C: WEIGHTED AVERAGE METHOD (PERPETUAL SYSTEM)

Date	Transaction	Units	Amount
Jan. 1	Inventory	300 @ $10.00	$ 3,000
Jan. 5	Issue	(100) @ 10.00	(1,000)
Jan. 5	Balance	200 @ 10.00	$ 2,000
Jan. 7	Purchase	800 @ 11.00	8,800
Jan. 7	Balance	1,000 @ 10.80	$ 10,800
Jan. 10	Issue	(400) @ 10.80	(4,320)
Jan. 10	Balance	600 @ 10.80	$ 6,480
Jan. 16	Purchase	400 @ 12.00	4,800
Jan. 16	Balance	1,000 @ 11.28	$ 11,280
Jan. 18	Issue	(600) @ 11.28	(6,768)
Jan. 18	Balance	400 @ 11.28	$ 4,512
Jan. 28	Issue	300 @ 11.28	3,384
Jan. 28	Balance	100 @ 11.28	$ 1,128
Jan. 30	Purchase	500 @ 13.00	6,500
Jan. 31	Balance (inventory value)	600 @ 12.71	$ 7,628

Under this method, the inventory is $7,628 and the cost of goods sold would be $15,472 ($23,100 − $7,628).

Comparison of Inventory Methods

In Example 10 below, the results of the FIFO, LIFO and weighted-average methods are compared. It is clear that each of these methods has a direct effect on profits (i.e. *understatement* of the ending inventory results in *overstatement* of cost of goods sold and *understatement* of net profits, and vice-versa), particularly in periods of steadily rising or falling prices. None of these methods is best for all firms; when choosing a method, therefore, it is important to consider carefully the potential effect of each upon the income statement and the balance sheet, taxable income and the selling price.

EXAMPLE 10.

In the following comparison of the FIFO, LIFO and weighted average methods, the goods available for sale is $23,100 for all methods and equals the total of inventory and cost of goods sold. The assumed annual sales are $23,500. Depending on the method used, the inventory costs ranged from $6,300 to $7,700 and the cost of goods sold ranged from $15,400 to $16,800, a spread of $1,400. The gross profit, of course, also varied by $1,400, from $6,700 to $8,100. As shown previously, in a corporation with an income tax rate of 50%, the method showing the highest profit (FIFO) would require a payment for this year of $700 more tax than the LIFO periodic system. Results under the weighted-average method clearly fall somewhere between these two extremes.

COMPARISON OF INVENTORY METHODS

Method	Inventory	Cost of Goods Sold	Sales	Gross Profit
First-in, First-out	$7,700	$15,400	$23,500	$8,100
Last-in, First-out				
Periodic system	6,300	16,800	23,500	6,700
Perpetual system	7,500	15,600	23,500	7,900
Weighted Average				
Periodic system	6,930	16,170	23,500	7,330
Perpetual system	7,628	15,472	23,500	8,028

Method 4. Specific Identification. When an inventory is composed of a small number of high-value items (such as automobiles or major appliances) whose costs can be traced to specific invoices, the specific identification method may be used in determining cost of goods sold and inventory on hand. It is not suitable for large quantity inventories where the identity of a particular unit may be lost, and has been criticized as providing an opportunity for manipulation of profits when units are acquired at varying prices.

7.7 OTHER COST PROCEDURES

In addition to the principal inventory methods discussed, there are other accepted costing procedures which are often variations of the principal methods. These are described below.

Standard Costs. These are predetermined costs based on a given level of operations and specified conditions. Actual costs are compared to standard costs and the difference summarized in variance accounts for materials, labor and manufacturing overhead which indicate a favorable or unfavorable effect. For example, excess materials used, inefficient labor and idle time would be unfavorable variances. To be most effective, standard cost data must be updated from time to time to reflect current material costs, labor rates and manufacturing overhead costs.

Direct Costing. Under this method, sometimes called *variable costing* or *marginal costing*, only variable costs incurred in production are included (e.g. direct materials, direct labor and variable manufacturing overhead). Costs that relate to time, such as depreciation, property taxes and supervisors' salaries, are excluded from inventory costs. They are considered period costs and are charged against income in the period in which incurred. Under this method, the cost of goods sold varies directly with sales and greater sales mean greater earnings. Under *full costing* or *absorption costing*, in which fixed costs are included, a high production volume usually means lower production unit costs and a higher profit rate even though sales are low. Direct costing has gained much support from management since it provides more meaningful information for planning and control. There has been objection to the use of direct costing for annual financial statements since fixed costs are excluded from inventory. This method is not acceptable for Federal income tax purposes or for statements submitted to the Securities and Exchange Commission.

Base Stock Method.   The method assumes a base stock of goods, fixed in price as a permanent asset. When there is any increase over the base amount, it is considered a temporary condition and is priced at current replacement cost. Any decrease is also considered to be temporary and is charged to revenue at current replacement cost. This method is not acceptable for income tax purposes and is not widely used.

Unit-LIFO.   Under the unit-LIFO method, units of inventory are segregated into pools or groups, if purchased, and according to process, if manufactured. To institute this method, the average unit cost within each pool is computed, and a quantity of units equal to the amount in the opening inventory, or pool, would be priced at the beginning unit costs. Purchases during the period are considered collectively as an incremental layer, and are priced in accordance with one of the principal inventory methods (see Section 7.6). Purchases in later periods are treated as separate incremental layers. Decreases in inventory from sales reduce the layers on a last-in, first-out basis until the original or base quantity is reached. This adaptation of the LIFO method reduces clerical detail when there are a large number of items and a great many transactions.

EXAMPLE 11.

Unit-LIFO valuation for an inventory pool using weighted-average unit costs for increments is illustrated below. The form reflects the following for 19X3: (1) all units acquired in the period were sold, (2) all units comprising Layer B were absorbed through sales and (3) Layer A was reduced by 200 units through sales.

INVENTORY: UNIT-LIFO METHOD

Year	Description	Units	Amount
19X1	Beginning inventory	2,000 @ $5.00	$10,000
19X1	Layer A added (1)	600 @ 5.83	3,500
19X1	Ending inventory	2,600	$13,500
19X2	Layer B added (2)	500 @ 6.70	3,350
19X2	Ending inventory	3,100	$16,850
19X3	Ending inventory	2,000 @ 5.00	$10,000
		400 @ 5.83	2,332
		2,400 units	$12,332

Computation of Unit Costs:

(1)   Layer A: 200 units @ $5.50 $1,100
                  400 units @ $6.00   2,400
                  ___   _____
                  600                    $3,500   Average cost = $5.83

(2)   Layer B: 300 units @ $6.50 $1,950
                  200 units @ $7.00   1,400
                  ___   _____
                  500                    $3,350   Average cost = $6.70

Dollar-value LIFO.   This is another procedure to reduce the clerical detail associated with the LIFO method. The ending inventory is priced at current cost and the *total* is then adjusted by means of a price index to the cost when LIFO was instituted. It can then be compared with the beginning inventory, also priced at base-year dollars, to determine the actual change in quantity. Generally, the index is based on the costs at the end of the particular year. Increases or decreases in inventory are costed at the rate prevailing at the end of the period in which the items were purchased.

EXAMPLE 12.

If the inventory value is $20,000 at the beginning of the year and $23,000 at the end of the year, it appears that there has been a 15% increase in quantity. However, if there has been a price increase of 15%, then the increase in the total dollar amount of inventory is due entirely to a price change, and the quantity remains the same.

EXAMPLE 13.

A dollar-value LIFO schedule showing the computation of ending inventory value over a four-year period is presented below. The base year is 19X1 and the cost index is as follows: 19X1 = 100, 19X2 = 120, 19X3 = 150 and 19X4 = 145.

DOLLAR-VALUE LIFO PROCEDURE
Years 19X1 through 19X4

Year	Inventory Year-end Cost	Cost Index	Inventory @ Base Cost	Computation of Inventory Layers		Dollar-value Inventory
19X1	$20,000	1.00	$20,000	$20,000 × 1.00		$20,000
19X2	36,000	1.20	30,000	20,000 × 1.00 / 10,000 × 1.20	$20,000 / 12,000	32,000
19X3	42,000	1.50	28,000	20,000 × 1.00 / 8,000 × 1.20	20,000 / 9,600	29,600
19X4	46,400	1.45	32,000	20,000 × 1.00 / 8,000 × 1.20 / 4,000 × 1.45	20,000 / 9,600 / 5,800	35,400

As can be seen above, the cost change factor for 19X2 is eliminated by dividing $36,000 by 1.20, which is $30,000 at base-year cost. This is an actual increase in quantity of $10,000 at base-year cost. The increment is valued at year-end cost of 1.20 or $12,000. This amount added to the base of $20,000 equals $32,000, the dollar-value LIFO inventory. For 19X3, the current cost of $42,000 is divided by the cost index of 1.50 and equals $28,000 in base-year dollars. Thus, there was really a reduction of physical goods on hand even though there was an increase of $6,000 in the inventory based on current costs. Any reduction is backed out of the latest increment; thus, $2,000 is taken off of the $10,000 increment from year 19X2. For 19X4, $46,400 divided by 1.45 equals $32,000, the inventory at base-year costs, and shows a physical increase of $4,000 over 19X3. This $4,000 valued at 1.45, the cost index, amounts to $5,800, which is added to the previous dollar-value inventory of $29,600 for a total of $35,400, the dollar-value LIFO inventory for 19X4.

Relative Sales Value. This method is used when there is a need to apportion the cost of different items purchased for a single sum on some equitable basis. It is a common procedure for realty companies which purchase undeveloped land, make improvements and then sell individual lots.

EXAMPLE 14.

Suppose that the Schooff Realty Company purchased 50 acres of land for $350,000. The cost of grading, landscaping, streets and water mains amounted to $250,000 for this property. There are three classes of lots: Class A, 100 lots to sell for $2,500 each; Class B, 150 lots to sell for $3,000 each; and Class C, 60 lots to sell for $5,000 each. Costs would be allocated according to relative sales values as shown in the schedule below.

INVENTORY: RELATIVE SALES VALUE METHOD

Lot Class	No. of Lots	Selling Price	Sales Value	%	Cost Allocation	Cost to Each Lot
A	100	$2,500	$ 250,000	25%	$150,000	$1,500
B	150	3,000	450,000	45%	270,000	1,800
C	60	5,000	300,000	30%	180,000	3,000
			$1,000,000	100%	$600,000	

Another approach is to determine the relationship between total costs and total sales and apply the resulting percentage to the individual lots. For example, $600,000 ÷ $1,000,000 = 60%. Therefore, the cost is 60% of the selling price, or, for Class A lots, $2,500 × 60% = $1,500; Class B lots, $3,000 × 60% = $1,800 and Class C lots, $5,000 × 60% = $3,000.

Summary

(1) Two important problems in accounting for inventories are the determination of _____ and _____ .

(2) The inventory system which calls for a physical count of goods at the end of the period is termed a_____system, while the system which requires a continuous record of receipts and issues is termed a _____system.

(3) When a number of distinct products are manufactured in limited quantities, a_____ _____system is generally used. When the type of products are manufactured in large quantities, a _____ system is generally used.

(4) When all fixed factory overhead items are excluded from inventory, the method is termed_____ .

(5) The four principal methods of inventory valuation are_____,_____, _____and _____ .

(6) The inventory turnover rate is the ratio of _____to _____ .

(7) Inventories are classified on the balance sheet as which type of asset? (a) Fixed, (b) perpetual, (c) current, (d) variable.

(8) Goods shipped to dealers on memorandum billing are termed (a) goods in transit, (b) consigned goods, (c) segregated goods, (d) none of the above.

(9) If prices are increasing, the use of LIFO rather than FIFO tends to result, in the current period, in a (a) higher ending inventory, (b) higher gross profit percentage, (c) lower cost of goods sold, (d) lower income taxes.

(10)   Two inventory methods that are not permissible for income tax purposes are (a) base stock and direct costing, (b) base stock and FIFO, (c) base stock and LIFO or (d) base stock and weighted average.

(11)   A company using dollar-value LIFO had a beginning inventory (base year) of $20,000 and an ending inventory of $28,750 with a price index of 115% of base-year cost. The real increase in inventory was (a) $8,750, (b) $5,000, (c) $4,375, (d) $10,000.

(12)   If current assets were $25,000 and current liabilities $10,000, what would be the effect on the current ratio if it were discovered that $5,000 of inventory had been overlooked in the final inventory count? (a) Ratio increase, (b) increase in working capital, (c) ratio decrease, (d) none of the above.

Answers: (1) quantity, dollar value; (2) periodic, perpetual; (3) job order cost, process cost; (4) direct costing; (5) FIFO, LIFO, weighted average, specific identification; (6) cost of goods sold, average inventory cost; (7) c; (8) b; (9) d; (10) a; (11) b; (12) c.

Solved Problems

7.1.   The inventory of the Valley Road Company at December 31, 19– was as follows:

(a)	Merchandise on hand, priced at 15% above cost	$215,600
(b)	Merchandise held on consignment, sales commission 25% of sales price included	3,000
(c)	Merchandise out on consignment, shown at selling price including 25% markup on selling price	4,000
(d)	Merchandise in transit, f.o.b. shipping point, estimated transportation $500, invoice cost	3,600
		$226,200

From the above information, compute the inventory valuation.

SOLUTION

(a)	215,600 ÷ 115%	$187,478
(b)	Excluded as it is not owned by the company	—
(c)	Should be included at cost	3,000
(d)	Transportation cost must be included	4,100
		$194,578

7.2.   The Hofstra Company's accountant reported net income or loss as indicated below. An audit of the company revealed that errors were made in computing final inventory in the years shown.

Year	Reported Net Income (Loss)	Inventory Overstated	Inventory Understated
19X1	$40,500	$2,000	
19X2	39,000		
19X3	16,000	4,000	
19X4	(5,000)		$3,500
19X5	19,000		1,000

Compute the correct net income for each year.

SOLUTION

Year	Reported Net Income (Loss)	Inventory Overstated	Inventory Understated	Correct Net Income
19X1	$40,500	$(2,000)		$38,500
19X2	39,000		$2,000	41,000
19X3	16,000	(4,000)		12,000
19X4	(5,000)		4,000	
			3,500	2,500
19X5	19,000	(3,500)	1,000	16,500

7.3. The Shorewood Company shows the following information for opening inventory and purchases of Product X for January, 19X1:

Date	Units	Cost
Jan. 1 Inv.	2,000	$ 5,000
6	1,000	3,000
15	500	1,550
22	1,000	3,500
30	1,000	4,000
Total available	5,500	$17,050

Compute the cost of goods sold if the closing inventory was 1,500 units, under (a) FIFO, (b) LIFO and (c) weighted average.

SOLUTION

If the total number of units available for January was 5,500 (opening inventory 2,000; purchases 3,500) and the closing inventory was 1,500, there were 4,000 units sold.

(a) FIFO:

Date	Units	Cost
Jan. 1	2,000	$ 5,000
6	1,000	3,000
15	500	1,550
22	500	1,750
	4,000	$11,300 (Unit cost: $2.83)

(b) LIFO:

Date	Units	Cost
Jan. 30	1,000	$ 4,000
22	1,000	3,500
15	500	1,550
6	1,000	3,000
1	500	1,250
	4,000	$13,300 (Unit cost: $3.33)

(c) WEIGHTED AVERAGE: Total available cost of $17,050 ÷ total available units of 5,500 is $3.10 per unit. Since there were 4,000 units sold, the weighted average cost of goods sold is $12,400 (4,000 × $3.10).

7.4. The A. Knowles Company uses the weighted-average method for valuing certain special materials. It is considering using the perpetual moving average method and asks for your advice, based on the following data for June, 197–:

	Units		Unit Price
Date	Purchases	Sales	
June 1 Inv.	1,400		$20
6		900	
12	1,000		23
15		1,100	
21	900		26
25		800	
27	1,200		30
30		700	

Compute the ending inventory value for June under (a) the periodic weighted average method and (b) the perpetual moving average method.

SOLUTION

(a) WEIGHTED AVERAGE:

	No. of Units	Unit Cost	Inventory Balance
June 1 Inventory	1,400	$20	$ 28,000
12	1,000	23	23,000
21	900	26	23,400
27	1,200	30	36,000
Inventory Available	4,500	$24.53	$110,400
Cost of Goods Sold	3,500 *	24.53	85,870 **
Ending Inventory	1,000	$24.53	$ 24,530

* Cost of goods sold equals $3,500 ($900 + $1,100 + $800 + $700).

** Inventory balance is slightly off since decimal was rounded to two places.

(b) MOVING AVERAGE:

	No. of Units	Unit Cost	Inventory Balance
June 1 Inventory	1,400	$20.00	$ 28,000
6 Sales	(900)	20.00	(18,000)
6 Balance	500	$20.00	$ 10,000
12 Purchase	1,000	23.00	23,000
12 Balance	1,500	$22.00	$ 33,000
15 Sales	(1,100)	22.00	(24,200)
15 Balance	400	$22.00	$ 8,800
21 Purchase	900	26.00	23,400
21 Balance	1,300	$24.77	$ 32,200
25 Sales	(800)	24.77	(19,816)
25 Balance	500	$24.77	$ 12,384
27 Purchase	1,200	30.00	36,000
27 Balance	1,700	$28.46	$ 48,384
30 Sales	(700)	28.46	(19,924)
30 Balance	1,000	$28.46	$ 28,460

7.5. The Wall's Beach Company makes all of its merchandise purchases at trade discounts of 15%, 10%, 5% and a cash discount of 2%. The list price of merchandise received in December 19X1 was $45,000 and 60% of this was sold in that month.

Compute the value of the ending inventory if cash discounts are treated as (a) reductions in purchase price or (b) other revenue.

SOLUTION

Trade discounts are used to convert a list price to the net price, or cost, to the buyer. In this case, the cost of merchandise to the Wall's Beach Company is computed as follows:

List price	$45,000.00
First discount, 15%	6,750.00
	$38,250.00
Second discount, 10%	3,825.00
	$34,425.00
Third discount, 5%	1,721.25
Invoice cost	$32,703.75

(a) COST OF INVENTORY:

Total purchases	$32,703.75
Less: 2% cash discount	654.08
Net purchases cost	$32,049.67
Cost of goods sold, 60%	19,229,80
Ending inventory	$12,819.87

(b) COST OF INVENTORY: When cash discounts are considered "other revenue," they are not credited to purchases and the invoice amount is used.

Total purchases	$32,703.75
Cost of goods sold, 60%	19,622.25
Ending inventory	$13,081.50

7.6. At December 31, 19X1, the Seawall Company took a physical inventory which was determined to be $35,600. The regular annual audit revealed the following errors requiring correction:

(1) Merchandise costing $1,525 was received on January 5, 19X2. The invoice disclosed that the merchandise was shipped f.o.b. supplier's factory on December 20, 19X1. It was not included in inventory.

(2) The invoice for merchandise costing $3,000 received December 27, 19X1, was not received until January 5, 19X2. The merchandise was included in inventory.

(3) The report of goods costing $8,000, held in a public warehouse at December 31, 19X1 was received January 10, 19X2. The amount was not included in inventory at December 31.

(4) Merchandise costing $2,375 was counted and included in physical inventory. It had been received December 21, 19X1 on consignment from the Barton Supply Company.

Prepare a schedule showing the correct inventory at December 31, 19X1.

SOLUTION

The Seawall Company
Correction of Inventory
December 31, 19X1

Physical inventory amount reported by Company			$35,600
Additions			
(1)	*Goods shipped f.o.b. factory.* Title passes when goods are delivered to carrier.	$1,525	
(3)	*Goods in public warehouse.* This amount is owned and should be included in inventory.	8,000	9,525
			$45,125
Deductions			
(4)	*Consigned goods on hand.* Such goods are owned by the consignor and should not be included in the inventory of the consignee.		2,375
			$42,750

NOTE:

(2) Invoices for all goods received prior to inventory date should be included in accounts payable even though they are received after the inventory date. The goods are already included.

7.7. The Bayville Realty Company purchased a tract of land for $420,000 for purposes of development. After deducting 15% for streets and parks, the tract was subdivided into 1,000 lots as follows:

Class	Quantity	Price
A	500	$900
B	300	700
C	100	400

Using the relative sales method, compute the inventory value at the end of the year, net of other cost, for the following unsold lots: Class A, 100; Class B, 100; and Class C, 50.

SOLUTION

Cost Based on Relative Sales Value

Class	Quantity	Price	Salable Total
A	500	$900	$450,000
B	300	700	210,000
C	100	400	40,000
	900		$700,000

The cost factor is 60% ($420,000 ÷ $700,000).

Inventory Valuation

Class	Selling Price	Cost (60%)	Unsold Lots	Inventory Valuation
A	$900	$540	100	$ 54,000
B	700	420	100	42,000
C	400	240	50	12,000
				$108,000

7.8. The Owens Siding Company opened on January 1 with 50 units of inventory at a cost of $5,000. The following purchases were made during the year:

Purchase No.	No. of Units	Cost	Unit Cost
1	120	$13,200	$110.00
2	100	11,500	115.00
3	130	15,600	120.00
4	150	18,750	125.00
	500	$59,050	

Inventory taken at the end of the year shows 100 units remaining in stock.

Based on the above information, compute (1) the ending inventory cost and (2) the cost of goods sold during the period, using (a) FIFO, (b) LIFO and (c) weighted average methods.

SOLUTION

Since ending inventory was 100 units, 450 units must have been used (50 + 500 − 100). Total goods available equaled $64,050 ($5,000 + $59,050).

(a)   FIFO:

Inventory Cost (1)			Cost of Goods Sold (2)	
Lot #4:	100 @ $125	$12,500	Goods Available	$64,050
			Less: Inventory	12,500
			(2)	$51,550

(b)   LIFO:

Inventory Cost (1)			Cost of Goods Sold (2)	
Beginning:	50 @ $100	$ 5,000	Goods Available	$64,050
Lot #1:	50 @ $110	5,500	Less: Inventory	10,500
		$10,500	(2)	$53,550

(c) WEIGHTED AVERAGE: $64,050 ÷ 550 = $116.45 per unit

Inventory Cost (1)		Cost of Goods Sold (2)	
Ending: 100 @ $116.45 $11,645		*Goods Available*	$64,050
		Less: Inventory	11,645
		(2)	$52,405

7.9. The Bigfoot Company uses material X in its principal product. Following is information on the activity of material X for the year 197–:

	Quantities			Unit
Date	Received	Issued	Balance	Price
Jan. 1			150	$2.50
28	175		325	3.25
Feb. 2		200	125	—
May 10	125		250	3.75
June 12		90	160	—
Sept. 18		60	100	—
Dec. 22	250		350	4.00
30		130	220	—

Compute the *closing inventory* using (a) periodic FIFO, (b) periodic LIFO, (c) perpetual FIFO and (d) perpetual LIFO.

SOLUTION

(a) The closing inventory of 220 under periodic FIFO would represent part of the 250 received on December 22 at $4.00 each. Thus, 220 × $4.00 = $880.00.

(b) The closing inventory of 220 under periodic LIFO would include 150 units in the opening inventory and 70 units received January 28.

$$\begin{aligned} 150 \text{ units @ } \$2.50 &= \$375.00 \\ 70 \text{ units @ } 3.25 &= \underline{227.50} \\ \underline{\underline{220}} \qquad\qquad && \underline{\underline{\$602.50}} \end{aligned}$$

(c) Under FIFO, the closing inventory amount will be the same whether the *periodic* or *perpetual* method is used. Each individual withdrawal is from the oldest inventory; the balance on hand is from the latest receipt, as shown in the table below.

COMPUTATION OF ISSUE PRICES

	Units Issued	Unit Price
Feb. 2	200 { 150	$2.50
	50	3.25
June 12	90	3.25
Sept. 18	60 { 35	3.25
	25	3.75
Dec. 30	130 { 100	3.75
	30	4.00
Closing inventory	220	4.00 = $880.00

(*d*) Under perpetual LIFO, the inventory amount may vary substantially from the amount obtained under periodic LIFO, depending on the *timing* of issues. Each individual issue must come from the latest receipt. When the issue amount exceeds the latest receipt, the next earliest receipt must be used, as illustrated in the following table.

COMPUTATION OF ISSUE PRICES

		Units Issued	Unit Price		
Feb. 2	200	175	$3.25		
		25	2.50		
June 12		90	3.75		
Sept. 18	60	35	3.75		
		25	2.50		
Dec. 30		130	4.00		
Closing inventory	220	100	2.50 =	$250.00	
		120	4.00 =	480.00	
				$730.00	

7.10. At the end of 19X0, the New-Gold Company decided to change to the dollar-value LIFO method of pricing its ending inventory. Inventories valued at year-end prices and a general price index for each year are provided below:

December 31	Inventory at Year-end Prices	Price Index at Year End
19X0	$45,000	100
19X1	60,000	120
19X2	70,000	125
19X3	55,000	110
19X4	65,000	125

Prepare a schedule showing the calculation of the ending inventory at LIFO cost for the years 19X1 through 19X4.

SOLUTION

		19X1	19X2	19X3	19X4
(1)	Beginning Inventory at LIFO	$45,000	$51,000	$58,500	$51,000
(2)	Ending Inventory at Year-end Prices	60,000	70,000	55,000	65,000
(3)	Cumulative Price Index	120	125	110	125
(4)	Ending Inventory at Base-year Prices (Lines 2 ÷ 3)	50,000	56,000	50,000	52,000
(5)	Beginning Inventory at Base-year Prices	45,000	50,000	56,000	50,000
(6)	Inventory Increase at Base-year Prices (Lines 4 − 5)	5,000	6,000	(6,000) × 125%	2,000
(7)	Inventory Increases at End-of-year Prices (Lines 3 × 6)	6,000	7,500	(7,500)	2,500
(8)	Ending Inventory at LIFO Cost (Lines 1 + 7)	$51,000	$58,500	$51,000	$53,500

Chapter 8

Inventory: Special Valuations

8.1 INTRODUCTION

When inventories present no special problems, the procedures discussed in Chapter 7 are appropriate for valuation purposes. However, there are some common situations which require special consideration in valuation; these are described in the following sections.

8.2 DAMAGED AND OBSOLETE GOODS

Goods which become damaged or shopworn over time and those which become obsolete due to changing styles or customer preference are usually sold *at prices below cost* to facilitate disposal. For good management control, the amount written down should be analyzed to determine whether it is reasonable (consistent with past experience) or whether some portion reflects poor purchasing practices needing correction in future periods.

In these cases, inventories are usually valued under the *lower of cost or market* rule; the amount of write-down may be costed at net realizable value, cash replacement cost or arbitrary percentage of original cost. It is preferable that any write-down for damaged or obsolete goods be segregated as a separate item in Cost of Goods Sold or Selling Expense, not included directly in Cost of Goods Sold. See Sections 8.3 and 8.4.

8.3 TRADE-INS AND REPOSSESSIONS

Inventory acquired in secondhand condition as a result of trade-ins or repossessions should be valued at a cost which provides for an established rate of profit. For example, automobile and large appliance dealers usually recondition traded-in items; the inventory costs must be set at amounts that, after inclusion of reconditioning charges, allow for the realization of normal profits. It is common practice to assign *floor* values in such cases (see Section 8.4).

8.4 LOWER OF COST OR MARKET

While generally accepted accounting principles require that inventory price increases not be recognized until the merchandise is sold, a *loss from a decline in the price of merchandise should be identified with the period in which the loss occurred*. This point is discussed in Accounting Research Bulletin No. 43, Chapter 4, as follows:

> Where there is evidence that the utility of goods, in their disposal in the ordinary course of business, will be less than cost, whether due to physical deterioration, obsolescence, changes in price levels, or other causes, the differences should be recognized as a loss of the current period. This is generally accomplished by stating such goods at a lower level commonly designated as *market*.

"MARKET" DEFINED

The AICPA states that the term *market* means *current replacement cost*, by purchase or by reproduction, as the case may be.   In ARB No. 43, Chapter 4, *market* is defined as follows:

(1)   Market should not exceed the net realizable value (i.e. estimated selling price in the ordinary course of business less reasonably predictable costs of completion and disposal); and

(2)   Market should not be less than net realizable value reduced by an allowance for an approximately normal profit margin.

FLOOR AND CEILING

The above definition establishes a range for market value between the *ceiling* and the *floor*.   The *ceiling* is the selling price less the *estimated cost* of completion and disposal. The *floor* is the selling price less completion and disposal costs *and the normal profit margin.* The following may help in determining market.

(1)   ***Replacement cost within range.*** The replacement cost is used as market if it falls between ceiling and floor limits.

(2)   ***Replacement cost below floor.*** The floor figure is used when the replacement cost is below the floor.

(3)   ***Replacement cost above ceiling.*** The ceiling figure is used when the replacement cost is above the ceiling.

EXAMPLE 1.

The application of the "lower-of-cost-or-market" procedure is shown in the table below.   The value to be used for inventory in each case is underlined.   The cost of completion and disposal is $10 in each case and the normal gross profit is 20% of the selling price.

	Product				
	1	**2**	**3**	**4**	**5**
Cost (original)	$14	$16	$30	$32	$24
Selling Price	25	30	35	40	45
Ceiling (selling price—$10)	15	20	25	30	35
Floor (selling price—20% profit—$10)	10	14	18	22	26
Replacement cost (market)	12	13	27	35	23

For Products 1, 2 and 3, the *replacement cost is less than the original cost.*

1   *Within range.*   Since replacement cost ($12) is within the ceiling-floor range ($15 to $10), it is used as market.

2   *Replacement cost below floor.*   Replacement cost ($13) is below the floor figure ($14).   The floor figure of *$14* is used since market cannot be less than the floor figure.

3   *Replacement cost above ceiling.*   Replacement cost ($27) is greater than the ceiling ($25).   As market cannot exceed the ceiling, the ceiling of *$25* is used.

For Product 4, the *replacement cost is greater than the original cost and the ceiling.*

4 Replacement cost ($35) exceeds both cost ($32) and the ceiling ($30). The ceiling cost ($30) is used here since market cannot exceed the ceiling.

For Product 5, the *replacement cost is lower than both cost and the floor figure.*

5 Since replacement cost ($23) is less than the floor ($26), the floor figure is considered market here. Cost ($24) is used since it is less than market. The normal profit will be earned upon sale and thus no loss will occur.

APPLICATION OF LOWER OF COST OR MARKET

The lower-of-cost-or-market method can be applied in three different ways: (1) *to each item of inventory,* (2) *to major groups or classifications of inventory,* or (3) *to the inventory as a whole.* The item-by-item treatment results in the lowest total inventory amount, while application to the inventory as a whole results in the highest inventory valuation (see Example 2).

EXAMPLE 2.

The variation which results from application of the lower of cost or market method to the three inventory categories is illustrated below. NOTE: Since the basis for this method is comparison, each item is initially priced at *both* cost and market.

| Inventory | Quanti-ties | Unit Cost | Market | Totals | | (1) Individual Items | (2) Inventory Groups | (3) Inventory as a Whole |
				Cost	Market			
Raw Material	(Pounds)							
#1	1,000	$ 1	$ 2	$ 1,000	$ 2,000	$ 1,000		
#2	500	3	5	1,500	2,500	1,500		
#3	2,000	2	4	4,000	8,000	4,000		
Total				$ 6,500	$12,500		$ 6,500	
Goods in Process	(Dozens)							
A	200	$ 6	$ 7	$ 1,200	$ 1,400	1,200		
B	600	10	8	6,000	4,800	4,800		
C	400	4	5	1,600	2,000	1,600		
Total				$ 8,800	$ 8,200		8,200	
Finished Goods	(Dozens)							
A	1,000	$12	$10	$12,000	$10,000	10,000		
B	3,000	15	12	45,000	36,000	36,000		
C	2,000	8	9	16,000	18,000	16,000		
Total				$73,000	$64,000		64,000	
				$88,300	$84,700			84,700
Inventory valuation						$76,100	$78,700	$84,700

In applying lower-of-cost-or-market procedures to manufacturing inventories, keep in mind that declines in raw material prices as well as direct labor and factory overhead must be carried to goods in process and finished goods. *Where an inventory item has been written down, it is carried at that value until disposition. If the price rises in a subsequent period, the item is still carried at the reduced figure.*

8.5　WRITE-DOWN OF INVENTORY

The write-down of inventory to a figure below cost may be made to each item or the total may be credited to an inventory valuation account. The latter approach is more efficient and makes the original inventory cost available. A valuation account is especially helpful where a perpetual inventory is used since it eliminates the need to adjust the inventory records for individual items.

EXAMPLE 3.

In Example 2, valuation on the individual item basis would entail a reduction in inventory cost of $12,200 ($88,300 − $76,100). The appropriate journal entry would be

Cost of Goods Sold	12,200	
Allowance for Inventory Write-down		12,200

The balance sheet would show the valuation account as follows:

Current Assets		
Inventory, at Cost	$88,300	
Less: Allowance for Inventory Write-down	12,200	$76,100

In the income statement, the reduced inventory figure may be shown in cost of goods sold as in (1) below, or the amount of reduction (in this case, $12,200) may be carried as a separate item following the determination of gross profit as in (2). The latter approach is desirable since it neither "buries" the loss in cost of goods sold nor distorts gross profit on sales.

(1)

Sales		$350,000
Cost of Goods Sold		
Beginning Inventory, at cost	$ 85,500	
Purchases	282,600	
Goods Available	$368,100	
Ending Inventory, at lower of cost or market	76,100	292,000
Gross Profit on Sales		$ 58,000
Operating Expenses		50,000
Net Income		$ 8,000

(2)

Sales		$350,000
Cost of Goods Sold		
Beginning Inventory (cost)	$ 85,500	
Purchases	282,600	
	$368,100	
Less: Ending Inventory (cost)	88,300	279,800
Gross Profit on Sales		$ 70,200
Loss on Inventory Write-down to Market	$ 12,200	
Operating Expenses	50,000	62,200
Net Income		$ 8,000

8.6 PURCHASE COMMITMENT LOSSES

When a purchase contract is placed with a supplier, the buyer is assured delivery of goods in future periods *at a fixed price*. However, such contracts are binding and cannot be cancelled if market prices fluctuate. The lower-of-cost-or-market rule, where used, also applies to commitment losses. The AICPA in ARB No. 43, Chapter 4, states:

> The recognition in a current period of losses arising from the decline in the utility of cost expenditures is equally applicable to similar losses which are expected to arise from firm, uncancellable, and unhedged commitments for the future purchase of inventory items.

The purchase commitment loss should be recognized in the period in which it occurs. The entries to record the loss and subsequent receipt of the goods are described in the following example.

EXAMPLE 4.

Assume that the Barton Company made a commitment by purchase contract in September to buy $50,000 of materials for delivery the following April. There was a price decline and at December 31 the market price of the order was only $40,000. The entries are as follows:

Dec. 31	Loss on Purchase Commitments	10,000	
	Liability on Purchase Commitments		10,000
April 30	Liability on Purchase Commitments	10,000	
	Purchases	40,000	
	Accounts Payable		50,000

8.7 VALUATION AT SELLING PRICE

The use of selling price for inventories is sometimes appropriate. However, there must be (1) market conditions that assure immediate sale at the price, and (2) an inability to arrive at reasonable costs.

Gold, silver and certain other metals may be carried on this basis since they can be sold immediately (i.e. the government will buy all gold mined at a fixed price). In cases where the selling price is established by a firm contract and sale is understood to follow completed production, such inventory may be valued at net selling price less disposition costs. Farmers, for example, are allowed to use current market prices less the direct cost of marketing.

8.8 LONG-TERM CONSTRUCTION

Long-term construction contracts present special inventory and profit recognition problems. Such contracts may cover several years and thus extend over a number of accounting periods. For these cases, there are two principal methods of inventory valuation and profit recognition: (1) *the completed-contract method* and (2) *the percentage-of-completion method*.

The Completed-Contract Method. Under this method, construction in progress is valued at cost and no profit is recognized until the contract is completed and the work accepted. A serious disadvantage of this method is that it tends to distort earnings since in one year there may be much construction but no revenue or profit recognition while in the next, although little actual work is done, the entire profit on the contract is recognized.

The direct costs of construction are accumulated in Construction in Progress, which is closed to expense after the job is completed and accepted. Customer billings are accumulated in the progress billings account.

If it appears that a contract will result in a loss, it is desirable to recognize the loss as soon as it is determined. The entry would be a debit to Loss on Long-term Contract and a credit to Construction in Progress.

EXAMPLE 5.

The Adams Construction Company signed a contract in 19X1 to construct a building to be completed in 19X3. The contract price was $500,000; the construction cost was estimated at $400,000. Profit is recognized only on completed construction. The pertinent data *for each year* is shown below.

Description	19X1	19X2	19X3	Total
1. Construction costs incurred	$ 60,000	$280,000	$ 75,000	$415,000
2. Estimated costs to complete	340,000	85,000	—	—
3. Progress billings to customers	45,000	375,000	80,000	500,000
4. Collected on billings	40,000	325,000	120,000	485,000
5. Operating expenses incurred	10,000	15,000	5,000	30,000

The entries to record the transactions each year are as follows:

COMPLETED-CONTRACT METHOD
JOURNAL ENTRIES

Entries	19X1 Dr.	19X1 Cr.	19X2 Dr.	19X2 Cr.	19X3 Dr.	19X3 Cr.
Construction in Progress	60,000		280,000		75,000	
Operating Expenses	10,000		15,000		5,000	
Materials, Cash, Payables		70,000		295,000		80,000
To record costs incurred.						
Accounts Receivable	45,000		375,000		80,000	
Progress Billings		45,000		375,000		80,000
To record billings on contract.						
Cash	40,000		325,000		120,000	
Accounts Receivable		40,000		325,000		120,000
To record collections on account.						
Progress Billings					500,000	
Cost of Construction					415,000	
Revenue Realized						500,000
Construction in Progress						415,000
To recognize revenue and construction costs upon acceptance of project.						

The balance sheet of the Adams Construction Company would have the following balances relating to long-term construction under the *completed-contract method*. The amounts for years 19X2 and 19X3 represent cumulative differences with respect to the date given in the above table.

Captions	19X1	19X2	19X3
Current Assets:			
Accounts Receivable (3 − 4)	$ 5,000	$55,000	$15,000
Inventories: Costs in Excess of Billings (1 − 3)	15,000	—	—
Current Liabilities:			
Billings in Excess of Costs (3 − 1)	—	80,000	—

Percentage-of-Completion Method.   The percentage-of-completion method allows for periodic recognition of profit over the life of the contract.   Two principal bases may be used: (1) the relationship between costs incurred to date and estimated total cost, or (2) engineering estimates.

Under the first basis, costs incurred to date are related to estimated total cost as a fraction, which is then applied to estimated total income.   The result is the amount of profit to be recognized in the current year.   This concept is expressed mathematically as

$$\frac{\text{COST TO DATE}}{\text{ESTIMATED TOTAL COST}} \times \text{ESTIMATED TOTAL INCOME}$$

$$= \text{PROFIT IN CURRENT YEAR}$$

The computations are illustrated in Example 6.

Under the second basis, qualified engineers or architects may submit estimates in terms of project completion.   Such estimates are applied to total contract price, and costs to date are subtracted from estimated revenue (see Example 7).   Mathematically, this is expressed

$$\text{ESTIMATED \% OF COMPLETION} \times \text{CONTRACT PRICE} - \text{COST TO DATE}$$

$$= \text{PROFIT IN CURRENT YEAR}$$

When contracts specify that a substantial portion of total materials required be ordered or on hand before actual work begins, engineering estimates may be superior to the relative cost basis for revenue recognition purposes.   However, since acquisition alone does not contribute to revenue realization, the AICPA has recommended in ARB No. 45 that in the beginning stages, the cost of materials and subcontracts be excluded from total cost in computing the percentage of completion.

EXAMPLE 6.

The data in Example 5 is now used to illustrate the percentage-of-completion method under the relative cost basis.

Gross Profit Earned
Years 19X1, 19X2 and 19X3

19X1	Contract price		$500,000	
	Less: Actual cost to date	$ 60,000		
	Estimated cost to complete	340,000	400,000	
			$100,000	
	Profit earned 19X1 ($60,000/$400,000 × $100,000)			$15,000
19X2	Contract price		$500,000	
	Less: Actual cost to date	$340,000		
	Estimated cost to complete	85,000	425,000	
			$ 75,000	
	Profit earned ($340,000/$425,000 × $75,000)		$ 60,000	
	Less: Profit recognized in prior period		15,000	
	Profit recognized in 19X2			$45,000
19X3	Contract price		$500,000	
	Less: Actual cost to date		415,000	
	Actual profit earned		$ 85,000	
	Profit earned		$ 85,000	
	Less: Profit recognized in prior periods		60,000	
	Profit recognized in 19X3			$25,000

The entries to record the transactions each year, including gross profit realized, are as follows:

PERCENTAGE-OF-COMPLETION METHOD
JOURNAL ENTRIES

Entries	19X1 Dr.	19X1 Cr.	19X2 Dr.	19X2 Cr.	19X3 Dr.	19X3 Cr.
Construction in Progress	60,000		280,000		75,000	
Operating Expenses	10,000		15,000		5,000	
Materials, Cash, Payables		70,000		295,000		80,000
To record costs incurred.						
Accounts Receivable	45,000		375,000		80,000	
Progress Billings		45,000		375,000		80,000
To record billings on contract.						
Cash	40,000		325,000		120,000	
Accounts Receivable		40,000		325,000		120,000
To record collections on account.						
Construction in Progress	15,000		45,000		25,000	
Gross Profit on Construction		15,000		45,000		25,000
To recognize profit.						
Progress Billings					500,000	
Construction in Progress						500,000
To record approval of project.						

The balance sheet would have the following balances relating to long-term construction under the *percentage-of-completion method.*

Captions	19X1	19X2	19X3
Current Assets:			
Accounts Receivable	$ 5,000	$55,000	$15,000
Inventories: Costs in Excess of Billings	30,000		
Current Liabilities:			
Billings in Excess of Costs		20,000	

Construction in Progress is part of inventories and so shown on the balance sheet. The inventory amount is the cumulative construction cost plus the gross profit earned to date less progress billings to date. For example, in 19X1 the cost excess is $30,000 ($60,000 + $15,000 − $45,000). In 19X2, the billing excess is $20,000 ($340,000 + $60,000 − $420,000).

EXAMPLE 7.

If the engineering estimate basis had been used in Example 6, and the percentage of completion supplied had been 14% in 19X1, 75% in 19X2 and 100% in 19X3, profit recognition would have been calculated for the accounts as follows:

Year	Computations	Revenue	Cost	Profit
19X1	14% × $500,000	$ 70,000	$ 60,000	$10,000
19X2	(75% × $500,000) − $70,000	305,000	280,000	25,000
19X3	$500,000 − ($70,000 + $305,000)	125,000	75,000	50,000
		$500,000	$415,000	$85,000

Summary

(1) Where the economic usefulness of an item has declined in value during a period due to change in style, technology, etc., it is termed _____ and the amount of decline is charged against revenue of the current period.

(2) Current replacement cost by purchase or by reproduction is generally considered the _____.

(3) The AICPA, in ARB No. 43, defined the upper level of market, called the _____ and the lower level, called the _____.

(4) In applying the lower-of-cost-or-market rule, "market" should not exceed _____ _____ or be less than _____.

(5) The two accepted methods of accounting for long-term contracts are the _____ _____ method and the _____ method.

(6) The two principal methods of estimating the portion of a contract that is completed are _____ and _____ _____.

(7) The lower-of-cost-or-market valuation may be applied to _____, _____ or _____.

(8) For lower of cost or market, market means current replacement cost except when that cost: (a) exceeds net realizable value, (b) exceeds changes in price level, (c) exceeds normal profit, (d) none of the above.

(9) When the lower of cost or market is applied to each inventory item, the total valuation of the inventory, as compared to the other methods, is: (a) higher, (b) the same, (c) lower, (d) none of the above.

(10) Assume that a long-term construction contract for $100,000 is estimated to be 75% complete and unbilled costs to date are $70,000. What inventory amount should be shown in the balance sheet if the percentage-of-completion method is used? (a) $70,000, (b) $75,000, (c) $25,000, (d) none of the above.

(11) Long-term construction contracts show costs of $250,000 and partial billings of $275,000. What amount should be shown as a current liability on the balance sheet? (a) $250,000, (b) $275,000, (c) $25,000, (d) none of the above.

Answers: (1) obsolescence; (2) market; (3) ceiling, floor; (4) net realizable value, net realizable value less normal profit; (5) completed-contract, percentage-of-completion; (6) engineering estimate, ratio of costs incurred to total estimated cost; (7) each inventory item, each inventory class, inventory as a whole; (8) *a*; (9) *c*; (10) *b*; (11) *c*.

Solved Problems

8.1. The Schwartz Company manufactures five products which are inventoried at cost or market price, whichever is lower. The company assumes a profit margin of 25% on all sales. From the data below, compute the floor and ceiling prices and determine the lower-of-cost-or-market value.

Schwartz Company
December 31, 197–

Item	Original Cost	Replacement Cost	Selling Cost	Expected Selling Price
A	$87.50	$105.00	$37.50	$200.00
B	35.00	30.00	10.00	60.00
C	22.50	23.00	13.00	50.00
D	52.00	45.00	20.50	95.00
E	95.50	100.00	15.00	110.00

SOLUTION

Schwartz Company
December 31, 197—

Item	Original Cost	Replacement Cost	Floor[1]	Ceiling[2]	LCM
A	$87.50	$105.00	$112.50	$162.50	$87.50
B	36.00	30.00	35.00	50.00	35.00
C	22.50	23.00	24.50	37.00	22.50
D	52.00	45.00	50.75	74.50	50.75
E	95.50	100.00	67.50	95.00	95.00

[1] Floor = 75% of expected selling price − selling cost.

[2] Ceiling = expected selling price − selling cost.

8.2. The Gold Corporation had a beginning inventory of $180,000 (valued at both cost and market) in January, 19X1. Its sales and inventory records for the years 19X1 through 19X3 are summarized below.

	19X1	19X2	19X3
Sales	$1,125,000	$975,000	$1,275,000
Net Purchases	780,000	675,000	900,000
Year-end Inventory			
At Cost	180,000	210,000	225,000
Market	135,000	246,000	165,000

Prepare partial income statements for each year at (a) lower of cost or market, and (b) cost.

SOLUTION

Gold Corporation
Partial Income Statement
Lower of Cost or Market

	19X1	19X2	19X3
Sales	$1,125,000	$975,000	$1,275,000
Cost of Goods Sold			
Beginning Inventory	$ 180,000	$135,000	$ 210,000
Purchases	780,000	675,000	900,000
Available for Sale	$ 960,000	$810,000	$1,110,000
Ending Inventory	135,000	210,000	165,000
Cost of Goods Sold	$ 825,000	$600,000	$ 945,000
Gross Profit	$ 300,000	$375,000	$ 330,000

Gold Corporation
Partial Income Statement at Cost

	19X1	19X2	19X3
Sales	$1,125,000	$975,000	$1,275,000
Cost of Goods Sold			
Beginning Inventory	$ 180,000	$180,000	$ 210,000
Purchases	780,000	675,000	900,000
Available for Sale	$ 960,000	$855,000	$1,110,000
Ending Inventory	180,000	210,000	225,000
Cost of Goods Sold	$ 780,000	$645,000	$ 885,000
Gross Profit	$ 345,000	$330,000	$ 390,000

8.3.   You are the accountant of a local stationery store which has an inventory composed of the items given below. The store's selling expense is 10% and normal profit is 25% of selling price.

Item	Original Cost	Selling Price	Replacement Cost
A	$ 4.00	$ 4.80	$ 3.80
B	15.00	22.50	15.75
C	2.15	3.00	2.00
D	3.41	3.25	3.00
E	4.20	4.80	4.00
F	7.30	9.00	7.50
G	3.80	4.20	3.75
H	9.00	10.00	6.40

Price all inventory at lower of cost or market according to AICPA recommendations.

SOLUTION

Item	Selling Price	Selling Expense	Profit	Original Cost	Replacement Cost	Ceiling	Floor	Inventory Value
A	$ 4.80	$ .48	$1.20	$ 4.00	$ 3.80	$ 4.32	$ 3.12	$ 3.80
B	22.50	2.25	5.62	15.00	15.75	20.25	14.63	15.00
C	3.00	.30	.75	2.15	2.00	2.70	1.95	2.00
D	3.25	.33	.81	3.41	3.00	2.92	2.11	2.92
E	4.80	.48	1.20	4.20	4.00	4.32	3.12	4.00
F	9.00	.90	2.25	7.30	7.50	8.10	5.85	7.30
G	4.20	.42	1.05	3.80	3.75	3.78	2.73	3.75
H	10.00	1.00	2.50	9.00	6.40	9.00	6.50	6.50

8.4. The Darby Company produces six types of widgets whose inventories are priced at the lower of cost or market. The selling expense is 10% of selling price and normal profit is 20% of selling price.

Item	Original Cost	Expected Selling Price	Replacement Cost
1	$ 3.00	$ 3.50	$ 3.20
2	4.90	5.00	4.80
3	2.30	4.00	2.50
4	11.40	16.00	11.00
5	7.80	8.00	7.40
6	6.50	6.00	5.80

Underline the unit value which should be used to price each of these items in accordance with the lower-of-cost-or-market rule.

SOLUTION

Item	Ceiling	Floor	Replacement Cost	Original Cost
1	$3.15	$ 2.45	$ 3.20	$ 3.00
2	4.50	3.50	4.80	4.90
3	3.60	2.80	2.50	2.30
4	14.40	11.20	11.00	11.40
5	7.20	5.60	7.40	7.80
6	5.40	4.20	5.80	6.50

8.5. The Snug Harbor Company had the following information in its inventory records at December 31, 19X1:

Department	Item Code	Quantity	Cost	Market
A	3535	20	$25.00	$28.00
	3537	25	15.00	10.00
	3539	25	19.50	19.30
	3541	30	9.83	9.69
B	154	9	12.75	15.00
	156	13	12.33	11.00
	158	17	9.88	9.88
C	7454	11	12.50	11.00
	7972	13	13.70	19.00
	7995	2	12.68	14.00

Price the inventory for the Snug Harbor Company using the lower-of-cost-or-market method applied to (1) each individual item in inventory, (2) major departments, and (3) the inventory as a whole.

SOLUTION

Determination of Inventory Value Using Lower of Cost or Market Applying the Three Methods

Dept.	Item	Units	Unit Cost	Market	Extension Cost	Extension Market	By Item	By Dept.	Inventory as a Whole
A	3535	20	$25.00	$28.00	$ 500.00	$ 560.00	$ 500.00		
	3537	25	15.00	10.00	375.00	250.00	250.00		
	3539	25	19.50	19.30	487.50	482.50	482.50		
	3541	30	9.83	9.69	294.90	290.70	290.70		
TOTAL					$1,657.40	$1,583.20		$1,583.20	
B	154	9	$12.75	$15.00	$ 114.75	$ 135.00	114.75		
	156	13	12.33	11.00	160.29	143.00	143.00		
	158	17	9.88	9.88	167.96	167.96	167.96		
TOTAL					$ 443.00	$ 445.96		443.00	
C	7454	11	$12.50	$11.00	$ 137.50	$ 121.00	121.00		
	7972	13	13.70	19.00	178.10	247.00	178.10		
	7995	2	12.68	14.00	25.36	28.00	25.36		
TOTAL					$ 340.96	$ 396.00		340.96	
TOTAL, All Depts.					$2,441.36	$2,425.16	$2,273.37	$2,367.16	$2,425.16

It should be noted that the item-by-item method produces the lowest inventory value while the application of cost or market to the inventory as a whole produces the highest inventory valuation.

8.6. The Brown Company uses the first-in, first-out method in computing cost of goods sold. However, because of rapidly rising prices the company is considering switching to last-in, first-out for 19X5 with inventories reported on a LIFO basis. The operations for 19X5 on a FIFO basis were

Sales	$350,000
Cost of Goods Sold	245,000
Gross Profit	$105,000
Operating Expenses	40,000
Income before Income Taxes	$ 65,000
Income Taxes (50%)	32,500
Net Income	$ 32,500

Inventories for the current year were

	FIFO	LIFO
January 1	$30,000	$25,500
December 31	36,500	26,300

Prepare a revised income statement for 19X5 based on LIFO valuations.

SOLUTION

Sales	*$350,000*
Cost of Goods Sold	*255,200*
Gross Profit	*$ 94,800*
Operating Expenses	*40,000*
Income before Income Taxes	*$ 54,800*
Income Taxes (50%)	*27,400*
Net Income	*$27,400*

The cost of goods sold was increased by $10,200 ($255,200 − $245,000) and there was a similar decrease in inventory due to repricing the ending inventory at LIFO ($36,500 − $26,300). The switch to LIFO resulted, after taxes, in a decrease in net income of $5,100 for the year.

8.7. Smitty's Refreshment Center placed a $500,000 purchase commitment for its major raw material on September 1, 19X1. There has been a severe drop in price so that the price of the commitment on December 31, 19X1 is $425,000. At the time of delivery, the total cost will probably be about $375,000. Present the journal entry at December 31, 19X1.

SOLUTION

Dec. 31	*Loss on Purchase Commitments*	*75,000*	
	Accrued Loss on Purchase Commitments		*75,000*
	To record loss on purchase commitments from $500,000 at Sept. 1, 19X1 to $425,000 at Dec. 31, 19X1.		

Also, the financial statement notes should include mention of a possible further loss of $50,000 at the date of delivery.

8.8. Paul's Recreation Center maintains its raw material records at standard cost. When purchases are made, the difference between standard and actual is accumulated in a price variance account for the period. Material A had 1,000 units at a standard cost of $8.00 at the beginning of 19X1. During 19X1, the following purchases were made: March 15, 400 units at $9.00; June 30, 600 units at $7.50; and October 31, 500 units at $9.50. There were 2,000 units issued during the period.

Show the journal entries for 19X1 and summarize the results for the period.

SOLUTION

March 15	*Raw Material*	*3,200*	
	Price Variance (400 × $1.00)	*400*	
	Accounts Payable		*3,600*
June 30	*Raw Material*	*4,800*	
	Price Variance (600 × $.50)		*300*
	Accounts Payable		*4,500*
Oct. 31	*Raw Material*	*4,000*	
	Price Variance (500 × $1.50)	*750*	
	Accounts Payable		*4,750*

SUMMARY

Beginning Inventory (1,000 × $8.00)		$ 8,000
Purchases, 19X1		
March 31 (400 × $9.00)	$ 3,600	
June 30 (600 × $7.50)	4,500	
Oct. 31 (500 × $9.50)	4,750	12,850
Total Available		$20,850
Issued (2,000 × $8.00)	$16,000	
Ending Inventory (500 × $8.00)	4,000	20,000
Price Variance (+400 − 300 + 750)		$ 850

8.9. The Pincus Construction Company contracted to build a highway complex over a two-year period for 5.4 million dollars. With the data given below, calculate the net income to be realized under (*a*) percentage-of-completion method, and (*b*) completed-contract method.

Year	Cost Incurred to Date	Estimated Cost to Complete
19X1	$1,500,000	$2,100,000
19X2	3,660,000	—

SOLUTION

Pincus Construction Company
Reporting of Income
Years 19X1 and 19X2

(*a*) PERCENTAGE-OF-COMPLETION METHOD

Year 19X1

Contract Price		$5,400,000
Costs Incurred to Date	$1,500,000	
Estimated Cost to Complete	2,100,000	3,600,000
Estimated Total Income		$1,800,000

Income to be recognized:

$$\frac{\$1,500,000}{\$3,600,000} \times \frac{\$1,800,000}{1} = \$750,000$$

Year 19X2

Contract Price		$5,400,000
Costs Incurred to Date	$3,660,000	
Estimated to Complete	—0—	3,660,000
Total Income		$1,740,000
Less: Income Recognized First Year		750,000
Income to be Recognized Second Year		$ 990,000

(*b*) COMPLETED-CONTRACT METHOD

Contract Price	$5,400,000
Cost Incurred	$3,660,000
Profit	$1,740,000

8.10. The Sam Construction Company has the following contracts in progress, as described, at December 31, 19XX:

Contract No.	Contract Price	Total Estimated Cost	Cost Incurred to Date
A	$ 150,000	$ 120,000	$ 80,000
B	3,000,000	3,150,000	1,575,000
C	300,000	225,000	67,500

Prepare a schedule of contract income for the company using the (a) completed-contract method and (b) percentage-of-completion method. Show estimated total costs and costs incurred.

SOLUTION

Sam Construction Company
Schedule of Contract Income

(a) COMPLETED-CONTRACT METHOD

Project	Provision for Losses	Income to be Reported
B	$150,000	($150,000)

(b) PERCENTAGE-OF-COMPLETION METHOD

Project	Revenue to be Reported	Costs Incurred	Provision for Loss	Income to be Reported
A	$ 100,000	$ 80,000		$ 20,000
B	1,500,000	1,575,000	$75,000	(150,000)
C	90,000	67,500		22,500

Computation of Revenue Recognized:

$$A: \quad \frac{80,000}{120,000} \times 150,000 = \$100,000$$

$$B: \quad \frac{1,575,000}{3,150,000} \times 3,000,000 = \$1,500,000$$

$$C: \quad \frac{67,500}{225,000} \times 300,000 = \$90,000$$

8.11. The partnership of Hebb and Epp Construction Company primarily builds large commercial buildings. In 19X1, they were engaged to build a new town hall for Lattingtown at a contract price of $450,000. The costs incurred to December 31, 19X1 were $270,000 and it was estimated that additional costs to complete the building would be $90,000. Compute the gross profit earned on the project under the percentage-of-completion method.

SOLUTION

Hebb and Epp Construction Company
Project Earnings
Year 19X1

Contract Price		*$440,000*
Estimated Cost of Building		
Costs Incurred in 19X1	*$270,000*	
Estimated Cost to Complete	*90,000*	*360,000*
Estimated Income		*$ 80,000*
Percentage of Completion ($270,000 ÷ $360,000)		*75%*
Gross Profit Earned		*$ 60,000*

Chapter 9

Inventories: Estimations

9.1 INTRODUCTION

Estimations of inventory valuations are widely used where detailed records are not maintained, where the data may not be readily available or where thousands of unit cost records may otherwise be required. They are used to establish inventory valuations or to verify amounts obtained through other methods. The principal estimation methods are described in the following sections.

9.2 GROSS PROFIT METHOD

Under the gross profit method, inventory value is determined by reducing the sales total at retail to the total equivalent amount at cost. Its essential feature is an accurate *gross profit percentage*, usually based on gross profit percentages for recent years, adjusted for any abnormalities. This method is used primarily to estimate (1) interim inventory amounts between physical counts, (2) inventory value when the inventory and related records have been destroyed or lost and (3) inventory value in order to verify the amount determined by other means.

The gross profit percentage may be expressed in terms of net sales or cost. When the *net sales* basis is used, the appropriate calculation is

$$\text{Sales (100\%)} - \text{Gross Profit Percentage} \;=\; \text{Cost of Goods Sold Percentage} \qquad (1)$$

then

$$\begin{array}{cc} \text{Net Sales} \times \text{Cost of Goods Sold} & = \quad \text{Cost of Goods Sold} \\ \text{(\$)} \qquad\qquad \text{(\%)} & \qquad\qquad \text{(\$)} \end{array} \qquad (2)$$

Alternatively, the value of cost of goods sold may be approximated from records of past periods and related to net sales for the same period as a ratio where

$$\begin{array}{cc} \text{Cost of Goods Sold} \div \text{Net Sales} & = \quad \text{Cost of Goods Sold} \\ \text{(\$)} \qquad\qquad \text{(\$)} & \qquad\qquad \text{(\%)} \end{array}$$

and the cost of goods sold percentage is applied to net sales as in equation (2).

EXAMPLE 1.   Gross Profit Percentage Based on Sales.

At the Nuttall Art Supply Company, physical inventories are taken semiannually at June 30 and December 31. At March 31, Mr. Nuttall decides to estimate the value of the inventory on hand rather than take a physical count. In reviewing the company records he finds that the physical inventory at December 31 was $25,000, net purchases in the first three months of the current year were $72,000, while net sales totaled $100,000. The cost of goods sold/net sales ratio was consistently about 67% for the past three years. The ending inventory computation is shown below.

Nuttall Art Supply Company
Estimated Inventory
March 31, 19X—

Beginning Inventory		$25,000
Net Purchases		72,000
Goods Available for Sale		$97,000
Less: Estimated Cost of Goods Sold		
Net Sales	$100,000	
Cost of Sales %	67%	67,000
Estimated Ending Inventory		$30,000

When the *cost* basis is used, the gross profit as a percentage of cost of goods sold is converted to the gross profit as a percentage of net sales. In this case, when

$$\begin{array}{ccc} \textbf{Cost of Goods Sold} & + & \textbf{Gross Profit} & = & \textbf{Net Sales} \\ \textbf{(100\%)} & & \textbf{(\%)} & & \textbf{(\%)} \end{array}$$

then

$$\begin{array}{ccc} \textbf{Net Sales} & \div & \textbf{Net Sales} & = & \textbf{Cost of Goods Sold} \\ \textbf{(\$)} & & \textbf{(\%)} & & \textbf{(\$)} \end{array}$$

or alternatively

$$\begin{array}{ccc} \textbf{Cost of Goods Sold} & \div & \textbf{Net Sales} & = & \textbf{Cost of Goods Sold as Percentage of Sales} \\ \textbf{(\%)} & & \textbf{(\%)} & & \end{array}$$

and cost of goods sold as a percentage of sales is applied to net sales as in equation (*2*) above.

EXAMPLE 2.   Gross Profit Percentage Based on Cost.

Assume the same conditions and amounts as in Example 1, except that the gross profit percentage is based on cost. Nuttall marks up his goods by 50%; therefore, sales are 150% of cost. Dividing $100,000 by 1.50, the cost of goods sold is $66,667 or approximately $67,000, and the ending inventory is computed as shown below.

Nuttall Art Supply Company
Estimated Inventory
March 31, 19X—

Beginning Inventory	$25,000
Net Purchases	72,000
Goods Available for Sale	$97,000
Less: Estimated Cost of Goods Sold	
Net Sales $100,000 ÷ 1.50, is approximately	67,000
Estimated Ending Inventory	$30,000

Alternatively, 100%/150% = 0.666 or 0.67 which, when applied to net sales of $100,000, yields the same results as in Example 1.

9.3   RETAIL METHOD

This method is widely used by department stores and other retail concerns as a means of converting the inventory value from retail to cost. The retail method is used primarily (1) to value an inventory when selling prices are the only reasonably accessible data, (2) to value an inventory between physical counts and (3) to determine if the inventory value at the end of the period is reasonable.

Under this method, purchase records and beginning inventory are both stated in terms of *cost and retail* to establish comparative goods available for sale figures, as follows:

Beginning Inventory at Cost + Net Purchases at Cost   =   Goods Available at Cost

Beginning Inventory at Retail + Net Purchases at Retail   =   Goods Available at Retail

The relationship between cost and retail can then be expressed as a percentage:

$$\frac{\text{Goods Available at Cost}}{\text{Goods Available at Retail}} \quad = \quad \text{Cost as Percentage of Sales}$$

To compute the estimated cost of ending inventory, the retail value is first established by subtracting sales (retail) from goods available for sale (retail). The cost percentage is then applied to the retail value of inventory, so that

Ending Inventory at Retail × Cost as Percentage of Sales   =   Ending Inventory at Cost

EXAMPLE 3.

In the calculations below, cost as a percentage of sales is 62.5% ($150,000 ÷ $240,000).

The EPP Company
Retail Method of Estimating Inventory
Current Year

	Cost	Retail
Beginning Inventory	$ 50,000	$ 90,000
Net Purchases	100,000	150,000
Goods Available for Sale	$150,000	$240,000
Less: Sales for the Year		136,000
Ending Inventory		
Retail		$104,000
Cost ($104,000 × 62.5%)	$ 65,000	

The reliability of the retail method requires that there be a uniform relation between cost and retail. The mix of goods in the ending inventory is assumed to be the same as the mix in the total goods available for sale during the period. Since this is not always the case, the retail method will generally be more accurate if it is applied to the individual departments of a business.

9.4 RETAIL METHOD TERMINOLOGY

For illustration, the previous examples used only the original sales price. However, it is frequently necessary, because of changes in customers' demands, inflation or other reasons, to mark up or mark down the original sales price. The following terms are used in applying the retail method.

(1) *Original sales price.* The price at which the article is first offered for sale.

(2) *Markup.* The difference between cost and original retail, which is sometimes called *markon* or *gross margin.*

(3) *Additional markup.* Any increase above the original sales price.

(4) *Markup cancellation.* A decrease that does not reduce sales prices below original retail.

(5) *Markdown.* A decrease below the original sales price.

(6) *Markdown cancellation.* An increase, following a markdown, which does not raise the price above the original sales price.

EXAMPLE 4.

Assume that the Epp Company marks up its merchandise 50%. Thus if an inventory item costs $100, the *original sales price* will be $150. The increase of $50 is the *markup*, which is 50% of cost or $33\frac{1}{3}\%$ of the sales price. Because of expected heavy demand, an *additional markup* of $40 is made, raising the selling price to $190. Later the price is cut to $175 representing a *markup cancellation* of $15. To close out the remaining stock, the price is dropped to $140 representing a *markup cancellation* of $25 and a *markdown* of $10. The few remaining items were sold at $145, a *markdown cancellation* of $5.

9.5 RETAIL METHOD APPLICATIONS

The classification of the various retail method components has a significant effect on inventory valuation. Of particular importance is the treatment of markups and markdowns, since these affect the relationship between the cost of goods available and the selling price (i.e. the cost to retail percentage).

The principal applications of the retail method are described below. In Examples 5 and 6, the following data will be used.

	Cost	Retail
Beginning inventory	$29,000	$53,000
Net purchases	48,000	85,000
Additional markups		18,000
Markup cancellations		2,000
Markdowns		15,000
Markdown cancellations		1,000
Net sales		80,000

Average Cost Basis.   Under this basis, the computation of retail goods available for sale includes *adding net markups* and *deducting net markdowns*.

EXAMPLE 5.

In the following calculation of ending inventory at average cost, the cost to retail percentage is 55% ($77,000 ÷ $140,000).

Ralph Addonizio Company
Ending Inventory, Average Cost Basis
Year 19X—

	Cost	Retail
Beginning Inventory	$29,000	$53,000
Net Purchases	48,000	85,000
Additional Markups, net ($18,000 — $2,000)		16,000
Less: Markdowns, net ($15,000 — $1,000)		(14,000)
Goods Available for Sale	$77,000	$140,000
Less: Net Sales		80,000
Ending Inventory		
Retail		$ 60,000
Average Cost ($60,000 × 55%)	$33,000	

Lower-of-Cost-or-Market Basis.   This basis, also called the conventional retail method, *excludes* net markdowns from the computation of retail goods available for sale. Net markups are added in deriving the retail total for the computation of the cost to retail percentage.

EXAMPLE 6.

The cost to retail percentage is 50% ($77,000 ÷ $154,000) in the lower-of-cost-or-market computations below.

Ralph Addonizio Company
Ending Inventory, Lower of Cost or Market
Year 19X—

	Cost	Retail
Beginning Inventory	$29,000	$ 53,000
Net Purchases	48,000	85,000
Additional Markups, net ($18,000 — $2,000)		16,000
Goods Available for Sale	$77,000	$154,000
Less: Net Sales		(80,000)
Net Markdowns		(14,000)
Ending Inventory		
Retail		$60,000
Lower of Cost or Market ($60,000 × 50%)	$30,000	

The feature which distinguishes net markups from net markdowns is *utility*. In the case of net markups, the higher market value represents increased utility. Net markdowns, on the other hand, reflect declines in market value, or utility, and are considered a current loss to be included in cost of goods sold.

A comparison of Examples 5 and 6 shows that the average cost basis, which assumes the same mix of items in goods available for sale and ending inventory, results in a higher cost to retail percentage and a higher ending inventory value. In contrast, the conventional retail method, by recognizing losses in the period, produces a lower percentage and an estimated ending inventory which approximates lower of cost or market, not average costs.

First-in, First-out Basis. Under this basis, which approximates cost, the oldest goods (i.e. the beginning inventory) are presumed shipped first. In most cases, the ending inventory will consist of some part of purchases plus changes in the period. This concept of inventory layers under the FIFO basis requires the following treatment:

(1) Cost to retail percentages for beginning inventory and purchases must be separately calculated.

(2) Both markups and markdowns are included in calculating the cost to retail percentage *for purchases.*

(3) The beginning inventory percentage is used in valuing ending inventory *only* when sales are *less than the beginning inventory at retail* (i.e. when the ending inventory is composed of some part of beginning inventory goods).

EXAMPLE 7.

The calculations below assume stable prices during the period. The beginning inventory percentage is 50% ($30,000 ÷ $60,000) and the purchases percentage is 60% ($54,000 ÷ $90,000).

Carlton Hammer Company
Ending Inventory, First-in, First-out Basis
Year 19X—

	Cost	Retail
Beginning Inventory	$30,000	$ 60,000
Net Purchases	54,000	80,000
Additional Markups, net ($15,000 — $1,000)		14,000
Less: Markdowns, net ($6,000 — $2,000)		(4,000)

Goods Available for Sale	$84,000	$150,000
Less: Net Sales		80,000
Ending Inventory		
Retail		$ 70,000
FIFO ($70,000 × 60%)	$42,000	

Last-in, First-out Basis. This cost basis is essentially the reverse of FIFO. The ending inventory is assumed to consist of the oldest purchases (i.e. the beginning inventory plus some part of purchases during the period). The calculations are the same as those for FIFO, except that the cost to retail percentage for *purchases* need be computed only when the retail value of the ending inventory increases during the period. When the ending inventory is equal to or less than the beginning inventory, its value at cost is calculated from the beginning inventory percentage.

EXAMPLE 8.

Again assuming stable prices during the period, the beginning inventory is 50% ($30,000 ÷ $60,000) and the purchases percentage is 60% ($54,000 ÷ $90,000).

Carlton Hammer Company
Ending Inventory, Last-in, First-out Basis
Year 19X—

	Cost	Retail
Beginning Inventory	$30,000	$ 60,000
Net Purchases	54,000	80,000
Additional Markups, net ($15,000 − $1,000)		14,000
Less: Markdowns, net ($6,000 − $2,000)		(4,000)
Goods Available for Sale	$84,000	$150,000
Less: Net Sales		80,000
Ending Inventory		
Retail		$ 70,000
LIFO: Beginning Inventory ($60,000 × 50%)	$30,000	
Layer added ($10,000 × 60%)	6,000	
Ending Inventory at LIFO Cost	$36,000	

Dollar-value LIFO. While the LIFO-retail method assumes stable prices in the period, this condition is not the usual case. When retail selling prices *fluctuate* during the period, the dollar value-LIFO approach (see Section 7.7) is used to determine inventory cost under the retail method.

The distinguishing feature of this method is that the ending inventory must be converted or deflated to beginning inventory retail prices to determine the *real* increase in inventory; that is, the increase in quantity. This is accomplished through the use of price indexes, as follows:

(1) Divide ending inventory at retail by year-end price index as a percentage to obtain value at beginning inventory price level.

(2) Subtract beginning inventory at retail from deflated ending inventory value (1). The remainder presents the real increase in inventory.

(3) Multiply real increase by price index percentage in (1) to determine value of increment at year-end prices.

The ending inventory at cost is the sum of the beginning inventory (at cost) and the increment at year-end prices reduced to cost through application of the cost to retail percentage for purchases.

EXAMPLE 9.

The computations below assume a retail price index of 100% at the beginning of the year (when LIFO was adopted) and an increase to 112% at year end. The figures in part (*a*) are the same as in Example 8; the cost to retail percentage is 60%. The real increase in inventory is computed in part (*b*). Part (*c*) illustrates the calculation of the ending inventory at cost.

Carlton Hammer Company
Ending Inventory, Dollar Value LIFO
Year 19X—

		Cost	Retail
(a)	Beginning Inventory	$30,000	$ 60,000
	Purchases (including markups and markdowns)	54,000	90,000
	Goods Available for Sale	$84,000	$150,000
	Less: Net Sales		80,000
	Ending Inventory at Retail		$ 70,000
(b)	Ending Inventory Deflated ($70,000 ÷ 1.12)		$ 62,500
	Less: Beginning Inventory at Retail		60,000
	Real Increase in Inventory		$ 2,500
	Increment at Year-end Prices ($2,500 × 1.12)		$ 2,800
(c)	Beginning Inventory Layer:		
	At Base Prices	$30,000	$ 60,000
	Add: Increase due to Inflation		7,200
	[($60,000 × 1.12) − $60,000]		
	Incremental Layer:		
	At Year-end Prices		2,800
	At Cost ($2,800 × 60%)	1,680	
	Ending Inventory	$31,680	$ 70,000

NOTE: The retail inventory calculations in part (*c*) include the restatement of beginning inventory to inflated year-end prices.

A comparison of ending inventory at cost in Examples 8 and 9 shows that the value of inventory is lower under the dollar-LIFO basis. In a period of rising prices, this basis is preferable because it reduces the amount of taxable income.

9.6 ESTIMATING MANUFACTURING INVENTORIES

The two principal systems for accumulating costs in a manufacturing company, the job order system and the process cost system, were described in Section 7.4. The allocation of costs between completed goods and goods in process is often difficult, especially where the process system is used.

When beginning and ending inventories are in process and are in different stages of completion, the flow of goods (in terms of quantity) through the system can be summarized by the following equation:

UNITS AVAILABLE DURING PERIOD (Input) = UNIT DISPOSITION DURING PERIOD (Output)

OPENING INVENTORY   UNITS COMPLETED OR TRANSFERRED
+ UNITS PUT INTO PRODUCTION   + ENDING INVENTORY

When any three terms in the flow equation are known, the missing piece of data can be computed from the equation itself.

To determine actual costs of the various categories of goods, all units must be converted to *a common denominator, equivalent completed units.* Proper costs can then be allocated to goods in process, finished goods inventory and cost of goods sold.

EXAMPLE 10.

The Suburban Paint Company had total production costs of $12,035 (materials, $4,160; direct labor, $2,700; and factory overhead, $5,175), and completed 2,000 units during the month of November. There were 400 units completed, however, which were started in October and 600 units that were started in November but not completed by the month end. The first step is to compute the equivalent completed units produced for November.

Suburban Paint Company
Computation of Equivalent Completed Units Produced
Month of November, 19X—

	EQUIVALENT COMPLETED UNITS	
	Materials	Labor and Overhead
Goods in Process, Nov. 1		
400 units with prior month's cost of $1,000, 70% complete as to materials and 50% complete as to direct labor and factory overhead. Added this month 120 (400 × 30%), and 200 (400 × 50%).	*120*	*200*
Units Started and Completed in November		
2,000 units completed, less 400 units in process at November 1.	*1,600*	*1,600*
Goods in Process, Nov. 30		
600 units, 60% complete as to materials 360 (600 × 60%), and 75% complete as to direct labor and factory overhead 450 (600 × 75%).	*360*	*450*
Equivalent Completed Units	*2,080*	*2,250*

The production cost for each *equivalent completed unit* during November was as follows:

	Production Cost	Equivalent Units	Unit Cost
Materials	*$ 4,160*	*2,080*	*$2.00*
Direct labor and factory overhead			
($2,700 + $5,175)	*7,875*	*2,250*	*3.50*
Total production costs	*$12,035*		*$5.50*

The unit costs can now be applied to the inventory components, on a first-in, first-out basis. There was no beginning inventory of finished goods. The ending inventory of finished goods was 500 units.

Suburban Paint Company
Cost of Inventory and Cost of Goods Sold
Month of November, 19X—

Finished Goods Inventory, Nov. 30 (500 units × $5.50)		*$2,750*
Goods in Process, Nov. 30		
Materials (600 units × 60% × $2.00)	*$ 720*	
Direct Labor and Factory Overhead (600 units × 75% × $3.50)	*1,575*	*$2,295*

Cost of Goods Sold, Month of November

Goods in Process, Nov. 1[1] *(400 units)*	$ 1,940
Units Started and Completed in November *(1,600 × $5.50)*	8,800
Goods in Process, Nov. 30 *(600 units)*	2,295
Total Cost of Goods in Process	$13,035
Less: Goods in Process, Nov. 30	2,295
Total Cost of Goods Completed (2,000 units)	$10,740
Less: Finished Goods Inventory, Nov. 30	2,750
Cost of Goods Sold[2] *(1,500 units)*	7,990

[1] Includes prior month's cost of $1,000 plus $940 added in November: materials, $240 (120 × $2.00) and direct labor and factory overhead, $700 (200 × $3.50).

[2] Calculated as follows under FIFO:

400 units @ $4.85	($1,940 ÷ 400)	$1,940
1,100 units @ $5.50	($6,050 ÷ 1,100)	6,050
1,500 units		$7,990

Summary

(1) Gross profit percentage on sales is a ratio of_____to_____.

(2) Gross profit percentages of 20%, 40% and 60% based on cost would be_____,_____, and_____based on sales.

(3) If there are several classes of goods with different markup percentages, the gross profit percentage should be applied to_____.

(4) A reduction in the retail price after there has been an additional markup is called a _____.

(5) Alternative terms for markup are_____ and_____.

(6) The major advantages of dollar-value LIFO are that it uses_____instead of physical units, and_____is less tedious and costly.

(7) The method of accounting for joint-product costs that results in the same gross profit rate for all products is the_____method.

(8) Estimates of inventory costs are ordinarily *not* desirable (a) between physical counts, (b) when records have been destroyed or lost, (c) to verify amounts determined by other means, and (d) to compute product costs.

(9) A markdown is a reduction in selling price to (a) below the original retail price, (b) below cost, (c) above cost, (d) eliminate profit.

(10) If total manufacturing costs of Product C in July were $12,000 and 8,000 equivalent units were manufactured in July, the cost of 500 units completed at July 31 would be (a) $600, (b) $800, (c) $750, (d) $375.

(11)   The Clark Company, which marks up its goods 30% on cost, has the following account balances at September 30: Inventory, September 1, $75,000; net purchases during the month, $45,000; and sales during the month, $65,000.   What is the estimated cost of the September 30 inventory? (a) $80,000, (b) $60,000, (c) $65,000, (d) 70,000.

Answers: (1) gross profit, sales; (2)16⅔%, 28⁴⁄₇, 37½; (3) each class; (4) markup cancellation; (5) markon, gross margin; (6) dollars, clerical work; (7) relative sales value; (8) *d*; (9) *a*; (10) *c*; (11) *d*.

Solved Problems

9.1.   The Marcketta Paint Company is trying to decide whether to mark up goods based on *gross profit on sales* or *gross profit on cost*. (a) If the gross margin percentages based on cost are 25%, 50% and 66⅔%, what would be the equivalent markup percentages based on selling price? (b) If the gross profit margin percentages based on selling price are 20%, 33⅓% and 40%, what would be the equivalent mark-up percentages based on cost?

SOLUTION

(a) *Gross Profit Based on Cost* (cost is 100%)

COST + GROSS PROFIT = SELLING PRICE

Percentage Based on Cost	Equation	Percentage Based on Selling Price
25%	100% + 25% = 125%, then 25/125	20%
50%	100% + 50% = 150%, then 50/150	33⅓%
66⅔%	100% + 66⅔% = 166⅔%, then 66⅔/166⅔	40%

(b) *Gross Profit Based on Selling Price* (selling price is 100%)

SELLING PRICE − GROSS PROFIT = COST

Percentage Based on Selling Price	Equation	Percentage Based on Cost
20%	100% − 20% = 80%, then 20/80	25%
33⅓%	100% − 33⅓% = 66⅔%, then 33⅓/66⅔	50%
40%	100% − 40% = 60%, then 40/60	66⅔%

9.2.   The Franklin Company's books showed the following data at March 15, 19X2.   The gross profit has averaged 25% on sales.

Year 19X2

Inventory, Jan. 1	$ 50,000
Purchases, Jan. 1 to March 15	110,000
Net sales Jan. 1 to March 15	100,000

The entire inventory was lost in a fire on March 15, 19X2.   What was the amount of the loss?

SOLUTION

Beginning Inventory		$ 50,000
Purchases		110,000
Goods Available		$160,000
Less: Cost of Goods Sold		
Sales	$100,000	
Less: Gross Margin (25%)	25,000	75,000
Inventory Lost in Fire		$ 85,000

9.3. The Post Company sells its merchandise at a gross profit of 30% on sales. Following are the purchases and sales figures for the last three months of 19–. The inventory at October 1 was $50,000.

Month	Purchases	Sales
October	$65,000	$100,000
November	75,000	120,000
December	90,000	150,000

Determine the inventory balance at the end of each month.

SOLUTION

	October	November	December
Inventory, at beginning	$ 50,000	$ 45,000	$ 36,000
Purchases	65,000	75,000	90,000
Goods Available	$115,000	$120,000	$126,000
Cost of Goods Sold[1]	70,000	84,000	105,000
Inventory, at end	$ 45,000	$ 36,000	$ 21,000

[1] 70% of sales.

9.4. The Suffolk Chemical Company has inventory information for 19X1 as follows:

	Cost	Retail
Inventory, January 1, 19X1	$ 45,000	$ 60,000
Purchases	100,000	125,000
Transportation-in	6,000	
Purchases allowances	1,800	
Purchases discounts	1,000	
Sales		116,500
Sales discount		1,500
Markups (net)		5,000
Markdowns (net)		3,000

The price level at December 31, 19X1 was 110, based on January 1, 19X1 as 100.

Compute (a) the conventional retail cost percentage for the inventory, and (b) retail and cost amounts for the December 31, 19X1 inventory, using retail-LIFO procedures.

SOLUTION

(a) Conventional Retail Cost Percentage

	Cost	Retail
Inventory, January 1, 19X1	$ 45,000	$ 60,000
Purchases	100,000	125,000
Transportation-in	6,000	
Purchases allowances	(1,800)	
Purchases discounts	(1,000)	
Markups (net)		5,000
	$148,200	$190,000

Retail cost percentage ($148,200 ÷ $190,000) = 78%

(b) Inventory at Retail and at Cost

	Retail	Index	Cost %	Cost
Inventory, January 1, 19X1	$ 60,000	100	75	$45,000
Net Purchases				
Retail ($125,000 + $5,000 −				
$3,000)	127,000			
Cost ($100,000 + $6,000 −				
$1,800 − $1,000 =				
$103,200)				
Available for Sale	$187,000			
Less: Net Sales	115,000			
Ending Inventory at Retail	$ 72,000			
Ending Inventory at Base				
($72,000 ÷ 1.10)	65,455			
Increment	$ 6,545	110	81.2[1]	5,846
Ending Inventory at Retail-LIFO				
($45,000 + $5,846)				$50,846
Composition of Inventory:				
Base Quantity	$ 60,000	100	75	$45,000
19X1 Layer	6,545	110	81.2	5,846
	$ 66,545			$50,846

[1] $103,200 ÷ $127,000 = 81.2%.

9.5. The Locust Valley Company has the following inventory data at December 31, 19X1:

	Cost	Retail
Inventory, January 1, 19X1	$ 62,000	$125,000
Purchases	372,000	620,000
Freight-in	15,200	
Purchases returns	5,200	11,000
Additional markups		15,000
Markup cancellations		9,000
Markdowns		12,000
Markdown cancellations		3,000
Gross sales		630,000
Sales returns		13,500
Estimated shrinkage		4,000

Calculate the ending inventory at sales price and at lower of average cost or market.

SOLUTION

	Cost	Retail
Inventory, January 1, 19X1	$ 62,000	$125,000
Purchases	372,000	620,000
Freight-in	15,200	
Purchase Returns	(5,200)	(11,000)
Additional Markups		15,000
Less: Markup Cancellations		(9,000)
	$444,000	$740,000
Cost to Retail Percentage		
($444,000 ÷ $740,000)	60%	
Less:		
Gross Sales		$630,000
Sales Returns		(13,500)
Markdowns		12,000
Markdown Cancellations		(3,000)
Estimated Shrinkage		4,000
		$629,500
Ending Inventory		
Retail		$110,500
Cost ($110,500 × 60%)	$ 66,300	

9.6. The conventional retail method is used by the Reed Food Company to control inventories at its stores. The estimated inventory at a location is not expected to vary more than 6% from the established normal amount. The normal amount for the Newton location at June 30 is $70,000.

	Cost	Retail
Net sales		$700,000
Beginning inventory	$150,000	200,000
Net purchases	431,000	600,000
Net additional markups		30,500
Net markdowns		20,000
Estimated shrinkage		5,000

Using the information provided above, calculate (a) the amount of the ending inventory at retail and at cost and (b) the percentage of variance from the expected normal amount.

SOLUTION

(a) Ending Inventory:

	Cost	Retail
Beginning Inventory	$150,000	$200,000
Net Purchases	431,000	600,000
Net Additional Mark-ups		30,500
	$581,000	$830,500

Ratio of Cost to Retail	70%	
Less: Sales		$700,000
Net Markdowns		20,000
Estimated Shrinkage		5,000
		$725,000
Ending Inventory	$ 73,850	$105,500

(b) Percentage of Variance:

Amount of variance: $3,850 ($73,850 − $70,000)

Percentage of variance: 5.5% ($3,850 ÷ $70,000)

9.7. The Kelsch Company sells two types of furniture: the Utility Brand on which it has a profit margin of 40% of sales, and the Premium Brand on which it has a profit margin of 30% of sales. On total business, the profit margin on sales has been 35%.

	Furniture Brand		
	Utility	**Premium**	**Total**
Beginning Inventory	$12,000	$ 20,000	$ 32,000
Purchases	22,000	63,000	85,000
Sales	50,000	110,000	160,000

The physical inventory total amounted to $10,000. However, the gross profit test indicated the inventory should be $13,000. The gross margins on the two brands have not changed.

Determine the inventory value using the gross profit test based on (a) the total inventory and (b) the individual brands.

SOLUTION

(a) Total Inventory:

Beginning Inventory		$ 32,000
Purchases		85,000
Goods Available		$117,000
Cost of Goods Sold		
Sales	$160,000	
Less: Profit Margin (35%)	56,000	104,000
Ending Inventory		$ 13,000

(b) Individual Brands:

	Utility	**Premium**
Beginning Inventory	$12,000	$ 20,000
Purchases	22,000	63,000
Goods Available	$34,000	$ 83,000
Cost of Goods Sold		
Sales	$50,000	$110,000
Less: Profit Margin	20,000 (40%)	33,000 (30%)
Cost of Goods	$30,000	$ 77,000
Ending Inventory	$ 4,000	$ 6,000

The gross profit margin on the total inventory was $56,000 ($160,000 × 35%). However, the gross margin on the individual brands was only $53,000, a difference of $3,000. The gross profit on the individual brands averaged only 33.12% due to the higher proportion of sales with lower markup.

9.8. On April 30, 19X1 the Nassau Chemical Corporation had an explosion which demolished its factory and the work in process. After the explosion an inventory was taken and it was found that raw materials on hand amounted to $20,000 and finished goods on hand amounted to $45,000. At January 1, 19X1 the inventories were: raw materials, $18,000; goods in process, $90,000 and finished goods, $80,000.

For the four months of 19X1 the raw material purchases were $45,000, direct labor was $35,000 and factory overhead was 70% of direct labor. Sales for the four months aggregated $240,000. The total sales for the last three years was $950,000 and the total gross profits during that period was $285,000.

Prepare a schedule showing the amount of the goods in process inventory lost in the explosion.

SOLUTION

Nassau Chemical Corporation
Schedule of Goods in Process Lost
April 30, 19X1

Raw Material		
Raw Material Inventory, January 1, 19X1	$18,000	
Raw Material Purchases, January–April	45,000	
Raw Material Available	$63,000	
Less: Raw Material on Hand After Explosion	20,000	
Raw Materials Placed in Production		$ 43,000
Direct Labor Cost		35,000
Factory Overhead ($35,000 × 70%)		24,500
Total Manufacturing Cost, January 1–April 30		$102,500
Goods in Process, January 1, 19X1		90,000
Total Cost of Production, January 1–April 30		$192,500
Less: Cost of Goods Completed[1]		133,000
Goods in Process, April 30, Lost in Explosion		$ 59,500

[1] *Cost of Goods Completed* (four months ended April 30, 19X1):

Finished Goods Inventory, April 30	$ 45,000
Cost of Goods Sold[†]	168,000
Total Available	$213,000
Less: Finished Goods Inventory, January 1, 19X1	80,000
Cost of Goods Completed in 19X1	$133,000

[†] *Cost of Goods Sold* (four months ended April 30, 19X1):
Computation of Gross Profit Percentage, past three years

$$\frac{\text{Gross profits past three years}}{\text{Sales profits past three years}} = \frac{\$285,000}{\$950,000} = 30\%$$

Computation of cost of goods sold (four months 19X1).
The cost of goods sold percentage is 70% (100 − 30%). Therefore,

SALES × COST OF GOODS SOLD % = COST OF GOODS SOLD
$240,000   70% $168,000

9.9. The Essex Company, a partnership, has the following inventory information on its books:

	Year Ended December 31, 19X1	Six Months Ended June 30 19X2
Sales (net)	$550,000	$300,000
Beginning inventory	190,500	160,500
Purchases	321,750	155,500
Transportation-in	45,000	25,000
Purchases returns	11,000	3,500
Purchases discounts	9,000	4,500
Ending inventory	160,500	
Selling expenses	75,000	35,000
General expenses	50,000	28,000

Prepare an income statement for the six-month period.

SOLUTION

Gross Profit 19X1

			Amount	Percent
Sales			$550,000	100.0%
Cost of Goods Sold				
Beginning Inventory		$190,500		
Purchases	$321,750			
Transportation-in	45,000			
	$366,750			
Less: Returns and Discounts	20,000	346,750		
Available for Sale		$537,250		
Less: Ending Inventory		160,500	376,750	68.5%
Gross Profit			$173,250	31.5%

Inventory June 30, 19X2

Inventory Jan. 1, 19X2		$160,500	
Purchases	$155,500		
Transportation-in	25,000		
	$180,500		
Less: Returns and Discounts	8,000	172,500	
Available for Sale		$333,000	
Cost of Goods Sold			
($300,000 × 68.5%)		205,500	
Inventory, June 30, 19X2		$127,500	

Essex Company
Income Statement
Six Months Ended June 30, 19X2

Sales (net)			$300,000
Cost of Goods Sold			
Inventory, January 1, 19X2		$160,500	
Purchases	$155,500		
Transportation-in	25,000		
	$180,500		
Less: Returns and Discounts	8,000	172,500	
Available for Sale		$333,000	
Less: Inventory, June 30, 19X2		127,500	205,500
Gross Profit			$ 94,500

Less: *Operating Expenses*		
Selling Expenses	$ 35,000	
General Expenses	28,000	$ 63,000
Net Income		$ 31,500

9.10. The Gridelli Confectionery Company uses a process cost system in its operations. For the month of June, direct labor was $10,000, and factory overhead was $12,500. Materials cost $2.75 per unit and are put into production at the beginning of the process. On June 1 there were 1,500 units, 60% completed as to direct labor and overhead. On June 30 there were 1,000 units 70% completed as to direct labor and overhead. During the month there were 15,200 units completed.

What is the cost of the goods in process at June 30?

SOLUTION

Equivalent Units Completed in June	
Beginning Goods in Process (1,500 × 40%)	600
Units Started and Completed in June	
(15,200 − 1,500)	13,700
Ending Goods in Process (1,000 × 70%)	700
Equivalent Full Units for the Month	15,000
Cost of Goods in Process, June 30	
Materials (1,000 × $2.75)	$2,750
Direct Labor and Factory Overhead	
(1,000 × 70% × $1.50)*	1,050
Total Cost of Goods in Process at June 30	$3,800
* Direct Labor and Overhead Per Unit	
($22,500 ÷ 15,000)	$1.50

9.11. From Problem 9.10, assume, for finished goods, no beginning inventory and an ending inventory of 1700 units at June 30. Assume further that the May cost structure for materials and overhead was identical to that in June. For the month of June, compute (a) unit and total production costs, (b) the finished goods ending inventory value, and (c) the cost of goods sold.

SOLUTION

(a)

	Production Cost	Equivalent Units	Unit Cost
Materials (units begun in June)	$40,425	14,700*	$2.75
Direct labor and factory overhead	22,500	15,000	1.50
Total production costs	$62,925		$4.25

* 13,700 units completed plus 1,000 units in ending inventory.

(b)

Finished Goods Inventory, June 30 (1,700 × $4.25)	$ 7,225

(c)

Cost of Goods Sold, June:	
Goods in Process, June 1[1] (1,500 units)	$ 5,475
Production Costs, Month of June	62,925
Total Cost of Goods in Process	$68,400
Less: Goods in Process, June 30 (1,000 units)	3,800
Cost of Goods Completed	$64,600
Less: Finished Goods Inventory, June 30 (1,700 units)	7,225
Cost of Goods Sold in June (13,500 units)	$57,375

[1] Materials (1,500 × $2.75)	$4,125	
Overhead (1,500 × 60% × $1.50)	1,350	
Goods in Process, June 1	$5,475	

Examination II
Chapters 5-9

Part I. *Circle T for true, F for false.*

1. T F Postage, IOUs and postdated checks are included as cash items.

2. T F Idle cash includes funds that are kept in the company vault and are not used.

3. T F The collection of an account written off in a previous year is ordinarily a debit to Accounts Receivable and a credit to Retained Earnings under the accrual method.

4. T F The customers account ledger should be maintained by someone who does not receive cash.

5. T F In a period of rising prices, the use of the LIFO inventory method tends to increase reported net income.

6. T F The moving-weighted-average method of determining inventory cost requires that goods received first should be moved out of storage first.

7. T F Equivalent full units represent the number of completed units that would have been produced if there had been no inventory at the beginning or end of the period.

8. T F Under the retail inventory method, the ending inventory amount is computed by multiplying the goods available for sale by the cost of goods sold.

9. T F A process cost system is generally used in manufacturing a homogeneous product.

10. T F Where two or more joint products are manufactured in a cost center, the costs are allocated to the products on the basis of relative cost values.

Part II. *Circle the letter identifying the best answer.*

1. The following item should be classified as cash on the balance sheet.
   a. cash in a special building account for construction
   b. blocked cash deposits in foreign banks
   c. demand deposit in a bank
   d. cash in an escrow account for purchase of property

2. Securities to be included as cash resources must:
   a. bolster business relations
   b. be held for control of a company
   c. be the company's own stock
   d. be readily salable

3. Which of the following methods of establishing and maintaining an Allowance for Uncollectible Accounts is not desirable? Basing the change or balance on:

    a. a percentage of sales

    b. an aged receivable trial balance

    c. a percentage of receivables balance

    d. a fixed dollar amount

4. An aging schedule disclosed that the Allowance for Uncollectible Accounts should be $4,000, even though there was a debit balance of $300 at the end of the period. What should be the amount of the adjustment? a. $4,300; b. $3,700; c. $4,000; d. $3,400.

5. The term *market* in inventory valuation means:

    a. the lower of cost or market

    b. the realizable value

    c. the price on the stock market

    d. the demand for the item

6. The percentage-of-completion method for recognizing profits on long-term contracts means that:

    a. profits are spread according to time periods

    b. a percentage of profits is held back until completion

    c. profits are related to the period in which the work is done

    d. a percentage of total contract price is withheld

7. Which of the following items should *not* be reported as part of inventory?

    a. goods sent to another plant for special processing

    b. goods in transit, FOB shipping point

    c. goods shipped out on consignment

    d. purchase orders outstanding

Part III. *Complete the following statements.*

1. The two forms used in reconciling bank accounts are (*a*) reconciling the _____ balance to the _____ balance and (*b*) reconciling both balances to a _____ balance.

2. An overdraft of the revolving fund account ____ be offset against a positive balance in the payroll account at the same bank.

3. Billing customers periodically by groups rather than altogether at the end of the month is called _____.

4. Shipments to sales agents are termed _____.

5. Shipments on the way but not yet received, with terms FOB shipping point should be _____ inventory; those with terms FOB destination should be _____ _____ inventory.

6. Deposits made by customers on long-term construction contracts is shown on the balance sheet as a _____.

7. Price indexes are generally used to arrive at inventory values under the _____ _____ method.

8. Under the retail method, a _____ is a reduction in the retail price after there has been an additional markup.

9. The gross profit test is generally more accurate when applied to _____ of inventory.

10. Dollar-value LIFO is most suited to companies having a _____ of items and a large _____ of shipments.

Part IV.   *Solve the following problems.*

1. The bank statement of the Brown Company disclosed a bank balance of $6,872.41 at July 31, 19X1, while the book balance at that date was $5,895.07. The following information was obtained from the records:

   (a) Check #102 for $238.25 was recorded on the books as $328.25.

   (b) R. Harter's note for $1,050, including interest, was collected by the bank and a collection charge of $5.00 deducted.

   (c) The following checks were outstanding on July 31:
   #106, $85.70; #107, $425,17; #108, $157.31; #109, $638.47.

   (d) The bank account had been charged $275.70 for an NSF check from customer James Smith.

   (e) Receipts of $1,175.20 for July 31 were deposited August 1.

   (f) Bank service charges for June were $13.41.

   Prepare a bank reconciliation at July 31, 19X1, using the form in which both bank and book balances are carried to a corrected cash balance.

2. The Barclay Company has just sold a used piece of heavy equipment for $10,000. A down payment of $1,000 is received and three notes of $3,000 each, at no interest, are due at the end of each of the next three years. The fair rate of interest is 10%. The equipment originally cost $15,000 and had a book value of $5,000 at date of sale.

   Prepare the entry for the recording of the sale as recommended in APB Opinion No. 21.

3. The Whyte Knight Company had inventory and purchases for the year as follows:

	Units	Cost	Amount
Inventory, January 1	2,000	$2.00	$ 4,000
Purchase No. 1	1,000	2.50	2,500
Purchase No. 2	1,500	2.75	4,125
Purchase No. 3	1,500	2.85	4,275
Purchase No. 4	2,000	3.00	6,000
	8,000		$20,900

The physical inventory count at December was 3,000 units. Compute the cost of the December 31 inventory based on the following inventory methods: (a) FIFO, (b) LIFO, and (c) Average Cost.

4. The Payne Company values its inventory by the retail method. The pertinent information for 19X1 is as follows:

	Cost	Retail
Inventory, January 1	$11,500	$15,750
Purchases	30,500	46,250
Net markups		8,000
Net markdowns		6,000
Sales		42,000
Inventory, December 31		22,000

Compute the inventory cost at December 31, using the conventional method.

Answers to Examination II

Part I

1. F, 2. F, 3. F, 4. T, 5. F, 6. F, 7. T, 8. F, 9. T, 10. F

Part II

1. c, 2. d, 3. d, 4. a, 5. b, 6. c, 7. d

Part III

1. (a) bank, book; (b) corrected; 2. can; 3. cycle billing; 4. consignments; 5. included in, excluded from; 6. liability; 7. dollar-value LIFO; 8. markup cancellation; 9. classes; 10. wide variety, number.

Part IV

1.
Brown Company
Bank Reconciliation
July 31, 19X1

Balance per Bank Statement, July 31, 19X1		*$6,872.41*
Add: Deposit in Transit, Receipts of July 31		*1,175.20*
Deduct: Outstanding Checks, #106, $85.70; #107, $425.17		*$8,047.61*
#108, $157.31; and #109, $638.47		*1,306.65*
Corrected Bank Balance		*$6,740.96*
Balance per Books		*$5,895.07*
Add: Error in Recording Check #102 ($328.25 − $238.25)	*$ 90.00*	
Collection of R. Harter's Note, Bank Fee: $5.00	*1,045.00*	*1,135.00*
		$7,030.07
Deduct: NSF Check, James Smith	*$ 275.70*	
Bank Service Charges	*13.41*	*289.11*
Corrected Book Balance		*$6,740.96*

2.   **Entry**

Cash	1,000.00
Notes Receivable*	7,460.54
Accumulated Depreciation Equipment	10,000.00
Equipment	15,000.00
Gain on Sale of Equipment	3,460.54

* Present value of notes:

Year 1 $3,000.00 \div 1.10 = \$2,727.27
Year 2 $2,727.27 \div 1.10 = 2,479.33
Year 3 $2,479.33 \div 1.10 = \underline{2,253.94}
                                     $7,460.54

<u>Present Value Method</u> (a shorter method)

Amount of annual notes	$3,000.00
Present value of ordinary annuity	
of $1 at 10% interest for three periods	2.4869
Present value of three notes (2.4869 × 3)	$7,460.70

* The slight difference of $0.16 is due to rounding
off of figures in annuity table.

3.   (a) **FIFO:** *$8,850 [(2,000 @ $3.00) + (1,000 @ $2.85) = $6,000 + $2,850]*

     (b) **LIFO:** *$6,500 [(2,000 @)$2.00) + (1,000 @ $2.50) = $4,000 + $2,500]*

     (c) **Average Cost:** *$7,830 [(3,000 @)$2.61), from ($20,900 \div 8,000 = $2.61)]*

4.

	Cost	Retail
Cost ($11,500 + $30,500)	$42,000	
Retail ($15,750 + $46,250 + 8,000)		$70,000
Goods Available for Sale	$42,000	$70,000

Cost to retail percentage: $42,000 \div $70,000 = 60%
Inventory, December 31; at cost: $22,000 × 0.60 = $13,200

Chapter 10

Plant and Equipment:
Acquisition and Retirement

10.1 NATURE OF PLANT AND EQUIPMENT

Plant and equipment refers to those long-lived assets acquired for use in the operation of a business and not for resale. These assets may also be called *fixed assets*; *property, plant and equipment*; *plant assets,* etc. They have physical existence, as distinguished from intangible assets, and are usually subject to depreciation. These assets turn over less frequently than current assets and are usually shown as a separate grouping among noncurrent assets.

The allocation of the cost of plant and equipment over the periods which receive benefits is discussed in Chapter 11, Plant and Equipment: Depreciation and Depletion. Assets of an intangible nature such as patents and goodwill are discussed in Chapter 12, Intangibles.

10.2 CLASSIFICATION OF PLANT AND EQUIPMENT

The classification most frequently found in financial statements is *land, buildings* and *equipment.*

Land. Unlike other classes of plant and equipment, land ordinarily does not deteriorate or become physically exhausted through use. Thus it is a nondepreciable asset. This category includes building sites, yards and parking areas. The cost of land incorporates all expenditures necessary to acquire and make the land ready for use (e.g. the purchase price, attorney's fees and recording fees incurred in obtaining title; also, expenses for razing, grading, draining or clearing the property). Assessments made for city permits, street lights, sewers and similar local improvements are also part of land costs.

Any receipts from salvage, sale of timber, etc. are considered reductions in land cost. Owner improvements such as landscaping, private driveways, walks, parking lots, etc. are best separated and shown as Land Improvements since they have limited life and are subject to depreciation. Finally, land held for future use is carried under *investments,* not plant and equipment, until it is used in current business operations.

Buildings. The cost of buildings includes all expenditures related to their acquisition or construction. When buildings are purchased, the cost includes the contract purchase price, the cost of remodeling for purposes of the owner, unpaid taxes assumed and various legal costs and closing fees. When buildings are constructed, the cost includes architects' and engineers' fees, cost of materials, labor and overhead, permit and license fees, etc. Financing costs, such as interest accrued and bond discount amortized during construction, may be included in cost.

Machinery and Equipment.   This category includes factory machinery and equipment, office machinery and equipment, furniture and fixtures, delivery equipment, etc. Its acquisition costs include any transportation costs, sales taxes, transit insurance, installation costs and, sometimes, breaking-in costs.

Machinery and equipment is generally subdivided for control purposes, and subsidiary ledgers may be established to provide cost allocation records (i.e. for maintenance, depreciation, etc.) by group. When this is done, individual records are identified by means of a fixed asset number (usually a metal tag or decal affixed to the asset item).

10.3   CAPITAL VERSUS REVENUE EXPENDITURES

An expenditure that benefits operations beyond the current period is a *capital expenditure,* and is included in the cost of the asset. Such expenditures are said to be *capitalized.* An expenditure that benefits only the current period is a *revenue expenditure,* that is, it is applied against current revenue and is an expense. It is important that capital and revenue expenditures be properly distinguished. For example, if a capital item (such as a machine costing $200) is charged to expense, *net income is understated.* If an expenditure is capitalized rather than charged to expense, *net income is overstated.* In the latter case, there should have been more expense and less net income.

In order to avoid the effort involved in depreciating items of small amount, most companies set an arbitrary limit on items to be capitalized. For example, if the limit were $100, an item costing $50 would be expensed. Such an amount is immaterial and would not distort net income for the period.

ACQUISITION OF PLANT AND EQUIPMENT

10.4   MEANS OF ACQUISITION

Plant and equipment may be acquired for cash, by noncash considerations or by exchange.

Cash Acquisitions.   Under this basis, plant and equipment is valued at cost, including all expenditures to make the asset ready for use, less any cash discounts.

EXAMPLE 1.

The Joseph Marcketta Company is considering the purchase of a machine priced at $3,000. Payment may be made as follows: (1) if paid within 10 days, a 2% discount is allowed; (2) if paid within 60 days the quoted price is payable, or (3) a down payment of $300 may be made and the balance paid in 12 monthly installments of $275. The entry for each type of payment is:

Entry 1	*Machinery*	*2,940*	
	Cash		*2,940*
Entry 2	*Machinery*	*2,940*	
	Discounts Lost	*60*	
	Accounts Payable		*3,000*
Entry 3	*Machinery*	*2,940*	
	Discount Lost	*60*	
	Interest Expense	*600*	
	Cash		*300*
	Installment Contracts Payable		*3,300*

EXAMPLE 2.

Mr. William Hankinson purchased land and contracted to have a building constructed. The expenditures made were as follows: land, $25,000; legal fees at closing of land title, $400; title insurance, $300; building contract, $200,000; architect's fees, $1,500; construction insurance, $1,000; assessment for street and sidewalk, $3,500; property taxes prior to construction, $1,300; interest on construction loan, $2,000. The cost of (1) land and (2) building is calculated below.

(1) Cost of Land

Land	$ 25,000
Street and sidewalk	3,500
Property taxes prior to construction	1,300
Legal fees	400
Title insurance	300
Total	$ 30,500

(2) Cost of Building

Building contract	$200,000
Construction insurance	1,000
Architect's fees	1,500
Interest on construction loan	2,000
Total	$204,500

Noncash Acquisitions. When plant and equipment is acquired by means of noncash considerations such as stocks, bonds or a trade-in, the value is the fair market value of the consideration given, or the fair market value of the asset acquired, whichever is more clearly evident. If there is a difference between the fair market value of the consideration given up and its book value, it should be recognized as a gain or loss on the exchange.

EXAMPLE 3.

The Dale Adams Company exchanged 1,000 shares of its common stock for a building site. The company's stock, par value $25, was selling on the market at $30 a share. The entry to record the acquisition is

Land	30,000	
Common Stock		25,000
Premium on Common Stock		5,000

EXAMPLE 4.

The William Smith Company has decided to trade in a large color machine for a later model. The old machine cost $14,000 and has accumulated depreciation of $8,000. The new machine costs $18,000 before the trade-in allowance of $8,000 and payment of the balance. (1) Give the entry to record the transaction, and (2) show the cost basis of the new equipment for income tax purposes.

(1)	Machinery	18,000	
	Accumulated Depreciation, Machinery	8,000	
	Machinery		14,000
	Gain on Trade-in		2,000
	Cash		10,000

Gain on trade-in, $2,000 ($8,000 − $6,000 book value, [$14,000 − $8,000])

(2)	Book value of old equipment ($14,000 − $8,000)	$ 6,000
	Cash paid	10,000
	Total	$16,000

10.5 GROUP PURCHASES

When two or more assets are purchased for a lump-sum price (sometimes called a *basket purchase*), it is necessary to separate the amount into proper classifications for accounting purposes and computation of depreciation. For example, for a land/building purchase, the amount allocated to land would not be subject to depreciation. Generally, allocation of cost is based on appraised values, tax assessments or market values. The following example illustrates an apportionment based on appraised values.

EXAMPLE 5.

For $40,000, Mr. William Englefield purchased property that included the site, a building, and productive machinery. The assets were appraised as follows: land, $5,000; building, $30,000; and machinery, $15,000. The apportionment of cost and the journal entry are as follows:

APPORTIONMENT OF COST

Assets	Appraisal	%	Cost
Land	$ 5,000	10	$ 4,000
Building	30,000	60	24,000
Machinery	15,000	30	12,000
	$50,000	100	$40,000

JOURNAL ENTRY

Land	4,000	
Building	24,000	
Machinery	12,000	
Cash		40,000

10.6 LEASEHOLD IMPROVEMENTS

In the previous sections, assets owned by the business or individual were discussed. This section is concerned with assets that are owned by someone else, the *lessor*, and leased to the business, the *lessee*. Any improvements made by the lessee usually remain with the property and thus are amortized over the remaining life of the lease. Where the lease is subject to renewal at the option of the lessee, the amortization period may be extended, but not beyond the normal life of the improvement. In many cases the improvements are written off over the first lease, since additional improvements may be required during the renewal period.

EXAMPLE 6.

The Robert Strauss Company leases a building for ten years and makes improvements including partitions, counters, display shelves, etc. costing $12,000. The journal entries to record (1) the asset and (2) the annual amortization are as follows:

Entry 1	Leasehold Improvements	12,000	
	Cash		12,000
Entry 2	Amortization of Leasehold Improvements (expense)	1,200	
	Leasehold Improvements		1,200

10.7 SELF-CONSTRUCTED ASSETS

Companies often construct their own buildings or special machinery. They may have a group of maintenance employees who can be used to construct assets as time permits and/or the cost and quality of the construction may be better controlled.

Accounting problems arise in determining which costs should be allocated to the self-constructed project. Costs that can be specifically identified with the project or would not have otherwise been incurred should be included in cost (capitalized). Generally, direct costs of this nature include material, labor, architect and engineering fees, etc. Factory overhead costs are more difficult to determine. How much heat, power, light, insurance, depreciation, property taxes, etc. should be assigned to construction? There are three principal ways of treating this problem:

(1) *Apply no overhead.* Generally this treatment is not realistic since there is at least some overhead incurred because of the construction.

(2) *Apply a portion of all overhead.* Under this treatment total factory overhead is related to total output (i.e. allocated proportionately to production cost and to construction cost).

(3) *Apply only incremental costs.* Under this treatment only costs which have increased because of construction are included, since fixed costs would have been incurred anyway. Generally this treatment does not distort the amount of overhead ordinarily applied to normal production, as (1) and (2) may do.

10.8 DEFERRED PAYMENT CONTRACTS

Plant and equipment are often purchased on long-term installment contracts (covering periods of from two or three years to ten or more). If the item has a cash purchase price, that is the cost to be used rather than the sum of the installment payments. If an interest rate is stipulated, then the cost is the present value of the future payments. Where no interest is stipulated or where the rate is unreasonably low, the interest is *imputed* and must be excluded from the cost of the item as required by APB Opinion No. 21, *Interest on Receivables and Payables.* Following are examples of the acquisition of assets (1) for cash and (2) under deferred payment contracts.

EXAMPLE 7.

The Edward Bates Company could buy a grinding machine at a stated price of (1) $3,000 (a similar machine could be bought from another dealer for $2,575 cash) or (2) with three payments of $1,000 at the end of each year, with interest at 8%.

(1) Entry at Acquisition — Cash. If immediate payment is to be made the entry is

Machinery	2,575	
Cash		2,575

(2) Entry at Acquisition — Installment Payment. If payments are to be made in installments, the amount to be recorded as cost is the present value of the installments. The present value table of an ordinary annuity shows that the present value of an annuity of $1 at 8%, payable in three annual installments, is $2.57710 (see Appendix, Table 2). The appropriate entry is

Machinery	2,577.10	
Installment Contracts Payable		2,577.10

Entries for Annual Payments. With reference to the table below, the payments of $1,000 each year are apportioned to interest expense and principal as follows. The interest rate (8%) is applied to the opening principal amount, $2,577.10, to find the interest expense in the first year ($206.17). Subtracting from $1,000, the payment balance, $793.83, is then applied against the principal ($2,577.10), reducing it to $1,783.27. The interest rate of 8% applied to $1,783.27 is $142.66 (the interest expense for the second year) and the payment balance of $857.34 is applied against the principal, reducing it to $925.93. Then, 8% of $925.93 (or $74.07) is the interest for the third year and the payment balance is $925.93. Note that the table columns show the total amount paid, the total interest, the total of payment balances and the present value.

TABLE OF INSTALLMENT PAYMENTS

Payable in Three Installments of $1,000 each

Year	Annual Payments	Interest Expense	Principal	
			Payments	Balance
Beginning				$2,577.10
1	$1,000.00	$206.17	$ 793.83	1,783.27
2	1,000.00	142.66	857.34	925.93
3	1,000.00	74.07	925.93	—0—
Total	$3,000.00	$422.90	$2,577.10	—0—

The entries for each year are as follows:

Year 1	Interest Expense	206.17	
	Installment Contracts Payable	793.83	
	Cash		1,000.00
Year 2	Interest Expense	142.66	
	Installment Contracts Payable	857.34	
	Cash		1,000.00
Year 3	Interest Expense	74.07	
	Installment Contracts Payable	925.93	
	Cash		1,000.00

10.9 DONATIONS OF PROPERTY

When cities make gifts of plant and equipment in order to attract industry to the area and provide jobs for the citizens, the donation must be recorded. If there is no cost to use as a basis of value, then the entry is recorded at the fair market value of the asset(s) donated. Depreciation should be taken in the same manner as if the property were purchased.

EXAMPLE 8.

The Adams Roofing Company received from Boca Raton land worth $50,000 and a specially constructed plant worth $150,000 as a gift for locating in that city. The donation was contingent on the company employing 300 people for the next five years. The journal entry to record the donation is

Land	50,000	
Building	150,000	
Donated Capital		200,000

10.10 INVESTMENT CREDIT

For income tax purposes, an investment tax credit of 7% is allowed by the Federal government against the cost of depreciable property other than buildings and components. The company is entitled to 7% reduction in its tax bill while the total cost of the asset may be depreciated for tax purposes over its life. Two methods may be used to record the investment credit:

(1) *Flow-through Method.*   This method reduces income tax expense by the amount of the investment credit in the year of purchase.   Immediate tax reduction is allowed, which is the intent of the law.

(2) *Deferred Method.*   The benefit of the tax credit is spread over the life of the asset, thereby reducing its effective cost.

EXAMPLE 9.

Corporate Management, Incorporated purchased a teletype machine for $50,000 and was eligible for an investment tax credit of $3,500.   The machine had a useful life of seven years and no salvage value; straight-line depreciation was planned.   In the year of purchase, the company had net taxable income of $25,000.   Assuming a 50% tax rate, the entry *to record payments of taxes* is as follows under (1) the flow-through method and (2) the deferred method.

Method 1	*Income Tax Expense*	*9,000*	
	Cash		*9,000*
Method 2	*Income Tax Expense*	*12,500*	
	Cash		*9,000*
	Deferred Investment Credit		*3,500*
	Deferred Investment Credit	*500*	
	Income Tax Expense		*500*

In the following year, with net taxable income at $25,000, the entries under the two methods are

Method 1	*Income Tax Expense*	*12,500*	
	Cash		*12,500*
Method 2	*Income Tax Expense*	*12,000*	
	Deferred Investment Credit	*500*	
	Cash		*12,500*

EXPENDITURES DURING SERVICE LIFE

10.11 ADDITIONS

The construction of an *addition* (i.e. a new wing or enlargement of an existing building) is considered an acquisition of new property.   The principal accounting problem occurs when a new addition causes a change in the old asset.   For example, a new addition might overload the air-conditioning system, requiring a new unit with a larger capacity.   Any loss on the old unit being retired (i.e. the difference between cost and accumulated depreciation) should be treated as an expense of the current period, not as an added cost of the new unit.

10.12 IMPROVEMENTS AND REPLACEMENTS

These expenditures add to the service life of the plant assets.   Generally the cost of the old unit, including accumulated depreciation, is removed from the books and the cost of new asset is added.   However, when the costs incurred represent modification rather than substitution of an asset, there may be a charge to Accumulated Depreciation or the asset account which, in effect, increases the asset's net book value.

10.13 REARRANGEMENTS

Very often it is desirable to rearrange certain machines or overall plant layout for increased efficiency.   Such costs should be recorded in a separate asset account and amortized over the benefitting periods on a short-term basis, since it may be necessary to make further rearrangements.

10.14   MAINTENANCE

Maintenance expenses are ordinary recurring expenditures made to maintain assets in operating condition.   Since they do not improve the asset or extend its life, they *should not* be capitalized.

RETIREMENT OF PLANT AND EQUIPMENT

10.15   RETIREMENT PROCEDURES

When use of an asset is discontinued, there are two steps to be taken to compute any gain or loss and complete the accounting entries: (1) bring the amount of depreciation taken up to the date of retirement and (2) remove the asset amount and its accumulated depreciation from the books.

EXAMPLE 10.

On July 10, 1975, the Thomas Costello Company sold for $1,850 a machine it had bought on January 8, 1969 for $5,000. The machine had been depreciated on the straight-line method at 10% a year. The entries to record (1), the depreciation for the current year and (2), the gain on the sale follow.

Entry 1	*Depreciation Expense*	*250*	
	Accumulated Depreciation, Machinery		*250*
	To record six months' depreciation on		
	machine sold ($5,000 × 10% × ½).		
Entry 2	*Cash*	*1,850*	
	*Accumulated Depreciation, Machinery**	*3,250*	
	Gain on Disposal of Machinery		*100*
	Machinery		*5,000*
	To record disposal of machine.		

* Accumulated Depreciation, $3,250 (5,000 × 10% × 6½). The month of purchase and month of sale were not included in computing the time period since both transactions occurred in the first half of the month. For practical purposes many companies do not split months in determining acquisition or retirements of plant and equipment. If an item is purchased before the 15th it will carry depreciation for that month; if purchased on the 15th or after, no depreciation will be taken for that month. The reverse situation would be the case where an item is sold.

According to APB Opinion No. 30, the gain or loss from disposal of machinery as shown above is to be included in income before extraordinary items. *It is not to be considered an extraordinary item.*

10.16   TRADE-INS

When a new asset is purchased by trading in an old asset as partial payment, accounting questions arise concerning the values of the assets exchanged and recognition of a gain or loss on the old asset's disposal.   These may be resolved by valuing the old asset at (1) book value, (2) trade-in allowance or (3) fair market value.

Book Value.   When the book value of the old asset (cost − accumulated depreciation) is used, the valuation basis for the new asset is *the book value of the old asset plus the balance paid in cash.*   This method is required for income tax purposes and is widely used.

Trade-in Allowance.   When the trade-in allowance is used as the value of the old asset, the gain or loss is equal to the difference between book value and trade-in value for the old asset, and the value of the new asset is *the trade-in allowance plus the balance paid*. Since the price of the new asset is frequently inflated to allow for a higher trade-in allowance than would otherwise be the case, this basis should be used only in the absence of more reliable values.

Fair Market Value. This basis recognizes any difference between fair market and book value as a gain or loss. The new asset is recorded at *the fair market value plus the balance paid.*

The three methods described above are illustrated in the following example.

EXAMPLE 11.

The Robert Strauss Company wants to trade in an old machine for a more efficient, later model. The values relating to the old asset are: (a) book value, $8,000, (b) trade-in allowance, $9,000 and (c) fair market value, $8,500. The new asset is priced at $20,000 and the balance to be paid in cash is $11,000.

(a) Under the *book value method*, the new asset is valued at the book value of the old asset plus the cash balance. Thus, it would be recorded at $19,000 ($8,000 + $11,000). No gain or loss would be recognized on the old asset.

(b) Under the *trade-in allowance method*, the new asset would be recorded at the trade-in allowance plus the balance paid. Since the trade-in allowance exceeds the book value, there would be a gain on the old asset, in this case, $1,000 ($9,000 − $8,000) and the new asset would be recorded at $20,000 ($9,000 + $11,000).

(c) Under the *fair market value method* the new asset would be recorded at the fair market value of the old asset plus the cash balance. In this case, it would be $19,500 ($8,500 + $11,000). There would be a gain on the old asset of the difference between fair market value and book value, in this case, $500 ($9,000 − $8,500).

Summary

(1) The major classifications of plant and equipment are _____, _____ and _____ _____.

(2) Expenditures that benefit future periods are termed _____ expenditures; those that benefit only the current period are termed _____ expenditures.

(3) Plant and equipment assets are recorded at _____ plus any expenditures necessary to prepare the asset for the purpose intended.

(4) Plant and equipment assets of more than one class purchased for a lump-sum price are called _____ purchases.

(5) When an asset is retired, there are generally two accounting steps to be taken: bring the _____ record up to date of retirement, and remove _____ _____ and _____ from the books.

(6) Plant assets are sometimes termed (a) short-term assets, (b) intangible assets, (c) a bundle of services, (d) a bundle of bricks.

(7) Cash discounts on purchased equipment (a) increase expense, (b) decrease asset cost, (c) decrease expenses, (d) increase asset cost.

(8)   Expenditures made to maintain assets in operating condition are (*a*) expensed, (*b*) capitalized, (*c*) suspensed, (*d*) debited to assets.

(9)   Which of the following is *not* part of the cost of production equipment?   (*a*) invoice price, (*b*) freight, (*c*) breaking-in costs, (*d*) interest on installment contract.

(10)   The cost to be recorded for a new machine purchased on an installment contract is (*a*) list price, (*b*) quoted price, (*c*) sum of the installment payments, (*d*) present value of the future payments.

Answers: (1) land, buildings and equipment; (2) capital, revenue; (3) cost; (4) group; (5) depreciation, the asset amount, accumulated depreciation: (6) *c*; (7) *b*; (8) *a*; (9) *d*; (10) *d*.

Solved Problems

10.1.   The Seiden Company is considering the purchase of equipment priced at $12,000. The manufacturer has offered the company three different financing plans. Prepare the initial entry for each of the following types of payment: (*a*) terms of 2/10, n/30; (*b*) payment at the end of thirty days; (*c*) down payment of $1,000 and 12 monthly payments of $1,000 each.

SOLUTION

(*a*)	Equipment ($12,000 × 98%)	11,760	
	Accounts Payable		11,760
(*b*)	Equipment ($12,000 × 98%)	11,760	
	Discounts Lost (interest expense)	240	
	Accounts Payable		12,000
(*c*)	Equipment ($12,000 × 98%)	11,760	
	Discount on Equipment Contract	1,240	
	Cash		1,000
	Equipment Contract Payable		12,000

10.2.   The Armiente Corporation purchased a new machine costing $15,000 with a trade-in allowance of $4,000 on an old machine.   The old machine had cost $10,000 and had accumulated depreciation to date of $7,000.   Prepare the entries to record the purchase according to: (*a*) generally accepted accounting principles and (*b*) income tax regulations.

SOLUTION

(*a*)	Machinery	15,000	
	Accumulated Depreciation	7,000	
	Machinery		10,000
	Cash		11,000
	Gain on Disposal of Machinery		1,000

(b)

Machinery	14,000	
Accumulated Depreciation	7,000	
Machinery		10,000
Cash		11,000

10.3. The M. H. Reed Company purchased land with a fair market value of $100,000 for $50,000 cash and 2,000 shares of $20 par value unlisted common stock. Prepare the necessary journal entry.

SOLUTION

Land	100,000	
Cash		50,000
Common Stock, Par $20		40,000
Paid-in Capital		10,000

10.4. The Boca Raton Company acquired undeveloped land for $40,000 cash and 3,000 shares of $25 par value common stock, selling on a national exchange at $20 a share. Prepare the appropriate journal entry.

SOLUTION

Land	100,000	
Discount on Common Stock	15,000	
Cash		40,000
Common Stock, $25 Par		75,000

10.5. The Bedaux Company was organized in June 19X1 to manufacture noonies and construction of a plant was begun shortly. At December 31, 19X1 the plant construction account showed the following entries.

Date	Description	Dr.	Cr.
June 30	Land and old building	$150,000	
30	Organization expenses	6,000	
30	Bond discount (10 years)	2,000	
July 15	Title search fees	1,500	
15	Demolishing old building	3,000	
Aug. 31	Scrap sales from demolition		$500
Dec. 1	Salaries of company executives	5,500	
31	Contract cost of new building	350,000	
31	Bond interest, six months	3,500	
31	Property taxes		
	(six months ending 12/31)	1,800	
		$523,300	$500
Balance	$522,800		

ADDITIONAL DATA: The company executives performed no services in construction of the new building. The old building was valued at $25,000.

Prepare a compound entry closing out the plant construction account and charging the proper accounts.

SOLUTION

Land (land and old building)*	154,000	
Building	350,000	
Property Taxes	1,800	
Bond Interest	3,500	
Amortization of Discount	100	
Organization Expenses	6,000	
Executive Salaries	5,500	
Unamortized Bond Discount	1,900	
Plant Construction Account		522,800

To close out plant construction account.

Certain costs incurred prior to the start of operations such as taxes, interest, salaries and similar expenses may be charged to expense, as was shown above, or may be capitalized.

* In the entry above, land = $150,000 + $1,500 + $3,000 − $500 = $154,000. If property taxes were capitalized, the land amount would be $155,800 ($154,000 + $1,800) and if bond interest and discount amortizations were capitalized the building amount would be $353,600 ($350,000 + $3,500 + $100). A portion of the executives' salaries may be charged to organization expenses and written off over a reasonably short period.

10.6. The Gibbons Company purchased the plant and equipment of the Whyte Company for $45,000. The land had been purchased by the Whyte Company some years before for $3,000, but is now estimated to be worth $20,000. The building, which had cost the Whyte Company $20,000 and had accumulated depreciation of $18,000, will be replaced with a modern efficient manufacturing plant. Some of the equipment can be overhauled and used in the new building. Expected equipment expenditures will be $10,000 which will then give the equipment a value of $40,000. The equipment had originally cost $45,000 and had accumulated depreciation of $20,000.

Prepare journal entries to (a) record the purchase and (b) record the overhaul of the equipment.

SOLUTION

(a)

Land	15,000	
Equipment*	30,000	
Cash		45,000

PRORATION OF COST

Assets	Estimated Value	Ratio	Amount
Land	$20,000	1 / 3	$15,000
Equipment	40,000	2 / 3	30,000
	$60,000		$45,000

* NOTE: The value before expenditures of $10,000 were made. Book values on previous books are not relevant.

(b)

Equipment	10,000	
Cash		10,000

10.7. At the time the Nanco Company decided to begin production of several new products, the volume of production of its regular products was slow. The company therefore decided to build the needed new equipment with its own employees. Following are the construction costs recorded for the project at completion.

Consulting engineering services	$ 7,000
Subcontractor payments	18,000
Labor (ordinarily used in production)	60,000
Labor (ordinarily used in maintenance)	50,000
Materials	125,000
	$260,000

ADDITIONAL DATA: Maintenance labor represents the idle time of nonproduction employees who ordinarily would have been paid for the time.   Employee fringe benefits are approximately 30% of labor cost and are included in factory overhead costs of $3,335,000 for the year.   Factory overhead is approximately 60% variable and is applied on the basis of production labor cost. The regular products had total production labor cost of $4,300,000 for the year.   General and administrative expenses include $15,000 of executive salaries and $5,000 of supplies, telephone calls and miscellaneous costs applicable to the project.

(a) Prepare a schedule showing the *full cost* of the construction project.

(b) Prepare a schedule showing the *incremental cost* of the construction project.

SOLUTION

(a)

Cost of Constructing Equipment
Stated at Full Cost

Consulting Engineering Services	$ 7,000
Subcontractor Payments	18,000
Production Labor	60,000
Maintenance Labor	50,000
Executive Salaries	15,000
Materials	125,000
*Factory Overhead (75% × $60,000)**	45,000
Fringe Benefits, Maintenance (30% × $50,000)	15,000
Supplies, Telephone and Miscellaneous	5,000
	$340,000

*COMPUTATION OF FACTORY OVERHEAD RATE

Adjustment of Factory Overhead

Total Factory Overhead		$3,335,000
Less: Maintenance Labor Used	$50,000	
Fringe Benefits, Maint.	15,000	65,000
		$3,270,000

Total Production Labor

Regular Products	$4,300,000
Self-construction Project	60,000
	$4,360,000

Factory Overhead Rate

$3,270,000 ÷ $4,360,000 = 75%

(b)

Cost of Constructing Equipment
Stated at Incremental Cost

Consulting Engineering Services	$ 7,000
Subcontractor Payments	18,000
Production Labor	60,000
Materials	125,000
Factory Overhead (60% × $45,000)**	27,000
Supplies, Telephone and Miscellaneous	5,000
	$242,000

** 60% of full factory overhead.

10.8. On June 30, 19X1, William Gnad sold property to Frank Cheatum for $50,000. The property had originally cost Gnad $32,000 and had accumulated depreciation of $7,000. Gnad keeps his books on the cash basis; Cheatum on the accrual basis. The escrow statements at June 30, 19X1 show the following:

Gnad's Escrow Statement

Charges:	
Cash	$21,000
First Mortgage (assumed by buyer)	27,000
Commission	2,500
Title Fee	125
Deed Recording	20
Taxes (this year unpaid)	160
Lease Deposits	300
	$51,105
Credits:	
Sales Price	$50,000
Fire Insurance (prorated)	1,105
	$51,105

Cheatum's Escrow Statement

Charges:	
Sales Price	$50,000
Title Fee	125
Recording	20
Fire Insurance (prorated)	1,105
	$51,250
Credits:	
Deposit	$23,790
First Mortgage Assumed	27,000
Taxes for Year	160
Lease Deposits	300
	$51,250

(a) Determine the gain or loss on Gnad's books, and (b) prepare the appropriate entries for Gnad's and Cheatum's books.

SOLUTION

(a)

Gain on Gnad's books

Sale Price			$50,000
Less: Book Value			
Original Cost	$32,000		
Accumulated Depreciation	7,000	$25,000	
Expense of Sale			
Commission	$ 2,500		
Title Fee	125		
Deed	20	2,645	27,645
Gain on Sale			$22,355

(b)

Journal Entries on Gnad's books

Cash	21,000	
First Mortgage Receivable	27,000	
Accumulated Depreciation	7,000	
Lease Deposits*	300	
Property Expense	160	
Gain on Sale		22,355
Property		32,000
Insurance Expense		1,105
To record sale of property on June 30, 19X1.		

* Rental Revenue may have been credited at the time of receipt since the cash basis is being used. Just a debit to Rental Revenue would then be justified.

Journal Entries on Cheatum's books

Property ($50,000 + $125 + $20)	50,145	
Prepaid Insurance	1,105	
Deposit		23,790
Mortgage Payable		27,000
Lease Deposits Payable		300
Property Tax Payable		160
To record purchase of property on June 30, 19X1.		

10.9. James Allen is the owner of a factory building which was completed January 1, 19X1 at a cost of $135,000. The land cost $40,000. Depreciation has been recorded by the straight-line method, assuming a 45-year life and no salvage value. Allen's fiscal year ends on December 31, and his books are maintained on the cash basis. Allen sells the property to Brown for $200,000. Partial payment is by a deferred payment contract. Payments of $5,000 are to be made quarterly, plus accrued interest on the unpaid balance. The following information is given:

	ALLEN		BROWN	
	Charges	Credits	Charges	Credits
Selling Price		$200,000	$200,000	
Down Payment	$ 35,000			$ 35,000
First Mortgage (assumed by buyer)	73,000			73,000
Second Mortgage (assumed by buyer)	72,000			72,000

Prorations:

Real Estate Taxes		$ 600	$	600
Interest		625		625

Fees:

Escrow	$ 125			125
Legal Fees	75			150
Amount in Escrow Account				$ 21,500
Real Estate Commission	12,000			
Amount Due Seller	9,025			
	$201,225	$201,225	$201,500	$201,500

The sale took place on June 30, 19X6. The land value is 30% of the purchase price.

(*a*) Prepare the journal entries for the above transactions on Allen's books and determine his gain on the sale.

(*b*) Prepare the journal entries for the purchase on Brown's books.

SOLUTION

(*a*)   **Journal entries on Allen's books**

Depreciation Expense, Building	1,500	
Accumulated Depreciation, Building		1,500
To record depreciation to June 30, 19X6.		

Cash (from seller $35,000 + $9,025)	44,025	
Accumulated Depreciation	16,500	
First Mortgage Receivable	73,000	
Second Mortgage Receivable	72,000	
Building		135,000
Land		40,000
Real Estate Taxes		600
Interest Expense		625
Gain on Sale		29,300
To record sale of building and property.		

Determination of Gain on Sale

Selling Price			$200,000
Less: Book Value			
Building Cost	$135,000		
Accumulated Depreciation	16,500*	$118,500	
Land		40,000	
Sale Expenses:			
Escrow	$ 125		
Legal	75		
Commission	12,000	12,200	170,700
Gain on Sale			$ 29,300

* Depreciation on the building:

$$\frac{\$135,000}{45 \text{ years}} = \$3,000 \text{ per year}$$

$ 3,000	
× 5.5 yrs.	
$16,500	

(b)   **Journal entries on Brown's books**

Building	140,193	
Land	60,082	
Real Estate Taxes	600	
Interest Expense	625	
Cash		56,500
First Mortgage Payable		73,000
Second Mortgage Payable		72,000

To record purchase of building and land.

Allocation of costs:

Purchase Price		200,000
Fees		
Escrow	125	
Legal Fees	150	275
Total Costs		$200,275
Allocated: Building (70%)		$140,193
Land (30%)		60,082

10.10. A fire occurred at the Albertson Company warehouse on June 19, 19X2, destroying the office and a substantial part of the inventory. All accounting records at the warehouse were destroyed except the general ledger. The company ends its fiscal year December 31. The following balances were taken from the general ledger as of May 31, 19X2.

Accounts	Dr.	Cr.
Accounts Receivable	$300,000	
Inventory, Beginning	487,000	
Accounts Payable		$468,000
Sales		882,400
Purchases	656,000	

The company had insured the inventory under the following policies:

Insurance Company	Face Value	Coinsurance Requirement
Mason	$240,000	90%
Richfield	160,000	70%
Blue	80,000	—

ADDITIONAL DATA: (1) Inventory costing $256,000 was not damaged. (2) Repairs to the office cost $10,250. (3) Customers reported $236,000 owed to the company at the time of the fire. This was accepted as a fair amount. (4) Suppliers reported purchases of $57,600 for the period June 1 through June 19. (5) The bank statement for June revealed the following for the period June 1 through June 19: deposits of $192,200 ($181,600 from customers; $10,600 refund from a supplier), and disbursements of $93,275 ($64,000 for accounts payable; $16,000 purchases in May and $13,275 for miscellaneous expenses). (6) The cost of goods sold has averaged 55% of sales since the company began operations. The insurance companies have accepted this percentage for 19X2.

(a) Prepare a schedule showing the amount of inventory lost. (b) Determine the amount to be claimed from each insurance company. (c) Prepare a partial income statement showing the extraordinary gain or loss resulting from the fire.

SOLUTION

(a)   **Estimation of Inventory Lost**

Inventory, Beginning	$ 487,000
Purchases ($656,000 + $57,600 − $10,600)	703,000
Goods Available for Sale	$1,190,000
Less: Estimated Cost of Goods Sold	
($1,000,000 × 55%)*	550,000
Approximate Ending Inventory	$ 640,000
Less: Amount of Inventory Recovered	256,000
Cost of Inventory Lost	$ 384,000

(b)   **Recovery From Each Insurance Company**

Mason Company: $\dfrac{\$240,000}{0.9(\$640,000)} \times \$384,000 \ = \ \$160,000$

Richfield Company: Coinsurance formula does not apply since the amount of insurance ($480,000) exceeds the coinsurance requirement ($448,000).   Therefore,

$$\frac{160}{480} \times \$384,000 \ = \ \$128,000$$

Blue Company: $\dfrac{80}{480} \times \$384,000 \ = \ \$64,000$

Calculation of Sales through June 19

Sales (to May 31)		$882,400
Sales (6/1 to 6/19)		
Accounts Receivable, 6/19	$236,000	
Collected on Account, 6/1 to 6/19	181,600	
Subtotal	$417,600	
Less: Accounts Receivable, 5/31	300,000	117,600
Total Sales		$1,000,000

(c)   **Partial Income Statement**

Extraordinary Loss Due to Fire		
Inventory Not Covered by Insurance*	$32,000	
Repair of Office Not Covered by Insurance	10,250	
Total Amount of Loss	$42,250	

* Loss: $384,000 − $352,000 ($160,000 + $128,000 + $64,000)

Plant and Equipment: Depreciation and Depletion

DEPRECIATION

11.1 DEPRECIATION DEFINED

The accounting term *depreciation* refers to a process of *cost allocation*, not asset valuation. With respect to tangible assets such as plant and equipment, depreciation expenses reflect a decline in the asset's service potential over its useful life. The various depreciation methods are described in the following sections.

11.2 ACCOUNTING FOR DEPRECIATION

Assets are recorded at cost; the estimated accumulated depreciation is a contra or offset account. Thus *book value* as indicated in the balance sheet is the net of *cost less accumulated depreciation*.

The periodic entry for depreciation is a debit to an expense account (*an income statement item*) and a credit to Accumulated Depreciation (*a balance sheet item*). There should be a separate expense account and a separate accumulated depreciation account for each class of plant and equipment. For example,

Depreciation Expense, Buildings

    Accumulated Depreciation, Buildings

Depreciation Expense, Machinery and Equipment

    Accumulated Depreciation, Machinery and Equipment

Depreciation Expense, Furniture and Fixtures

    Accumulated Depreciation, Furniture and Fixtures

Each function of the business should be charged its proper share of depreciation. For example, if the sales department occupies 25% of the area of the building, it would be charged with 25% of the building depreciation expense. Generally, for assets such as machinery and equipment or furniture and fixtures, there would be separate groupings according to function (i.e. those assets used for production, those used for sales, and those used for general administrative purposes).

EXAMPLE 1.

On January 1, 19X1 Joseph Kelso, the proprietor of a small company, purchased two machines, one costing $9,500 and the other costing $4,500. The freight cost was $500 for each machine and the scrap value at the end of the ten-year service life was estimated at 10% of cost. The calculation of annual depreciation and the appropriate journal entry are shown below.

Cost of Machine	#1	#2
Invoice cost	$ 9,500	$4,500
Freight-in	500	500
	$10,000	$5,000
Less: scrap value (10%)	1,000	500
Depreciable amount	$ 9,000	$4,500
Annual depreciation (10 years)	$ 900	$ 450

Depreciation Expense, Machinery and Equipment	1,350	
Accumulated Depreciation, Machinery and Equipment		1,350

EXAMPLE 2.

Continuing with Example 1, assume that machine #1 was used by the sales department while machine #2 was used by the general administrative department. The annual depreciation entry would be

Sales Department, Depreciation	900	
General Administrative Department, Depreciation	450	
Accumulated Depreciation, Machinery and Equipment		1,350

11.3 ESTIMATING DEPRECIATION

In estimating the periodic expense for depreciation, there are three factors that must be considered:

(1) *Cost of the Asset.* Cost includes all expenditures related to the acquisition and preparation of the asset for use, i.e. transportation costs, installation costs, title fees, attorney fees, grading, etc. (See Section 10.2.)

(2) *Residual Value.* This is the estimated sales value, or scrap value, at the end of an asset's useful life. When the asset is expected to have significant value at the end of its projected service life (for example, when a company trades in equipment, such as automobiles, every two years), the residual value should be deducted from cost and the resulting *depreciable value* spread over the period of service (see Example 1). In practice, however, it may be difficult to estimate the residual value of an asset fifteen or twenty years hence, and in many cases, the residual value is minimal after offset by removal costs. In other cases, the cost of dismantling and removing an asset may even be greater than the residual value. In such instances, residual values may be ignored in computing periodic depreciation unless they are significant.

(3) *Service Life.* This is the period of time or output over which the depreciable cost is to be spread. The proper measure of an asset's service life is affected by both *physical* and *functional* factors. Physical factors relate to wear and tear due to use and deterioration, such as rust or rot due to the elements. Functional or economic factors such as obsolescence or inadequacy may dictate that an asset, although in good condition, should be replaced. For example, a new machine with greater production capacity may make present equipment obsolete.

11.4 METHODS OF DEPRECIATION

The depreciation method used should be the one which most equitably spreads asset cost over the periods of its use. There are four principal methods of depreciation: straight-line, sum-of-the-years'-digits, double-declining-balance, and units-of-output.

Straight-line Method.   Under this method, an equal portion of asset cost is allocated to each year of use. The annual charge is computed as follows:

$$\text{Annual Depreciation Charge} = \frac{\text{Cost} - \text{Residual Value}}{\text{Useful Life (years)}}$$

EXAMPLE 3.

The Hennessy Company purchased a machine for $6,000 with an expected life of four years. The residual or scrap value was expected to be $1,000. The annual depreciation rate is 25%. From

$$\frac{\$6,000 - \$1,000}{4} = \$1,250 \text{ per year}$$

the entry to record annual depreciation is

Depreciation Expense, Machinery	1,250	
Accumulated Depreciation, Machinery		1,250

Sum-of-the-Years'-Digits Method.   This is one of two accelerated methods under which a greater amount is depreciated in the early years of the asset's life. The annual amounts are based on a series of fractions having the sum of the years' digits as the common denominator. The largest digit is used as the numerator for the first year, the next largest digit for the second year, etc.

EXAMPLE 4.

We may use the same data as above for the Hennessy Company: cost of machine, $6,000; residual value, $1,000; useful life, 4 years. The denominator (the sum of the years' digits) is: $1 + 2 + 3 + 4 = 10$. The fraction each year, *applied in reverse order* to the depreciable amount of $5,000, is

Year	Fraction		Amount	Depreciation
1	4/10	×	$5,000	$2,000
2	3/10	×	5,000	1,500
3	2/10	×	5,000	1,000
4	1/10	×	5,000	500
			Total	$5,000

The entry for the first year is

Depreciation Expense, Machinery	2,000	
Accumulated Depreciation, Machinery		2,000

The entry for the second year is

Depreciation Expense, Machinery	1,500	
Accumulated Depreciation, Machinery		1,500

Note that this method, for this particular case, permits depreciation of 40% ($2,000 ÷ $5,000) in the first year and 30% ($1,500 ÷ $5,000) in the second year. Thus, in two years, or half the life of the asset, 70% of the asset's cost is written off.

Declining-Balance Method. The declining-balance method is the other of the two accelerated methods. Under this method a *fixed rate* is applied to the *declining book value* of the asset each year, and estimated residual value is ignored. As the book value declines, the depreciation charge becomes smaller and the book value at the end of the period becomes the scrap value. For Federal income tax purposes, certain assets may be depreciated under this method at double the straight-line rate.

EXAMPLE 5.

From Example 3, the Hennessy Company's straight-line rate of 25% would be doubled to 50%. This fixed rate would be applied to the declining balance of the asset as follows:

Year	Book Value	Rate	Depreciation
1	$6,000	50%	$3,000
2	3,000	50%	1,500
3	1,500	50%	750
4	750	50%	375
		Total	$5,625

The book value $375 ($6,000 − $5,625) at the end of the fourth year becomes the scrap value.

The entry for the first year is

| Depreciation Expense, Machinery | 3,000 | |
| Accumulated Depreciation, Machinery | | 3,000 |

The entry for the second year is

| Depreciation Expense, Machinery | 1,500 | |
| Accumulated Depreciation, Machinery | | 1,500 |

Under this method, 50% ($3,000 ÷ $6,000) of the Hennessy Company's asset cost is written off in the first year and 25% ($1,500 ÷ $6,000) is written off in the second year. Thus, in the first half of the asset's life, 75% of cost is written off.

Units-of-Output Method. For some assets (such as production machines, trucks, and other mobile equipment), the units of output (i.e. number of units of production or miles driven) may be a more logical method of depreciation. This method is particularly suitable where there is a wide difference in use of the asset each year. Its depreciation equations are

$$\text{Unit Depreciation} = \frac{\text{Cost} - \text{Residual Value}}{\text{Estimated Units of Output during Lifetime}}$$

and

$$\text{Annual Depreciation} = \text{Total Units of Output per Year} \times \text{Unit Depreciation}$$

An important advantage of this method is that the depreciation expense is directly related to income. The more units produced, the more income and the more depreciation expense is charged.

EXAMPLE 6.

Assume that the asset of the Hennessy Company is a truck which is expected to have a life of 100,000 miles. The unit depreciation cost would be

$$\frac{\$6,000 - \$1,000}{100,000 \text{ miles}} = \$0.05 \text{ per mile}$$

If the miles driven for the four years were 40,000, 20,000, 30,000 and 10,000 respectively, the depreciation per year would be $2,000, $1,000, $1,500 and $500.

The entry for the first year would be

Depreciation Expense	*2,000*	
Accumulated Depreciation, Machinery		*2,000*

11.5   COMPARISON OF METHODS

The annual depreciation for the Hennessy Company under each of the four principal methods is shown below.

Year	Annual Depreciation Charge				Accumulated Depreciation			
	Straight-Line (1)	Sum-of-Digits (2)	Declining-Balance (3)	Units-of-Output (4)	% of Total			
					(1)	(2)	(3)	(4)
1	$1,250	$2,000	$3,000	$2,000	25	40	50	40
2	1,250	1,500	1,500	1,000	50	70	75	60
3	1,250	1,000	750	1,500	75	90	88	90
4	1,250	500	375	500	100	100	94	100

11.6   SPECIAL DEPRECIATION METHODS

Two other depreciation methods which are used by special industries such as public utilities or railroads are the retirement and replacement methods, and the compound interest methods.

Retirement and Replacement Methods.   Under these methods, depreciation is not recorded until the unit is replaced. Under the retirement method, the cost of the *old asset,* less residual value, is recorded as depreciation when it is replaced. Under the replacement method the cost of the *new asset,* less residual value of the old asset, is recorded as depreciation when it is replaced. These methods have two serious defects in that (1) no depreciation is charged until retirement, thereby overstating income on the income statement and overstating book value on the balance sheet, and (2) the amount of depreciation depends on the assets replaced, which may vary with the availability of funds or with a management decision.

Compound Interest Methods.   Compound interest principles are used in the annuity and sinking fund methods. These methods are covered in the Advanced Accounting course.

11.7   GROUP AND COMPOSITE DEPRECIATION

In order to avoid the clerical work involved in computing depreciation on numerous individual assets, many companies establish classes of assets and apply a depreciation rate to the total acquisition cost for the class. If the assets in the class are similar, the depreciation computed is termed *group depreciation*; the appropriate rate is determined from the following equation:

$$\text{Group Depreciation Rate} = \frac{1}{\text{Estimated Average Life of Class}}$$

and is then applied to the total acquisition cost. If class consists of dissimilar assets, the depreciation computed is termed *composite depreciation*. In this case, annual depreciation is computed for each asset on a straight-line basis, and the total annual depreciation for the class is related to total acquisition costs to provide the depreciation rate:

$$\text{Composite Depreciation Rate on Cost} = \frac{\text{Total Annual Depreciation}}{\text{Total Acquisition Costs}}$$

EXAMPLE 7.   Group Depreciation.

Frank Weag, proprietor of the Monmouth Dairy Company, uses three delivery trucks costing $3,000, $5,000 and $7,000. The estimated residual values are $250, $500, and $750, respectively. All trucks have an expected service life of 5 years.

Computation of Truck Depreciation
Group Basis
Service Life 5 Years

Truck No.	Acquisition Cost	Residual Value	Depreciable Amount
1	$ 3,000	$ 250	$ 2,750
2	5,000	500	4,500
3	7,000	750	6,250
	$15,000	$1,500	$13,500

Group Depreciation Rate $= 1 \div 5 = 20\%$
Annual Depreciation $= 20\% \times \$15,000 = \$3,000$

EXAMPLE 8.   Composite Depreciation.

Ray Lanuto, proprietor of the Seaview Beach Electric Supply Company, uses three production machines: #1, a sanding machine costing $4,000, with a residual value of $500 and estimated service life of 5 years; #2, a drill press costing $8,000, with a residual value of $300 and estimated service life of 7 years; #3, a cutting machine costing $12,000, with a residual value of $1,200 and estimated service life of 9 years.

Computation of Machine Depreciation
Composite Rate Basis

Machine No.	Acquisition Cost	Residual Value	Depreciable Amount	Service Life	Annual Depreciation
1	$ 4,000	$ 500	$ 3,500	5	$ 700
2	8,000	300	7,700	7	1,100
3	12,000	1,200	10,800	9	1,200
	$24,000	$2,000	$22,000		$3,000

Composite Depreciation Rate on Cost $= \$3,000 \div \$24,000 = 12\frac{1}{2}\%$

The composite rate of $12\frac{1}{2}\%$ is applied to the asset account balance at the beginning of the year to determine the annual depreciation expense.

Under group or composite procedures, there is no record of accumulated depreciation for individual assets. If an asset is retired, the cost is removed from assets and the difference between cost and proceeds received is charged to Accumulated Depreciation. Thus, if machine #2 were sold at the end of the sixth year for $1,500, the entry would be as follows:

Cash	1,500	
Accumulated Depreciation	6,500	
Machinery		8,500

11.8 DEPRECIATION RECORDS

It is desirable for financial analyses and for various reports to maintain records showing original cost data. The principal depreciation records are (1) property records and (2) depreciation schedules.

Property Records.   Information concerning individual units of fixed assets is required when depreciation rates are being established, when fixed assets are sold and in general planning for business operations.   A record should be maintained for each asset unit and should show its original cost, additions, freight charges, installation charges, location, class and basis of depreciation.   Other pertinent information should be included where applicable, such as name of manufacturer, serial number, salvage value, etc.

Most companies maintain these detailed or *unit property records* in a subsidiary property ledger under a general ledger control account.   The detailed record may be kept on ledger sheets, ledger cards, magnetic tape, or in computer memory systems.

Depreciation Schedules.   Depreciation schedules, or *lapsing* schedules, aid in computing depreciation each year.   Generally, such schedules are established for asset classes and typically show, for each asset, acquisition cost, salvage value, depreciable amount and about five years depreciation data spread or lapsed across the form.

EXAMPLE 9.

If a sanding machine is purchased on January 1, 19X1 for $3,000 and has a salvage value of $300 and a three-year service life, the depreciation would be $900 a year.   The entries for this machine are given on the first line of the lapsing schedule below.

Class: Sanding Equipment
Lapsing Schedule

Date Acquired	Manufacturer	Life	Cost	Salvage	Net	Annual Depreciation 19X1	19X2	19X3	19X4	19X5	19X6
19X1											
1/1/X1	Cross	3	$3,000	$300	$2,700	$ 900	$ 900	$ 900			
7/2/X1	Precision	4	5,200	400	4,800	600	1,200	1,200	$1,200	$ 600	
19X2											
4/1/X2	Stanley	4	3,700	500	3,200		600	800	800	800	$200
10/1/X2	Brown	3	2,000	200	1,800		150	600	600	450	
19X3											
1/3/X3	Excel	4	2,100	100	2,000			500	500	500	500
1/5/X3	Cross (retired)	—	—	—	—			(900)			
1/5/X3	Cross	3	3,500	200	3,300			1,100	1,100	1,100	
						$1,500	$2,850	$4,200	$4,200	$3,450	$700

As can be seen above, the columns for each year are added to obtain the total annual depreciation. When an asset is traded in or retired before being fully depreciated, the remaining depreciation charges are subtracted in the applicable columns.   For example, the machine manufactured by the Cross Company was purchased January 1, 19X1 and had an expected life extending through 19X3.   However, on January 5, 19X3 it was decided to trade this machine in for a newer model.   Thus, the depreciation which had been recorded in the lapsing schedule on acquisition must be deleted for 19X3.   This is done by crediting ( ) the amount at date of retirement.   If there had been more than one year of remaining life, the depreciation for any additional life would also be credited on the schedule.   The entries for removing the cost and applicable depreciation and any gain or loss are discussed fully in Sections 10.15 and 10.16.   The listing by individual assets would be practical only in smaller companies.   Other companies would use class totals.

DEPLETION

11.9 NATURE OF DEPLETION

Depletion refers to the exhaustion of natural resources held as assets and the associated reduction in their cost or value. These resources (i.e. coal or oil deposits) are called *wasting assets* and become *depleted* as the resources are removed. Any value assigned to land after the resources have been removed is accounted for separately; the remaining portion is subject to depletion.

11.10 COMPUTING DEPLETION

The cost to be depleted includes the cost of the resource *plus* all other costs incurred (i.e. exploring, excavating and other costs required to remove the resource). These costs, usually called *development costs*, are amortized in proportion to the units removed. When the working of the resource extends over many years and certain structures or equipment have a service life less than the resource, these assets are amortized over their particular service lives.

While any of the depreciation methods may be used in calculating depletion, the *units-of-output basis* is usually the most logical choice since the exhaustion of natural resources relates to physical output rather than the passage of time. There are usually some restoration costs to prepare the land for other use and these should be considered in determining the residual cost. The depletion equation is

$$\text{Depletion} = \frac{\text{Cost} - \text{Net Residual Value}}{\text{Total Expected Units}}$$

EXAMPLE 10.

The Bernard Franklin Company purchased a wasting asset at a cost of $250,000. It was estimated that 100,000 units could be produced after which the land would have a residual value, after restoration costs, of $50,000. During the current year 15,000 units were produced and 10,000 units were sold. The depletion unit cost and the cost of goods sold are computed as shown below.

Depletion Cost per Unit:

$$\text{Depletion} = \frac{\$250,000 - \$50,000}{100,000 \text{ units}} = \$2.00 \text{ per unit}$$

Cost of Goods Sold	Total	Per Unit
Depletion (15,000 units × $2.00)	$30,000	$2.00
Materials, Labor and Overhead	45,000	3.00
Depreciation of Equipment	15,000	1.00
Total Production Cost (15,000)	$90,000	$6.00
Less: Ending Inventory (5,000 units @ $6.00)	30,000	
Cost of Goods Sold (10,000 units @ $6.00)	$60,000	

When estimated recoverable amounts are revised and additional costs incurred, the depletion rate should be revised. The unamortized cost, including additional development costs, should be divided by the new estimate of recoverable units.

Summary

(1) The process of allocating the cost of assets to the periods in which services are received from the asset are termed: for plant and equipment, _____, for intangible assets, _____, and for natural resources, _____.

(2) In estimating depreciation expense the following factors must be considered: _____, _____, and _____.

(3) The principal methods of computing depreciation are_____, _____, _____, _____ and _____.

(4) The process of taking depreciation on a collection of depreciable assets is called, for similar assets, _____ depreciation, for dissimilar assets, _____ depreciation.

(5) Decreases in the service lives of assets may be related to _____ causes or to _____ causes.

(6) The units-of-output method would be suitable where (a) production is constant, (b) production fluctuates widely, (c) obsolescence occurs, (d) cost is increasing.

(7) An accelerated method of depreciation is the (a) units-of-output, (b) retirement and replacement, (c) declining-balance, (d) compound interest.

(8) If the sum-of-the-years'-digits method of depreciation is used rather than the straight-line method for an asset with a 10-year life, (a) depreciation expense will be lower the first year, (b) income taxes will be higher the first year, (c) income will be lower the second year, (d) expense will be higher the tenth year.

(9) A wasting asset is a natural resource that is (a) destroyed quickly, (b) not economically used, (c) not consumed, (d) exhausted through consumption.

(10) Plant and equipment donated to the company should (a) be depreciated, (b) not be depreciated, (c) be written off immediately, (d) not be recorded.

(11) A lapsing schedule for plant and equipment lists, for each asset, (a) those that have lapsed, (b) depreciation over its estimated life, (c) possible obsolescence, (d) estimated tax savings.

Answers: (1) depreciation, amortization, depletion; (2) cost, residual value, service life; (3) straight-line, sum-of-the-years'-digits, declining-balance, units-of-output; (4) group, composite; (5) physical, functional; (6) *b*; (7) *c*; (8) *c*; (9) *d*; (10) *a*; (11) *b*.

Solved Problems

11.1. On January 1, 19X1, the A. M. Hughes Bicycle Company purchased a machine priced at $15,000 cash. The machine has an estimated life of 10 years or 200,000 units. It was decided to finance the purchase as follows:

Cash	$ 2,000
Old machine traded in	3,000
Installment payables, 10 monthly payments of $1,100	11,000
	$16,000

Assuming that the salvage value of the machine is $1,000, determine the depreciation for 19X1 and 19X2 under the following methods: (a) Straight-line, (b) Sum-of-the-years'-digits, (c) Double-declining-balance and (d) Units-of-output (15,000 and 25,000 respectively in 19X1 and 19X2).

SOLUTION

		19X1	19X2
(a)	Straight-line	$1,400	$1,400
(b)	Sum-of-the-years'-digits	2,545	2,291
(c)	Double-declining-balance	3,000	2,400
(d)	Units-of-output	1,050	1,750

Calculations [depreciation base: $14,000 ($15,000 − $1,000)]

(a) $14,000 \times 10\% = \$1,400$

(b) $14,000 \times 10/55 = \$2,545, \quad \$14,000 \times 9/55 = 2,291$

(c) $15,000 \times 20\% = \$3,000, \quad \$12,000 \times 20\% = \$2,400$

(d) $\$14,000 \times \dfrac{15}{200} = \$1,050, \quad \$14,000 \times \dfrac{25}{200} = \$1,750$

11.2. The Hofstra Company maintains its records of production machines on a composite basis. The following machines were purchased December 31, 19X4:

Machine	Cost	Salvage Value	Service Life
A	$17,000	$2,000	15
B	13,000	1,000	10
C	10,000	1,000	10
D	4,500	500	5

Compute (a) the composite life of the assets, (b) the composite depreciation rate and (c) the annual depreciation.

SOLUTION

(a) 10.26 years ($40,000 ÷ $3,900)

(b) 8.76% ($3,900 ÷ $44,500)

(c) $3,900

Computations:

Machine	Cost	Salvage Value	Depreciable Cost	Service Life	Annual Depreciation
A	$17,000	$2,000	$15,000	15	$1,000
B	13,000	1,000	12,000	10	1,200
C	10,000	1,000	9,000	10	900
D	4,500	500	4,000	5	800
	$44,500	$4,500	$40,000		$3,900

11.3. The Johnson Company shows the following entries in its Plant Property account at the end of 19X5.

Debits

Jan. 15	Cost of building site	$18,500
15	Cost of razing old building	2,500
Oct. 6	Contract price for building completed July 6	80,000
15	Other direct construction costs	6,000
	Total debits	$107,000

Credits

Mar. 31	Sale of old building salvage	$ 2,000
Dec. 31	Depreciation for 19X5*	4,200
	Total credits	$ 6,200
	Balance in Plant Property account, Dec. 31, 19X5	$100,800

* Depreciation was incorrectly calculated on balance ($107,000 − $2,000 = $105,000 × 4% = $4,200). The charge was made to Depreciation Expense.

(a) Prepare a compound correcting entry at December 31, 19X5 based on a new building life of 25 years and depreciation on the straight-line method for the current year.

(b) Compute the amount of depreciation for 19X5 under (1) the sum-of-the-years'-digits method and (2) the double-declining-balance method.

SOLUTION

(a)

Land	*19,000*	
Building	*86,000*	
Plant Property		*100,800*
Accumulated Depreciation		*1,720*
Depreciation Expense		*2,480*

Computations for correcting asset accounts:

Land: Cost of building site	$18,500
Cost of razing old building	2,500
Less: Sale of old building salvage	(2,000)
Cost of land	$19,000

Building: Contract price for building	$80,000
Other direct construction costs	6,000
Cost of building	$86,000

Computations for correcting depreciation amount:

Depreciation: $\$86,000 \times 4\% \times 6/12 = \$1,720$

Reduction: $\$4,200 - \$1,720 = \$2,480$

(b)   **(1)   Sum-of-the-Years-Digits Method**

$$\$86,000 \times \frac{25}{325} \times \frac{6}{12} = \$3,308$$

(2)   Double-Declining-Balance Method

$$\$86,000 \times 4\% \times 2 \times \frac{6}{12} = \$3,440$$

11.4. The Lloyd Smith Company used group depreciation for the automobiles used by its salesmen. A four-year life is used with an estimated trade-in value of 20% of cost. The purchases, all for cash, are as follows:

Date	Purchases		Less: Total Trade-in Allowance		
	No. of Cars	Total Cost	No. of Cars	Purch. Date	Amount
Jan. 19X1	15	$52,500			
Jan. 19X2	8	30,400			
Jan. 19X3	3	12,000	3	19X1	$5,000
Jan. 19X4	10	40,000	10	19X1	6,000

Prepare the entries for the purchase, trade-in and depreciation for 19X1 through 19X4.

SOLUTION

19X1

January 31	*Automobiles*	*52,500*	
	Cash		*52,500*
	Bought 15 cars.		

December 31	*Depreciation Expense, Automobiles*	*10,500*	
	Accumulated Depreciation, Automobiles		*10,500*
	Depreciation: ($52,500 × 20%)*.		

* *Group rate: (100% − 20% salvage) ÷ 4-year life = 20%*

19X2

January 31	*Automobiles*	*30,400*	
	Cash		*30,400*
	Bought 8 cars.		

December 31	*Depreciation Expense, Automobiles*	*16,580*	
	Accumulated Depreciation, Automobiles		*16,580*
	Depreciation: $82,900 × 20%, where $82,900 = $52,500 + $30,400.		

19X3

January 31	*Automobiles*	*12,000*	
	Accumulated Depreciation, Automobiles	*5,500*	
	Automobiles		*10,500*
	Cash		*7,000*
	Bought 3 cars for $12,000; received trade-in of $5,000 for 3 cars bought in 19X1 for $10,500.		

December 31	*Depreciation Expense, Automobiles*	*16,880*	
	Accumulated Depreciation, Automobiles		*16,880*
	Depreciation:		
	$84,400 \times 20\%$, where $84,400 = 82,900 + 12,000 - 10,500$.		

19X4

January 31	*Automobiles*	*40,000*	
	Accumulated Depreciation, Automobiles	*29,000*	
	Automobiles		*35,000*
	Cash		*34,000*
	Bought 10 cars for $40,000; received trade-in of $6,000 for 10 cars bought in 19X1 for $35,000.		
December 31	*Depreciation Expense, Automobiles*	*17,880*	
	Accumulated Depreciation, Automobiles		*17,880*
	Depreciation:		
	$89,400 \times 20\%$, where $89,400 = 84,400 + 40,000 - 35,000$.		

11.5. The bookkeeper for the Roberta Harter Decorating Company was inexperienced and made incorrect entries in the equipment account. Service life is estimated to be 5 years but 20% of the balance in the account each year has been taken as depreciation. Scrap value is estimated to be: Unit M, $800; unit N, $1,200; and unit O, $2,000.

Debits

Jan.	5, 19X1	Purchased Unit M	$ 8,000
	9, 19X1	Installed Unit M	800
Aug.	20, 19X1	Purchased Unit N	12,000
Apr.	10, 19X2	Purchased Unit O	20,000
May	5, 19X3	Storm damage	4,000
			$44,800

Credits

Dec.	31, 19X1	Depreciation for year	$ 4,160
Dec.	31, 19X2	Depreciation for year	7,328
May	2, 19X3	Sale of Unit M	4,000
Dec.	31, 19X3	Depreciation for year	5,862
			$21,350
	Balance, Dec. 31, 19X3		$23,450

(*a*) Prepare a depreciation (lapsing) schedule, using straight-line depreciation, through December 31, 19X3.

(*b*) Prepare a compound entry to correct the accounts at December 31, 19X3.

SOLUTION

(*a*) See Fig. 11-1 below.

Roberta Harter Decorating Company
Depreciation Schedule
Equipment

Date Bought or Sold	Unit	Asset Debit or (Credit)	Asset Balance	Accumulated Depr. Debit or (Credit)	Accumulated Depr. Balance	Est. Scrap Value	Depr. Base	Serv. Life	Depreciation Expense 19X1	19X2	19X3	19X4	19X5	19X6	19X7
19X1															
Jan. 5–9	M	$ 8,800	$ 8,800			$ 800	$ 8,000	5	$1,600	$1,600	$1,600	$1,600	$ 1,600		
Aug. 20	N	12,000	20,800			1,200	10,800	5	($\frac{1}{3}$) 720	2,160	2,160	2,160	$ 2,160	$1,440	
Deprec.				$(2,320)	$(2,320)				$2,320						
19X2															
Apr. 10	O	20,000	40,800			2,000	18,000	5		($\frac{2}{5}$)2,400	3,600	3,600	3,600	3,600	$1,200
Deprec.				(6,160)	(8,480)					$6,160					
19X3															
May 2 (sold)	M	(8,800)	32,000	3,733[1]	(4,747)[2]						($\frac{2}{5}$)(1,067)	(1,600)	(1,600)		
Deprec.				(6,293)	(11,040)[3]						$ 6,293				

[1] $3,733 ($1,600 + $1,600 + $1,600 − $1,067)

[2] $4,747 ($8,480 − $3,733)

[3] $11,040 ($4,747 + $6,293)

Fig. 11-1

(*b*) **Correcting Entry**

Equipment ($32,000 − $23,450)	8,550	
Storm Damage	4,000	
Loss on Disposal ($8,800 − $3,733 − $4,000)	1,067	
Depreciation Expense ($6,293 − $5,862)	431	
Accumulated Depreciation (see footnote 3, Fig. 11-1)		11,040
Correction, Prior Years' Depreciation (as below)		3,008

To correct accounts according to lapsing schedule.

Depreciation correction:

Depreciation taken 19X1–19X2 ($4,160 + $7,328)	$11,488
Correct Depreciation 19X1–19X2 ($2,320 + $6,160)	8,480
Understatement in income 19X1–19X2	$ 3,008

11.6. In September 19X4, the A. Knowles Mining Company acquired substantial mining property for $1,200,000. During that year $350,000 was spent in development costs. Geologists estimated that the mine would yield 1,250,000 tons of ore and would have a value of $200,000 after the ore deposit was exhausted.

The capital investment, exclusive of development costs, for 19X5 was

	Cost	Service Years
Railroad and hoisting equipment	$412,500	25
Mine buildings	150,000	35
Miscellaneous mining equipment	110,000	10

The miscellaneous mining equipment can be moved and used elsewhere. The rest of the capital equipment cannot be economically removed.

The costs and production for year 19X5 were

Operating expenses (exclusive of depreciation and depletion)	$1,600,000
Selling and administrative expenses	$260,000
Tons of ore mined	600,000
Tons of ore sold ($6.00 a ton, at mine)	570,000

Income taxes were $275,000 for the year, after deducting percentage depletion.

(*a*) Prepare an income statement for the Knowles Mining Company.

(*b*) Compute the cost per ton for depletion.

(*c*) Compute the cost per ton for depreciation.

SOLUTION

(a)

A. Knowles Mining Company
Income Statement
year 19X5

Sale of Ore (570,000 tons @ $6.00)		$3,420,000
Cost of Ore Sold		
Operating Expenses	$1,600,000	
Depletion (600,000 × $1.08)*	648,000	
Depreciation of Buildings and Equipment (600,000 × $0.45)**	270,000	
Depreciation of Miscellaneous Equipment (10%)	11,000	
Total Production Cost (600,000 tons @ $4.215 per ton)	$2,529,000	
Less: Ending Inventory (30/600 × $2,529,000)	126,450	2,402,550
Gross Profit		$1,017,450
Selling and Administrative Expenses		260,000
Income from Operations		$ 757,450
Income Taxes		275,000
Net Income		$ 482,450

(b)   **Depletion Cost per Ton**

Mining property		
Land	$1,200,000	
Development costs	350,000	
	$1,550,000	
Less: Residual value	200,000	
Depletion base	$1,350,000	
Estimated tons in deposit	1,250,000	
* Depreciation cost per ton		
($1,350,000 ÷ 1,250,000)	$1.08	

(c)   **Depreciation Cost per Ton**

Capital investment		
Railroad and hoisting equipment	$ 412,500	
Mine buildings	150,000	
Total cost	$ 562,500	
** Depreciation cost per ton		
($562,500 ÷ 1,250,000)	$0.45	

11.7. The Silver Express Company purchased land and buildings on January 2, 19X4.   The transaction was recorded in the accounts with the entry below:

Land	200,000	
Buildings: Cost	400,000	
Buildings: Appraisal Increase	60,000	
Cash		150,000
Note Payable		450,000
Appraisal Capital		60,000

Depreciation on the buildings, using the straight-line method and a useful life of 25 years, is recorded each year as follows:

Depreciation Expense	18,400	
Appraisal Capital	2,400	
Accumulated Depreciation		16,000
Accumulated Depreciation: Appraisal Increase		2,400
Retained Earnings: Appropriated for		
Plant Replacement Increase		2,400

In April 19X7, $100,000 was borrowed, mortgaging the land and the buildings. In 19X9, the Silver Express Company decided to sell the property, and on June 30, the following transaction was completed:

Sales Price		$520,000
Add: Insurance Transferred to Buyer		320
Property Taxes Charged to Buyer		3,300
		$523,620
Less: Mortgage Assumed	$75,000	
Commissions	26,000	
Interest on Mortgage	225	101,225
Cash Received		$422,395

Interest on the mortgage has not been recorded on the books, and the insurance and property taxes accounts are carried as assets.

(a) Record depreciation for 19X9.

(b) Make a compound entry to record the sale. How was the gain or loss on the sale computed?

SOLUTION

(a)

Depreciation Expense ($460,000 ÷ 25 × $\frac{1}{2}$ yr.)	9,200	
Appraisal Capital ($60,000 ÷ 25 × $\frac{1}{2}$ yr.)	1,200	
Accumulated Depreciation ($400,000 ÷ 25 × $\frac{1}{2}$ yr.)		8,000
Accumulated Depreciation: Appraisal Increase		1,200
Retained Earnings: Appropriated for Plant		
Replacement Increase		1,200

(b)

Accumulated Depreciation	88,000	
Accumulated Depreciation: Appraisal Increase	13,200	
Appraisal Capital	46,800	
Mortgage Payable	75,000	
Interest Expense	225	
Cash	422,395	
Loss on Sale of Land and Buildings*	18,000	
Buildings: Cost		400,000
Buildings: Appraisal Increase		60,000
Land		200,000
Prepaid Taxes		3,300
Prepaid Insurance		320

*Loss on Sale of Land and Buildings

Buildings: Cost	$ 400,000		Sales Price	$520,000
Accumulated Depreciation	(88,000)		Less: Commissions	26,000
Book Value of Building	$ 312,000			$494,000
Land	200,000		Less: Land and Buildings	512,000
Total	$ 512,000		Loss on Sale	$ 18,000

11.8. The Miliano Corporation purchased a building five years ago at a cost of $270,000. The useful life was estimated to be 15 years, and the company uses the straight-line method of depreciation. When the building was appraised at the beginning of the sixth year, it was found that it had a sound value of $240,000 based on a total useful life of 20 years. In recording the appraisal in the accounts, the company does not correct depreciation charges in prior years. The entry to record depreciation in each of the remaining years will consist of a portion of the present book value applicable to the remaining years of useful life and a portion of the appraisal increase based on the revised estimate of useful life. The portion of the appraisal increase that is realized each year is not transferred to retained earnings.

(a) Make an entry to record the revaluation in the accounts.

(b) Record the depreciation on the building at the end of the 6th year.

(c) Show how the building would be reported on the balance sheet at the end of the 6th year.

(d) Did the Miliano Corporation follow proper accounting procedures to record the revaluation and depreciation? Explain.

SOLUTION

(a)

Building: Appraisal Increase*	50,000	
Accumulated Depreciation on		
Building: Appraisal Increase*		12,500
Appraisal Capital		37,500

* Appraisal Increase, Building: $50,000 ($320,000 − $270,000)

  Appraisal Increase, Accumulated Depreciation: $12,500 ($50,000 × 5/20)

	Per Books	Per Appraisal
Cost	$270,000	$320,000
Service Life	15 yrs.	20 yrs.
Depreciation for 5 Years	$90,000	$80,000
Book Value	$180,000	$240,000

(b)

Depreciation Expense: Building	14,500	
Accumulated Depreciation on Building		12,000
Accumulated Depreciation on Building: Appraisal Increase		2,500

Accumulated Depreciation on Building = $180,000 ÷ 15

Accumulated Depreciation on Building: Appraisal Increase = $37,500 ÷ 15

(c)

	Cost	Appraisal Increase	Total
Building	$270,000	$50,000	$320,000
Accumulated Depreciation	102,000	15,000	117,000
Book Value	$168,000	$35,000	$203,000

(d) No. The appraisal capital amount should be decreased over the remaining years of useful life.

11.9. The DeGennaro Manufacturing Company purchased equipment on January 3, 19X0 at a cost of $720,000. Because new improvements were being made in this type of equipment each year, the company felt it would be obsolete within 5 years, and began depreciating it on the straight-line basis at 20% per year. However, it was found in 19X1 that the equipment could be modernized by adding an electronic device. The new addition was installed on June 30, 19X2 at a cost of $80,000. During 19X2, the company depreciated the entire cost at the 20% rate. At the end of 19X3 it was estimated that the equipment had a remaining service life of 6 years, would cost $20,000 to dismantle, and would have a net salvage value of $3,500.

(a) Assuming that the depreciation will be based upon the revised estimate, make the entry for depreciation at the end of 19X2.

(b) What entry would be made to correct past errors in depreciation?

SOLUTION

(a)

Depreciation Expense	79,100	
Accumulated Depreciation		79,100

(b)

Accumulated Depreciation	212,900	
Depreciation Expense		212,900

Computations:

	Old Estimate			Revised Estimate		
	1/X0 Equipment	6/X2 Addition	Total	1/X0 Equipment	6/X2 Addition	Total
Cost	$720,000	$80,000	$800,000	$720,000	$80,000	$800,000
Salvage, etc.	—	—		20,000	(3,500)	16,500
Total Base	$720,000	$80,000	$800,000	$740,000	$76,500	$816,500
Life	5 yrs.	5 yrs.		10 yrs.	7.5 yrs.	
Annual Deprec.	$144,000	$16,000		$ 74,000	$10,200	
19X0	$144,000	—	$144,000	$ 74,000		$ 74,000
19X1	144,000	—	144,000	74,000		74,000
19X2	144,000	$ 8,000	152,000	74,000	$ 5,100	79,100
19X3	144,000	16,000	160,000	74,000	10,200	84,200

	Old Estimate	Revised Estimate	Difference
Cost	$800,000	$800,000	$572,900
Accumulated Depreciation	440,000	227,100	360,000
Book Value at 12/31/X2	$360,000	$572,900	$212,900

11.10. Equipment which cost the Triple E Company $213,000 was being depreciated on the sum-of-the-years'-digits method with an estimated useful life of four years. Salvage value at the end of this time was estimated to be $3,000. At the end of the third year it was found that the equipment would have a remaining life of three years, a revised total of six years. Net income for the three years has averaged $150,000 per year.

Two different plans for handling the depreciation problem have been submitted to the president for his consideration:

1. *Correct the book value.* After correcting the book value, record depreciation during the remaining three years based on an original six-year life.

2. *Use present book value.* Use the same method of depreciation on the present book value over the remaining three years.

As the company's CPA and at the president's request, evaluate each of the plans and provide supporting data.

SOLUTION

In order to derive the amount of excess depreciation indicated under Plan 1, it is necessary to compare the present book value under the method now used (four-year life) with the book value at the end of three years for the revised period (6-year life). The following schedule shows the book value of $21,000 at present. The revised schedule shows a book value of $60,000 at the end of three years. The difference of $39,000 is the basis for the suggested entry in Plan 1.

Four-year Life: Based on a $210,000 depreciable amount ($213,000 − $3,000).

Year	Fraction	Depreciation Expense	Accumulated Depreciation	Book Value
1	4/10*	$84,000	$ 84,000	$126,000
2	3/10	63,000	147,000	63,000
3	2/10	42,000	189,000	21,000
4	1/10	21,000	210,000	—

Six-year Life (*revised*): Based on a $210,000 depreciable amount.

Year	Fraction	Depreciation Expense	Accumulated Depreciation	Book Value
1	6/21**	$60,000	$ 60,000	$150,000
2	5/21	50,000	110,000	100,000
3	4/21	40,000	150,000	60,000
4	3/21	30,000	180,000	30,000
5	2/21	20,000	200,000	10,000
6	1/21	10,000	210,000	—

Fractions: *Sum-of-the-years'-digits denominators*

$$*1 + 2 + 3 + 4 = 10$$
$$**1 + 2 + 3 + 4 + 5 + 6 = 21$$

Plan 1. Under this plan, depreciation based on the latest information would be used and net income would not be distorted by any errors in previous years. However, to correct the book value it would be necessary to debit Accumulated Depreciation and credit Retained Earnings for excess depreciation in prior periods. The amount would be $39,000 ($60,000 − $21,000). This would be a material amount in relation to net income per year of $150,000, favoring such an adjustment. However, recent APB Opinions have clarified the point involved here and this treatment would violate APB Opinion Nos. 9, 20 and 30. The transaction is not a prior period adjustment since APB Opinion No. 9 specifically *does not* include normal recurring corrections or adjustments resulting from estimates that are necessary in accounting. Under this plan the revised book value, based on six years, of $60,000 would be spread over the remaining life, as follows:

Year	Fraction	Depreciation Expense
4	3/21	$30,000
5	2/21	20,000
6	1/21	10,000
		$60,000

A disadvantage of this plan is that a total of $249,000 in depreciation charges is reported ($189,000 + $60,000) which is offset by $39,000 to net $210,000.

Plan 2. Under this plan, the present book value of $21,000, based on a four-year life, would be spread over the remaining life, as follows:

Year	Fraction	Depreciation Expense
4	3/6	$10,500
5	2/6	7,000
6	1/6	3,500
		$21,000

APB Opinion No. 30 further clarified and limited the definition of extraordinary items described in APB Opinion No. 9. The later opinion required that both the following criteria must be met. The transaction must be distinguished by its *unusual nature* and *infrequency of occurrence*. The transaction relating to depreciation would apply to the ordinary activities of the business and would be expected to recur from time to time. A transaction covered by APB Opinion No. 9 would be a major casualty such as a flood or earthquake. Transactions such as a change in estimate of years of service life for equipment would be included in current operations; that is, before arriving at *net income before extraordinary items*.

APB Opinion No. 20 relating to accounting changes states that a change in accounting principle, such as a change in the method of depreciation, for example, from a sum-of-the-years'-digits method to a straight-line method would require a prior period adjustment. However, the opinion specifically states that a change in an *estimate* does not require adjustment of prior period amounts.

Another consideration of this plan is that it is in accordance with income tax regulations and, therefore, book treatment and tax treatment will be the same.

Chapter 12

Intangibles

12.1 GENERAL DISCUSSION

For accounting purposes, the classification *intangible assets* refers to nonphysical assets such as patents, copyrights, franchises, leaseholds, goodwill, etc.

The basic value of these assets is derived from their potential earning power for the business. Whether this earning potential is ever realized is, of course, another matter.

12.2 VALUATION OF INTANGIBLE ASSETS

As with other assets, the valuation basis for this category is *cost*. The value of the intangible is written off over its useful life and charged against the revenue it produces.

When an intangible is acquired by purchase, its cost includes all associated acquisition expenses (i.e. technical drawings, legal and consulting fees, license applications, etc.). When such assets are acquired by exchange (i.e. for nonmonetary assets), the fair market value of the asset exchanged or that of the intangible, whichever provides clearer evidence, is used to assign a cost to the asset acquired.

With respect to internally developed intangibles, the difficulty in distinguishing revenue expenditures from capital expenditures has resulted in several acceptable treatments of research and development costs:

(1) Where research and experimental costs can be associated with a specific project, they are summarized and included with all other development expenses in the reported cost of the intangible.

(2) Research and development costs which may or may not benefit revenue in future periods may be *expensed as incurred*, according to function (i.e. sales, manufacturing, etc.). Tax laws encourage this approach as a stimulus to economic growth.

(3) An alternative to (2) above is the capitalization of research and development costs and the subsequent amortization of such amounts over the useful lives of those projects having profitable results.

12.3 AMORTIZATION OF INTANGIBLES

The process of writing off the cost of intangibles is called *amortization*. However, not all intangibles are subject to amortization; thus, two distinct categories of intangible assets are generally recognized.

(1) *Limited Existence.* Some intangibles have a limited term of existence as a result of governmental laws, regulation or contractual arrangement. This category includes patents, copyrights, leases, fixed-term franchises and goodwill for which there is evidence of a limited life.

These assets are amortized over their useful service lives (i.e. in the same manner as depreciable assets). The straight-line method is generally used, although an accelerated method may be substituted if there is evidence that a greater part of the value will be lost in the earlier years than in the later ones.

(2) **Unlimited Existence.** This category includes such intangibles as goodwill, trade names, subscription lists and perpetual franchises which possess no indication or evidence of limited existence. Although no amortization would seem the logical treatment for these assets, APB Opinion No. 17 states that it is an acceptable accounting principle to write them off over some time period for balance sheet purposes, and that the time period selected should be not more than forty years. It specifies, however, that "the cost of each type of intangible asset should be amortized on the basis of the estimated life of that specific asset and should not be written off in the period of acquisition."

12.4 IDENTIFIABLE INTANGIBLE ASSETS

This section deals with the various intangibles which can be identified as distinct and separate property rights. These assets can be contrasted to others, e.g. goodwill, which by virtue of being specifically unidentifiable, require special accounting considerations (see Section 12.5).

(1) **Patents.** Granted by the Federal government, patents give the owner an exclusive right to manufacture and sell, or otherwise control, a particular invention or discovery for a period of 17 years. At such time, the invention or discovery enters the *public domain*, and is available for use by others without payment of any royalty or license fees. Patents are not renewable; however, new patents may be obtained on the basis of improvements in the original invention or discovery.

Patents may be amortized over their legal lives; however, since a patent's economic usefulness is generally less than 17 years, shorter amortization periods are the usual case.

(2) **Copyrights.** Unlike patents, copyrights give the owner an exclusive right to a literary or artistic creation for a period of 28 years which is renewable for an additional 28-year period. Rights to copyrighted material may be leased, assigned or sold.

In theory, copyright costs should be amortized against total revenues resulting from the copyrighted work. However, since such revenues are difficult to estimate, the amortization period is generally short and in some cases, copyright costs may be written off against the first revenues received.

(3) **Trademarks and Trade Names.** These distinctive means of identification, together with symbols, labels and design, represent important property rights to the owner inasmuch as they are forms of advertising having great impact on a product's reputation and consumer confidence in it. They can be bought and sold in their own right.

While developing this particular asset requires great monetary investment, a value is usually *not* assigned unless there has been a purchase acquisition. Even in such cases, the value is typically written off over a period shorter than the 40-year limit, or the asset may be carried at a valuation of $1 just to call attention to it in the balance sheet.

(4) **Organization Costs.** This category encompasses expenses incurred in the formation of a business (i.e. creative, legal, accounting and incorporation fees, etc.). Since it is assumed that these will be recovered through profitable operations, they are considered an asset rather than a reduction in capital. Theoretically, organization costs are an asset as long as the business continues in existence; however, practical considerations dictate that they be amortized over a relatively short life (typically, five years for income tax purposes) in the balance sheet.

Organization costs *do not* include operating losses in initial years of operation, initial advertising costs, bond discount and issuance costs, etc. Such expenses should be deducted from revenues, classified as deferred charges or deducted from security face value and amortized over the life of the obligation.

(5) **Leaseholds and Leasehold Improvements.** A *leasehold* is a right granted to a *lessee* (business or individual) for the use of real property owned by a *lessor* (landlord). Leaseholds cover a specified time period and require the payment of rent. *Leasehold improvements* are betterments of rented property (i.e. resurfaced lots, building modification, new structures, etc.) effected by the lessee. When the estimated useful life of the improvement exceeds the life of the leasehold, it is amortized over the life of the lease as ownership reverts to the lessor when the lease expires. Otherwise, the useful life of the improvement is used as the amortization basis. (See Problem 1.7.)

(6) **Deferred Charges.** This catch-all category covers significant expenditures expected to benefit future periods, although they do not directly result in assets, intangible or otherwise. Research and development costs, plant rearrangement costs and mineral exploration costs are examples of such charges; they are amortized over their useful lives. Because the term deferred charges does not clearly identify the nature of the asset(s), modern accounting theory discourages its use in favor of more specific account titles (see Problem 12.4).

12.5 GOODWILL

For accounting purposes, the term *goodwill* refers to the difference between the value of the business entity as a whole and the sum of the valuations of its identifiable parts. The increased earning power represented by goodwill is attributed to a variety of unidentifiable factors (i.e. superior management, more desirable location, substantial consumer following, etc.) which, by their very natures, would never appear on a company's books.

A difference between value as a whole and value of the parts, or a portion thereof, may have more specific origins, such as (1) undervaluation due to errors in the accounting records or (2) unrealized appreciation of assets which is seldom recorded on the books as a revaluation. However, once such questions have been satisfactorily resolved, any remaining difference (or goodwill) is considered evidence of a firm's ability to earn a rate of return on its net assets (invested capital) in excess of a normal rate.

EXAMPLE 1.

River View Industries is for sale, and its balance sheet shows the following: Total Assets, including cash, receivables, inventories and fixed assets, $100,000; Total Liabilities (all current), $20,000; Stockholders' Equity, $80,000. Annual earnings of $15,000 (after taxes and owners' salaries) are expected to continue indefinitely. Thus, the business can be valued as a whole, as a going concern, rather than according to the value of its collective assets.

The ultimate sales price or value of River View, given this data, relates to the question: How much money need be invested now to earn $15,000 annually? If it is known that similar investments can earn a 10% return, the necessary investment is computed by *capitalizing the earnings* of River View: $15,000 ÷

10% = \$150,000. As a result, River View's value as a going concern (\$150,000) differs from the sum of its identifiable parts (\$80,000) by \$70,000. Assuming that all accounting errors have been corrected and any unrealized appreciation recognized, this figure must represent goodwill, or River View's ability to earn profits in excess of a normal rate of return (at the normal 10% rate, the business would earn \$8,000, not \$15,000, annually). Essentially, if the intangibles represented by goodwill could be identified and added to total assets, River View's book value would be \$150,000 and the \$15,000 in annual earnings would represent a normal rate of return; there would be no superior earning power, and no goodwill with respect to the value of this business.

RECOGNITION OF GOODWILL

The prerequisite for recording goodwill on a company's books is that its value be established by means of an arm's-length transaction, such as acquisition by purchase of a business entity. Goodwill *cannot* be sold or acquired in and of itself, nor does it appear in the balance sheet when internally developed.

EXAMPLE 2.

The new owners of River View Industries, having paid \$150,000, would record \$70,000 of this investment as Purchased Goodwill. Since the new owners paid for anticipated earnings in excess of the normal rate, if only \$70,000 of excess earnings materialize, this amount would represent only a recovery of investment, not income.

ESTIMATING GOODWILL

The purchase price of a business is essentially the result of a bargaining process between the buyer and seller. Accountants are often called upon to assist in estimating goodwill and thereby setting a value on the business. The process of estimating goodwill involves five separate steps:

(1) *Determine the net asset value.* While some of a company's assets may approximate market value (i.e. cash, receivables, FIFO inventories), there are usually differences between book and market values of others (i.e. plant assets, LIFO inventories) which require adjustment. These should be carefully considered, along with any unrecorded intangibles and/or liabilities, so that, after appraisal,

NET ASSET VALUE = TOTAL ASSETS − LIABILITIES TO BE TRANSFERRED

(2) *Forecast average future earnings.* Assuming a going concern, future net earnings are usually estimated on the basis of immediate past performance (i.e. an average of earnings over the past three to six years). Such projections should take into consideration any internal or external conditions having a potentially material effect on future earnings.

(3) *Select an appropriate rate of return.* The rate of return is a function both of relative risks and investment alternatives. It is essential in capitalizing profits and in separating superior from normal earnings. Thus, the rate selected should be comparable to those for similar companies in a particular industry (figures for which are readily available from government or trade association publications).

(4) *Compute superior (excess) earnings.* With respect to the variables discussed above,

EST. FUTURE SUPERIOR EARNINGS

    = EST. AVERAGE FUTURE EARNINGS − (% RETURN × NET ASSET VALUE)

(5) **Determine the goodwill amount.** The present value of expected annual superior earnings (goodwill) may be calculated by any of the following methods:

(i) *Capitalization of average net earnings.* Using the required rate of return on the investment,

$$\text{EST. VALUE OF PURCHASE} \; = \; \frac{\text{NET ASSET VALUE}}{\text{RATE OF RETURN}}$$

then

$$\text{GOODWILL} \; = \; \text{EST. VALUE OF PURCHASE} - \text{NET ASSET VALUE}$$

(ii) *Capitalization of average superior earnings.* A distinction is often made between the expectation of a normal rate of return on a company's net assets and a superior rate of return on excess earnings recognizing increased risk, so that

$$\text{RETURN ON NET ASSETS} = \text{EST. NET EARNINGS} \times \text{NORMAL RATE OF RETURN}$$

and

$$\text{SUPERIOR EARNINGS} = \text{EST. NET EARNINGS} - \text{NORMAL RETURN ON NET ASSETS}$$

where

$$\text{GOODWILL} \; = \; \text{SUPERIOR EARNINGS} \div \text{EST. SUPERIOR RATE OF RETURN}$$

from which

$$\text{PURCHASE PRICE} \; = \; \text{NET ASSETS} + \text{GOODWILL}$$
(value of net assets)

(See Problem 12.3*b*.)

(iii) *Discount of future excess earnings.* This method assumes that while superior earnings can be anticipated only for a limited period, the risks associated with any investment require an adequate return. Given a specific time period (number of years) and a required rate of return, the present value of $1 can be obtained. Then,

$$\text{GOODWILL} \; = \; \text{ANNUAL SUPERIOR EARNINGS} \times \text{PRESENT VALUE OF \$1}$$

(iv) *Number of years' purchase.* This method also limits the recognition of superior earnings to a specific time period. (See Problem 12.3*a*.) It provides the same results as the capitalization method when the number of years used equals the reciprocal of the capitalization rate (five years is equal to a 20% rate, since $1 \div 20 = 5$). The equation is

$$\text{GOODWILL} \; = \; \text{ANNUAL SUPERIOR EARNINGS} \times \text{NUMBER OF YEARS}$$

It is important to note that the higher the rate, the lower goodwill. The value ultimately placed on this intangible usually falls somewhere between the two extremes.

AMORTIZATION OF GOODWILL

There are two schools of thought with respect to the amortization of goodwill:

(1) Since it has an indefinite life, it should not be written off unless there is clear evidence that it no longer exists. In this case, a large amount could be deducted as a lump-sum write-off.

(2) Because goodwill is essentially the purchase of excess earnings for a limited time period, it should be amortized over that period.

While both arguments concur that goodwill should be written off or down at some point in time, the one for periodic amortization is more realistic since it prevents the distortion of asset and capital balances and presents excess earnings as a return on capital rather than income.

For tax purposes, goodwill is considered a permanent asset, and no deduction for amortization is permitted. However, if the operations of a business are terminated or sold, a deduction equal to the unrealized portion of the asset (or investment) may be taken.

Summary

(1)   The valuation basis for intangibles is _____.

(2)   The process of writing off intangibles is called _____.

(3)   The Federal government gives the owner exclusive rights in a patent for a period of ____ years and in a copyright for a period of ____ years.

(4)   Intangible assets may be categorized as those having _____ existence and those having _____ existence.

(5)   Additions or alterations made to leased property by the lessee are called _____ improvements.

(6)   Expenses incurred in the formation of a business are called (*a*) start-up costs, (*b*) organization costs, (*c*) beginning costs, (*d*) official costs.

(7)   The difference between the value of the business as a whole and the values of its identifiable parts is called (*a*) goodwill, (*b*) negative goodwill, (*c*) appreciation, (*d*) unrealized gain.

(8)   The exclusive right to conduct particular activities in a given area is called (*a*) an exclusive right, (*b*) a lease, (*c*) a covenant, (*d*) a franchise.

(9)   Goodwill should be written off (*a*) over 5 years, (*b*) over 10 years, (*c*) over period benefited, not exceeding 40 years, (*d*) against retained earnings.

(10)   A covenant not to compete means that (*a*) the buyer will have to live in a different territory, (*b*) the seller will not engage in the same business in that territory for a specified period, (*c*) a contract has been signed, (*d*) the seller will never open the same type of business.

Answers: (1) cost; (2) amortization; (3) 17, 28; (4) limited, unlimited; (5) leasehold; (6) *b*; (7) *a*; (8) *d*; (9) *c*; (10) *b*.

Solved Problems

12.1. The owners of Makewell Corporation are contemplating selling their business to new interests. For the year 19X5, the earnings of Makewell (before taxes) amounted to $250,000. Included in this determination of net income were the following:

Depreciation of building	$56,000
Amortization of goodwill	20,000
Extraordinary gains	70,000
Extraordinary losses	25,000
Amortization of intangibles	22,500
Profit-sharing payments to employees	30,000

The building is worth approximately twice as much as its book value, and the new owners intend to increase its remaining life by 100%. The new owners also intend to continue the profit-sharing payments to employees, which are based on earnings before depreciation and amortization.

Compute the earnings for the year 19X6 for purposes of measuring the possible existence of superior earnings.

SOLUTION

The solution to this problem involves the concept of normal earnings, which are defined as *recurring earnings*, and tends to exclude any items of an extraordinary nature.

Earnings for 19X5 as reported		$250,000
Less: Extraordinary Gains	$70,000	
Additional Depreciation based on fair market value and adjusted for new, estimated remaining life (see below)	—0—	70,000
		$180,000
Add: Extraordinary Losses	$25,000	
Amortization of Goodwill	20,000	45,000
Normal Projected and Adjusted Earnings for 19X6		$225,000

Additional depreciation computation:

Projected new depreciation charge ($56,000 \times 2 \times \frac{1}{2}$)	$56,000
Depreciation as recorded	56,000
Additional depreciation	$ —0—

The amortization of goodwill is added back to earnings since we are trying to determine what the goodwill is for purposes of amortization. Obviously the profit-sharing arrangement with employees is a normal expense of operations, as is the amortization of intangibles.

12.2. In 19X3, the Electronic Corporation acquired a patent at a cost of $18,600, with a remaining life of 12 years and an estimated useful life of 8 years. Early in 19X6 the company paid $2,000 to an inventor who claimed that this particular patent infringed on one of his inventions.

Prepare the necessary entries to record (a) the acquisition of the patent, (b) the payment of $2,000 on the patent infringement suit and (c) amortization of the patent for 19X6.

SOLUTION

(a) **19X3**   *Patents*   *18,600*

            Cash   *18,600*

      To record the payment for a patent in 19X3.

(b) **19X6**   *Patents*   *2,000*

            Cash   *2,000*

      *To record the payment of $2,000 for the purpose of protecting
      the patent.*

(c) **19X6**   *Patent Amortization Expense*   *2,725*

            Patents   *2,725*

      Computation of 19X6 patent amortization:

      Original cost in 19X3   *$18,600*

      *Amortization of patent for 19X3, 19X4 and 19X5
        based on an estimated useful life of 8 years
        ($2,325 per year × 3)*   *6,975*

      Book value, early 19X6   *$11,625*

      Payment in 19X6 to protect the patent   *2,000*

      Remaining cost to be amortized over 5 years   *$13,625*

      Amortization for 19X6 ($13,625 ÷ 5)   *$ 2,725*

12.3. Company A is negotiating to purchase Company B. Past earnings of Company B
have averaged $25,000 per year. The executives of Company A feel that they can
increase the earnings of B by 30%. Normal earnings for Company B are set at
$20,000 per annum.

   Compute the amount that Company A would pay for goodwill, (a) if goodwill is
equal to the sum of superior earnings for 5 years or (b) if superior earnings are capitalized at $12\frac{1}{2}\%$.

SOLUTION

(a)   *Estimated Future Earnings ($25,000 × 1.3)*   *$ 32,500*
           Normal Earnings as given   *20,000*
           Superior Earnings   *$ 12,500*
           Goodwill ($12,500 × 5)   *$ 62,500*

(b)   *Goodwill ($12,500 ÷ 0.125)*   *$100,000*

12.4. The trial balance of Masters, Incorporated includes the following balance sheet items
as of June 30, 19X6:

Discount on bonds payable	$20,000
Organization costs	5,000
Patents	10,200
Prepaid advertising costs to promote the corporate name	5,000
Excess of cost over book value of net assets of the acquired subsidiary	30,000

   Prepare the intangible assets section of the balance sheet.

SOLUTION

Intangible Assets

Excess of cost over book value of net assets	
of acquired corporation	*$30,000*
Patents	*10,200*
Organization Costs	*5,000*
Total Intangible Assets	*$45,200*

Prepaid advertising costs are more properly a current asset and should be listed as a Prepaid Expense. Discount on bonds payable is more properly listed as an offset to the bonds payable account in the liability section of the balance sheet.

12.5. The Small Corporation purchased the entire business of Lou's Lumber for $350,000 in cash. As part of the purchase, Small agreed to assume the liabilities of Lou's Lumber. On the date of purchase, the balance sheet of Lou's Lumber is as shown below:

Assets	*$400,000*	*Liabilities*	*$150,000*
		Lou Magna, Capital	*250,000*
Total	*$400,000*	*Total*	*$400,000*

After the purchase, the Small Corporation revalued the tangible assets at $430,000 and restated the liabilities at $175,000. The purchase agreement also included a stipulation that Magna could not operate a competing business within the present locality for a period of three years. The purchase price therefore included a payment of $75,000 for this covenant not to compete.

Record the purchase of Lou's Lumber on the books of the Small Corporation.

SOLUTION

Assets	*430,000*	
Covenant Not to Compete	*75,000*	
Goodwill	*20,000*	
Liabilities		*175,000*
Cash		*350,000*
To record the purchase of Lou's Lumber.		

12.6. Early in 19X6, the Stonewell Corporation was considering the acquisition of the Martin Company. As a part of the negotiations, the Martin Company made available to the executives of Stonewell the following information relating to its operations and current position:

Net assets	$300,000
Total assets (as per the latest balance sheet)	450,000
Earnings for the three prior years	180,000
Cash dividends for the three prior years	45,000

Part of the selling price to Stonewell represents a patent which has proven to be quite valuable and which has not been recorded on the books of the Martin Company. This patent has an estimated useful life of no more than five years and is to be sold to Stonewell for $75,000. The other assets are fairly valued. From all indications, earnings of the Martin Company for the next four years are conservatively estimated to average at least 15% more than the average earnings for the past three years (before taking into consideration any additional patent cost amortization).

Estimate the amount of goodwill if (*a*) the minimum earnings rate on net assets at appraised value is considered to be 13% and goodwill is estimated at three years superior earnings and (*b*) earnings at the rate of 14%, based on net assets at appraised value, are considered minimal for this type of business. Goodwill is estimated to be equal to average superior earnings capitalized at 25%.

SOLUTION

Preliminary computations:

Computation of average estimated earnings for the next four years:

Average earnings per year for prior three years		
(180,000 ÷ 3)		$60,000
Projected increase of 15%		9,000
		$69,000
Less: Amortization of patent during next four years		
(75,000 ÷ 5)		15,000
Average estimated earnings per year (revised)		$54,000

Computation of adjusted net asset value:

Net assets of Martin Company as reported	$300,000
Add: Value of patent	75,000
Adjusted net asset value	$375,000

(*a*)	*Average Estimated Future Earnings*	$54,000	
	Minimum Earnings Required (13% of $375,000)	48,750	
	Superior Earnings	$ 5,250	
	Goodwill ($5,250 × 3)		$15,750
(*b*)	*Average Estimated Future Earnings*	$54,000	
	Minimum Earnings (14% of $375,000)	52,500	
	Superior Earnings	$ 1,500	
	Goodwill ($1,500 ÷ 0.25)		$ 6,000

12.7. The Phoenix Candy Company is being audited as of December 31, 19X5, the end of its first full year of operations. An examination of the intangibles account includes the following:

Debits

Jan.	2	*Incorporation fees*	$ 7,500
	4	*Cost of stock certificates*	2,000
	9	*Organizational legal fees*	5,000
Feb.	28	*First year advertising campaign*	12,500
July	1	*Operating loss for first six months*	9,600
	8	*Research and development costs on abandoned products*	13,000
Aug.	1	*Goodwill set up by a credit to Retained Earnings pursuant to estimates of future favorable earnings*	65,000

Sept. 18   Cost of developing EDP software
            (to be amortized over a period of
            4 years beginning Oct. 1, 19X5) $ 5,000

Nov. 1   Purchased a patent with a five-year
            useful life   15,750

Dec. 27   Bonus to supervisor   2,500
            Total debits $137,850

Credits

Jan. 15   Premium on sale of capital stock $47,500

Oct. 1   Proceeds of sale of patentable
            new design   8,500
            Total credits   56,000

Dec. 31   Balance $ 81,850

(a) Prepare the necessary journal entries to correct the accounts, assuming that the books are still open for 19X5. Amounts allocated to organization costs should be amortized over five years.

(b) Prepare the intangible assets section of the balance sheet as of December 31, 19X5.

SOLUTION

(a) **Adjusting and correcting entries**

Organization Costs	10,000	
Amortization of Organization Costs	2,500	
Intangibles		12,500

To record incorporation fees, $7,500, and legal fees, $5,000, in connection with organization, in an Organization Costs account. Amortization for 19X5 = 1/5 of $12,500.

Premium on Capital Stock	2,000	
Advertising Expense	12,500	
Operating Loss (income summary)	9,600	
Research and Development Expenses	13,000	
Intangibles		37,100

To transfer expense and operating loss accounts applicable to current operations from the intangibles account, and to record the cost of stock certificates as an offset to Premium on Capital Stock recorded below.

Retained Earnings	65,000	
Intangibles		65,000

To reverse entry improperly made to recognize goodwill.

Deferred Costs of EDP Program	4,687.50	
EDP Program Expense	312.50	
Intangibles		5,000

To record the unamortized cost of the EDP program and to recognize amortization on such expenditure for 19X5 $(3/48 \times \$5,000)$.

Patents	15,225	
Amortization of Patent Expense	525	
Intangibles		15,750

To record patents and applicable amortization for 19X5 $(2/60 \times \$15,750)$.

Bonus Expense	*2,500*	
Intangibles		*2,500*

To record bonus paid to a supervisor as an expense of the period.

Intangibles	*56,000*	
Premium on Capital Stock		*47,500*
Research and Development Expense		*8,500*

To transfer the premium on capital stock to its own account and to reclassify the proceeds on the sale of design data to offset research and development costs for the year.

(*b*) **Intangible Assets**

Patents, unamortized cost	*$15,225.00*
Organization Costs, amortized over a five-year period starting Jan. 1, 19X5	*10,000.00*
Deferred Costs of EDP Program	*4,687.50*
Total Intangibles	*$29,912.50*

12.8. Northern Television Company owns and operates two television stations in two cities approximately 200 miles apart. On September 1, 19X6, the company contracted with a national film distributor to air certain films over its TV stations. The contract gives the company the right to run the films as follows: 39 initial weekly telecasts during a nine-month period beginning October 12, 19X6; 13 weekly reruns of the best films during the summer of 19X7; and 52 more reruns during the period from October, 19X7 to September, 19X8. The expected revenue from advertisers on both TV stations resulting from the films is estimated by management as follows:

Revenue original 39 weeks (prime time)	$350,000
Revenue summer reruns (late show)	90,000
Revenue second-year reruns (late, late show)	60,000
Total anticipated revenue, 19X6–19X8	$500,000

The cost of the film contract to Northern is $200,000, which the company may elect to pay in installments over a two-year period at a monthly rate of $15,000 during the first year and $3,000 per month during the second year.

(*a*) Prepare the entry to record the contract, assuming that Northern elects the installment payments.

(*b*) Prepare a schedule showing amortization of the rental cost per telecast over the two-year period.

(*c*) Prepare the necessary entries to record:

(1) the first payment on the contract (assuming amortization of the discount on the contract payable by the straight-line, weighted-average method)

(2) amortization of the film rental at the end of January, 19X6 (after 16 telecasts have been run).

SOLUTION

(*a*) **Journal entry to record the contract:**

Film Rights	*200,000*	
Discount on Contract Payable	*16,000*	
Contract Payable, Film Rights		*216,000*

To record a contract payable for film rights to be paid as follows:

Year 1: $15,000 per month	$180,000
Year 2: $3,000 per month	36,000
	$216,000
Less: Amount applicable to rental	200,000
Presumed Interest	$ 16,000

(b) **Schedule for amortizing cost of film rights:**

Expected Revenue	Amount	% of Total
First 39 Telecasts	$350,000	70
Summer Telecasts	90,000	18
Second Year	60,000	12
Totals	$500,000	100

AMORTIZATION OF COSTS
(Total Cost = $200,000)

Period	Percent of Revenue	Amortization of Total Cost	Number of Telecasts	Cost Per Telecast
First 39 Telecasts	70%	$140,000	39	$3,590
Summer Telecasts	18	36,000	13	2,769
Second Year	12	24,000	52	462
Totals	100%	$200,000		

(c) **Journal entries:**

Entry 1

Contract Payable	15,000	
Interest Expense	1,111	
Discount on Contract Payable		1,111
Cash		15,000

To record the first payment on the film rights contract and to amortize the discount on a straight-line, weighted-average basis. (The amortization of the discount can be secured by solving the following equation).

$$\frac{\$15,000 \times 12}{\$216,000} \times \$16,000 = \frac{\$180,000}{\$216,000} \times \$16,000$$

$$= \$13,333 \text{ discount for year 1}$$

$$\frac{\$13,333}{12} = \$1,111$$

Entry 2

Amortization of Film Rights Expense	57,440	
Film Rights		57,440

To record the amortization of film rights for the first 16 telecasts at $3,590 per telecast.

12.9. The Meltronics Corporation was organized early in 19X3 to manufacture a new electronic device patented by C. Barlow. Barlow had been offered $42,000 for his patent, but at about this time, his wife inherited $70,000 and he decided to form his own company to exploit his invention. At the inception of the company, Barlow issued himself 750 shares of $50 par value common stock in exchange for $30,000 and his patent rights, which he recorded at $7,500 on the company records. For the years 19X3 to 19X6 inclusive, the operating results showed the following:

19X3	Net loss	$13,500
19X4	Net loss	21,000
19X5	Net loss	3,200
19X6	Net profit (before taxes)	31,000

In the middle of 19X3, Barlow established a research and development department in the business to continue work on improving the original patent and to develop other patents and products. Expenses allocated to this department were: 19X3, $8,600; 19X4, $18,000; 19X5, $21,000; 19X6, $28,000.

At the beginning of 19X7, Barlow is trying to interest a friend in investing additional capital in the business to finance a contemplated expansion. Barlow believes that the statements prepared by his accountant do not fairly reflect the operating results of the company to date, and he asks you to prepare a revised statement of operating income for the last four years. Barlow feels that the patents developed to date are worth more than the $7,500 now shown on the books. To support his statement, he has prepared an analysis of research costs and he is prepared to demonstrate that costs directly related to the development of the new patents are: improvement of original device in 19X4, $11,800; in 19X5, $3,200 and costs of improvements on new components in 19X4, $9,000; in 19X5, $9,000. In addition, he points out that $20,000 of research costs charged to expense in 19X6 relate directly to a new process which appears to be very promising at the end of 19X6, and which he expects will result in a valuable patent sometime in 19X7.

(a) Prepare a schedule showing the revised yearly operating results (before taxes) of Meltronics for the years 19X3 through 19X6. Assume that the patents are to be amortized on a sum-of-the-years'-digits basis based on an estimated useful life of five years, and that a full year's amortization is to be recorded in 19X3 on the original patent, a full year on the improvements starting in 19X5, and a full year on the new components starting in 19X6.

(b) Prepare the adjusting journal entry that should be recorded on the books of Meltronics as of January 1, 19X7 to reflect the adjustments summarized in (a). Ignore income taxes.

SOLUTION

(a)

REVISED NET INCOME BEFORE TAXES

	19X3	19X4	19X5	19X6
Net Income per Books as Reported	$(13,500)	$(21,000)	$(3,200)	$ 31,000
Adjustments				
Amortization of Original Patent (Note 1)	$(14,000)	$(11,200)	$(8,400)	$(5,600)
Capitalization of Research Costs on Improvements		11,800	3,200	
Amortization of Improvements (Note 2)			(5,000)	(4,000)
Capitalization of Costs of New Components			9,000	9,000
Amortization of Costs of New Components (Note 3)				(6,000)
Deferred Research and Development Costs				20,000
Net Adjustment to Reported Income	$(14,000)	$ 600	$(1,200)	$ 13,400
Revised Net Income Before Taxes	$(27,500)	$(20,400)	$(4,400)	$ 44,400

NOTE 1: Based on a valuation for the patent of $42,000 (the offer to Mr. Barlow).
Sum of the digits 1 through 5 = 15. $42,000 ÷ 15 = $2,800 × years of
remaining life.

NOTE 2: Total research costs on improvements = $15,000.
Amortization = $15,000 ÷ 15 × years of remaining life.

NOTE 3: Research costs on new components = $18,000.
Amortization = $18,000 ÷ 15 × years of remaining life.

(b) Journal entry as of January 1, 19X7:

Deferred Research and Development Costs	*20,000*	
*Patents**	*13,300*	
Correction of Prior Years' Profits	*1,200*	
Paid-in Capital in Excess of Par Value		*34,500*

*To correct capital for increase in value of original patent
($42,000 − $7,500) and to correct earnings for the years
19X3 through 19X6.*

* *Adjustment of patent account:*

Original patent, fair market value	*$42,000*	
Cost of improvements	*15,000*	
Cost of components	*18,000*	*$75,000*

Less: Amortization to January 1, 19X7

Year	Original Patent	Improvements	Components	Total	
19X3	*$14,000*			*$14,000*	
19X4	*11,200*			*11,200*	
19X5	*8,400*	*$5,000*		*13,400*	
19X6	*5,600*	*4,000*	*$6,000*	*15,600*	
Totals	*$39,200*	*$9,000*	*$6,000*		*54,200*

Adjusted book value of patents at January 1, 19X7	*$20,800*
Less: Value of original patent as recorded	*7,500*
Net adjustment as above	*$13,300*

12.10. The following represents information taken from the books of Radial Corporation and
Little Corporation as of December 31, 19X5.   The information was developed in connection with a proposed merger between the two companies.

	Radial Corporation	Little Corporation
Assets other than goodwill	$437,500	$270,000
Liabilities	162,500	120,000
Average net income before income taxes for the years 19X1–19X5	68,000	46,000

The values of all assets, including goodwill, are to be determined as follows:
20% is considered a reasonable pre-tax return on net assets, excluding goodwill; average pre-tax income for 19X1–19X5 in excess of 20% on net assets at December 31,
19X5 is to be capitalized at 25% in determining goodwill.   Before determining the
value of each company, the following adjustments to average pre-tax income are
required:

(1)   Included in the income of Little Corporation for the years 19X1–19X5 are
extraordinary gains of $7,750 and extraordinary losses of $16,500.

(2) In 19X3, Little Corporation charged off to revenue a perpetual franchise. The cost of the franchise was $9,000.

(3) Radial Corporation has equipment in use which is estimated to be worth $25,000 more than book value. This equipment has a remaining estimated useful life of 10 years.

Prepare a schedule showing for each company the valuation of (a) net assets other than goodwill and (b) goodwill.

SOLUTION

		Radial Corporation	Little Corporation
(a)	Valuation of Net Assets Other Than Goodwill		
	Total Assets Other Than Goodwill	$437,500	$270,000
	Less: Liabilities	162,500	120,000
	Net Assets Other Than Goodwill, per books	$275,000	$150,000
	Add: Increase in Value of Equipment	25,000	—
	Adjusted Net Assets Other Than Goodwill	$300,000	$150,000
(b)	Estimate of Goodwill		
	Average Income Before Income Taxes, 19X1–19X5	$ 68,000	$ 46,000
	Add: Perpetual Franchise Written Off ($9,000 ÷ 5)		1,800
	Extraordinary Losses for Five Years ($16,500 ÷ 5)		3,300
	Less: Additional Depreciation Expense on Increased Value of Equipment ($25,000 ÷ 10)	(2,500)	
	Extraordinary Gains for Five Years ($7,750 ÷ 5)		(1,550)
	Adjusted Average Net Income Before Income Taxes for the Years 19X1–19X5	$ 65,500	$ 49,550
	Less: Normal Return on Adjusted Net Assets Other Than Goodwill:		
	$300,000 × 20%	60,000	
	150,000 × 20%		30,000
	Average Superior Income Before Income Taxes	$ 5,500	$ 19,550
	Capitalization Rate for Average Superior Income Before Income Taxes	25%	25%
	Estimated Goodwill	$ 22,000	$ 78,200
	Valuation Summary for Each Company		
	Adjusted Net Assets Other Than Goodwill	$300,000	$150,000
	Estimated Goodwill, as above	22,000	78,200
	Total Value of Each Company	$322,000	$228,200

12.11. From the solution to Problem 12.10, (a) calculate goodwill for the Radial Corporation on the capitalization of net average earnings basis if the required rate of return is 20%. (b) What is its total value in this case?

SOLUTION

(a)
Capitalized Net Earnings ($65,500 ÷ 20%)	$327,500
Less: Net Asset Value	300,000
Estimated Goodwill	$ 27,500

(b)
Net Asset Value	$300,000
Add: Estimated Goodwill	27,500
Total Value of Radial Corporation	$327,500

12.12. With reference to the Little Corporation figures in Problem 12.10, (a) estimate good-will by discounting annual future excess earnings. Assume that the 20% return is expected to continue for 5 years. (Present value table appears in Appendix.) (b) What is the total value of the Little Corporation in this case?

SOLUTION

(a) Since the present value of $1 at 20% for five years equals 2.99,

$$\text{Goodwill} = \$19,550 \times 2.99$$
$$= \$58,455 \text{ (rounded)}$$

(b)

Net Asset Value	*$150,000*
Add: Estimated Goodwill	*58,455*
Total Value	*$208,455*

Chapter 13

Long-term Investments

13.1 CHARACTERISTICS OF LONG-TERM INVESTMENTS

Long-term investments are made for the purpose of improving the operating performance of the investing corporation and controlling one or more affiliates, for periods in excess of one year. They are thus distinguished from short-term investments of idle funds designed to be converted into cash as needed (see Section 5.4).

Motivation for long-term investments, which typically involves intercorporate transactions, may reflect an interest in securing sources of raw materials, favorable sales outlets or the services of operating executives. Alternatively, an interest in diversifying corporate operations may provide the investment stimulus.

Long-term investments generally include stocks, bonds and/or special funds.

13.2 ACCOUNTING FOR LONG-TERM INVESTMENTS

The cost of securities purchased includes the purchase price plus any brokerage fees, transfer taxes and other expenditures necessary for their acquisition. If securities are acquired in exchange for other assets whose dollar value is unknown, the market price of the shares at the time of the transaction can be used to determine the value of the assets given up in exchange. If the value of the asset given in exchange is known and the value of the securities acquired is not, the value of the asset(s) surrendered will determine the cost recorded.

When two or more securities are purchased for a lump-sum amount, the total cost should be allocated between classes (i.e. preferred and common). If market prices are available for both securities, these serve as the allocation basis. If a market price is available for only one class, the difference between this and the acquisition amount is assigned to the other.

EXAMPLE 1.

Company A acquires 1,000 shares of common stock and 200 shares of preferred stock of Company B directly from Company B for a total purchase price of $45,000. The allocation of the total cost between common and preferred is

	Market Value	Allocation Percentage	Allocated Cost
Common: 1,000 shares			
(market value per share, $40)	$40,000	$66\frac{2}{3}\%$	$30,000
Preferred: 200 shares			
(market value per share, $100)	20,000	$33\frac{1}{3}\%$	15,000
Totals	$60,000		$45,000

The allocation of costs between classes is necessary for the determination of a profit or loss upon subsequent disposition. The shares sold may be identified by a certificate number; in cases where a group purchase is identified by a single certificate number but is not sold as a unit, the cost of securities sold may be determined by FIFO, LIFO or the average cost method. When specific identification of securities is not possible, tax laws require that FIFO be used in measuring the gain or loss.

13.3 CONVERTIBLE SECURITIES

Convertible securities are those preferred stocks and bonds which can be converted into common stock of the issuing corporation at the shareholder's option. While they retain the characteristics of preferred securities, their market prices fluctuate in recognition of the value of the common stock into which they may be converted.

With respect to the resulting valuation problem (i.e. whether or not to recognize the difference between the cost of the securities at acquisition and the value of the common stock upon conversion), there are currently two schools of thought:

(1) Such securities should be carried at acquisition cost despite conversion and recognize no gain or loss, since no sale has been made. This viewpoint receives support from the IRS in the form of regulating provisions, and is the typical procedure.

(2) Recognize the gain or loss on the conversion in the face of objective evidence, since conversion is made for the specific purpose of obtaining a more valuable security.

13.4 VALUATION OF INVESTMENT SECURITIES

Securities held for investment purposes are generally carried at cost. When significant and relatively permanent declines in their values occur, departures from the cost principle must be made in recognition of asset's decreased value.

EXAMPLE 2.

Declines in the market value of long-term securities may be stated parenthetically:

Investment in Common Stock of ABC, Inc. (market value $40,000)	*$50,000*

or as a contra account established by the entry

Loss on Market Decline of Securities	*10,000*	
Allowance for Decline in Investment		*10,000*

and presented in financial statements as

Investment in ABC, Inc.	*$50,000*	
Less: Allowance for Decline in Investment	*10,000*	*$40,000*

In cases where the value of long-term securities has increased, a parenthetical notation may reflect the higher value; however, such increases do not normally affect financial statement figures.

STOCK INVESTMENTS

13.5 MEASURING THE RETURN ON INVESTMENT

Revenue from long-term securities generally takes the form of (1) regular dividends, (2) liquidating dividends and (3) stock dividends and splits.

Regular Dividends

Regular dividends are those which arise from the earnings of the issuing corporation, and are usually distributed in cash. While ownership of dividends transfers to the shareholder as of *the date of record* (i.e. the date on which the stock records of the issuing corporation are closed for the purpose of determining dividend distribution), dividend income is normally recorded at the time payment is received. Where a corporation's assets consist almost entirely of investments, the accrual system, which recognizes income as earned, would prevail.

A gain or loss is recorded only in the period in which securities are sold. Thus, the principle of objective evidence dictates recognition of a change in value, regardless of when that change actually occurred.

Liquidating Dividends

Liquidating dividends represent returns on invested capital to the shareholder from the sale or liquidation by a corporation of all or part of its assets.

EXAMPLE 3.

Suppose that a corporation has an unprofitable division which is draining the rest of the organization of its working capital. In order to protect the corporation, its management and stockholders agree to sell the unprofitable division and distribute the revenue from said sale to stockholders on a pro-rata basis. Since such revenue represents neither accumulated nor current earnings, its distribution clearly represents a return of capital, or a liquidating dividend.

Complications often arise in cases where complete corporations are liquidated, since there may be accumulated earnings as of the liquidation date. Then, the funds realized by the investor are said to come from two sources: (1) accumulated earnings and (2) proceeds of the liquidation itself. On the records of the stockholder, the particular investment account should be closed, the revenue recorded and a profit or loss recognized on the investment.

See Section 13.8 for instances of liquidating dividends arising from accumulated earnings.

Stock Dividends and Splits

Stock dividends and splits have no effect on stockholder equity; they do, however, increase the number of shares held on a pro-rata basis and decrease the market value and the cost per share. Therefore, no income is recognized by the stockholder when such dividends are issued, and receipt is noted simply by a memorandum entry recording the additional shares acquired. A sale of such accumulated stock, however, is based on the adjusted cost per share, as is any recognized gain or loss.

EXAMPLE 4.

ABC, Incorporated purchased 10,000 shares of Parsons Lumber Company at $55 per share ($550,000). A 10% dividend was subsequently issued, resulting in an adjusted cost per share of $50. ABC later elected to sell 5,000 shares of its Parsons stock at the original cost per share and thereby recognized a gain of $25,000 [(5,000 × $55) − (5,000 × $50)].

13.6 STOCK WARRANTS AND STOCK RIGHTS

A corporation sometimes issues *stock warrants* or certificates giving its stockholders *rights* to purchase additional shares at a specific price within a specific time period (otherwise they become worthless). Generally, one right is offered for each share originally held and more than one right is required for each new share at the specified price. Warrants may also be traded on the market as a form of stock option. In this case, they may become valuable for long periods of time and may thus be considered long-term investments.

When warrants are acquired in the open market, the cost is determined in the same manner as for other security purchases. When warrants are acquired as a part of a package along with other securities, the total cost of the package must be allocated to the various securities within the package. A simple example will serve to illustrate the accounting treatment of these two instances.

EXAMPLE 5.

On July 1, 19X3 the ABC Manufacturing Corporation purchases $200 worth of warrants for Mellot Corporation stock, and on the same day pays out $50,000 to acquire 100 units of Consolidated Distribution, Incorporated securities. Each unit consists of (1) a $500 debenture bond, (2) five shares of common stock and (3) a warrant to acquire 10 shares of common stock at $5 per share. At the date of purchase, the common stock of Consolidated Distribution is selling for $4 per share, the warrant to acquire 10 shares of stock is selling for $30 per warrant, while the bond is not traded on the market at all. The entries to record these transactions are

Investment in Mellot Warrants	200	
Cash		200
To record the purchase of Mellot Corporation warrants.		

Investment in Consolidated Distribution Warrants	3,000	
Investment in Consolidated Distribution Common Stock	2,000	
Investment in Consolidated Distribution Bonds	45,000	
Cash		50,000

   To record the investment of $50,000 in securities of Consolidated Distribution, Incorporated consisting of the following: 100 warrants at a fair market value of $30; 500 shares of common stock at a fair market value of $4 each; and $50,000 face value bonds at an allocated cost of $45,000.

At a later date, ABC sells the Mellot warrants for $180 in cash and exercises its Consolidated Distribution warrants to buy an additional 1,000 shares of common stock having a market value of $15 per share. The entries to record these facts are

Cash	180	
Loss on Sale of Mellot Warrants	20	
Investment in Mellot Warrants		200
To record the sale of Mellot Corporation warrants.		

Investment in Consolidated Distribution Common Stock	8,000	
Cash		5,000
Investment in Consolidated Distribution Warrants		3,000

   To record the additional investment in Consolidated common resulting from the exercise of warrants.

13.7 ACCOUNTING FOR THE RECEIPT OF STOCK RIGHTS

From the point of view of the issuing corporation, accounting for stock rights is similar to the issuance of a stock dividend. Suffice to say that the corporation has not distributed any assets of its own, although it will eventually realize additional capital from the exercise of these rights.

From the point of view of the investor, the receipt of stock rights means that, if he does not exercise them, his proportionate interest in the company will change. Theoretically, therefore, the cost of the original investment should be apportioned over these two parts of his total investment based upon relative market prices, as expressed by the equation

$$Y = \frac{A}{B + A} \times C$$

where: Y = cost assigned to one (1) right

A = market value of one (1) right

B = market value of one share of stock, ex right

C = cost of original investment

EXAMPLE 6.

Fairview Industries owns 100 shares of Electronic Computer Systems, Incorporated (ECS), for which it paid $20,000. ECS later issues rights; market values are $246 per stock share and $4 per right.

The cost of Fairview's 100 rights, allocated over the $20,000 original investment, is

$$Y = \frac{4}{250} \times \$20,000 = \$320$$

If one additional share of stock can be purchased for $200 plus 10 rights, the holder can purchase 10 additional shares of stock at a cost of $2,320 ($2,000 cash outlay plus $320 allocated cost of rights). If the holder sells these rights for $350 he will have a $30 profit on the sale, and the original investment will have a new cost basis of $19,680 ($20,000 cost less $320 allocated to the rights).

13.8   ACCOUNTING FOR INVESTMENTS IN SUBSIDIARY COMPANIES

There are two principal methods of accounting for investments: *the equity method* and *the cost method*. The one used depends on the nature of the investment and the degree of control exercised by the *investor* (the owning or parent corporation) over the *investee* (the owned or subsidiary corporation).

The AICPA, in APB Opinion No. 18, lowered the ownership requirement for accounting purposes. Thus, the prerequisite went from more than 50% and a *controlling financial interest* (APB Opinion No. 10) to more than 20% and the *exercise of significant influence* over the operations of the subsidiary. The equity method is now required except in cases where ownership is 20% or less.

Equity Method. This method is distinguished by the changes in the parent company's investment account which result from changes in the value of a subsidiary's net assets. When the subsidiary earns a profit, the parent corporation picks up its proportionate share as an increase in the investment and a credit to income, recognizing revenue. When dividends are declared or losses are recognized, the parent corporation credits the value of its investment on a pro-rata basis.

The chief argument for the equity method is that the investment as shown by the parent company agrees with the net assets as shown by the subsidiary. In cases where the parent-subsidiary relationship exists, reality is only achieved by means of *consolidated financial statements* which ignore the legal implications of separate corporate entities and concentrate on the economic realities.

EXAMPLE 7.

The Bates Company invests $600,000 on January 1, 19X5 for 75% of the outstanding stock of the Southime Corporation. Earnings for the Southime Corporation for that year were $60,000 and cash dividends paid were $40,000. The parent corporation's entries are

Acquisition of Stock

Investment in Southime Corporation	*600,000*	
Cash		*600,000*

The investment is recorded at cost but adjusted for earnings and dividends as shown below.

Earnings of Subsidiary

Investment in Southime Corporation	45,000	
Investment Income		45,000

The investment account is *increased* by the proportionate part of the subsidiaries' earnings (75% of $60,000).

Receipt of Dividends

Cash	30,000	
Investment in Southime Corporation		30,000

The investment account is *decreased* by the proportionate part of the subsidiaries' dividends (75% of $40,000).

Cost Method.   Under this method, the parent corporation records investments in subsidiaries at cost and recognizes dividends only as received or if a portion of the investment is sold.   Profits or losses affecting the subsidiary's net worth are ignored unless a significant and permanent decline in the value of stock occurs.   A departure from the cost method may result from

(i)   Dividends declared by the subsidiary out of retained earnings existing prior to acquisition which are considered a return of capital (a liquidating dividend). In this event, the investment account is reduced by the dividend amount.   In the case of individual investors or corporate investors with relatively small holdings, such dividends would normally be considered as earnings.

(ii)   Determination of a substantial and permanent decline in the value of the stock, as a result of operating losses, is recognized as a loss of part of the investment by reducing the value of the investment account.

EXAMPLE 8.

The Englefield Company invests $800,000 on January 1, 19X1, for 60% of the outstanding stock of the Adams Corporation.   Earnings for the Adams Corporation for 19X1 were $80,000 and cash dividends paid were $50,000.   The entries are as follows on the parent's books.

Acquisition of Stock

Investment in Adams Corporation	800,000	
Cash		800,000

The investment is carried at cost.

Earnings of Subsidiary   *No Entry*

Under the cost method no recognition of earnings is made until dividends are received.

Receipt of Dividends

Cash	30,000	
Dividend Income		30,000

The parent company receives 60% of the dividends of the subsidiary company.

BOND INVESTMENTS

13.9   THE NATURE OF BONDS

A bond is an obligation to pay a sum of money (the face value) at some future date (maturity) plus a fixed series of interest payments over the life of the obligation.   Since a bond carries a fixed rate of return (the amount of actual interest to be paid in cash), the cost of such securities to the investor may be greater or smaller than the face value because of investor expectations as to the rate of interest they wish to earn on the investment.

EXAMPLE 9.

If the market rate of interest (investor expectations) is 8% while a bond carries a 7% coupon, investors will purchase this bond only at a cost below face value so that at maturity, the difference between the face value and the actual purchase price, when added to the total amount of interest received during the holding period, yields the expected 8%.

On the other hand, if the market rate of interest is 6%, while the bond carries a 7% coupon, the investor will generally pay a price in excess of face value, for exactly the same reason.

There are, of course, other factors which affect market prices for bonds, and there are numerous kinds of bonds (i.e. guaranteed, secured, mortgage, debenture, etc.). However, as the safety of such investments increases, with respect to interest and/or principal, the investor generally has to accept a lower rate of interest.

13.10 ACQUISITION BETWEEN INTEREST DATES

Interest on bonds is generally paid by the issuing corporation (the seller) at specific dates. If the investor purchases bonds between interest dates, the seller receives the market price as agreed between them *plus* the interest accrued on such bonds since the last interest payment. The new holder (the buyer) will receive from the seller the total amount of interest due on the bonds *since the last interest payment made*. Thus, the buyer is really only reimbursing the seller for the actual amount of time he held the security.

EXAMPLE 10.

On July 1, the ABC Investment Company purchases $50,000 face value bonds of the XYZ Manufacturing Company for $45,000. Interest on these bonds is payable by XYZ on April 1 and October 1 of each year at 7% per annum. ABC will make the following entry on July 1:

Investment in XYZ Manufacturing Company Bonds	45,000	
Accrued Interest Receivable	875	
Cash		45,875
To record the purchase of $50,000 face value bonds of XYZ Manufacturing Company for $45,000 plus accrued interest.		

On October 1, when ABC Investment Company receives a check from XYZ Manufacturing in the amount of $1,750, it will make the following entry:

Cash	1,750	
Accrued Interest Receivable		875
Interest Income from Bonds		875

Thus, ABC's income account reflects the actual amount of interest earned on $50,000 of face value bonds at 7% for three months.

13.11 DISCOUNT AND PREMIUM ON BOND INVESTMENTS

The initial entry for the acquisition of bonds, at either a premium or a discount, charges the investment account for the cost of the bonds acquired, including any brokerage or other fees, but excluding the accrued interest. Another acceptable possibility is to set up the investment in bonds account at the face value of the bonds acquired with a separate discount or premium account.

EXAMPLE 11.

ABC Corporation purchases $2,000 face value bonds of XYZ Manufacturing Company for $1,914.68, payable in five years. The coupon rate of interest is 5% and the yield to maturity is 6%. The entry to record the purchase of the bonds under each of the methods described is:

Method 1.　Bonds carried at cost.

Investment in XYZ Bonds	*1,914.68*	
Cash		*1,914.68*

Method 2.　Bonds carried at face value.

Investment in XYZ Bonds	*2,000.00*	
Discount on Bonds		*85.32*
Cash		*1,914.68*

Both methods in Example 11 are acceptable for accounting purposes; however, the cost method is used more extensively. While both methods will be illustrated in the next section, subsequent sections will use only the first.

13.12　DISCOUNT ACCUMULATION OR PREMIUM AMORTIZATION: STRAIGHT-LINE

Under the straight-line method, the discount or premium is spread uniformly over the life of the bond investment. This method is simple in application and avoids the necessity of determining the yield to maturity. The main objection to it is that a constant revenue is produced each year. However, if the bond has a relatively few years to maturity and a small discount or premium, the straight-line method will produce a close approximation of the true interest revenue.

EXAMPLE 12.

Using the same figures as presented in Example 11, the entry for the collection of the first period's interest will be as follows:

Method 1

Cash	*50.00*	
Investment in Bonds	*8.53*	
Interest Income Earned		*58.53*
To record interest income for the six-month period with the discount on a straight-line basis.		

Method 2

Cash	*50.00*	
Discount on Bonds	*8.53*	
Interest Income Earned		*58.53*

EXAMPLE 13.

If the bonds purchased in Example 11 had been acquired instead at a premium cost of $2,056.75, the entry to record interest income and premium amortization for the first six months under Method 1 would have been

Cash	*50.00*	
Investment in Bonds		*5.67*
Interest Income Earned		*44.33*

13.13　DISCOUNT ACCUMULATION OR PREMIUM AMORTIZATION: EFFECTIVE YIELD

This method is designed to produce a constant *rate* of return on the investment in contrast to the straight-line method, which produces a constant *amount* of return. It involves the application of the yield rate to the book value of the investment for each interest period. Then, the book value is equal to the original cost of the bond plus the discount accumulation *or* less the premium amortization.

EXAMPLE 14.

Continuing with the figures in Example 11, the entry for the accumulation of discount under the effective yield method for the first six months is

Cash	*50.00*	
Investment in Bonds	*7.44*	
Interest Income Earned		*57.44*

To record interest income earned on $1,914.68 at a yield of 3% semiannually. Bond carrying value per books is now $1,922.12.

At the next interest payment date the entry would be

Cash	*50.00*	
Investment in Bonds	*7.66*	
Interest Income Earned		*57.66*

To record interest income earned on $1,922.12 at a yield of 3% semiannually. Bond carrying value is now $1,929.78.

EXAMPLE 15.

Applying the effective yield method to the bonds purchased at a premium (Example 13), the entry for interest income and premium amortization is

Cash	*50.00*	
Investment in Bonds		*11.70*
Interest Income Earned		*38.30*

To record interest income earned on $2,056.75 at a yield of 3% semiannually. Bond carrying value is now $2,045.05.

The entry at the next interest date is

Cash	*50.00*	
Investment in Bonds		*11.35*
Interest Income Earned		*38.65*

To record interest income earned on $2,045.05 at a yield of 3% semiannually. Bond carrying value per books is now $2,033.70.

13.14   ACCOUNTING FOR INVESTMENTS BETWEEN INTEREST DATES

The important dates for accruing interest income earned are (1) the interest payment date, (2) the end of the accounting period for the investor and (3) the specific date of any transaction involving the bonds which may not coincide with the regular interest payment date.

Thus, the interest on bond investments must be accrued at the end of the accounting period and before the bonds may be sold. Furthermore, it makes no difference whether the straight-line method or the effective yield method is used. Accrual of interest earned between interest dates is always computed on the straight-line basis.

EXAMPLE 16.

Using the figures in Example 14, assume that interest payment dates are May 1 and November 1 and that the bonds are still held at December 31, the end of the accounting period. The year-end adjustment is

Accrued Interest Receivable	*16.67*	
Investment in Bonds	*2.55*	
Interest Income Earned		*19.22*

To accrue interest income earned as follows:

Total interest income (3% on $1,922.12 for 2 months)	*$19.22*
Interest receivable (5% × $2,000 for 2 months)	*16.67*
Increase in bond investment account	*$ 2.55*

If the bonds are sold on December 31 for $1,950 plus accrued interest, the initial entry is the same as above. An additional entry is required to handle the sale, as follows:

Cash	1,966.67	
Investment in Bonds		1,924.67
Accrued Interest Receivable		16.67
Profit on Sale of Bonds		25.33

13.15 BOND REDEMPTION PRIOR TO MATURITY

Some bonds are *callable* at the option of the issuer after a specified date has been reached or a certain amount of time has passed. This "call" or retirement privilege is usually accompanied by a requirement that the issuer pay a premium above the face amount of the bond to the holder. The redemption premium is usually set as a declining amount and decreases to zero near the actual maturity date.

The accounting problems of bonds that have been called are similar to those where the bonds have been sold by the holder, or investor. That is, the investor must first accrue his interest plus the amortization of premium or discount up to the date of the redemption call. At that point any gain or loss on redemption can be measured and recognized. A loss resulting from an unexpected redemption of bonds is properly recorded as a loss of the period in which such redemption occurs.

SPECIAL-PURPOSE FUNDS

13.16 INVESTMENTS IN SPECIAL-PURPOSE FUNDS

Special-purpose funds may be used to pay off a liability (e.g. bonded indebtedness) or to acquire specific assets (e.g. a building, additional plant equipment, etc.). Such funds are generally invested in securities. If the fund so invested is the result of contractual obligation and is not available to management for day-to-day operations, it is generally classified as a long-term investment. On the other hand, a fund of a sizable amount is classified as a current asset provided that management has created it voluntarily and may liquidate it for operating purposes within the operating cycle.

13.17 ACCOUNTING FOR FUNDS

Whether special-purpose funds are administered by corporate personnel or by a trustee, the accounting problems in connection with the fund are the same: (1) the transfer of assets, generally cash; (2) the investment of the assets; (3) the collection of revenue and the payment of expenses and (4) the use of the funds for their intended purpose.

Periodic deposits to the fund are generally established within the document creating the fund. They may be (1) set as a stated amount each period, (2) set as a stated amount less whatever earnings are realized from fund assets or (3) related directly to the level of operations. Where the liability to be paid from fund assets is smaller than the fund balance, the corporation, in effect, does not have any liability; in such cases, the balance sheet shows neither a liability nor asset balance for the fund. Most employee pension plans and supplementary unemployment benefit plans are of this nature.

The most usual type of special-purpose fund is the *bond sinking fund*, whose purpose is the accumulation of cash for the redemption of bonded indebtedness, in whole or in part, at specific time periods. Since the outstanding bond liability will always be greater than the sinking fund, the indebtedness must be shown among the liabilities and the sinking fund is shown among the assets. For balance sheet purposes, however, the fund is not offset against the bond liability.

Typically, funds are accumulated by depositing a given sum of money at periodic intervals with a trustee. Using compound interest formulas and an assumed rate of interest, it is possible to compute the periodic deposit needed to accumulate sufficient funds at a given point in time to pay off the liability. Since these funds are generally invested in fixed-income securities for comparatively long periods of time, the assumptions concerning the interest to be earned by the fund are generally well within range of the actual earnings.

All transactions of the fund relating to the purchase and sale of securities and the collection and recording of income can be accounted for in the same way as those transactions relating to general investments. The sole difference lies in the fact that transactions utilizing fund assets will generally be found in some subsidiary financial record and, therefore, will not go through the general corporate records (see Problem 13.9 for accumulation of fund balances).

13.18 CASH SURRENDER VALUE OF LIFE INSURANCE

A corporation will commonly insure the lives of its key executives, naming itself as beneficiary, so that in the case of untimely death, any funds necessary to train a successor or repurchase its stock from the deceased's estate will be available. Thus, the utilization of corporate assets to pay the premiums on such policies is, in effect, the creation of a fund which will be realized only if the specific event occurs.

One or two years after inception, however, most policies begin to accumulate a *cash surrender value* which is available for the corporation's use under specific circumstances (i.e. policy cancellation, loan collateral, etc.). While such accumulated funds remain in the hands of the insurance company, they represent a form of savings for the corporation and should be carried as an asset on the corporation's balance sheet.

EXAMPLE 17.

ABC purchases a $50,000 ordinary life insurance policy for one of its chief operating officers. The yearly premium is $1,480. The entries for the first two years are

Year 1	Insurance Expense	1,480	
	Cash		1,480
	To record the payment of a life insurance premium.		
Year 2	Insurance Expense	1,348	
	Cash Surrender Value of Life Insurance	132	
	Cash		1,480

Since an insurance policy is a contract specifying the terms of the agreement between the parties involved, tables of cash surrender values are included within its provisions.

If the insured officer should die after the second premium is paid, the firm would collect the entire $50,000. The entry to record this would be

Cash	50,000	
Cash Surrender Value of Life Insurance		132
Gain on Settlement of Life Insurance Policy		49,868
To record the collection of life insurance policy.		

FINANCIAL STATEMENT PRESENTATION

13.19 THE BALANCE SHEET

Long-term investments are generally classified as noncurrent assets. Their placement on the balance sheet may vary; if material in total, they are placed before plant assets; if relatively unimportant, after plant assets. However, material investments in subsidiaries are shown in a separate classification, such as "Investments in and Advances to Subsidiary Companies."

Current valuations of long-term investments are not as essential as they are for short-term investments, and minor variations in market values may safely be ignored. However, if there is objective evidence of any material value decline, such information should be fully disclosed through a parenthetical notation or a valuation allowance account.

13.20 THE INCOME STATEMENT

Profits or losses on the sale of long-term investments are generally reported in the income statement as a net figure. The general practice is to show them separately from Gross Sales as part of the revenue section.

Dividends received from investments in stocks and interest received on investments in bonds are treated as income for statement purposes. Generally these are shown after Net Income from Operations. Where the equity method of accounting for investments in subsidiaries is used, the income statement of the parent corporation should reflect its pro-rata share of the earnings of the subsidiaries. If the cost method is used, the parent's income statement would reflect only dividends actually received from the subsidiary.

Summary

(1)   The classification as a long-term asset or a short-term asset (marketable securities) depends on the _____ in owning the securities.

(2)   When capital stock is exchanged for an asset of _____ value, it is recorded at the value of the asset transferred; if exchanged for an asset of _____ value, it is recorded at market value of the stock.

(3)   Under the _____ method, the investment is initially recorded at cost, but is increased for the investee's net income and decreased for the investee's dividends or losses; while under the _____ method the investment is initially recorded at cost and remains at cost.

(4)   _____ represents the privilege of stockholders to purchase additional shares at a stated price.

(5)   For discount or premium amortization on bonds, the _____ method produces a constant *amount* of return on investment while the _____ method produces a constant *rate* of return.

(6) When stock and bond units are purchased for a lump sum and both securities are quoted, the cost should be allocated on the basis of (a) relative yields, (b) relative market value, (c) relative cost, (d) relative number of units.

(7) In the case of a stock dividend, (a) the shares are split, (b) inventory is distributed, (c) the investee's proportionate share in the investee is unchanged, (d) Gain on Investment is credited.

(8) If the issuing corporation declares a cash dividend, when does the investor normally record dividend income? (a) At date of declaration, (b) at date of record, (c) at date payment is mailed, (d) at date payment is received.

(9) When convertible bonds are exchanged for common stock, the investor usually considers it as (a) a change in form of investment, (b) a gain or loss, (c) a saving of taxes, (d) a higher tax base.

(10) The portion of premium paid for insurance on the lives of key executives and carried as an asset is called (a) insurance premium, (b) cash surrender value, (c) insurance expense, (d) gain on insurance.

Answers: (1) purpose; (2) known, unknown; (3) equity, cost; (4) stock rights; (5) straight-line, effective yield; (6) b; (7) c; (8) d; (9) a; (10) b.

Solved Problems

13.1. From the following information, prepare the necessary general journal entries to record the transactions of Dixie, Incorporated:

Jan. 25   Purchased 2,000 shares of Western Transportation, Inc. common stock at $44 per share.

Feb. 18   Western Transportation, Inc. issued 10% stock dividend to common stockholders.

May 31   Western Transportation, Inc. issued rights to common stockholders enabling the purchase of one additional share at $45 for every five shares held. The stock was trading ex-rights at $57 per share and the rights had a market value of $3 each.

June 15   Dixie, Inc. exercised 2,000 rights to acquire new shares.

June 17   The remaining rights were sold for $5.50 each.

Sept. 19   Dixie, Inc. sold 800 shares of Western Transportation, Inc. for $55 per share. The shares sold came from the lot purchased on January 25.

SOLUTION

Jan. 25	*Investment in Common Stock*	*88,000*	
	Cash		*88,000*
	To record the purchase of 2,000 shares of Western Transportation, Inc.		

Feb. 18	*Memorandum: Received 200 additional shares of*		
	Western Transportation as a stock dividend.		
	New basis = $88,000/2,200 shares = $40 per share.		

| May 31 | Investment in Rights, Western Transportation | 4,400 | |
| | Investment in Common Stock | | 4,400 |

To allocate portion of investment in stock rights based on relative sales value:

$$\frac{\$3}{\$60} \times \$88,000 = \$4,400$$

Basis per right: $4,400/2,200 = $2 per right

June 15	Investment in Common Stock	22,000	
	Investment in Rights		4,000
	Cash		18,000

To record the acquisition of 400 shares of Western Transportation by exercising 2,000 rights at subscription price of $45 per share.

June 17	Cash	1,100	
	Investment in Rights, Western Transportation		400
	Profit on Sale of Rights		700

To record the sale of the remaining 200 rights at a profit of $3.50 per right.

Sept. 19	Cash	44,000	
	Investment in Common Stock		30,400
	Profit on Sale of Common Stock Investment		13,600

To record the sale of 800 shares of Western Transportation, Inc.
Basis = ($88,000 − $4,400)/2,200 shares = $38 per share.

13.2. The following events relate to Landboard Corporation's long-term investment in 20th Century Development Company:

Mar. 10   Purchased 1,000 shares of common stock at $20 per share, plus brokerage commission and transfer costs of $600.

May 15   Purchased 2,000 shares of common stock at $27 per share, plus brokerage commission and transfer costs of $700.

July 25   20th Century Development distributed a 20% stock dividend.

(a) Prepare journal entries on Landboard's books to record the events.

(b) Compute the basis per share of the investment in 20th Century if (1) the two purchases are treated as separate lots to permit the use of FIFO, or (2) a weighted average is computed for the investment as a whole.

(c) Prepare a journal entry to record the sale of 1,600 shares at $23 per share, if the cost of the shares sold is determined by (1) FIFO, and (2) Weighted Average.

SOLUTION

(a) **Journal entries**

| Mar. 10 | Investment in 20th Century Development Company | 20,600 | |
| | Cash | | 20,600 |

Computation:

1,000 shares @ $20	$20,000	
Costs	600	
Total cost	$20,600 ($20.60 per share)	

May 15   *Investment in 20th Century Development Company*   54,700
                       Cash   .   54,700

                   Computation:

2,000 shares @ $27	$54,000	
Costs	700	
Total cost	$54,700	($27.35 per share)

July 25   *Memorandum: Received 600 shares as a stock dividend, as follows:*

                 Mar. 10 purchase: 200 shares; total 1,200 shares
                 May 15 purchase: 400 shares; total 2,400 shares
                   Total shares held   3,600

(b) Computation of basis per share

(1) FIFO

$$\text{Mar. 10 lot}\quad \frac{\text{Total cost}}{\text{Total shares}} = \frac{\$20,600}{1,200} = \$17.17 \text{ per share}$$

$$\text{May 15 lot}\quad \frac{\text{Total cost}}{\text{Total shares}} = \frac{\$54,700}{2,400} = \$22.79 \text{ per share}$$

(2) Weighted Average

Total cost of investment: $20,600 + $54,700 = $75,300
Total number of shares held: 3,600
Cost per share: $75,300/3,600 = $20.92 per share

(c) Sale of 1,600 shares

(1) FIFO

Cash   36,800
        Investment in 20th Century Development Co.   29,717
        Profit on Sale of Securities   7,083

    Computed as follows:

Selling price of 1,600 shares		$36,800
Cost of shares:		
Mar 10 lot: 1,200 shares	$20,600	
May 15 lot: 400 shares (1/6 of total)	9,117	
Total cost (rounded to nearest dollar)		29,717
Profit on sale (FIFO)		$ 7,083

(2) Weighted Average

Cash   36,800
        Investment in 20th Century Development Co.   33,472
        Profit on Sale of Securities   3,328

    Computed as follows:

Selling price of 1,600 shares	$36,800	
Cost: 1,600 shares × $20.92 per share	33,472	
Profit on sale	$ 3,328	

13.3. The information presented below represents the beginning of an amortization table prepared by a CPA for his client, County Financing Corporation, to account for the company's investment in $100,000 face value bonds issued by City Construction Corporation which mature in twenty years.

Year	Interest Received	Interest Income	Discount Accumulated	Carrying Value of Investment
				$85,805.00
1	$7,000.00	$7,293.43	$293.43	86,098.43
2	7,000.00	7,318.37	318.37	86,416.80
3	7,000.00	7,345.43	345.43	86,762.23

On the basis of the above information,

(a) Is the discount being accumulated by the straight-line or the effective interest method?

(b) What is the contract rate of interest paid on the bonds?

(c) What is the effective yield, or interest rate, on the bonds?

(d) Prepare a journal entry to reflect County's interest income in Year 3.

(e) Compute the amounts to be entered in each column of the table for Year 4.

(f) What would be the interest revenue recognized per year if the discount were accumulated by the straight-line method?

(g) Compute the percentage return on the carrying value of the investment in Years 1 and 3, assuming that the discount was accumulated by the straight-line method.

SOLUTION

(a) The discount is being accumulated by the effective interest method since the discount accumulation is increasing.

(b) $7,000/$100,000 = 0.70 or 7%

(c) $7,293.43/$85,805.00 = 0.085 or 8.5%

(d)
Cash	7,000.00	
Investment in Bonds	345.43	
Interest Income		7,345.43
To record interest income for Year 3.		

(e)
Interest Received:	$ 7,000.00	
Interest Income:	7,374.79	($86,762.23 × 0.085)
Discount Accumulation:	374.79	
Carrying Value:	87,137.02	($86,762.23 + $374.79)

(f) Interest revenue using the straight-line method

Interest received		$7,000.00
Amortization of discount		
Face value of bonds	$100,000.00	
Amount paid	85,805.00	
Discount on bonds	$ 14,195.00	
Yearly accumulation ($14,195/20)		709.75
Total interest income per year		$7,709.75

(g) **Year 1**

$$\frac{\text{Interest Income}}{\text{Carrying Value}} = \frac{\$7,709.75}{\$85,805.00} = 9\% \text{ rounded}$$

Year 3	*Interest Income*		$ 7,709.75
	Carrying value		
	Original	*$85,805.00*	
	Discount accumulation for years		
	1 and 2 ($709.75 × 2)	*1,419.50*	
	Carrying value, end of year 2		*$87,224.50*

$$\$7,709.75/\$87,224.50 \; = \; 8.8\% \;(\text{rounded})$$

13.4. On December 1, the Black Company acquired 6% convertible debenture bonds with a par value of $1,000,000 for $1,100,000 plus accrued interest. The debentures pay interest semiannually on March 1 and September 1 and mature in 10 years and 4 months from date of acquisition. Each bond is convertible on any interest date into seven shares of common stock at the option of the holder.

On September 1, 600 bonds are converted into common stock. On that date the common stock was selling for $200 per share. On October 1, a 10% stock dividend is declared on the common stock to be distributed on November 10 to stockholders of record on October 20. On January 1, Black Company sells 2,310 shares for $210 per share.

Record the above transactions, including the receipt of interest, in general journal form. Assume that the conversion of bonds into common stock is handled at cost.

SOLUTION

Dec. 1	*Investment in Convertible Bonds*		1,100,000	
	Accrued Interest Receivable		15,000	
	Cash			1,115,000

        To record the purchase of 6% convertible bonds as follows:

	Price paid for bonds	*$1,100,000*
	Accrued interest to 9/1:	
	$1,000,000 × 0.06 × 0.25	*15,000*
	Total price paid	*$1,115,000*

Mar. 1	*Cash*		30,000	
	Accrued Interest Receivable			15,000
	Interest Income			15,000

        To record the receipt of interest on $1,000,000 bonds at 6% for 6 months.

| Sept. 1 | *Cash* | | 30,000 | |
| | *Interest Income* | | | 30,000 |

        To record the receipt of semiannual interest.

| | *Investment in Common Stock* | | 660,000 | |
| | *Investment in Convertible Bonds* | | | 660,000 |

        To record the conversion of $600,000 face value bonds into 4,200 shares of common stock. Cost of stock is $157.14 per share.

| Nov. 10 | *Memo entry: To record the receipt of 420 shares of common stock as the result of a 10% stock dividend. Total shares now held is 4,620. Cost per share is now $142.86 (rounded).* |

Jan. 1	*Cash*		485,100	
	Investment in Common Stock			330,000
	Profit on Sale of Common Stock			155,100

        To record the sale of 2,310 shares of common stock (50% of total holdings) at $210 per share.

NOTE: The premium of $100,000 on the purchase of the bonds may or may not be subject to amortization. In dealing with convertible bonds in real life situations, any premium paid is considered really as applying to the convertibility feature—in other words, to the stock which is acquired. The solution to this problem, therefore, has taken the view that the premium should not be amortized but should be assigned to the value of the common stock purchased by conversion, as an additional cost of such stock.

13.5. Prepare the necessary journal entries to record the following events relating to the investments of International Finance, Incorporated:

Mar. 31 Purchased $70,000 face value, 9% bonds issued by Wheel Corporation, at a cost of $72,200 plus accrued interest. These bonds pay interest semiannually on February 1 and August 1, and mature 110 months from the date of acquisition.

June 10 Purchased for the lump sum of $200,000 a package of securities consisting of 500 shares of 6%, $100 par, preferred stock and 1,500 shares of common stock of Triangle Corporation. On this date the preferred and common were trading for $90 and $120 per share respectively.

Aug. 1 Received semiannual payment of interest on bonds of Wheel Corporation. (Amortization is handled at year end only).

Sept. 15 Received the quarterly dividend on the preferred stock of Triangle Corporation, $1.50 per share.

Oct. 15 Received 1,500 additional shares of common from Triangle resulting from a 2 for 1 stock split.

Dec. 31 End of fiscal year. Make all adjusting entries. Premium on bonds is to be amortized on the straight-line method.

SOLUTION

Mar. 31	*Investment in Bonds*		*72,200*	
	Accrued Interest Receivable		*1,050*	
	Cash			*73,250*

To record the purchase of Wheel Corporation bonds as follows:

Price paid for bonds	*$72,200*	
Accrued interest ($70,000 × 0.09/6)	*1,050*	
Total cash outlay	*$73,250*	

June 10	*Investment in Preferred Shares*		*40,000*	
	Investment in Common Shares		*160,000*	
	Cash			*200,000*

To record the purchase of 500 shares of preferred stock and 1,500 shares of common stock of Triangle Corporation for $200,000. The cost of each type of security is assigned on the basis of relative values, as follows:

Preferred: 500 shares × $90 (market value)	*$ 45,000*	*20%*
Common: 1,500 shares × $120 (market value)	*180,000*	*80%*
Totals	*$225,000*	*100%*

Cost allocation:

Preferred (20% × $200,000)	*$ 40,000*
Common (80% × $200,000)	*160,000*
	$200,000

Aug. 1	Cash	3,150	
	Accrued Interest Receivable		1,050
	Interest Income		2,100
	To record the receipt of semiannual interest from Wheel Corporation.		

Sept. 15	Cash	750	
	Dividend Income		750
	To record the receipt of the quarterly dividend on preferred stock from Triangle Corporation. $1.50 per quarter per share.		

Oct. 15	Memo entry: Received an additional 1,500 shares of common from Triangle Corporation as the result of a 2 for 1 stock split.		

Dec. 31	Accrued Interest Receivable	2,625	
	Interest Income		2,625
	To accrue five months interest on Wheel Corporation bonds ($70,000 × 0.09 × 5/12).		

	Interest Income	180	
	Investment in Bonds		180
	To amortize premium on Wheel Corporation bonds for nine months. Premium of $2,200/110 months = $20 per month.		

13.6. In the early part of 19X6, Brown Corporation purchased three lots of common stock in Meznick Electronics, as follows:

Lot	Number of Shares	Price per Share*	Total Cost
1	2,000	$27.50	$ 55,000
2	1,200	38.50	46,200
3	1,800	33.00	59,400
	5,000		$160,600

* Includes brokerage and other costs

On June 10, Meznick Electronics issued a 10% stock dividend. On September 15, Meznick issues stock rights to common stockholders entitling them to purchase one new share at $41 for every ten shares held. On September 15, the common stock of Meznick was selling ex-rights for $54 and the rights at $1. On that date, Brown sold 500 rights at $1.20, less brokerage and other costs of $15, and exercised the remaining rights.

(a) Compute the gain or loss on the sale of rights using (1) FIFO, (2) LIFO, and (3) Average Cost to determine the cost of the rights sold. Round off the cost per right to the nearest cent.

(b) Prepare a schedule showing the number of shares in each lot, the total cost of each lot, and the unit cost per share of each lot, assuming the use of FIFO in part (a), and considering the shares bought through the exercise of rights as Lot 4.

SOLUTION

(a) **Preliminary Computations:**

(i) *Determination of number of shares of stock held.*

	Shares Purchased	10% Stock Dividend	Total Owned
Lot 1	2,000	200	2,200
Lot 2	1,200	120	1,320
Lot 3	1,800	180	1,980
Totals	5,000	500	5,500

(ii) *Calculation of cost per right by lot.*

Lot	Cost of Stock before Rights Allocation	Cost Assigned to Shares 54/55*	Cost Assigned to Rights 1/55	Number of Rights	Cost per Right
1	$ 55,000	$ 54,000	$1,000	2,200	$0.45
2	46,200	45,360	840	1,320	0.64
3	59,400	58,320	1,080	1,980	0.55
Totals	$160,600	$157,680	$2,920	5,500	$0.53

* Market value per share, ex-rights	$54
Market value of right	1
Total market value	$55

PROFIT OR LOSS ON SALE OF RIGHTS

	FIFO	LIFO	Average Cost
Cost per right	$0.45	$0.55	$0.53
Cash received from sale of rights			
(500 × $1.20 − $15)	$585	$585	$585
Cost of rights as assigned	225	275	265
Profit on sale	$360	$310	$320

(b) **CALCULATION OF COST PER SHARE BY LOT**

	Number of Shares Held	Total Cost of Shares	Cost Per Share
Lot 1	2,200	$ 54,000	$24.55
Lot 2	1,320	45,360	34.36
Lot 3	1,980	58,320	29.45
Lot 4 (see Note 1)	500	23,195	46.39
Totals	6,000	$180,875	

NOTE 1: Determination of cost of shares in Lot 4

Cost assigned to 5,500 rights	$ 2,920
Less: Cost of rights sold (FIFO)	225
Remaining cost of rights (5,000)	$ 2,695
Cash payment to acquire 500 shares using above rights (500 shares × $41 per share)	20,500
Cost of 500 shares	$23,195

13.7. The following transactions took place in the long-term investment portfolio of Prentiss, Incorporated during 19X4:

Jan. 12   Purchased 2,500 shares of National Farm, Inc., par value $5, common stock at $31.50 per share.

Feb. 9   Received a dividend of 25¢ per share from National Farm, Inc.

Apr. 2   Purchased $100,000 of Burnoil Co. debentures at par plus accrued interest. The 9% interest is payable semiannually on March 1 and September 1. The bonds mature in ten years from March 1, 19X4 and are callable at 104 anytime.

May 9   Received a dividend of 25¢ per share from National Farm, Inc., plus a 5% stock dividend.

July 15   Sold the National Farm shares received as a stock dividend on May 9 for $37 per share. Purchased $40,000 face value bonds of Herbert's, Inc. at 95. The bonds carry an interest rate of 6% and interest is payable on July 15 and January 15. The bonds mature in 10 years.

Aug. 9   Received a dividend of 50¢ per share from National Farm, Inc.

Sept. 1   Received semiannual interest from Burnoil Co.

Nov. 9   Received a dividend of 25¢ per share from National Farm, Inc.

(a) Record the above transactions in general journal form and make any adjustments necessary at December 31, the end of the corporation's fiscal year. Amortize premiums and discounts on the straight-line method. Round off all computations to the nearest dollar.

(b) Prepare a schedule of investments as they would appear on the balance sheet at December 31.

SOLUTION

(a) **Journal entries**

Jan. 12	*Investment in Common Stock*	*78,750*	
	Cash		*78,750*

To record the purchase of 2,500 shares of common stock of National Farm, Inc. at $31.50 per share.

Feb. 9	*Cash*	*625*	
	Dividend Income		*625*

To record the receipt of a cash dividend of 25¢ per share from National Farm, Inc.

Apr. 2	*Investment in Bonds*	*100,000*	
	Accrued Interest Receivable	*750*	
	Cash		*100,750*

To record the purchase of $100,000 face-value, 9% bonds of Burnoil, Inc. at par plus accrued interest for one month.

May 9	*Cash*	*625*	
	Dividend Income		*625*

To record the receipt of dividend of 25¢ per share from National Farm, Inc.

Memo entry: Received 125 additional shares of National Farm, Inc. as the result of a 5% stock dividend.

July 15 Cash   4,625

        Investment in Common Stock   3,750
        Profit on Sale of Common Stock   875

        Sold the shares of National Farm received on May 9
        for $37 per share. Basis of stock sold is as follows.

Original purchase	2,500 shares @ 31.50	$78,750	
Stock dividend	125 shares	—	
	2,625 shares @ 30.00	$78,750	

    Investment in Bonds   38,000
        Cash   38,000

        To record the purchase of $40,000 face-value bonds of
        Herbert's Inc. at 95 and due in 10 years.

Aug. 9 Cash   1,250

        Dividend Income   1,250

        Received dividend of 50¢ per share on stock of National
        Farm, Inc.

Sept. 1 Cash   4,500

        Accrued Interest Receivable   750
        Interest Income   3,750

        To record interest for six months on bonds of Burnoil Co.
        ($100,000 × 0.09/2).

Nov. 9 Cash   625

        Dividend Income   625

        To record dividend received on stock of National Farm, Inc.
        at 25¢ per share.

Dec. 31 **Adjusting entries**

    Accrued Interest Receivable   4,100
        Interest Income   4,100

        To record interest accrued on the following bond investments:

Burnoil, Inc. ($100,000 × 0.09 × 4/12)	$3,000	
Herbert's Inc. (40,000 × 0.06 × $5\frac{1}{2}$/12)	1,100	
Total	$4,100	

    Investment in Bonds   92
        Interest Income   92

        Discount on bonds of Herbert's Inc. ($2,000) amortized over a ten-
        year period. For the period July 15 to December 31, the discount
        amounts to $200 × $5\frac{1}{2}$/12 = $92 (rounded to nearest dollar).

(b) **Balance sheet presentation of long-term investments**

    Investments, at cost

National Farm, Inc., Common Stock (Note 1)	$ 75,000	
Burnoil, Inc., Bonds	100,000	
Herbert's, Inc., Bonds (Note 2)	38,092	
Total Long-term Investments		$213,092

    Note 1:

Original investment	$ 78,750
Less: Cost assigned to stock dividend shares sold	3,750
Remaining value	$ 75,000

Note 2:

Original investment	*$ 38,000*
Amortization of bond discount for $5\frac{1}{2}$ months	*92*
Total carrying value at December 31	*$ 38,092*

13.8. Horizon Realty acquired 30% of the outstanding capital stock of Suburban Realty and Development Corporation on July 1, 19X6 at a cost of $270,000. The book value of the stock purchased by Horizon was only $210,000, according to the financial reports issued by Suburban as of June 30. Horizon is willing to pay this excess for three reasons, which they consider to be of overriding importance:

(1) An appraisal had indicated that Suburban owned depreciable assets with an estimated remaining life of ten years that were worth at least $25,000 more than book value.

(2) Suburban owned some very valuable pieces of real property acquired at least ten years ago and which, in today's market, were worth at least $125,000 more than book value.

(3) Horizon is also convinced that Suburban has a fine organization which would work nicely with their own to their mutual benefit; that this goodwill did in fact exist. However, Horizon also followed the policy of amortizing any such goodwill over a ten-year period.

Both companies closed their books on December 31, 19X6. For that year ended, Suburban earned a profit of $210,000, spread uniformly over the entire year. Also, on December 31, 19X6, Suburban paid a dividend of $140,000.

(a) Compute the total amount of goodwill Horizon believes Suburban to possess, based upon the price paid by Horizon for their share of the stock.

(b) Prepare the necessary journal entries on the books of Horizon relating to this investment in Suburban for the year ended Dec. 31, 19X6, based on the assumption that the investment is carried on the books of Horizon on the cost method.

(c) Prepare the necessary journal entries on the books of Horizon relating to this investment in Suburban for the year ended Dec. 31, 19X6, based on the assumption that the investment is carried on the books of Horizon using the equity method.

SOLUTION

(a) **Computation of goodwill**

Imputed total value of Suburban's net assets ($270,000/0.3)	*$900,000*
Book value of Suburban's net assets ($210,000/0.3)	*700,000*
Excess of total value over book value	*$200,000*
Excess attributable to undervaluation of depreciable assets	*25,000*
Balance	*$175,000*
Excess attributable to the increased value of land	*125,000*
Imputed goodwill	*$ 50,000*

(b) **Journal entries under Cost Method**

July 1

Investment in Suburban Realty and Development Corp.	270,000	
Cash		270,000

To record the acquisition of 30% of the outstanding shares of Suburban Realty & Development Corp.

Dec. 31

Cash	42,000	
Investment in Suburban Realty & Development		10,500
Dividend Revenue		31,500

To record the receipt of a dividend of $42,000 from Suburban Realty of which $10,500 is deemed to represent a return of capital computed as follows:

Dividend received by Horizon (30% × $140,000)		$42,000
Presumed earnings of Suburban for the period July 1, 19X6 to December 31, 19X6 ($210,000/2)	$105,000	
Share of those earnings belonging to Horizon (at 30%)		31,500
Part of dividend presumed to be a return of capital		$10,500

(c) **Journal entries under Equity Method:**

July 1

Investment in Suburban Realty & Development	270,000	
Cash		270,000

Acquired 30% of Suburban.

Dec. 31

Investment in Suburban Realty & Development	31,500	
Investment Income		31,500

To record 30% of net income of Suburban for the period 7/1–12/31/X6.

Dec. 31

Cash	42,000	
Investment in Suburban Realty & Development		42,000

Cash dividend received from Suburban.

Dec. 31

Investment Income	1,125	
Investment in Suburban Realty & Development		1,125

To adjust the income recognized from Suburban for the amortization of goodwill and the depreciation of fixed assets undervalued on the books of Suburban as follows:

Amortization ($50,000/10 × 0.5 × 0.3)	$ 750
Depreciation ($25,000/10 × 0.5 × 0.3)	375
	$1,125

13.9. Kimball Electronics is considering the issuance of $150,000 of 8%, 10-year bonds, with interest to be paid annually. Present plans call for the establishment of a sinking fund to which Kimball will make annual payments of $11,925.68 at the end of each year. This sinking fund is to be invested at 5% per annum.

In addition to the sinking fund, the corporation plans to take out a $150,000 life insurance policy on Sam Kimball, the company's president. The terms of the policy are as follows:

Year	Gross Premium	Projected Dividend	Guaranteed Cash Value
1	$3,185	—	—
2	3,185	$416	—
3	3,185	470	$ 2,534
4	3,185	525	5,193
5	3,185	581	7,883
6	3,185	639	10,599
7	3,185	698	14,160
8	3,185	755	16,937
9	3,185	813	19,746
10	3,185	872	22,589

(*a*) Prepare a fund accumulation schedule for the sinking fund for the first three years.

(*b*) Prepare a schedule to determine the net cash outlay, and the effect upon net income, of the insurance contract for the first three years.

(*c*) Prepare the necessary journal entries for all transactions involving the bonds, the sinking fund and the insurance contract for each of the first three years.

(*d*) Compute (1) the net cash outlay and (2) the cumulative effect on net income of all the transactions in (*c*) above for the entire three-year period.

SOLUTION

(*a*) *Accumulation schedule for three years for sinking fund*

Year	Payment	Interest Earned	Fund Balance
1	$11,925.68	—0—	$11,925.68
2	11,925.68	$ 596.28	24,447.64
3	11,925.68	1,222.38	37,595.70

(*b*) *Schedule of net cash outlays for insurance policy*

Year	Gross Premium	Dividend	Net Cash Outlay	Increase in Cash Surrender Value	Decrease in Net Income
1	$3,185	—	$3,185	—	$3,185
2	3,185	$416	2,769	—	2,769
3	3,185	470	2,715	$2,534	181

(*c*) *Journal entries*

Year 1   *Cash*   150,000

            Bonds Payable   150,000

            To record the issuance of bonds.

            Interest Expense   12,000

               Cash   12,000

            To record the payment of interest on bonds.

            Sinking Fund   11,925.68

               Cash   11,925.68

            To record the annual payment to sinking fund.

Insurance Expense   3,185
　　Cash   3,185
　　To record the payment of annual insurance premium.

Year 2　　Interest Expense   12,000
　　Cash   12,000
　　To record the payment of annual interest charges on bonds.

Sinking Fund   12,521.96
　　Cash   11,925.68
　　Interest Income   596.28
　　To record annual payment to sinking fund and income earned.

Insurance Expense   2,769
　　Cash   2,769
　　To record the payment of net insurance premium.

Year 3　　Interest Expense   12,000
　　Cash   12,000
　　To record the payment of annual interest on bonds.

Sinking Fund   13,148.06
　　Cash   11,925.68
　　Interest Income   1,222.38
　　To record the annual payment to the sinking fund and the
　　earnings of the fund for the year.

Insurance Expense   181
Cash Surrender Value of Life Insurance   2,534
　　Cash   2,715
　　Payment of net insurance premium and increase in cash
　　surrender value.

(d)

	Net Cash Outlay	Effect on Net Income (Decrease)[1]
Bond interest payments ($12,000 × 3)	$36,000.00	$(36,000.00)
Sinking fund		
Payments ($11,925.68 × 3)	35,777.04	
Interest earned ($596.28 + $1,222.38)		1,818.66
Insurance contract		
Net cash payments ($3,185 + $2,769 + $2,715)	8,669.00	
Expense ($3,185 + $2,769 + $181)		(6,135.00)
Totals	$80,446.04	$(40,316.34)

[1] Before taxes.

13.10. At the beginning of its current year of operations, August 1, 19X6, Peblum, Incorporated has two investments on its books. The first represents an investment made four years ago in which Peblum acquired 70% of the 20,000 outstanding shares of El Matador, Inc., at a total cost of $1,120,000. This cost exceeded Peblum's share of the underlying book value by $80,000, which was considered to be a purchase of unrecorded goodwill. This investment is carried on the equity basis and the unrecorded goodwill has been amortized over a forty-year basis to adjust the income that Peblum receives from El Matador. During this four-year period, El Matador has reported earnings of $1,200,000 and has paid dividends of $1,000,000.

Three years ago, Peblum purchased 10% of the 500,000 shares of Miller, Inc. at a cost of $1,200,000. During this three-year period, Miller reported profits of $1,800,000 and paid dividends of $1,350,000. This investment is carried on the cost basis.

During the fiscal year beginning August 1, 19X6, the following events relating to the long-term investment account took place:

19X6

Aug. 31   Purchased $100,000 face value bonds of Pierrpont Co., 9% coupon, for the sum of $102.17 plus accrued interest. The bonds pay interest on November 1 and May 1 and mature 62 months from date of purchase.

Oct. 31   El Matador paid a dividend of $1.50 per share; Miller paid a dividend of $0.25 per share.

Nov. 1   Interest due on Pierrpont Co. bonds was collected.

19X7

Jan. 31   El Matador paid a dividend of $1.50 per share; Miller paid a dividend of $0.25 per share.

Apr. 30   El Matador paid a dividend of $1.50 per share; Miller, Inc., paid a dividend of $0.25 per share.

May 1   Interest due on Pierrpont Co. bonds was collected.

July 31   El Matador, Inc. reported a net loss of $10,000 for the year ended July 31, consisting of ordinary income of $100,000 and an extraordinary loss of $110,000; it paid a dividend of $1.50 per share. Miller, Inc. reported net income of $240,000 and paid a dividend of $0.25 per share.

(a) Reconstruct the long-term investment accounts as they would appear on the balance sheet of Peblum, Inc. as of July 31, 19X6. (If necessary, round to the nearest dollar.)

(b) Show, in tabular form, the total earnings and dividends paid by El Matador, Inc., and by Miller, Inc., from the date Peblum acquired its interest in each to the end of the current year (July 31, 19X7).

(c) Journalize on Peblum's books all transactions and adjustments involving the events relating to the long-term investment accounts as presented. Any amortization of premium or discount is to be done by the straight-line method.

(d) Illustrate the balance sheet presentation of all items relating to Peblum's long-term investments at July 31, 19X7.

SOLUTION

(a)

Peblum, Inc.
Partial Balance Sheet
July 31, 19X6

Long-term Investments		
Investment in Stock of El Matador, Inc. (equity basis)[1]	$1,252,000	
Investment in Stock of Miller, Inc. (cost basis)	1,200,000	
Total Long-term Investments		$2,452,000

[1] Original investment	$1,120,000	
Add: Share of profits (70% × $1,200,000)	840,000	
	$1,960,000	

Less: Share of dividends (70% × $1,000,000)　　　$700,000

　　　　Amortization of goodwill for 4 years　　　8,000　　708,000

　　Balance, July 31, 19X6　　　　　　　　　　　　　$1,252,000

(b) **Schedule of earnings and dividends**

	El Matador, Inc.	Miller, Inc.
Earnings		
Prior years	$1,200,000	$1,800,000
Current year ended July 31, 19X7	(10,000)	240,000
Total reported earnings	$1,190,000	$2,040,000
Dividends		
Prior years	$1,000,000	$1,350,000
Current year ended July 31, 19X7	120,000	500,000
Total dividends paid	$1,120,000	$1,850,000

(c) **Journal entries:**

19X6

Aug. 31	Investment in Bonds	102,170	
	Accrued Interest Receivable	3,000	
	Cash		105,170

To record the purchase of $100,000, 9% Pierrpont Co. bonds at $102.17 plus four months accrued interest.

| Oct. 31 | Cash | 21,000 | |
| | 　　Investment in El Matador, Inc. | | 21,000 |

Received $1.50 per share on 14,000 shares.

| | Cash | 12,500 | |
| | 　　Dividend Income | | 12,500 |

Received 25¢ per share on 50,000 shares of Miller, Inc.

Nov. 1	Cash	4,500	
	Accrued Interest Receivable		3,000
	Interest Income		1,500

Received semiannual interest on Pierrpont Co. bonds ($100,000 × 0.09 × 0.5).

19X7

| Jan. 31 | Cash | 21,000 | |
| | 　　Investment in El Matador, Inc. | | 21,000 |

Received $1.50 per share on 14,000 shares.

| | Cash | 12,500 | |
| | 　　Dividend Income | | 12,500 |

Received 25¢ per share on 50,000 shares of Miller, Inc.

| Apr. 30 | Cash | 21,000 | |
| | 　　Investment in El Matador, Inc. | | 21,000 |

Received $1.50 per share on 14,000 shares.

| | Cash | 12,500 | |
| | 　　Dividend Income | | 12,500 |

Received 25¢ per share on 50,000 shares of Miller, Inc.

May 1   Cash   4,500
                   Interest Income   4,500
             Semiannual interest on Pierrpont Co. bonds.

July 31   Investment Loss   7,000
                   Investment in El Matador, Inc.   7,000
             70% of reported loss of $10,000.
             (NOTE: Another possible solution would be to pick up as Invest-
             ment Income, 70% of $100,000 = $70,000, and then pick up as an
             Extraordinary Investment Loss, 70% of $110,000 = $77,000. The
             net credit to the investment account, however, would be exactly
             the same.)

July 31   Investment Loss   2,000
                   Investment in El Matador, Inc.   2,000
             Amortization on $80,000 for 40 years.

             Cash   21,000
                   Investment in El Matador, Inc.   21,000
             Received $1.50 per share on 14,000 shares.

             Cash   12,500
                   Dividend Income   12,500
             Received 25¢ per share on 50,000 shares.

             Accrued Interest Receivable   2,250
                   Interest Income   2,250
             Accrued interest on Pierrpont Co. bonds for
             3 months at 9%.

             Interest Income   385
                   Investment in Pierrpont Co. Bonds   385
             Amortization of premium paid on Pierrpont Co. bonds
             [($102,170 − $100,000) × 11/62].

(d)   **Peblum, Inc.**
                             Partial Balance Sheet
                                July 31, 19X7

Current Assets
   Accrued Interest Receivable $ 2,250
Long-term Investments
   Investment in Pierrpont Co. Bonds (Note 1) $ 101,785
   Investment in El Matador Stock, equity basis (Note 2)   1,159,000
   Investment in Miller, Inc. Stock, cost basis   1,200,000
Total Long-term Investments   2,460,785

   NOTE 1:
   Original amount invested Aug. 31, 19X6 $102,170
   Less: Amortization of premium paid   385
   Carrying value, July 31, 19X7 $101,785

   NOTE 2:
   Carrying value, July 31, 19X6 [see solution, part (a)] $1,252,000
   Less: Share of net loss for period $ 7,000
         Dividends received Aug. 1, 19X6–July 31, 19X7   84,000
         Amortization of goodwill for year ended July 31   2,000   93,000
   Carrying value, July 31, 19X7 $1,159,000

Chapter 14

Current Liabilities

14.1 INTRODUCTION

A liability is an obligation to convey assets or perform services at some future date. For purposes of balance sheet analysis, it is important to make a distinction between short-term or *current liabilities* and *long-term liabilities* (treated in Chapter 15).

14.2 THE NATURE OF CURRENT LIABILITIES

Current liabilities include (1) those obligations which will require payment from existing current assets and (2) all other obligations that are to be paid from current assets within one year. Generally, current liabilities arise from day-to-day business operations (i.e. Accounts Payable, Salaries Payable, etc.). Others may result from the need for short-term loans (i.e. Notes Payable) and still others from management-created long-term obligations having a definite relationship to a short-term period (i.e. current maturity values of long-term loans).

Proper recognition and accurate measurement of all current liabilities are necessary in order to avoid overstatement of assets, long-term liabilities or net income (i.e. the entire balance sheet equity section). Further, current and long-term liabilities must be accurately distinguished so that net working capital will be properly stated. Finally, the preparation of meaningful cash budgets (see Sections 5.2 and 5.3) requires that a complete record of *all* current liabilities be kept.

14.3 VALUATION OF CURRENT LIABILITIES

Current liabilities (i.e. legal debts and obligations) are generally recorded in the accounts and reported in financial statements *at face value*. In those rare instances where exact amounts are not available, estimates are made to determine the present value of a future outlay, using the discount method described in APB Opinion No. 21, "Interest on Receivables and Payables."

Four distinct categories can be identified with respect to the element of uncertainty which affects the valuation of these *future* payments as current liabilities: *definitely determinable liabilities, liabilities arising from operating results, estimated liabilities* and *contingent liabilities*.

14.4 DEFINITELY DETERMINABLE LIABILITIES

These liabilities generally originate from contracts or legal statutes which fix the amount of the obligation and its due date rather precisely. Therefore, the basic accounting problem is determining that the obligation does in fact exist and that it is properly recorded.

Trade Accounts and Notes Payable. Procedures for handling the recording and control of trade accounts and trade notes payable center around purchase journals, voucher registers, accounts payable ledgers or open invoice files, etc. Generally these records, or any combination of them, will yield ample evidence as to the existence, amount and due date of unpaid obligations. For statement purposes it is important that particular attention be paid to transactions occurring near the end of one accounting period and the beginning of the next so that the liability for goods received is recorded in the same period as the merchandise is included in inventory.

EXAMPLE 1.

Suppose that merchandise with a valuation of $1,000 is received a few days before the end of one accounting period. If it is included in the inventory at the end of that period but is not included among that period's liabilities, the liabilities for that period will be understated and the net profit for the period will be overstated by $1,000.

Cash discounts applicable to vendors' invoices should be anticipated and recognized by a debit to Allowance for Purchase Discounts, a contra account against Accounts Payable-Trade on the balance sheet. This procedure is similar to that for the valuation of accounts receivable.

Loan Obligations. Items of this type include notes and loans payable and any portion of long-term debt that will mature during the coming operating cycle. However, if such portion of long-term debt will not require the use of current funds (such as retirement through the operation of a special-purpose sinking fund), the debt should be reported as noncurrent with an appropriate note.

According to APB Opinion No. 21, if no interest is explicitly stated, or if the rate of interest is unreasonably low, then interest must be *imputed* (that is, it is understood to be included in the total). If adequate interest is not included, the cost of the asset will be overstated and interest expense understated. The APB opinion does not apply to payables or receivables arising with suppliers or customers in the normal course of business which are due *on ordinary trade terms.*

EXAMPLE 2.

On June 30, 19X1, the Bishop Company issues a $15,000, one-year, non-interest-bearing note to the Adams Roofing Corporation for the purchase of a roofing machine. If the machinery and note payable are recorded at the face value of the note, both the asset and the liability will be overstated. If the prevailing rate of interest is $8\frac{1}{2}\%$, the present value of the note is $13,824.88 ($15,000 ÷ 1.085). The entry on June 30 is

Machinery	13,824.88	
Discount on Notes Payable	1,175.12	
Notes Payable		15,000.00

To record the present value of a non-interest-bearing note of $15,000.00 to the Adams Roofing Corporation. Present value of note is $13,824.88.

For financial statements prepared before the maturity of the note, Interest Expense and reduction of Discount on Notes Payable must be recognized. At December 19X1, the entry is

Interest Expense	587.56	
Discount on Notes Payable		587.56

To record interest on note to December 31, 19X1.

For balance sheet presentation, the balance of Discount on Notes Payable is subtracted from Notes Payable.

Dividends Payable. Dividend obligations are created only by action of a company's board of directors. The declaration by the board represents a legal obligation to pay the cash dividend in the amount specified at the specified time. It always creates a current liability.

Accumulated but undeclared dividends on cumulative preferred stock create no liability; however, the existence of such accumulated dividends in arrears should be disclosed by footnote.

Accrued Liabilities. Unpaid obligations resulting from contractual commitments (e.g. payrolls) or government legislation (e.g. taxes) are referred to as *accrued liabilities* or *accrued expenses.* Taxes are generally material in nature and are usually shown under a separate heading among current liabilities. Some accruals (e.g. accrued interest) are often combined with their respective liabilities, while most others are shown in a combined form under a single heading. Some types of accruals require special attention:

Payroll and Payroll Related Liabilities. Generally, employees are paid after services have been performed, thus creating a liability as of the end of any accounting period for amounts earned but not paid. In addition, employers are required by law to withhold certain amounts from the salaries or wages of employees to cover various tax obligations, and may be authorized by employees to withhold from their compensation certain amounts for such matters as union dues, group life and health insurance, savings bonds, etc.

(i) *Social Security and Withholding Taxes.* Old age and survivors' benefits (pensions) for qualified employees and members of their families are provided for by the Federal Insurance Contributions Act (FICA). This requires employers to withhold an amount equal to a specified rate from employees' *gross earnings* up to a specified level (in 1975, the rate was 5.85% on the first $14,100 of earnings), and to match that amount. In addition, the Internal Revenue Code requires that employers must also withhold from employee compensation an estimated amount of Federal income taxes due. The amount withheld for tax purposes can be determined by a formula or obtained from tax tables.

With respect to the combined amount of social security (FICA) and income taxes withheld, that in excess of $200 must be transferred to an authorized depository, generally a bank, usually on a monthly basis. Failure to do so may result in an additional liability for interest and penalty charges to the Federal government. Taxes of less than $200 may be remitted when Federally required quarterly tax returns showing earnings and taxes withheld are filed.

In the past decade, many states and municipalities have enacted their own income tax laws which also require withholding and monthly remittances.

(ii) *Federal Unemployment Insurance.* The Federal Unemployment Tax Act, which established a system of unemployment insurance in cooperation with the various states, subjects *employers* to a tax at a specified level of gross salary for each employee. However, this act provides a tax credit of up to 2.7% against the tax, depending on the amount paid to an accredited state plan (in 1975, the tax rate of 3.2% on the first *$4,200* of gross salaries, less the 2.7 credit, yielded an effective Federal rate of 0.5%). The tax is payable annually by January 31.

(iii) *State Unemployment Insurance.* The various state unemployment insurance laws are different from the Federal law and from each other. Variables include classes of exempt employees, number of employees required to establish the tax liability, the tax rate and the level of taxable earnings per employee. All such laws, however, contain a *merit-rating plan* under which tax rates are fixed according to employment records (i.e. the more stable the employment record, the lower the tax rate).

(iv)   *Vacation Pay.*   The creation of this liability more often results from a company's economic obligation to its employees than from any legal obligation. The schedule of paid vacation time generally depends on length of company service.

EXAMPLE 3.

If a company has 100 employees, each earning $150 per week and eligible for a two-week paid vacation, the rate at which vacation pay accrues is 4% (2 weeks/50 work weeks). The annual obligation to the employer would be $30,000 (100 × $150 × 50 = $750,000 × 4%), which should be recorded as a liability on a pro-rata basis in each accounting period.

Property Taxes.   These annual taxes arise from the ownership and/or use of real or personal property, and should be recorded as a pro-rated liability over the established tax year.

EXAMPLE 4.

For the fiscal year beginning July 1, 19X1, the ABC Lighting Company owes New York City $24,000 in real property taxes, payable in equal installments on the first of September, December, March and June. The company plans to write the liability off at the rate of $2,000 per month. The appropriate entries up to the first installment are

July 1	*Deferred Property Taxes*	*24,000*	
	Property Taxes Payable		*24,000*
	To establish property tax liability for year beginning		
	July 1, 19X1.		
July 31	*Property Taxes Expense*	*2,000*	
	Deferred Property Taxes		*2,000*
	To record monthly property tax expenses.		
September 1	*Property Taxes Payable*	*6,000*	
	Cash		*6,000*
	To record payment of first installment.		
September 31	*Property Taxes Expense*	*2,000*	
	Deferred Property Taxes		*2,000*
	To record monthly property tax expenses.		

14.5   LIABILITIES ARISING FROM OPERATING RESULTS

Some liabilities cannot be measured until the results of operations are known. In these cases, the basic accounting problem is estimating appropriate amounts for interim monthly or quarterly statements.

Income Taxes.   This liability applies only to corporate, estate and trust income. Earnings from the operation of sole proprietorships and partnerships are treated as personal income of the parties involved, and generally require no disclosure of a liability.

When a corporate Federal income tax liability is expected to exceed a specified amount, advance payment of that excess amount is required according to established tax law schedules; nonpayment is subject to penalty. Any liability not covered by the advance payment is due at specified dates in the following taxable year.

EXAMPLE 5.

Currently, the specified amount is $100,000. Any excess is to be paid in quarterly installments beginning April 15 of the taxable year, subject to a 6% nonpayment penalty. Any tax not covered by the advance payment (i.e. $100,000 ± difference between expected and actual liability for year) is due in equal installments on the 15th of March and June in the following year.

Amended declarations of estimated annual tax must be filed by a given date if it becomes obvious that the initial declaration was in error, and installment payments are then adjusted accordingly. Such estimated payments are entered as debits to Estimated Income Taxes Payable when the accrued liability has been previously recorded; otherwise, they are recorded as Prepaid Income Taxes.

While estimating the annual liability can be done with reasonable accuracy, the progressive nature of the corporate income tax makes estimates for interim statement purposes more difficult. The question of whether to annualize net income and compute a proportionate share as the tax liability or estimate the tax as operating results become evident was clarified in 1973 by APB Opinion No. 28. This opinion recommends that, at the end of each interim period, a company should make its best estimate of the effective tax rate applicable to the full fiscal year, and use that rate in computing the tax liability on a year-to-date basis.

Bonus Agreements. This category includes contractual obligations covering a variety of periodic items such as rents, royalties and additional employee compensation (i.e. profit-sharing). Bonuses which depend on *revenues* can be easily computed.

EXAMPLE 6.

A retailer's lease provides for a fixed rental of $500 per month, plus 2% of annual net sales in excess of $250,000. The fixed rental of $500 per month accrues at the beginning of each month whereas the additional rental depends on the net sales for a particular year. If the retailer has net sales of less than $250,000 for any year, no additional rental liability exists. If the retailer has net sales of $300,000 for the year, an additional rental of $1,000 [$0.02 \times (\$300,000 - \$250,000)$] is due the landlord.

Bonus arrangements which depend upon *net income* are more complicated, since net income is generally an *after-tax* figure and the bonus is a deductible item in computing taxable income. Bonus terms usually fall into four distinct categories which may require the use of mathematical formulas for computation: (1) net income *before* income taxes and the bonus (see Problem 14.11*a*), (2) net income *after* the bonus but *before* income taxes (see Problem 14.11*b*), (3) net income *after* taxes but *before* the bonus (see Problem 14.2*b*) and (4) net income *after* taxes and the bonus (see Problem 14.2*a*).

14.6 ESTIMATED LIABILITIES

This category refers to liabilities which are indeterminate as to amount and due date, but which exist and can be estimated with a reasonable degree of accuracy as long as there is objective evidence on which to base the amount of such obligation. Such liabilities may be either current or long term. The two main groups of estimated liabilities are discussed below.

Liabilities for Premiums and Other Customer Advances. Premium coupons, tokens, tickets, certificates, etc. which entitle the holder to merchandise, cash, or the performance of a service at some future time are considered customer advances. Such obligations should appear as an estimated liability on the balance sheet of the issuing company.

EXAMPLE 7.

If a company sells an item for $10 which carries a coupon worth 25¢, the entry for the sale on its books should read

Cash	10.00	
Estimated Premium Claims Outstanding		0.25
Sales		9.75

As the coupons are redeemed, a debit is made to the estimated liability account with an offsetting credit to either a revenue account (if the redemption value is greater than the cost of the item) or to a premium inventory account (if the redemption value is equal to the cost of the item).

Actual claims are generally a small percentage of the total amount available for redemption. At year end, therefore, the estimated liability for premium claims and/or the estimated amount of forfeited claims must be determined. Forfeited claims are easily calculated when a specified expiration date occurs during the year. However, where claims must be honored indefinitely, both estimates must be based on the company's past experience. For example, if a company's records indicate that redemptions average 40% of outstanding premium coupons, the estimated liability account must be reduced with an offsetting credit to an income account.

Liabilities under Guarantees and Warranties. This liability group arises from product sales (e.g. cars, televisions, etc.) or contracts (e.g. rentals where the lessee must restore property to a specified condition on termination). Although such liabilities may originate at the point of sale or as contracts mature and premises are used, it is always necessary to estimate the company's liability (and make periodic entries debiting an expense account and crediting an account for the estimated liability), even if the account amount must be adjusted once final performance costs are determined.

For tax purposes, these estimates are deductible *only* when performance costs have been incurred. However, tax considerations in this case should be minimally considered in the preparation of periodic financial statements, since to do otherwise might overstate income and understate liabilities, particularly when such liabilities are material in amount.

Service contracts for major appliances covering specified time periods constitute another aspect of this liability category. In this case, the price of a service contract is treated as deferred revenue which is recorded on a prorated basis over the contract's life. Estimates of periodic income realized may be based on a company's past experience.

EXAMPLE 8.

If a company sells a twelve-month contract for the servicing of a washing machine, the entry at the time of sale would be a debit to Cash and a credit to an account such as Deferred Service Contract Revenue. One twelfth of the contract amount would then be realized as income each month, while actual service costs would be charged to expense as incurred.

14.7 CONTINGENT LIABILITIES

The term *contingent liabilities* refers to potential *future* obligations which may or may not in fact materialize. It is thus distinguished from *estimated liabilities*, which do exist but are uncertain as to amount, due date and/or payee. Typical contingent liabilities include:

(1) ***Pending Lawsuits.*** Litigation against a company is carried as a contingent liability until such time as the claim is actually settled (i.e. after all appeals, upon out-of-court agreement). Lawsuits pending as of the balance sheet date are generally included as footnotes without mentioning dollar values.

(2) ***Endorsements.*** When recourse is involved in discounting notes receivable or assigning accounts receivable, the company endorses such debts and may become liable in the event that the original debtor defaults.

(3) ***Income Taxes.*** In the event that the IRS fails to accept a company's tax return as submitted and assesses additional taxes, a contingent liability is created pursuant to an audit. Specific disclosure need be made; frequently, however, a footnote noting IRS examination and final determination of tax liability for certain

years may be included.   Except in cases of fraud or failure to file a tax return, the statute of limitations prevents the IRS from auditing returns more than three years old.

In reporting contingent liabilities, the sole objective is adequate disclosure of such contingency and if determinable, the amount involved. Disclosure in financial statements may be made by (1) a parenthetical comment following the item heading, (2) footnote, (3) inclusion of item among liabilities without extending a dollar amount or (4) appropriation of retained earnings.

14.8 CURRENT LIABILITIES IN THE BALANCE SHEET

There are two considerations with respect to current liabilities in the balance sheet:

(1) *Listing Order.*   Current liabilities are generally listed according to amount (largest to smallest), although they may be listed by due dates when differences in maturity are significant.   Liquidation priorities (i.e. taxes, wages, etc.) should be ignored in the interest of the going-concern assumption.

(2) *Detail of Disclosure.*   The kinds of headings used under Current Liabilities will depend on the purpose of the balance sheet. The following classification is generally acceptable:

> *Notes Payable to Banks*
> *Notes Payable to Trade Creditors*
> *Accounts Payable to Trade Creditors*
> *Other Notes and Accounts Payable*
> *Estimated Income Taxes Payable*
> *Other Accrued Liabilities*
> *Amounts Due to Officers and Employees*
> *Other Current Liabilities*

Liabilities which will be liquidated by the issuance of capital stock should be included under stockholders' equity.

Summary

(1) To be classified as a current liability, the obligation must be paid for from existing _____ or through the creation of other _____ and be settled within _____ or within the normal business cycle, whichever comes first.

(2) Potential future obligations which may or may not materialize are referred to as _____ liabilities.

(3) Amounts that are received in advance of being earned are termed _____ _____.

(4) Liabilities resulting from contractual commitments or government regulations are referred to as _____.

(5) Current liabilities are listed in the balance sheet according to _____ or _____, if significant.

(6) Which of the following would *not* be reported as a current liability on the balance sheet? (*a*) Bank overdraft, (*b*) accrued vacation pay, (*c*) stock dividends, (*d*) stamps redeemable for premiums.

(7) Which of the following is *not* a contingent liability? (*a*) Pending lawsuits, (*b*) endorsement of notes, (*c*) additional income taxes assessed, (*d*) warranties.

(8) Bonus terms are *not* usually based on net income (*a*) before income taxes and bonus, (*b*) after cost of goods sold, but before bonus, (*c*) after bonus but before income taxes, (*d*) after income taxes and bonus.

(9) The Brown Company issues a long-term non-interest-bearing note for a machine and records the note at face value. What is the effect? (*a*) Asset cost will be overstated, (*b*) liability will be understated, (*c*) interest expense will be overstated, (*d*) depreciation expense will be understated.

(10) Accrued liabilities include (*a*) income tax expense, (*b*) accrued vacation pay, (*c*) contingent liabilities, (*d*) deposits paid.

Answers: (1) current assets, current liabilities, one year;   (2) contingent;   (3) deferred revenues;   (4) **accrued liabilities**;   (5) amount, maturity;   (6) *c*;   (7) *d*;   (8) *b*;   (9) *a*;   (10) *b*.

Solved Problems

14.1. On March 31, 19X6, the R & R Salvage Company issued a two-year, non-interest-bearing note with a face value of $11,449 for the purchase of supplies. The original transaction was as follows:

Purchases	*11,449*	
Notes Payable		*11,449*

Prepare a correcting entry at March 31, 19X6, the end of the company's fiscal year, assuming that a fair rate of interest is 7% per annum.

SOLUTION

The solution to this problem involves the concept of *imputed interest*. The theory is that all contracts and obligations, even those stating that no interest is payable, have a present value measured by an interest rate (see Section 14.4). Thus, this correcting entry requires that the face value of the note be discounted back to the original date of March 31, 19X6, as follows:

Face value of note at maturity, March 31, 19X8	*$11,449*
Value of note at March 31, 19X7 ($11,449 divided by 1.07)	*10,700*
Value of note at March 31, 19X6 ($10,700 divided by 1.07)	*10,000*
Discount on note payable ($11,449 − $10,000)	*1,449*

Journal entry

Discount on Notes Payable	*1,449*	
Purchases		*1,449*

To correct purchase account for "imputed interest" included in the face amount of a two-year, non-interest-bearing note.

14.2. Sanders has a contract with his company in his position as general manager whereby he receives a bonus of 25% of all income in excess of $150,000. For the year 19X5, income before income taxes amounts to $390,000. Taxes are 50% of taxable income.

Compute the amount due Sanders if the bonus is based on excess income (a) after taxes and bonus expense and (b) after taxes but before bonus expense.

SOLUTION

(a) Letting B = bonus and T = income taxes,

$$B = 0.25(\$390,000 - \$150,000 - T - B)$$
$$T = 0.5(\$390,000 - B)$$
$$B = 0.25[\$390,000 - \$150,000 - 0.5(\$390,000 - B) - B]$$
$$B = 0.25(\$240,000 - \$195,000 + 0.5\,B - B)$$
$$B = \$11,250 + 0.125\,B - 0.25\,B$$
$$1.125\,B = \$11,250$$
$$B = \$10,000$$

PROOF

Net income before taxes and bonus	$390,000
Less: Bonus	10,000
Net income subject to tax	$380,000
Income tax at 50%	190,000
Net income after tax	$190,000
Less: Income on which bonus does not apply	150,000
Income subject to bonus	$ 40,000
Bonus (25% of income subject to bonus)	$ 10,000

(b)

$$B = 0.25[\$390,000 - \$150,000 - 0.5(\$390,000 - B)]$$
$$B = 0.25(\$240,000 - \$195,000 + 0.5\,B)$$
$$B = \$60,000 - \$48,750 + 0.125\,B)$$
$$0.875\,B = \$11,250$$
$$B = \$12,857$$

PROOF

Net income before taxes and bonus	$390,000
Less: Taxes [0.50($390,000 − $12,857)]	188,571
Net income	$201,429
Less: Income on which bonus does not apply	150,000
Income subject to bonus	$ 51,429
Bonus (25% of income subject to bonus)	$ 12,857

14.3. The Premium Oil Company offers a coupon with each gallon of fuel oil purchased. After the customer accumulates 250 coupons he is given a choice of prizes consisting of a fishing reel, a tennis racquet or a basketball. These prizes cost the company $5 each. At the time of redemption, the promotional expense account is charged; this account is also charged at the end of the fiscal year when an estimate is made of outstanding coupons expected to be redeemed.

Prepare the necessary journal entries for each of the following summary transactions for the year ended April 30, 19X6: (a) Purchased 500 coupon books, each containing 1,000 coupons, for a total cost of $750. Paid cash. (b) Issued 300,000 coupons to customers. (c) Purchased for cash, 1,500 assorted prizes. (d) Issued 800 prizes to customers. (e) It is estimated that of the remaining coupons outstanding approximately 40% will be redeemed.

SOLUTION

(a)   Inventory of Coupons   750
                  Cash   750
             Purchased 500 coupon books for cash.

(b)   Promotional Expense   450
                  Inventory of Coupons   450
             Issued 300 coupon books to customers (300,000 coupons).

(c)   Inventory of Prizes   7,500
                  Cash   7,500
             Purchased 1,500 assorted prizes at $5.

(d)   Promotional Expense   4,000
                  Inventory of Prizes   4,000
             Issued 800 prizes to customers at $5 each.

(e)   Promotional Expense   800
                  Estimated Liability for Outstanding Coupons   800
             Computed as follows:
                  Total coupons issued   300,000
                  Redeemed (800 × 250)   200,000
                  Outstanding   100,000
                  40% thereof   40,000   (40,000 ÷ 250 = 160 prizes @ $5)

14.4. The North Equipment Company sells a machine early in 19X5 for $2,300, with a one-year warranty. Past history indicates that the actual cost of maintenance on such machines during the warranty period amounts to $150.

Make the necessary entries to record the sale of the machine and the subsequent expenditure of $110 to service it during the warranty period, under the assumption that the warranty expense account is charged at the time of sale. (The sale is recorded at $2,300.)

SOLUTION

             Cash   2,300
             Warranty Expense   150
                  Sales   2,300
                  Estimated Liability under Warranty   150
             To record the sale of a machine and the estimated cost of
             servicing it during the one-year warranty period.

             Estimated Liability under Warranty   110
                  Cash (or Parts, Labor, etc.)   110
             To record the actual costs incurred in servicing the machine
             during the warranty period.

The balance of $40 in the liability account at the end of the period should be reviewed to determine if it represents a reasonable estimate of potential claims at that time. If not, the appropriate adjustment should be made.

14.5. The S & R Company offers all officers the right to buy 7% bonds, redeemable at the holder's request at any time after two years from the date of issue. All bonds presently outstanding were issued more than two years ago. During the past few years, bonds redeemed amounted to less than 5% of bonds outstanding and there is no evidence to indicate that the bonds will be redeemed within a year.

The company also has a bank loan outstanding which is due within two months of the balance sheet date. This short-term loan, secured by the cash surrender value of an executive's life insurance policy, has been renewed for the past four years. The present intention is to renew it indefinitely.

How would you classify (a) the bonds payable, (b) the bank loan and (c) the cash surrender value of life insurance on the balance sheet of the S & R Company at the end of the current year? Explain.

SOLUTION

(a) **Bonds.** Should the *intent* of the creditors be allowed to govern the classification of the bond liability? The creditors *may* ask for redemption but there is no evidence that they intend to do so within the next accounting period. The bonds may be shown as noncurrent with an accompanying footnote explaining that the holders have the option of redemption at any time.

(b) **Bank loan.** Since the loan is secured by a noncurrent asset, its classification as a current liability depends primarily on management's intent. Generally a company will not surrender such a policy to pay a loan, and the classification rests on the *intent* of both parties. Presently it is the intent of both parties to keep the loan renewed, but conditions change and the bank may later pull in some of its loans. An acceptable treatment would be to classify the loan as noncurrent with an explanation in a footnote.

(c) **Cash surrender value of life insurance.** Since it is not the intent of management to convert the policy into cash, it cannot be classified as a current asset. Furthermore, it cannot be surrendered for cash since that act would destroy the purpose for which the policy was purchased. Classify it as an investment.

14.6. Selmer Furniture Company operates its only facility in a state which levies a flat tax of 12% on corporate income and allows the Federal income tax as a deduction in computing income subject to state tax. The state tax, in turn, is an allowable deduction in computing the amount subject to Federal income tax. The Federal tax rate is 40% of taxable income. For the year 19X5, the Selmer Furniture Company had net income of $325,750 before either state or Federal income taxes.

(a) Compute the company's liability for both state and Federal income taxes for 19X5. Prove that the amounts computed are correct by preparing the necessary schedule. Round all amounts to the nearest dollar.

(b) Prepare a schedule computing net income after all income taxes.

(c) Prepare journal entries to record the income tax liabilities.

SOLUTION

(a) *Computation of tax liabilities.*

Letting F = Federal income tax liability and S = state income tax liability,

$F = 0.40(\$325,750 - S)$

$S = 0.12(\$325,750 - F)$

$F = 0.4[\$325,750 - 0.12(\$325,750 - F)]$

$F = 0.4(\$325,750 - \$39,090 + 0.12 F)$

$F = \$130,300 - \$15,636 + 0.048 F$

$0.952 F = \$114,664$

$F = \$120,445$

$S = 0.12(\$325,750 - F)$

$S = 0.12(\$325,750 - \$120,445)$

$S = 0.12(\$205,305)$

$S = \$24,637$

PROOF

Income before income taxes	$325,750	Income before income taxes	$325,750
Less: State income taxes	24,637	Less: Federal income taxes	120,445
Taxable income, Federal	$301,113	Taxable income, state	$205,305
Tax at 40%	$120,445	Tax at 12%	$ 24,637

(b)	Net Income before State and Federal Income Taxes		$325,750
	Less: Provision for Federal Income Tax	$120,445	
	Provision for State Income Tax	24,637	145,082
	Net Income for the Period		$180,668

(c)	Provision for Federal Income Taxes	120,445	
	Federal Income Tax Payable		120,445
	To record liability for Federal income tax.		
	Provision for State Income Taxes	24,637	
	State Income Tax Payable		24,637
	To record liability for state income taxes.		

14.7. The transactions described below are those of the Latham Company during 19X5:

(1) During June, sold $18,000 in gift certificates (worth $2.50 each and redeemable against all items for sale). Redeemed certificates with a value of $14,400. The average markup on all goods for sale is 40%. Experience indicates that 3% of the certificates issued will never be redeemed.

(2) For May, salaries and wages amounted to $340,000, of which $70,000 was for earnings exceeding $7,000, and $210,000 for earnings exceeding $4,200. Income tax withholdings were $36,000, and FICA withholdings were 5.5% on wages up to $7,000. The state unemployment tax rate is 2.9% and the Federal unemployment tax is 0.5% (on wages up to $4,200). The payroll entry including the tax liabilities is recorded in a compound entry.

(3) For August, sales were $187,465, including $150,000 on open account. There is a 5% sales tax on all items except food. Food sales represented 28% of total sales before sales taxes.

(4) Under its rental contract, the company must pay $500 in advance plus 8% of the net income earned by store A, net of total rent and a 45% provision for income taxes. For the month of August, net operating income of store A, before rent or income taxes, amounted to $25,000. (Compute rent expense.)

Prepare journal entries for the above transactions.

SOLUTION

(1)	Cash	18,000	
	Liability for Gift Certificates Outstanding	14,940	
	Liability for Gift Certificates Outstanding		18,000
	Sales		14,400
	Forfeited Gift Certificates Income		540
	Issuance of gift certificates for $18,000 and redemption of $14,400 during June and reduction of the liability account for certificates not expected to be redeemed.		

(2)   Salary Expense   340,000
            FICA Tax Expense (5.5% × $270,000)   14,850
            State Unemployment Tax Expense (2.9% × $130,000)   3,770
            Federal Unemployment Tax Expense (0.5% × $130,000)   650
                    Liability for Income Taxes Withheld   36,000
                    FICA Taxes Payable (11% × $270,000)   29,700
                    State Unemployment Tax Payable   3,770
                    Federal Unemployment Tax Payable   650
                    Accrued Payroll   289,150
            Accrued payroll and payroll taxes for May.

(3)   Accounts Receivable   150,000
            Cash   37,465
                    Sales*   180,951
                    Sales Tax Payable**   6,514
            Sales and sales taxes for August, computed as follows:

                    *N = sales net of sales taxes

                    $187,465 = 0.28 N + 0.72 N(1.05)$

                    $187,465 = 0.28 N + 0.756 N$

                    $187,465 = 1.036 N$

                    $N = \$187,465/1.036$

                    $N = \$180,951$

                ** $\$180,951 \times 72\% \times 5\% = \$6,514$

(4)   Rent Expense   500
                    Cash   500
            Advance rent paid for August.

            Rent Expense   1,033
                    Rent Payable   1,033
            Additional rent for August computed as follows:

                    R = monthly rent

                    T = income taxes

                    $R = \$500 + 0.08(\$25,000 - R - T) = \$500 + \$2,000 - 0.08 R - 0.08 T$

                    $T = 0.45(\$25,000 - R) = \$11,250 - 0.45 R$

                    $R = \$500 + \$2,000 - 0.08 R - 0.08(\$11,250 - 0.45 R)$

                    $R = \$2,500 - 0.08 R - \$900 + 0.036 R$

            $1.044 R = \$1,600$

                    $R = \$1,533$

        Additional rent = $\$1,533 - \$500 = \$1,033$

14.8. The Nearland Trucking Corporation leases land to the Farland Mining Company, and
       has received minimum annual royalties of $30,000 in the preceding four-year period.
       The lease contains the following royalty provisions:

       (1)   The basis for earned royalties is 10 cents per ton shipped from the mine
             plus a per ton amount equal to 4% of the amount that the market value of
             the ore at the mine exceeds $6 per ton.   Operations in the current year are
             summarized below:

Quarter	Tons Shipped	Market Value at Dest., per Ton	Freight from Mine to Dest., per Ton
1	120,000	$12	$4.10
2	none		
3	none		
4	210,000	11	4.50

(2) Minimum annual royalty is $10,000, with a minimum of $2,500 payable quarterly. Unearned minimum royalties may be recovered in any subsequent period from earned royalties in excess of minimum royalties.

(a) Compute the royalty amount due Nearland for the current year and the amount of unearned minimum royalty at year end.

(b) How should the unearned minimum royalty payment in part (a) be reported on Farland's balance sheet at year end?

SOLUTION

(a)

	Royalties Paid to Nearland Trucking Corporation	Balance of Recoverable Unearned Minimum Royalties
Balance, Beginning of Current Year		$ 30,000
First Quarter:		
Minimum Quarterly Royalty	$ 2,500	32,500
Unearned Minimum Royalty Recovered (Schedule A)		(21,120)
Balance		$ 11,380
Second Quarter, Minimum Royalty	2,500	13,880
Third Quarter, Minimum Royalty	2,500	16,380
Fourth Quarter, Royalty Paid (see Schedule B)	8,820	(16,380)
Royalties Paid for the Current Year	$16,320	
Recoverable Unearned Minimum Royalties at Year End		$ —0—

SCHEDULE A
COMPUTATION OF EARNED ROYALTIES

	First Quarter	Fourth Quarter
Additional Royalty per Ton:		
Market Value per Ton at Destination	$ 12.00	$ 11.00
Less: Freight to Destination	4.10	4.50
Market Value at Mine	$ 7.90	$ 6.50
Base Price for Rate Computation	6.00	6.00
Basis for Additional Royalty	$ 1.90	$ 0.50
Additional Royalty at 4%	$ 0.076	$ 0.02
Base Royalty Rate	0.10	.10
Total Royalty Rate per Ton	$ 0.176	$ 0.12
Tons Shipped in Quarter	120,000	210,000
Total Royalty Earned during the Quarter	$ 21,120	$ 25,200

SCHEDULE B
ROYALTY PAYMENT FOR FOURTH QUARTER

Royalty Earned in Fourth Quarter (Schedule A)	$25,200
Less: Balance of Recoverable Unearned Minimum Royalty	
at Beginning of Fourth Quarter	16,380
Royalty Payment, Fourth Quarter	$ 8,820

(b) If the unearned minimum royalty is expected to be recovered during the subsequent time period, it is properly classified as a prepaid royalty. What is not clear from the problem is that these minimum royalties will be recovered, or are recoverable, in the future. The only thing that is clear is that the company must continue paying at least the minimum of $2,500 per quarter. If these minimum payments are not recoverable, they should be written off as paid.

14.9. The R & M Electronics Company manufactures a line of radio transistors which it markets under a six-month guarantee to replace defective units at no charge. Each transistor is stamped with a date at the time of sale so that the warranty may be properly administered. At the beginning of the company's fiscal year, April 1, 19X5, the company's balance sheet showed an Estimated Liability for Product Warranty of $247,500. By August 31, 19X5, this account had been reduced to $42,250 by charges for the net cost of defective transistors returned which had been sold in the previous year. The net cost of replacing defective transistors sold in the current year (April through July) was recorded in the product warranty expense account.

For the first four months of the current year, unit returns under the warranty are expected to run to 8% of sales revenue. On August 1, 19X5, the company introduced a new type of transistor and, therefore, increased this estimate to 10% as of that date. It is assumed that no units sold during a given month are returned in that month.

The following table represents R & M's projection of the likely sales return pattern for the six-month period of the warranty, beginning with the month following the sale.

Month after Sale	Expected Percentage of Total Returns
1st	*30*
2nd	*20*
3rd	*20*
4th–6th (at 10% each month)	*30*

Gross sales of transistors for the first six months of the year are

April	*$1,800,000*	*July*	*$1,425,000*
May	*1,650,000*	*August*	*1,000,000*
June	*2,050,000*	*September*	*980,000*

The warranty covers not only the transistor but the shipping cost on the defective unit and on the new one sent out as a replacement. The shipping cost averages approximately 10% of the sales price. The cost to manufacture is roughly about 80% of the sales price, and the salvage price runs about 15% of the sales price. Inventories at April 1, 19X5, therefore, included returned transistors valued at 15% of their original sales price.

Prepare (a) a schedule of estimated product warranty liability at September 30, 19X5 and (b) the required adjusting journal entries as of that date. (AICPA adapted.)

SOLUTION

(a)

Month of Sale	Gross Sales	Expected Returns %	Expected Returns Amount	Estimated Potential Returns at September 30 %	Estimated Potential Returns at September 30 Amount
April	$1,800,000	8	$144,000	10	$ 14,400
May	1,650,000	8	132,000	20	26,400
June	2,050,000	8	164,000	30	49,200
July	1,425,000	8	114,000	50	57,000
August	1,000,000	10	100,000	70	70,000
September	980,000	10	98,000	100	98,000
Sales Value of Potential Returns at September 30					$315,000

ESTIMATED LIABILITY AT SEPTEMBER 30

Estimated Cost of Tubes Returned ($315,000 × 0.80)	$252,000
Estimated Freight Charges ($315,000 × 10%)	31,500
	$283,500
Less: Salvage Value ($315,000 × 15%)	47,250
Estimated Liability at September 30	$236,250

(b) **ADJUSTING ENTRY**

Product Warranty Expense	194,000	
Estimated Product Warranty Liability		194,000
To adjust liability account to amount needed as follows:		
Amount required at September 30	$236,250	
Balance of account at September 30	42,250	
Required addition	$194,000	

NOTE: This solution is based on the assumption that all incurred costs in making good on warranties relating to sales of tubes to September 30 have already been charged to Product Warranty Expense. Note that the problem specifies that the charges relating to the net cost of replacing defective tubes for the period April 1 to July 31 have been charged to this account.

14.10. At March 31, 19X6 the account balances relating to liabilities, and other data relating to obligations and commitments of the Suffolk Corporation, showed the following:

Accounts payable, trade	$ 94,200
Property taxes payable	900
Discount on notes payable	1,350
Allowance for purchase discounts	1,500
Notes payable	30,000
Bonds payable, $50,000 due annually at September 30	400,000
Accrued payroll	3,250
Payroll taxes payable	850
Liability for income taxes withheld	1,275
Income taxes payable	12,600
Estimated liability for outstanding coupons	6,000
Deferred service contract revenue (contracts are for one year)	8,000

Accounts receivable, excluding $30,000 which
    have been sold to a factor on *recourse* basis $150,000

Stock dividends, at par   5,000

Deferred income taxes payable   80,000

Loans payable to officers   75,000

On November 20, 19X5 the company had signed a contract for the purchase of merchandise in the latter part of 19X6 at a fixed price of $150,000. At March 31, 19X6, the merchandise had a market value in excess of $175,000.

Prepare the current liability section of the balance sheet at March 31, 19X6. Include in your answer any contingent liabilities and/or commitments which should be disclosed on that date.

SOLUTION

Suffolk Corporation
Current Liabilities
March 31, 19X6

Current Liabilities		
Notes Payable	$30,000	
Less: Discount on Notes Payable	1,350	$ 28,650
Accounts Payable, Trade	$94,200	
Less: Allowance for Purchase Discounts	1,500	92,700
Current Portion of Long-term Debt		50,000
Income Taxes Payable		12,600
Deferred Service Contract Revenue		8,000
Other Accrued Liabilities		
Accrued Payroll	$ 3,250	
Payroll Taxes Payable	850	
Liability for Income Taxes Withheld	1,275	
Property Taxes Payable	900	
Estimated Liability for Outstanding Coupons	6,000	12,275
Total Current Liabilities*		$204,225

* **Contingent Liabilities.** At March 31, 19X6 the company is contingently liable to the extent of $30,000 as a result of a sale of accounts receivable to a factor on a *recourse* basis. In addition the company has signed a contract to purchase merchandise during the coming months at a fixed price of $150,000. Based upon current information, the market value of this merchandise is approximately $175,000.

NOTE: The stock dividend to be distributed is more properly included in the equity section of the balance sheet since no current assets are involved in the proposed distribution. Deferred income taxes are properly classifiable as a long-term liability in the absence of more specific information. Loans payable to officers could be classified as a current liability if it is the intent of the company to repay those loans currently. The solution here assumes that these loans are, and will be, renewable. Note further that while deferred service contract revenue is listed separately, the estimated liability for outstanding coupons is listed among the accrued liabilities. The former account is a more definite one—hence the treatment.

14.11. The Harkness Theatre Group, Incorporated has as part of its staff contract a profit-sharing clause stating that 20% of income in excess of $50,000 will be distributed equally to staff members at the end of each season. For the current season, the staff totaled 25, income before taxes and bonus was $125,000 and the applicable income tax rate was 40%.

Compute the total amount set aside for distribution of profits if that amount were based on excess income (a) before taxes and bonus and (b) after the bonus but before taxes. (c) What was each staff member's bonus for the season in each case?

SOLUTION

(a) Letting $B =$ bonus,

$$B = 0.20(\$125,000 - \$50,000)$$
$$B = 0.20(\$75,000)$$
$$B = \$15,000$$

(b)

$$B = 0.20(\$125,000 - \$50,000 - B)$$
$$B = \$25,000 - \$10,000 - 0.2B$$
$$1.2B = \$15,000$$
$$B = \$12,500$$

Proof: Net income less bonus ($125,000 − $12,500) exceeds $50,000 by $62,500. Thus, 20% of $62,500 equals the bonus, $12,500.

(c) According to the terms in (a), each staff member receives a $600 bonus; in (b), $500.

Chapter 15

Long-term Liabilities

15.1 INTRODUCTION

Liabilities that do not require the use of current funds (i.e. current assets) are designated as *long-term* and are shown as a separate balance sheet category immediately following Current Liabilities. Typically, this category includes bonds, notes, mortgages, obligations to affiliated companies and other obligations of a long-term nature. Pensions and deferred compensation agreements as well as long-term lease obligations are also considered long-term liabilities; these will be covered in detail in Intermediate Accounting II.

Long-term liabilities are generally based on written contracts which detail the rights and obligations of both the lender and the borrower. Contract provisions cover such matters as the amount borrowed, the interest rate, the due date of the obligation, interest payment dates, property pledged as security (if any) and various restrictions on the debtor while the debt is outstanding. Obligations which have property pledged as collateral are called *secured* obligations. The security may be real property (mortgages), equipment (equipment notes or chattel mortgages), or other securities (collateral trust bonds). Unsecured obligations, those that are backed only by the general credit of the issuing corporation, are called *debentures*.

While short-term obligations generally do not have an interest factor (except for bank obligations or notes), the same cannot be said for long-term obligations. In the latter case, the interest factor is generally of great importance and must be carefully considered.

15.2 BONDS PAYABLE

The sale of bonds as a means of raising funds for a business enterprise has the advantage of dividing a large obligation into smaller units. Although bonds are generally issued in denominations of $1,000 each, smaller denominations (as low as $100) are becoming increasingly available. This can be of great importance to a borrower since it is now possible to raise funds from many sources instead of a relative handful of traditional credit sources. The contract, which specifies agreement terms between the issuer and the buyer, is called an *indenture*. Generally, this document is held by a *trustee* who acts as an intermediary to protect the rights of the bondholders as well as the borrower.

Bonds may be *registered* [interest and principal (or face value) payable to holder of record only] or *bearer* (interest and principal payable to whoever presents periodic interest coupon and bond at maturity) obligations. They may mature in installments (*serial bonds*) or at a specific time (*term bonds*).

Some bond issues rank behind others and are known as *subordinated debentures* or *second mortgage bonds*. They may be *guaranteed* by other companies, *callable* at the option of the issuing corporation, or *convertible* into common or preferred stock at the option of the holder. *Income* bonds pay periodic interest only if such interest is earned. *Revenue bonds* pay interest from specific revenue sources and are generally issued by governmental units.

The entire bond issue may be placed with a single financial institution or sold to investment bankers who, in turn, retail the bonds to individuals or other investors. These investment bankers may *underwrite* the issue (that is, guarantee a certain price to the issuer and assume the risk of reselling the bonds), or they may simply agree to sell the bonds on a commission basis.

All bond issues are based upon a formal authorization by the board of directors and/or the stockholders. Where the bond issue is underwritten, the entire issue is recorded as sold at the time of sale to the underwriters. When the entire issue is not sold at one time, the balance sheet should disclose both the amount of bonds authorized as well as the portion sold.

15.3   ACCOUNTING FOR ISSUANCE OF BONDS

Bond contracts contain two kinds of future payments: (1) a fixed sum called the *face* or *maturity value* at a specific date and (2) *interest payable*, generally at six-month intervals, which is usually expressed as a percentage of face value. This is the *contractual* rate of interest and is generally referred to as the *nominal* or *coupon* rate. It is set at a level sufficient to attract the required funds based upon the issuing company's future expectations. However, the money or capital markets tend to have their own expectations as to bond issues (see Section 13.9). If the market is willing to take these bonds at their nominal rate, the bond will sell at face value. If the market rate of interest is greater than the coupon rate, the bonds will sell at a *discount*. If the market rate is lower than the nominal rate, the bonds will sell at a *premium*. The *yield* or *effective rate* of interest is the rate actually earned by the bondholders on their investment.

EXAMPLE 1.

Assume that a corporation issues $100,000 face value bonds, payable in five years and carrying a 7% coupon interest rate with semiannual interest payments of $3,500. The proceeds realized by the issuing corporation will vary according to the yield rate expectations of investing underwriters or syndicates:

Amount bid for bonds assuming a yield rate of 6%		**Amount bid for bonds assuming a yield rate of 8%**	
Present value of $100,000 due in 5 years @ 6%, with interest paid semiannually	$ 74,410	*Present value of $100,000 due in 5 years @ 8%, with interest paid semiannually*	$67,560
Present value of $3,500 every six months for 5 years @ 6% (3% semiannually)	29,856	*Present value of $3,500 every six months for 5 years @ 8% (4% semiannually)*	28,388
Proceeds of bond issue	$104,266	*Proceeds of bond issue*	$95,948

The proceeds realized by the issuing corporation is the price paid by the underwriters, who then resell the bonds publicly at a higher price but lower yield, thus insuring their own profit margin. The entries on the issuing corporation's books to record the sale at premium or discount are

Effective Rate — 6%

Cash	104,266	
Premium on Bonds Payable		4,266
Bonds Payable		100,000

Effective Rate — 8%

Cash	95,948	
Discount on Bonds Payable	4,052	
Bonds Payable		100,000

The issuing corporation generally incurs other bond-issue related expenses (e.g. accounting, legal, printing, promotional, etc.).   According to APB Opinion No. 21, these should be treated separately as deferred costs (i.e. debited to a deferred expense account such as Unamortized Bond Issue Expense and charged to revenue over the life of the issue). Thus, in the balance sheet, such costs would be classified under Assets rather than Long-term Liabilities.

15.4 ACCOUNTING FOR BOND INTEREST EXPENSE

It is obvious from the preceding discussion that the total interest expense to the issuing corporation will be greater or smaller depending on the effective interest rate.

EXAMPLE 2.

If the bonds in Example 1 are sold to yield 6%, the premium received of $4,266 serves to reduce the average interest expense to $3,074 per semiannual period ($35,000 total interest less $4,266 premium/10 interest periods).   If sold to yield 8%, the discount given of $4,052 serves to increase the average interest expense to $3,905 per semiannual interest period ($35,000 total interest plus $4,052 discount/10 interest periods).   The entries to record the semiannual payment of interest under this straight-line amortization are

Bonds Sold at a Premium

Interest Expense	3,074	
Premium on Bonds Payable	426	
Cash		3,500

Bonds Sold at a Discount

Interest Expense	3,905	
Discount on Bonds Payable		405
Cash		3,500

15.5 STRAIGHT-LINE VERSUS EFFECTIVE RATE AMORTIZATION

The straight-line method of interest amortization described in Example 2 results in an equal interest amount incurred each period over the life of the bond issue.   Theoretically, the recorded interest expense should equal the effective interest expense, thus indicating the real cost of the money used by the issuing corporation.

EXAMPLE 3.

If the bonds in Example 1 are priced to yield 6%, the premium of $4,266 can be said to represent an advance paid by bondholders for the right to receive larger periodic interest checks and, therefore, can be viewed as a reduction in the actual interest cost to the corporate borrower.   In effect, the book value of the debt decreases as the bonds approach maturity until, at maturity, the bonds reach $100,000.   Thus while the straight-line method of premium amortization indicates that the semiannual interest expense is computed at $3,074, the interest expense using the effective interest rate method presented below shows that the semiannual interest expense would amount to $3,128 for the first interest period and $3,015 for the tenth interest period.

Bonds Sold at a Premium
Accounting for Interest Expense, Effective Interest Method

($100,000, 5-year bonds, annual interest of 7%, payable semiannually,
sold at $104,265, to yield 6% compounded semiannually)

Interest period	(1) Interest paid (3½% of $100,000)	(2) Effective interest expense (3% of bond book value)	(3) Premium amortization (1 − 2)	(4) Bond premium balance (4 − 3)	(5) Book value of bonds ($100,000 + 4)
At time of issue				$4,265	$104,265
1	$3,500	$3,128	$372	3,893	103,893
2	3,500	3,117	383	3,510	103,510
3	3,500	3,105	395	3,115	103,115
4	3,500	3,093	407	2,708	102,708
5	3,500	3,081	419	2,289	102,289
6	3,500	3,069	431	1,858	101,858
7	3,500	3,056	444	1,414	101,414
8	3,500	3,042	458	956	100,956
9	3,500	3,029	471	485	100,485
10	3,500	3,015	485	—	100,000

A similar table can be constructed for bonds issued at a discount. The first interest period would show a cash payment of $3,500 for interest, actual interest expense of $3,838 (4% of $95,944), amortization of discount $338, and bond book value of $96,282.

15.6   REPORTING BOND ISSUES

As of the issue date, the issuing corporation's obligation can be measured by the actual cash received. Thus, bond discount and premium are valuation accounts relating to the bonds payable account. As of the date of issue, therefore, bonds payable would be presented on the balance sheet as follows (assuming the sale at a premium):

> *Long-term Debt*
> *7% Bonds Payable, Due in 5 Years:*
> > *Maturity Value* $100,000
> > *Add: Bond Premium*   4,266
> > *Net Liability* $104,266

APB Opinion No. 21 requires, in connection with notes, and equally applicable to bonds, that *premium or discount should be added or deducted from the face amount.* It should not be shown on the balance sheet as a deferred charge or deferred credit.

In periods of sharply fluctuating interest rates, a *call* provision may be put into the contract. This provision entitles the borrower to "pay off" or "call" the bonds prior to maturity and is useful when more favorable financing (a smaller interest cost) can be secured. To compensate the lender for the loss of future interest payments, a *call premium* is generally paid by the borrower; these are usually established at decreasing values as the bonds move closer to maturity.

Since financial statements are prepared under the going-concern assumption, the retirement of long-term debt as of the balance sheet date is not normally expected. However, if a decision to call the bonds has been made, it must be disclosed in the statements. This is generally accomplished by moving the liability up to Current Liabilities, unless the bonds are to be paid from a sinking fund. In that case, a parenthetical notation or a footnote giving the essential details of the contemplated redemption is sufficient.

15.7 BONDS ISSUED BETWEEN INTEREST DATES

Generally, bond interest payments are made semiannually on dates specified in the indenture. However, when bonds are sold between interest dates, the amount of accrued interest since the last interest date is added to the price of the bond. The buyer then receives the full six-month interest payment at the next semiannual interest payment date.

EXAMPLE 4.

Assume that MGC, Incorporated issues $300,000 in twenty-year, 6% bonds, with interest payable semiannually on May 1 and November 1. The bonds are sold on July 1 for $321,420 plus accrued interest for two months. The bonds are dated May 1 and the borrower incurs various issue costs amounting to $3,570.

Since the actual borrowing time is 19 years and 10 months, or 238 months, proper accounting for this debt should reflect this fact. The average interest expense per month may be calculated as follows:

Actual interest payments for 20 years (20 × $18,000)		*$360,000*
Less: Premium received at issue date	*$21,420*	
Accrued interest received (May 1–July 1)	*3,000*	*24,420*
Total interest expense for 19 years, 10 months		*$335,580*
Average interest expense per month ($335,580 ÷ 238 months)		*$ 1,410*

The monthly interest accrual amounts to $1,500. However, since the average interest cost is only $1,410, the monthly premium amortization will amount to the difference, or $90 ($21,420 ÷ 238 months) and issue costs would be amortized at $15 per month ($3,570 ÷ 238 months). If the amortization of interest costs and premium are recorded at the end of the year, the entries relating to the bond issue for the first year of issuance are

Various Dates as Costs are Incurred

Bond Issue Costs	*3,570*	
Cash		*3,570*

July 1 (Issue Date)

Cash	*324,420*	
Bonds Payable		*300,000*
Bond Interest Expense		*3,000*
Premium on Bonds Payable		*21,420*

November 1 (First Interest Payment)

Bond Interest Expense	*9,000*	
Cash		*9,000*

December 31 (End of First Fiscal Year)

Bond Interest Expense	*2,460*	
Bond Issue Expense (15 × 6 mos.)	*90*	
Premium on Bonds Payable	*540*	
Bond Issue Costs		*90*
Bond Interest Payable		*3,000*

Computations:

Interest expense for 2 mos. (Nov. 1–Dec. 31)	$3,000
Less: Premium amortization for 6 mos. @ $90	540
Net interest expense for 2 mos.	$2,460

15.8 ACQUISITION AND RETIREMENT OF TERM BONDS

An issuing corporation may often acquire its own bonds and hold them in the treasury, as part of a sinking fund, or retire them permanently.   The transaction cycle is completed by such acquisition and the debt no longer exists for the corporation.   Thus, a gain or loss must be recognized equal to the difference between the amount paid to retire the bonds and their book value (maturity value plus bond premium less issue costs and discount).

EXAMPLE 5.

Assume that $75,000 of MGC, Incorporated bonds described in Example 4 are retired on December 1 of the second year.   If the bonds are retired at 103 plus accrued interest of $375, the following entries would be required.

February 1 (17 Months after Issuance)

Premium on Bonds Payable	247.50	
Bond Issue Expense	41.25	
Bond Interest Expense		247.50
Bond Issue Costs		41.25

To record amortization on $75,000 of bonds for the period
January 1 to December 1.
Amortization of premium:
$247.50 [(11/238) × $21,420 × $75,000/$300,000].
Bond issue costs: $41.25 [(11/238) × $3,570 × $75,000/$300,000].

Bonds Payable	75,000.00	
Premium on Bonds Payable	4,972.50	
Bond Interest Expense	375.00	
Cash ($75,000 × 103 + $375 accrued interest)		77,625.00
Bond Issue Costs		828.75
Gain on Bond Retirement		1,893.75

To record retirement of $75,000 of bonds at 103 plus
accrued interest for one month as follows:

Original proceeds (25% of $321,420)	$80,355.00
Less: Original portion of issuance costs (25% × $3,570)	892.50
Book value at date of issuance	$79,462.50
Less: Amortization of premium for 17 mos.	382.50
	$79,080.00
Add: Amortization of bond issue costs for 17 mos.	63.75
Book value of bonds at retirement date	$79,143.75
Amount paid to retire bonds ($75,000 × 103)	77,250.00
Gain on bond retirement	$ 1,893.75

If bonds are acquired but not formally retired, Treasury Bonds may be debited for their face value.   However, a gain or loss must still be recognized in the manner illustrated above.   This account, Treasury Bonds, is not generally considered an asset and should be deducted from Bonds Payable on the balance sheet.   Treasury bonds do not pay interest unless they are held as an investment by a company-sponsored fund, such as an employee pension fund.   According to APB Opinion No. 26, "Early Extinguishment of Debt," gains or losses (net of income taxes), if unusual and infrequent, should be reported as extraordinary items in the period of retirement.   Such gains and losses should not be amortized to future periods.

15.9 SERIAL BONDS

In contrast to term bonds with fixed maturity dates, *serial bonds* provide repayment of principal in periodic installments. The two main advantages of serial bond issues are

(1) Periodic debt repayment is geared to the issuing corporation's periodic cash inflow from current operations. Thus, the need for sinking funds or appropriations from retained earnings to repay bonded indebtedness is eliminated.

(2) The shorter maturities usually sell at lower yields, thus reducing the issue's average interest rate.

15.10 DISCOUNT AND PREMIUM ON SERIAL BONDS

Since the terms of all bonds in a serial issue are identical except for the maturity date, the varying yield rate for each maturity results in varying discount or premium amounts. When the effective interest rates are known, each maturity should be treated as a separate bond issue.

EXAMPLE 6.

Suppose that $200,000 in five-year, 5% serial bonds are issued to be repaid at the rate of $40,000 per year, and each maturity sells at a price reflecting a different yield rate. Proper accounting would treat this sale as five separate bond issues of $40,000, maturing in one, two, three, four and five years, respectively. Each maturity would have a related premium or discount account, and interest expense as well as premium or discount amortization for each maturity would be calculated as described in Sections 15.5 and 15.6.

However, when entire serial bond issues are acquired for resale (as by underwriters) at a lump-sum price, the ultimate yield rates of the various maturities are often undeterminable by the borrower, who must then assume that the same yield rate applies to all maturities in the issue. Since, in such cases, the straight-line method of premium or discount amortization has a distorting effect on interest expense, the effective interest method, or alternatively, the *bonds outstanding method* should be used. The latter method results in a decreasing amount of premium or discount amortization each period in proportion to the decrease in the bonded indebtedness.

EXAMPLE 7.

To illustrate the bond outstanding method of amortization of premium or discount, we shall assume that the Henry Company issues $200,000 of five-year, 5% serial bonds, to be repaid at the rate of $40,000 each year. For purposes of simplicity, assume further that interest payments are made once a year. If the bonds are sold at an average yield rate of 6%, the proceeds will amount to about $194,750, resulting in a discount of $5,250. The discount and interest expense are prorated over the life of this entire issue under the *bonds outstanding method* as shown below. (The student may find it worthwhile to construct a similar table using the effective interest method, which results in a constant rate of interest expense relative to the book value of outstanding debt.)

Bonds Outstanding Method

Year	Bonds outstanding (maturity value)	Fraction of total of bonds outstanding	Amortization of discount ($5,250 × fraction)	Interest payments (5% of bonds outstanding)	Total interest expense
1	$200,000	20/60	$1,750	$10,000	$11,750
2	160,000	16/60	1,400	8,000	9,400
3	120,000	12/60	1,050	6,000	7,050
4	80,000	8/60	700	4,000	4,700
5	40,000	4/60	350	2,000	2,350
	$600,000	60/60	$5,250	$30,000	$35,250

If the straight-line method had been used in the above example, discount amortization would amount to $1,050 per year. Obviously, had the life of the bonds been longer or the discount greater, there would have been a much larger discrepancy between years.

The bonds outstanding method, however, is itself a variation of the straight-line method since the amount of discount amortization per $1,000 of maturity value of bonds outstanding is a constant figure [in Example 7, $8.75 ($5,250 ÷ $600,000) × $1,000]. Once this constant has been computed, the amortization amount at the end of each year can be readily calculated [in Example 7, the amortization at the end of the third year is the product of $120,000 (bonds outstanding at the beginning of the year) times $8.75 per $1,000, or $1,050].

15.11   ACQUISITION AND RETIREMENT OF SERIAL BONDS

When serial bonds are retired at maturity, Bonds Payable is debited and Cash is credited. Since the retirement is generally at par, no gain or loss is created. However, if serial bonds are acquired by the issuing corporation prior to maturity, a gain or loss on retirement is generally created since there is usually a difference between the acquisition price and book value. Book value at date of retirement of serial bonds is computed in the same manner as for single-maturity bonds (i.e. par value plus the related premium or less the related discount and issuance costs).

EXAMPLE 8.

Assume that $20,000 of the Henry Company bonds described in Example 7 are retired at the end of Year 2, two years ahead of schedule. The bonds are retired at 101 and interest has been paid for Year 2. Since the discount amortization on these bonds amounted to $8.75 per $1,000 per year, the discount amount to be written off can be readily computed as $350 ($20,000 × $8.75 per $1,000 × 2 = $350). Thus, bonds with a book value of $19,650 ($20,000 − $350 discount) are retired for $20,200, creating a loss of $550. The entry to record the retirement is

Bonds Payable	20,000	
Loss on Bond Retirement	550	
Discount on Bonds Payable		350
Cash		20,200

The original discount table must now be revised to reflect the elimination of $350 by the retirement of $20,000 face-value bonds.

15.12   BOND REFUNDING

The process of *refunding* represents the retirement of one bond issue with the proceeds of another. If refunding occurs at the maturity of the old debt, the two transactions (retirement of the old and issuance of the new) can be handled in the normal manner. However, when refunding occurs prior to the maturity date of the old issue (usually when interest rates have fallen), the call price of the old bonds will generally be different than book value, resulting in either a gain or a loss on retirement.

EXAMPLE 9.

Assume that the Leonard Corporation has outstanding $200,000 in 8% bonds having a remaining life of 5 years and a book value of $196,000 ($200,000 maturity less $4,000 discount). These bonds are called at $102½ and redeemed by the issuance of new 10-year bonds issued at par and bearing an interest coupon of 6%. The cancellation of bonds having a book value of $196,000 for $205,000 creates a loss of $9,000.

The APB, in Opinion No. 26, "Early Extinguishment of Debt," states that gains or losses on refunding, net of the tax effect, should be recognized currently and identified as a separate item. According to APB Opinion No. 30, these gains and losses are not *extraordinary* items as they are usual and recurring for companies having long-term debt. Such gains or losses, where material, should be reported as a separate item of income from operations.

15.13 CONVERTIBLE BONDS

Convertible bonds are those obligations issued by a corporation which may, at the option of the holder, be converted into either common or preferred stock. A portion of the proceeds of such bonds may, therefore, be attributable to the conversion privilege, a factor that is usually reflected in a lower coupon rate of interest. Theoretically, the conversion feature proceeds should be accounted for as paid-in capital and an amortizable bond discount (or reduced premium) recorded. However, APB Opinion No. 14, "Accounting for Convertible Debt and Debt Issued with Stock Purchase Warrants," which superseded APB Opinion No. 10 in this regard, states that when convertible debt is sold at a price or with a value at issuance not significantly in excess of the face amount, no portion of the proceeds should be attributable to the conversion feature.

15.14 BOND SINKING FUNDS

The creation of a sinking fund for the eventual redemption of outstanding bonds is generally required by the indenture, although some corporations may create them voluntarily. To avoid the reduction in working capital which results from sinking fund deposits and dividend payments, an appropriation of retained earnings is generally created to restrict the amount of such accumulated earnings available for the declaration of dividends. Such restrictions should be thoroughly disclosed in the financial statements.

15.15 MISCELLANEOUS LONG-TERM LIABILITIES

Other types of long-term liabilities frequently found in the financial statements of business concerns include Notes Payable, Mortgages Payable, Equipment Contracts Payable, etc. The primary accounting considerations relating to these liabilities are similar to those for bonds (see Sections 15.2-15.14). Where notes and mortgages are involved, APB Opinion No. 21 requires that if no interest is specified or if the rate is unreasonably low, then interest must be *imputed* to the debt and properly accounted for.

In highly condensed balance sheets, a variety of deferred credit or *quasi-liability* items are frequently reported as long-term liabilities. These range from unearned revenue items (unrealized profit on installment sales, rentals received in advance, etc.) to Federal income taxes deferred and deferred investment tax credits.

15.16 REPORTING LONG-TERM LIABILITIES ON THE BALANCE SHEET

Long-term liabilities should be fully disclosed in either the balance sheet itself or in the accompanying notes. For example, some companies may have large amounts of long-term debt with varying interest rates and maturities. Generally this would be presented as one amount under the balance sheet heading, Bonds Payable; however, this figure would be supported by a supplementary schedule showing the details of each issue. Furthermore, any assets pledged or intended for use in liquidating long-term liabilities should be shown in the asset section of the balance sheet. Any portion of long-term debt which will mature within one year should be shown as a current liability, unless its retirement will not require the use of current assets.

Summary

(1) Liabilities that do not require the use of current assets are termed _____ liabilities.

(2) Unsecured obligations backed only by the general credit of the issuing corporation are called _____.

(3) If the coupon rate of a bond is 6% and the yield is 6.75%, the bond will sell at a _____ ; if the yield is 5.50%, the bond will sell at a _____.

(4) When $500,000, 6%, 10-year bonds are issued and subsequently sold at 103, the average annual interest cost will be _____; if they are sold at 96, it will be_____.

(5) On the balance sheet the premium on bonds should be _____ par value, the discount should be _____ par value; while bond issue costs should be included under _____.

(6) Long-term liabilities do *not* include (a) bonds, (b) notes, (c) dividends payable, (d) mortgages.

(7) Bonds do *not* include the following types: (a) registered, (b) serial, (c) term, (d) convertible, (e) debenture, (f) income, (g) expense.

(8) An accepted method of interest amortization is (a) double-declining balance, (b) bonds outstanding, (c) last-in, first-out, (d) average cost.

(9) APB Opinion No. 14 requires the following practice in valuing the conversion feature of convertible bonds: (a) no value assigned to conversion feature, (b) prorata portion of cost, (c) present value, (d) incremental cost.

(10) When bonds carry detachable warrants, the warrants should carry (a) no value, (b) prorata cost, (c) incremental cost, (d) an assigned value.

Answers: (1) long-term; (2) debentures; (3) discount, premium;

           (4) $28,500 ($500,000 face value + $300,000 interest − $515,000 proceeds = $285,000 ÷ 10), $32,000 ($500,000 + $300,000 − $480,000 = $320,000 ÷ 10);

           (5) added to, deducted from, Other Assets; (6) c; (7) g; (8) b; (9) a; (10) d.

Solved Problems

15.1. On April 1, 1976, the Y Company issued $4,500,000 of serial bonds to be redeemed at the rate of $900,000 per year for the next five years. The discount on the issue amounted to $236,250.

(a) Show how the discount of $236,250 would be amortized under the bonds outstanding method.

(b) Compute the amount of discount that would be amortized during the fiscal year ending May 31, 1978.

SOLUTION

(*a*) Under this method, discount amortization is accomplished by charges to the interest expense account based upon the ratio of bonds outstanding during the period to total bonds outstanding over the entire period (see Example 7). In this problem, the constant amortization amount would be computed as follows:

Year	Dates	Outstanding at Beginning of Year
1	April 1, 1976–March 31, 1977	$ 4,500,000
2	April 1, 1977–March 31, 1978	3,600,000
3	April 1, 1978–March 31, 1979	2,700,000
4	April 1, 1979–March 31, 1980	1,800,000
5	April 1, 1980–March 31, 1981	900,000
	Total	$13,500,000

$236,250/$13,500 = $17.50 per $1,000 of bonds outstanding

(*b*) **Computation of amortization for fiscal year ended May 31, 1978**

June 1, 1977–March 31, 1978	
($17.50 × $3,600 × 10/12)	$52,500
April 1, 1978–May 31, 1978	
($17.50 × $2,700 × 2/12)	7,875
Amortization for the period	
June 1, 1977–May 31, 1978	$60,375

15.2. The Lyle Corporation is planning to issue $2 million, 9% bonds due in 15 years with interest on these bonds payable annually. Compute the proceeds Lyle can expect to receive from the proposed bond issue if the market rate of interest is (*a*) 8% and (*b*) 10%.

SOLUTION

The solution to this and other problems involving present value demands that the accountant be familiar with the arithmetic involving interest computations and have available the necessary tables for the purposes indicated. The solution to this particular problem, for example, involves two different interest tables. Table 1 is called "Present Value of $1 at Compound Interest Due in *n* Periods" and applies to the entire face value of $2,000,000. From Table 2, "Present Value of an Ordinary Annuity of $1 per Period," the annuity is represented by the periodic payment of the interest charge on $180,000 (see Appendix).

(*a*) **Market rate of interest 8%**

Present value of $2,000,000 due in 15 years at 8%	
($2,000,000 × 0.3152)	$ 630,400
Present value of an annuity of $180,000 (annual interest charge) for 15 years at 8% ($180,000 × 8.5595)	1,540,710
Expected proceeds of bond issue at a market rate of 8%	$2,171,110

(*b*) **Market rate of interest 10%**

Present value of $2,000,000 due in 15 years at 10%	
($2,000,000 × 0.2394)	$ 478,800
Present value of an annuity of $180,000 for 15 years at 10% ($180,000 × 7.6061)	1,369,098
Expected proceeds of bond issue at a market rate of 10%	$1,847,898

15.3. At June 30, 1976, the balance sheet of the Rivers Corporation included the following:

9% Convertible Debentures, due June 30, 1992 $1,000,000

Discount on Convertible Debentures   30,000

At the time the bonds were issued, no value had been assigned to the conversion feature. Under the terms of the bond indenture, each $1,000 bond is convertible into 40 shares of $5 par value common stock. On July 1, 1976, all of the bondholders decide to convert their holdings into the common stock when the common is selling for $30 per share.

Record the conversion of the bonds into common stock at July 1, 1976.

SOLUTION

Since APB Opinion No. 14 states that "no portion of the proceeds from the issuance of...convertible debt securities...should be accounted for as attributable to the conversion feature," the appropriate entry in the absence of an assigned value to the conversion feature is

9% Convertible Debentures	1,000,000	
Discount on Convertible Debentures		30,000
Common Stock $5 Par Value (40,000 shares)		200,000
Paid-in Capital in Excess of Par Value		770,000

To record the conversion of $1,000,000 in debentures into 40,000 shares of $5 par value common.

15.4. On June 30, 1976, Royal Corporation has outstanding $20,000,000 of 7%, 20-year bonds due in eight years and nine months. On April 1, 1976, the unamortized discount on these bonds amounted to $882,000. On July 1, 1976, Royal called $2,000,000 of these bonds for redemption at 101 plus accrued interest for three months.

(a) Give the journal entry to record the accrual of interest and the amortization of bond discount under the straight-line method for the three-month period ended June 30, 1976.

(b) Give the journal entry to record the call of $2,000,000 of these bonds on July 1, 1976 at 101 plus accrued interest for three months, assuming that reversing entries are not used.

SOLUTION

(a)

Bond Interest Expense	374,500	
Discount on Bonds Payable		24,500
Bond Interest Payable		350,000

Computed as follows:

Interest = $20,000,000 × 0.07 × $\frac{1}{4}$ = $350,000

Amortization of discount = $882,000/36 quarters to maturity = $24,500

(b)

Bonds Payable	2,000,000	
Bond Interest Payable	35,000	
Loss on Retirement of Bonds	105,750	
Discount on Bonds Payable		85,750
Cash		2,055,000

To record the recall of $2,000,000 face-value bonds outstanding plus accrued interest for three months. At the call date, the unamortized discount on the bonds called was equal to 10% ($882,000 − $24,500), or $85,750.

15.5. On July 1, 1976, the Fairfield Corporation sold 20,000, $100 par value bonds for $2,056,701. As part of the bond issue, the corporation attached thereto detachable warrants. Immediately upon issuance, the bonds were quoted at 97 and the warrants had a total market value of $160,000.

Prepare the journal entry to record the sale of the bonds. Accrued interest on the bonds is not a factor.

SOLUTION

The solution to this problem involves the application of APB Opinion No. 14, "Accounting for Convertible Debt and Debt Issued with Stock Purchase Warrants." See Section 13.6 for a discussion of this topic.

Cash	2,056,701	
Discount on Bonds Payable	100,000	
Bonds Payable		2,000,000
Paid-in Capital Stock Purchase Warrants		156,701

To record the sale of bonds with stock warrants attached.

The values assigned were computed as follows:

Market value assigned to bonds	$1,940,000
Market value of warrants	160,000
Total market value of bonds and warrants	$2,100,000

The total proceeds of $2,056,701 are assigned as follows:

Bonds: $2,056,701 × (1,940,000/2,100,000) = $1,900,000

Warrants: $2,056,701 × (160,000/2,100,00) = $156,701

15.6. The balance sheet of Consolidated Trousers, Incorporated showed the following at June 30, 1975:

8% Bonds Payable, maturing June 30, 1990	$500,000
Discount on Bonds Payable	7,500
Unamortized Bond Issuance Costs	2,865

(a) Compute the annual interest expense, including the amortization of bond discount and bond issuance costs. Use straight-line amortization.

(b) Prepare the entry to record the retirement of $200,000 face value bonds at 104 on July 1, 1980.

(c) Show how the accounts relating to bonds payable would appear on the balance sheet at June 30, 1985.

SOLUTION

(a) **Computation of Annual Interest Expense**

Annual interest paid to bondholders (8% × $500,000)	$40,000
Annual bond discount amortization ($7,500/15)	500
Amortization of bond issuance costs ($2,865/15)	191
Total bond interest expense per annum	$40,691

(b) **Retirement of Bonds on July 1, 1980**

8% Bonds Payable	200,000	
Loss on Retirement of Bonds	10,764	
Cash		208,000
Discount on Bonds Payable		2,000
Unamortized Bond Issuance Costs		764

To record the redemption of $200,000 of outstanding bonds at 104 and to write off portions of the bond discount and unamortized bond issuance costs account as follows:

	Bond Issuance Costs	Bond Discount
Amounts as of July 1, 1975	$2,865	$7,500
Write-off for the five-year period ended June 30, 1980	955	2,500
Balance, July 1, 1980	$1,910	$5,000
Applicable to bonds redeemed (40% of total issue)	764	2,000
Balance after write-off	$1,146	$3,000

(c) **Balance Sheet Presentation at June 30, 1985**

Deferred Charges		
Unamortized Bond Issuance Costs		$ 573
Long-term Debt		
8% Bonds Payable	$300,000	
Less: Discount on Bonds Payable	1,500	$298,500

NOTE: At June 30, 1985, 50% of the balance in the bond discount account and in the unamortized bond issuance cost account, as they appear after the July 1, 1980 redemption, would have been written off to operations.

15.7. The Board of Directors of Frizbee International authorized the issuance of $40,000,000 of 9%, 15-year bonds on January 1, 1975. The bonds were to be dated March 1 of that year and interest was to be paid semiannually on March 1 and September 1. Because of the size of the bond issue, the bonds were sold through an underwriting syndicate on May 1 of the same year.

Prepare all journal entries to record the issuance of the bonds, adjusting entries at June 30 (the end of the corporation's fiscal year), the entries to record the first two semiannual interest payments, and the adjusting entry at the end of the following fiscal year (round all figures to the nearest dollar, if necessary), assuming that:

(a) The bonds are sold to the underwriters at 96 plus accrued interest which the corporation records in Bond Interest Payable.

(b) The bonds are sold to the underwriters at 104.45 plus accrued interest which the company records in the Bond Interest Payable account.

SOLUTION

(a) **Sale to Underwriters at 96**

NOTE: Bonds will run from May 1, 1975 to February 28, 1990 (178 months). Total discount = $1,600,000. Write-off per month = $8,989 (rounded).

1975

May 1	Cash	39,000,000	
	Discount on Bonds Payable	1,600,000	
	Bonds Payable 9%		40,000,000
	Bond Interest Payable		600,000

To record the issuance of $40,000,000, 9%, 15-year bonds due February 28, 1990, at 96 plus accrued interest for two months.

June 30	Bond Interest Expense	617,978	
	Discount on Bonds Payable		17,978
	Bond Interest Payable		600,000

To record interest accrued for May and June, 1975 and to amortize discount for those two months at $8,989 per month.

Sept. 1	Bond Interest Expense	600,000	
	Bond Interest Payable	1,200,000	
	Cash		1,800,000

To record the payment of semiannual interest (9% × $40,000,000/2).

1976

| Mar. 1 | Bond Interest Expense | 1,800,000 | |
| | Cash | | 1,800,000 |

To record the payment of semiannual interest.

June 30	Interest Expense	1,307,868	
	Bond Interest Payable		1,200,000
	Discount on Bonds Payable		107,868

To accrue interest for 4 months and to write off discount for 12 months at $8,989 per month.

(b) Sale to underwriters at 104.45

NOTE: Total premium on bonds = $1,780,000.
        Premium write-off per month = $10,000.

1975

May 1	Cash	42,380,000	
	9% Bonds Payable		40,000,000
	Premium on Bonds Payable		1,780,000
	Bond Interest Payable		600,000

To record the issuance of $40,000,000, 9%, 15-year bonds at 104.45 plus accrued interest from March 1.

June 30	Bond Interest Expense	580,000	
	Premium on Bonds Payable	20,000	
	Bond Interest Payable		600,000

To record accrued interest payable for May and June, 1975 and to write off premium at the rate of $10,000 per month for the same period.

Sept. 1	Bond Interest Payable	1,200,000	
	Bond Interest Expense	600,000	
	Cash		1,800,000

Payment of semiannual interest expense (9%/2 × $40,000,000).

1976

| Mar. 1 | Bond Interest Expense | 1,800,000 | |
| | Cash | | 1,800,000 |

Semiannual interest expense.

June 30	Bond Interest Expense	1,080,000	
	Premium on Bonds Payable	120,000	
	Bond Interest Payable		1,200,000

To accrue interest expense for 4 months and to write off premium for 12 months at $10,000 per month.

15.8. On January 1, 1975, Frank Corporation issued $20,000,000 of 9% serial bonds. The bonds mature at the rate of $4,000,000 per year starting December 31, 1979. Net proceeds of the bond issue amounted to $20,420,000.

(a) Journalize the transaction for the issuance of the bonds.

(b) Prepare a schedule showing the amortization of the premium and the net interest expense for each year over the life of the bonds.

(c) Assume that on December 31, 1981, the following bonds were retired:

    (1) $4,000,000 due on December 31, 1981, at par

    (2) $ 200,000 due on December 31, 1982, at $102

    (3) $ 400,000 due on December 31, 1983, at $103

Prepare a compound entry to record the retirement of the bonds, assuming that all interest on them has already been paid and recorded.

SOLUTION

(a) **Journal entry**

Cash	20,420,000	
Premium on Bonds Payable		420,000
Bonds Payable		20,000,000

To record the issuance of serial bonds dated Jan. 1, 1975 at an interest rate of 9% per annum.

(b) **Amortization of premium and computation of interest expense**

Year	Bonds Outstanding (par value)	Fraction of Total Bonds Outstanding	(1) Amortization of Premium ($420,000 × Fraction)	(2) Interest Payments (9% of Bonds Outstanding)	Net Interest Expense (2 − 1)
1975	$ 20,000,000	20/140	$ 60,000	$ 1,800,000	$ 1,740,000
1976	20,000,000	20/140	60,000	1,800,000	1,740,000
1977	20,000,000	20/140	60,000	1,800,000	1,740,000
1978	20,000,000	20/140	60,000	1,800,000	1,740,000
1979	20,000,000	20/140	60,000	1,800,000	1,740,000
1980	16,000,000	16/140	48,000	1,440,000	1,392,000
1981	12,000,000	12/140	36,000	1,080,000	1,044,000
1982	8,000,000	8/140	24,000	720,000	696,000
1983	4,000,000	4/140	12,000	360,000	348,000
	$140,000,000		$420,000	$12,600,000	$12,180,000

Amortization of premium is equal to $300 per year
per $100,000 of bonds outstanding ($420,000/$1,400).

(c) **Journal entry to record retirement of bonds at Dec. 31, 1981**

Bonds Payable	4,600,000	
Premium on Bonds Payable	3,000	
Loss on Bond Retirement	13,000	
Cash		4,616,000

To record the retirement of $4,600,000 face-value bonds as follows:

Face Value of Bonds Retired	Due Date	Price	Cash Paid	Unamortized Premium*
$4,000,000	12-31-81	100	$4,000,000	—0—
200,000	12-31-82	102	204,000	$ 600
400,000	12-31-83	103	412,000	2,400
$4,600,000			$4,616,000	$3,000

* Based on $300 *per year* per $100,000 of face value bonds.

15.9. On April 2, 1976, the Board of Directors of the Sonora Wine Corporation authorized the issuance of $2,000,000 of 6% convertible debentures to fall due on April 30, 1986, with interest payable on April 30 and October 31 of each year. The indenture stated that each $1,000 denomination bond was convertible into 10 shares of $10 par value common and was callable at any time prior to maturity at a specified diminishing call premium.

On May 31, 1976, the bonds were sold to an underwriting syndicate for $1,982,400 plus accrued interest for one month. In addition, Sonora incurred $30,000 of issuance costs. At the date of issue, the conversion feature was considered to be of dubious value.

On June 1, 1977, the directors saw an opportunity to decrease the number of bonds outstanding and authorized the purchase of 100 of these bonds on the open market for $98,000 plus accrued interest for one month.

On November 1, 1984, the corporation decided to call the remaining bonds for retirement. All of the bondholders, with one exception, decided to convert their bondholdings into common stock. The sole exception owned $95,000 face value of these bonds; this bondholder was mailed a check for $95,950, the call value of the bonds. On November 1, 1984 the common stock of Sonora, which had been split three for one in 1979, was selling for $40 per share.

(a) Prepare the necessary journal entries as of May 31, 1976 to record the issuance of the bonds and the payment of bond issuance costs.

(b) Prepare the necessary journal entries as of October 31, 1976 to record the payment of interest and to record the amortization of bond issuance and discount costs on the straight-line method.

(c) Prepare the necessary journal entry for the purchase and retirement of the bonds acquired on June 1, 1977.

(d) Prepare the necessary journal entries for the recall and conversion of the bonds retired on November 1, 1984.

SOLUTION

(a) **Journal Entries, May 31, 1976**

Cash	1,992,400	
Bond Discount and Issuance Costs	17,600	
Bond Interest Payable		10,000
Bonds Payable		2,000,000

Issuance of $2,000,000 face value bonds; $1,982,400 plus accrued interest of $10,000 for one month ($2,000,000 × 0.06 × 1/12).

(b) **Journal Entry, October 31, 1976**

Bond Interest Payable	10,000	
Bond Interest Expense	52,000	
Cash		60,000
Bond Discount and Issuance Costs		2,000

Computed as follows:

Interest paid: 6% × $2,000,000 for six months

Amortization: $47,600 ($17,600 + $30,000) × 5/119

(c) **Journal Entries, June 1, 1977**

Bond Interest Expense	140	
Bond Discount and Issuance Costs		140

Amortization of bond discount and issuance costs for the period Nov. 1, 1976 to June 1, 1977 on $100,000 of bonds retired on this date ($47,600 × 7/119 × 1/20).

Bond Interest Expense	500	
Bonds Payable	100,000	
Loss on Bond Retirement	140	
Bond Discount and Issuance Costs		2,140
Cash		98,500

To record the retirement of $100,000 face-value bonds $98,000 plus interest for one month, calculated as follows:

Interest: $100,000 × 0.06 × 1/12 = $500

Amortization of bond discount and issuance costs:

Original write-off (total months)	119
Written off	12
Remaining number of months	107

$47,600 × 107/119 × 1/20 = $2,140

(d) **Journal Entries, November 1, 1984**

Bonds Payable	95,000	
Loss on Bond Retirement	1,292	
Bond Discount and Issuance Costs		342
Cash		95,950

To record the redemption of $95,000 face value bonds for $95,950 (see computations below).

Bonds Payable	1,805,000	
Bond Discount and Issuance Costs		6,498
Capital Stock, $3⅓ par		180,500
Paid-in Capital in Excess of Par		1,618,002

To record conversion of $1,805,000 face-value bonds into common stock (see computations below).

Carrying Value of Bonds at November 1, 1984

	Bonds Redeemed	Bonds Converted	Total
Total bonds outstanding at Nov. 1, 1984	$95,000	$1,805,000	$1,900,000
Less: Bond discount and issuance costs applicable at Nov. 1, 1984 (see note)	342	6,498	6,840
Carrying value at November 1, 1984	$94,658	$1,798,502	$1,893,160

NOTE: On November 1, 1984 the bonds had 18 months left to maturity. The computation of the portion of bond discount and issuance expense remaining on that date can be made as follows: $47,600 × 18/119 × 95% = $6,840. 5% of $6,840 represents the portion of such bond discount and issuance expense applicable to the bonds redeemed in cash.

Loss on Bond Retirement

Amount paid to bondholder	$95,950
Carrying value of bonds redeemed	94,658
Loss on bond retirement	$ 1,292

Details of Bond Conversion

Carrying value of bonds redeemed	$1,798,502
Credited to capital stock account (1,805 bonds × 30 shares per bond = 54,150 shares × $3⅓ par value)	180,500
Credited to paid-in capital	$1,618,002

15.10. On January 1, 1976, the Rostand Company issued $1,000,000, 7% bonds in a private placement with an insurance company, with interest payable semiannually on June 30 and December 31. The bonds are due in four years and were sold to the insurance company for $966,336.28, a price which represents the current effective interest cost of 8% per annum, or 4% semiannually.

(a) Prepare an amortization table showing the interest expense for each six-month period on an effective interest basis.

(b) Using the data in the above table, prepare the necessary journal entries to record the issuance of the bonds, the interest payments at the end of the first six months and the last six months of the bond issue, and the retirement of the bonds at December 31, 1979.

SOLUTION

(a) **Amortization Table**

Year	(A) Interest Paid Semiannually	(B) Semiannual Interest Expense (4% of Carrying Value)	(C) Discount Amortization (B − A)	(D) Carrying Value End of Period (D + C)
				$ 966,336.28
1976	$35,000.00	$38,653.45	$3,653.45	969,989.73
	35,000.00	38,799.59	3,799.59	973,789.32
1977	35,000.00	38,951.57	3,951.57	977,740.89
	35,000.00	39,109.64	4,109.64	981,850.53
1978	35,000.00	39,274.02	4,274.02	986,124.55
	35,000.00	39,444.98	4,444.98	990,569.53
1979	35,000.00	39,622.78	4,622.78	995,192.31
	35,000.00	39,807.69	4,807.69	1,000,000.00

(b) **Journal Entries**

1976

Jan. 1	Cash	966,336.28	
	Discount on Bonds	33,663.72	
	Bonds Payable		1,000,000

To record the sale of four-year, 7% bonds at a price to yield 4% semiannually. Interest payable June 30 and December 31 each year.

June 30	Bond Interest Expense	38,653.45	
	Discount on Bonds		3,653.45
	Cash		35,000.00

To record payment of semiannual interest expense at June 30, 1976.

1979

Dec. 31	Bond Interest Expense	39,807.69	
	Discount on Bonds		4,807.69
	Cash		35,000.00

To record the final payment of interest at Dec. 31, 1979.

| | Bonds Payable | 1,000,000 | |
| | Cash | | 1,000,000 |

To record the payment of the bonds at Dec. 31, 1979.

Examination III
Chapters 10-15

Part I. *Circle* T *for true,* F *for false.*

1. T   F   Cost plus accumulated depreciation equals book value.

2. T   F   The book value of an old building that was razed to make way for a new building is included in the cost of land.

3. T   F   The units-of-output method of depreciation would be used where there is not a wide variation in use each year.

4. T   F   Depletion occurs where physical units are removed from wasting assets.

5. T   F   Intangible assets include patents, copyrights, trademarks, organization costs, goodwill and cash surrender value of life insurance.

6. T   F   The classification as a marketable security (short-term asset) or a long-term asset depends on the purpose of the investment.

7. T   F   Current liabilities must be paid from current assets or from other current liabilities.

8. T   F   Contingent liabilities are potential obligations which may come into existence upon the occurrence of a future event.

9. T   F   Preferred dividends in arrears should be reported as current liabilities.

10. T   F   Interest accrued at purchase date may be credited to Bond Interest Expense.

Part II. *Circle the letter identifying the best answer.*

1. For how many years should a leasehold improvement be depreciated if it has a useful life of 13 years but the lease has only a single life of 10 years?

    a. 10   b. 13   c. $11\frac{1}{2}$ d. 23

2. One of the best methods of determining overhead for self-constructed assets is to apply:

    a. no overhead

    b. an estimated amount

    c. only incremental overhead

    d. an amount based on direct costing

3. Which of the following is not an accepted method of depreciation?

    a. straight-line

    b. LIFO

    c. declining-balance

    d. units-of-output

4. If depreciation is applied to a class of similar assets, the depreciation is termed:

    a. composite

    b. declining balance

    c. FIFO

    d. group

5. The periodic write-off of intangible assets is termed:

    a. depreciation

    b. amortization

    c. depletion

    d. obsolescence

6 APB Opinion No. 17 states that goodwill should be written off over not more than:

    a. 5 years   b. 10 years   c. 20 years   d. 40 years

7. Employer payroll taxes do not include:

    a. FICA taxes

    b. Federal unemployment taxes

    c. income taxes

    d. state unemployment taxes

8. Which of the following items should not be included in current liabilities?

    a. accrued salaries

    b. stock dividends payable

    c. income taxes payable

    d. interest payable

9. When bonds are issued at a premium, the carrying value of the debt as bonds approach maturity:

    a. decreases

    b. increases

    c. remains the same

    d. is refunded

10. Bonds maturing within one year that are to be converted into stock or repaid from a sinking fund should be reported as a:

    a. current liability

    b. long-term liability

    c. deferred charge

    d. contingent liability

Part III. *Complete the following statements.*

1. Costs incurred upon acquisition to put assets in good operating condition should be _____ .

2. The purchase of a $5,000 machine for $4,000 cash, a saving of $1,000, will _____ the current ratio.

3. In accounting, depreciation is a process of _____ rather than asset valuation.

4. In estimating periodic depreciation, the factors that must be considered are _____ , _____ and _____ .

5. The excess of the value of a business as a whole over the value of its identifiable parts is called _____ .

6. Under the equity method, the investor will _____ the investment account for investee's net income and _____ the investment account for _____ received.

7. An _____ in accrued liabilities usually causes an _____ in stockholders' equity.

8. Obligations which definitely exist but are uncertain as to amount and date of payment are termed _____ liabilities.

9. The group contract between the corporation and the bondholders is called a bond _____ .

10. If the effective rate of interest is higher than the nominal rate, the bonds are sold at a _____ .

Part IV. *Complete the following exercises.*

1. In the space below, note the effect of the described transaction or event on the various account groups, using the following symbols.

O = overstated, U = understated, NE = no effect

(a)

Description	Cost			Expenses	Income
	Land	Building	Equipment		
(1) Equipment purchase charged to expense.					
(2) Ordinary repairs charged to building.					
(3) Accrued taxes on land purchased charged to expense.					
(4) Book value of old building razed charged to new building.					
(5) Depreciation on equipment not recorded.					
(6) Depreciation for second year was computed on straight-line rather than declining-balance method.					

(b)

Description	Assets	Liabilities	Expenses	Income
(1) Organization costs charged to expense.				
(2) Research expenditures capitalized rather than expensed as prescribed.				
(3) Discount on bonds payable reported as asset.				
(4) Investor using equity method did not accrue for investee earnings.				
(5) An extraordinary expense treated as a prior period item.				

2. Indicate the proper classification of the following items by placing a check ($\sqrt{}$) in the appropriate column.

Description	Current Liabilities	Noncurrent Liabilities	Total Assets	Capital Section
(a) Large credit balance in Accounts Receivable.				
(b) Bonds due in two months, covered by sinking fund.				
(c) Stock dividend.				
(d) Preferred dividends in arrears.				
(e) Premium on bonds.				
(f) Issue cost of bonds.				

Part V. *Solve the following problems.*

1. A machine which originally cost $25,000 has a book value at December 31, 19X5 of $10,000. The cost of a replacement machine is $40,000, the trade-in allowance on the old machine is $13,000, and the balance is payable in cash. (a) Prepare the entry to record the transaction and (b) show the income tax basis for the new machine.

2. The Eugene Thompson Company paid $620,000 for coal mining property in 19X0 that will be worth $60,000 after removing the estimated supply of 400,000 tons of coal. For 19X1 and 19X2, the operations were as follows:

Year	Development Costs	Tons Mined
19X1	$80,000	100,000
19X2	95,000	125,000

Near the end of 19X2 a geologist's survey revised the estimated tons available to 300,000 at December 31, 19X2.

Prepare (a) calculations of depletion for 19X1 and 19X2 and (b) entries for both years.

3. The Hofstra Development Company is considering a bonus plan for its vice-president of operations. Under the proposal the bonus rate will be 12%. Income taxes are 50% of taxable income. The net income for 19X1 is estimated to be $200,000, before both bonus and income taxes. Compute the bonus based on income (a) before taxes and bonus, (b) after bonus but before taxes and (c) after both taxes and bonus.

Answers to Examination III

Part I

1. F, 2. T, 3. F, 4. T, 5. F, 6. T, 7. T, 8. T, 9. F, 10. T

Part II

1. a, 2. c, 3. b, 4. d, 5. b, 6. d, 7. c, 8. b, 9. a, 10. b

Part III

1. capitalized; 2. decrease; 3. cost allocation; 4. cost, scrap value, service life; 5. goodwill; 6. increase, decrease, dividends; 7. understatement, overstatement; 8. estimated; 9. indenture; 10. discount.

Part IV

1. (a)

| | Cost | | | | |
Description	Land	Building	Equipment	Expenses	Income
(1) Equipment purchase charged to expense.	NE	NE	U	O	U
(2) Ordinary repairs charged to building.	NE	O	NE	U	O
(3) Accrued taxes on land purchased charged to expense.	U	NE	NE	O	U
(4) Book value of old building razed charged to new building.	U	O	NE	NE	NE
(5) Depreciation on equipment not recorded.	NE	NE	NE	U	O
(6) Depreciation for second year was computed on straight-line rather than declining-balance method.	NE	NE	NE	U	O

(b)

Description	Assets	Liabilities	Expenses	Income
(1) Organization costs charged to expense.	U	NE	O	U
(2) Research expenditures capitalized rather than expensed as prescribed.	O	NE	U	O
(3) Discount on bonds payable reported as asset.	O	O	NE	NE
(4) Investor using equity method did not accrue for investee earnings.	U	NE	NE	U
(5) An extraordinary expense treated as a prior period item.	NE	NE	U	O

2.   Current Liabilities: *a*
     Noncurrent Liabilities: *b, e*
     Total Assets: *f*
     Capital Section: *c, d*

Part V

1.   (*a*)

Machinery	40,000	
Accumulated Depreciation, Machinery	15,000	
Machinery		25,000
Gain on Disposal of Machinery		3,000
Cash		27,000

     (*b*)

Book value of old machine	$10,000
Cash paid	27,000
Income tax cost basis	$37,000

2.   (*a*)   **Depletion Calculation**

19X1   ($620,000 − $60,000 + $80,000 = $640,000 ÷ 400,000 = $1.60)
Depletion amount: 100,000 tons mined × $1.60 = $160,000

19X2   ($620,000 − $60,000 + $80,000 − $160,000 + $95,000 = $575,000 ÷ 425,000* = $1.35)
Depletion amount: 125,000 tons × $1.35 = $168,750

* 125,000 tons mined in 19X2 + 300,000 estimated at end of year = 425,000 tons

     (*b*)   **Entries**

19X1	*Depletion Expense*	160,000	
	Accumulated Depletion		160,000
19X2	*Depletion Expense*	168,750	
	Accumulated Depletion		168,750

3.   Letting *B* = bonus, *T* = income taxes:

     (*a*) $B = 0.12 \times \$200,000 = \$24,000$

     (*b*)

$B = 0.12(\$200,000 - B)$
$B = \$24,000 - 0.12\,B$
$1.12\,B = \$24,000$
$B = \$21,429$

Proof

Income before bonus and taxes	$200,000
Less: Bonus	21,429
Income before taxes	$178,571
Bonus (12%)	$ 21,429

     (*c*)

$B = 0.12(\$200,000 - B - T)$
$T = 0.5(\$200,000 - B)$
$B = 0.12[\$200,000 - B - 0.5(\$200,000 - B)]$
$B = 0.12(\$200,000 - B - \$100,000 + 0.5\,B)$
$B = \$24,000 - 0.12\,B - \$12,000 + 0.06\,B$
$1.06\,B = \$12,000$
$B = \$11,321$

Proof

Income before bonus and taxes	$200,000
Less: Bonus	11,321
Taxable income	$188,679
Income taxes (50%)	94,339
Net income	$ 94,340
Bonus (12%)	$ 11,321

Appendix

TABLE 1
Present Value of $1 at Compound Interest Due in n Periods

n = number of periods	i = interest rate per period									
	2.0%	2.5%	3.0%	4.0%	5.0%	6.0%	8.0%	10.0%	15.0%	20.0%
1	0.9804	0.9756	0.9709	0.9615	0.9524	0.9434	0.9259	0.9091	0.8696	0.8333
2	0.9612	0.9518	0.9426	0.9246	0.9070	0.8900	0.8573	0.8264	0.7561	0.6944
3	0.9423	0.9286	0.9151	0.8890	0.8638	0.8396	0.7938	0.7513	0.6575	0.5787
4	0.9238	0.9060	0.8885	0.8548	0.8227	0.7921	0.7350	0.6830	0.5718	0.4823
5	0.9057	0.8839	0.8626	0.8219	0.7835	0.7473	0.6806	0.6209	0.4972	0.4019
6	0.8880	0.8623	0.8375	0.7903	0.7462	0.7050	0.6302	0.5645	0.4323	0.3349
7	0.8706	0.8413	0.8131	0.7599	0.7107	0.6651	0.5835	0.5132	0.3759	0.2791
8	0.8535	0.8207	0.7894	0.7307	0.6768	0.6274	0.5403	0.4665	0.3269	0.2326
9	0.8368	0.8007	0.7664	0.7026	0.6446	0.5919	0.5002	0.4241	0.2843	0.1938
10	0.8203	0.7812	0.7441	0.6756	0.6139	0.5584	0.4632	0.3855	0.2472	0.1615
11	0.8043	0.7621	0.7224	0.6496	0.5847	0.5268	0.4289	0.3505	0.2149	0.1346
12	0.7885	0.7436	0.7014	0.6246	0.5568	0.4970	0.3971	0.3186	0.1869	0.1122
13	0.7730	0.7254	0.6810	0.6006	0.5303	0.4688	0.3677	0.2897	0.1625	0.0935
14	0.7579	0.7077	0.6611	0.5775	0.5051	0.4423	0.3405	0.2633	0.1413	0.0779
15	0.7430	0.6905	0.6419	0.5553	0.4810	0.4173	0.3152	0.2394	0.1229	0.0649
16	0.7284	0.6736	0.6232	0.5339	0.4581	0.3936	0.2919	0.2176	0.1069	0.0541
17	0.7142	0.6572	0.6050	0.5134	0.4363	0.3714	0.2703	0.1978	0.0929	0.0451
18	0.7002	0.6412	0.5874	0.4936	0.4155	0.3503	0.2502	0.1799	0.0808	0.0376
19	0.6864	0.6255	0.5703	0.4746	0.3957	0.3305	0.2317	0.1635	0.0703	0.0313
20	0.6730	0.6103	0.5537	0.4564	0.3769	0.3118	0.2145	0.1486	0.0611	0.0261

TABLE 2
Present Value of an Ordinary Annuity of $1 per Period

n = number of periods	i = interest rate per period									
	2.0%	2.5%	3.0%	4.0%	5.0%	6.0%	8.0%	10.0%	15.0%	20.0%
1	0.9804	0.9756	0.9709	0.9615	0.9524	0.9434	0.9259	0.9091	0.8696	0.8333
2	1.9416	1.9274	1.9135	1.8861	1.8594	1.8334	1.7833	1.7355	1.6257	1.5278
3	2.8839	2.8560	2.8286	2.7751	2.7232	2.6730	2.5771	2.4869	2.2832	2.1065
4	3.8077	3.7620	3.7171	3.6299	3.5460	3.4651	3.3121	3.1699	2.8550	2.5887
5	4.7135	4.6458	4.5797	4.4518	4.3295	4.2124	3.9927	3.7908	3.3522	2.9906
6	5.6014	5.5081	5.4172	5.2421	5.0757	4.9173	4.6229	4.3553	3.7845	3.3255
7	6.4720	6.3494	6.2303	6.0021	5.7864	5.5824	5.2064	4.8684	4.1604	3.6046
8	7.3255	7.1701	7.0197	6.7327	6.4632	6.2098	5.7466	5.3349	4.4873	3.8372
9	8.1622	7.9709	7.7861	7.4353	7.1078	6.8017	6.2469	5.7590	4.7716	4.0310
10	8.9826	8.7521	8.5302	8.1109	7.7217	7.3601	6.7101	6.1446	5.0188	4.1925
11	9.7868	9.5142	9.2526	8.7605	8.3064	7.8869	7.1390	6.4951	5.2337	4.3271
12	10.5753	10.2578	9.9540	9.3851	8.8633	8.3838	7.5361	6.8137	5.4206	4.4392
13	11.3484	10.9832	10.6350	9.9856	9.3936	8.8527	7.9038	7.1034	5.5831	4.5327
14	12.1062	11.6909	11.2961	10.5631	9.8986	9.2950	8.2442	7.3667	5.7245	4.6106
15	12.8493	12.3814	11.9379	11.1184	10.3797	9.7122	8.5595	7.6061	5.8474	4.6755
16	13.5777	13.0550	12.5611	11.6523	10.8378	10.1059	8.8514	7.8237	5.9542	4.7296
17	14.2919	13.7122	13.1661	12.1657	11.2741	10.4773	9.1216	8.0216	6.0472	4.7746
18	14.9920	14.3534	13.7535	12.6593	11.6896	10.8276	9.3719	8.2014	6.1280	4.8122
19	15.6785	14.9789	14.3238	13.1339	12.0853	11.1581	9.6036	8.3649	6.1982	4.8435
20	16.3514	15.5892	14.8775	13.5903	12.4622	11.4699	9.8181	8.5136	6.2593	4.8696

INDEX

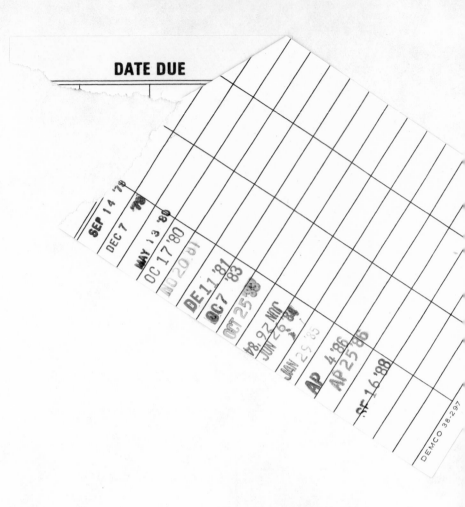